Books in the Security Series

Computer Security Fundamentals
ISBN: 0-13-171129-6

Information Security: Principles and Practices
ISBN: 0-13-154729-1

Firewalls and VPNs: Principles and Practices
ISBN: 0-13-154731-3

Security Policies and Procedures: Principles and Practices
ISBN: 0-13-186691-5

Network Defense and Countermeasures: Principles and Practices
ISBN: 0-13-171126-1

Intrusion Detection: Principles and Practices
ISBN: 0-13-154730-5

Disaster Recovery: Principles and Practices
ISBN: 0-13-171127-X

Computer Forensics: Principles and Practices
ISBN: 0-13-154727-5

Computer Security Fundamentals

CHUCK EASTTOM

Upper Saddle River, New Jersey 07458

Vice President and Publisher: Natalie E. Anderson
Executive Acquisitions Editor, Print: Stephanie Wall
Executive Acquisitions Editor, Media: Richard Keaveny
Editorial Project Manager: Emilie Herman
Editorial Assistants: Brian Hoehl, Bambi Dawn Marchigano, Alana Meyers, Sandra Bernales
Senior Media Project Manager: Cathi Profitko
Senior Media Project Manager: Steve Gagliostro
Marketing Manager: Sarah Davis
Marketing Assistant: Lisa Taylor
Managing Editor: Lynda Castillo
Production Project Manager: Vanessa Nuttry
Manufacturing Buyer: Natacha Moore
Design Manager: Maria Lange
Art Director: Blair Brown
Interior Design: Blair Brown
Cover Design: Blair Brown
Cover Illustration/Photo: Gettyimages/Photodisc Blue
Composition/Full-Service Project Management: Custom Editorial Productions Inc.
Cover Printer: Phoenix Color
Printer/Binder: Courier/Stoughton

Pearson Education LTD.
Pearson Education Singapore, Pte. Ltd
Pearson Education, Canada, Ltd
Pearson Education–Japan
Pearson Education Australia PTY, Limited
Pearson Education North Asia Ltd
Pearson Educación de Mexico, S.A. de C.V.
Pearson Education Malaysia, Pte. Ltd

10 9 8 7 6 5 4 3
ISBN 0-13-171129-6

Contents in Brief

Table of Contents

Security Series Walk-Through

The Prentice Hall Security Series prepares students for careers in IT security by providing practical advice and hands-on training from industry experts. All of the books in this series are filled with real-world examples to help readers apply what they learn to the workplace. This walk-through highlights the key elements in this book created to help students along the way.

Chapter Objectives. These short-term, attainable goals outline what will be covered in the chapter text.

Chapter Introduction. Each chapter begins with an explanation of why these topics are important and how the chapter fits into the overall organization of the book.

Chapter Objectives

After reading this chapter and completing the exercises, you will be able to do the following:

- Evaluate an organization's security policy.
- Create a basic security policy.
- Update a target system's patches.
- Shut down unnecessary ports.
- Scan a system for vulnerabilities.
- Activate port filtering in Windows 2000 or Windows XP.
- Use a port scanner.

Introduction

As you learn more about computer security you will learn new techniques for securing a particular system. However it is critical to be able to assess a system's security. This chapter discusses the essential steps in assessing a system for vulnerabilities. It is also important to assess a system's security level prior to implementing any security measures. Information about the current state of affairs will help you appropriately address any vulnerabilities.

IN PRACTICE: Using NetCop

Let us begin with NetCop, since it is one of the easiest to use port scanners available. IT can be obtained from many sites. You can download NetCop at http://www.cotse.com/pscan.htm.

When you download NetCop you get a simple self-extracting executable that will install the program on your machine and will even put a shortcut in your program menu. When you launch NetCop, it has a very simple and intuitive screen.

You can type in a single IP address, or a range of IP addresses. That makes this tool particularly useful for network administrators that wish to check for open ports on their entire network. Four our purposes we will begin by scanning a single IP address, our own machine. You can either type your machines actual IP address, or simply the loop back address (127.0.0.1). When you type in a single IP address and click on scan now, you can see it checking each and every port. This is very methodical but also a bit slow.

You can, of course, stop the scan at any time you desire. These results are from a machine the author used specifically for this book. You would, of course, get different results on different machines.

You can see that NetCop gives you useful information about open ports. Before you choose to close any port, you should make sure that the port is not one that you actually need for system operations. The following websites list all well-known ports.

In Practice. Takes concepts from the book and shows how they are applied in the workplace.

FYI. Additional information on topics that go beyond the scope of the book.

FYI: The Microsoft Patch

Go to http://www.microsoft.com and on the left hand side of the website you will find a link under the sub heading Resources, entitled Windows Update. If you select that option and follow the very clear instructions you will be able to correct any and all Windows patch issues on a target machine.

7

twork is to probe the network. This means using
for vulnerabilities. These tools are often the same
ttempting to breach your security, so it is critical
n this section we will use three separate analysis
other tools freely available on the Internet, and
ever these three are the most commonly used. We
er, NetBrute, and NetCop. Also this section will
ions in this book. We will conduct the exercise
d of the chapter. The reason for this is simply that
tical aspects of applying these tools Additional
f the chapter.

Caution

Security Audit

When conducting a security audit, it's critical that you document the specific steps taken during the audit, any flaws found, and what corrective actions where taken.

1

Caution. Critical, not-to-be forgotten information that is directly relevant to the surrounding text.

Test Your Skills

Each chapter ends with exercises designed to reinforce the chapter objectives. Four types of evaluation follow each chapter.

Multiple Choice Questions. Test the reader's understanding of the text.

Exercises. Brief, guided projects designed around individual concepts found in the chapter.

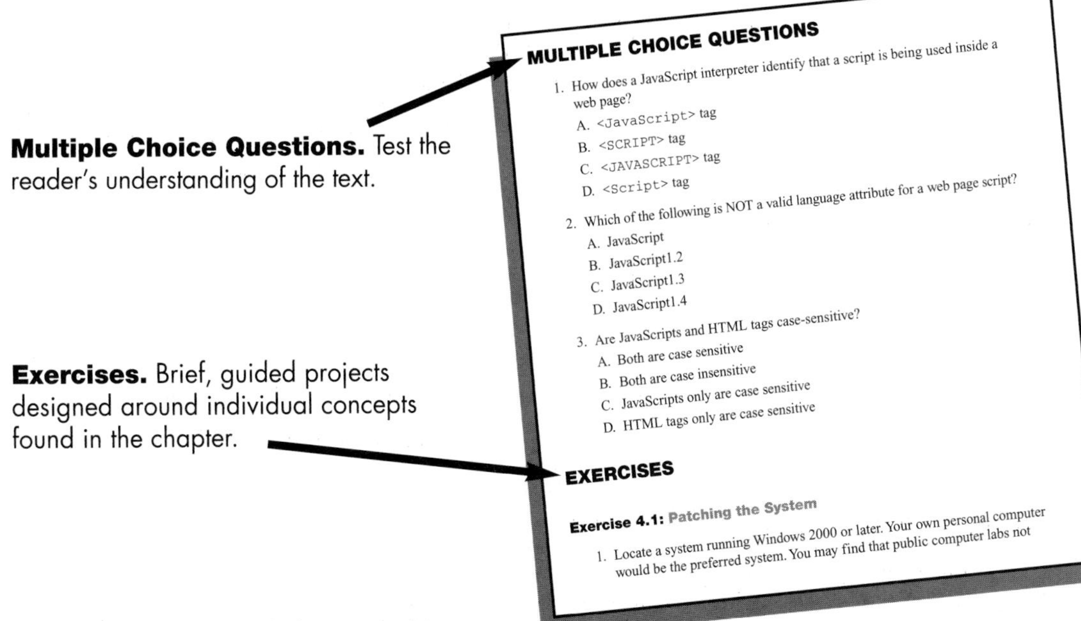

MULTIPLE CHOICE QUESTIONS

1. How does a JavaScript interpreter identify that a script is being used inside a web page?
   A. <JavaScript> tag
   B. <SCRIPT> tag
   C. <JAVASCRIPT> tag
   D. <Script> tag
2. Which of the following is NOT a valid language attribute for a web page script?
   A. JavaScript
   B. JavaScript1.2
   C. JavaScript1.3
   D. JavaScript1.4
3. Are JavaScripts and HTML tags case-sensitive?
   A. Both are case sensitive
   B. Both are case insensitive
   C. JavaScripts only are case sensitive
   D. HTML tags only are case sensitive

EXERCISES

Exercise 4.1: Patching the System

1. Locate a system running Windows 2000 or later. Your own personal computer would be the preferred system. You may find that public computer labs not

Projects. Longer, guided projects that combine lessons from the chapter.

PROJECTS

Project 4.1: Personal Policy Password System

1. Analyze or develop a personal policy password system for your PC and online accounts.

"<P>Welcome to Internet Banking</P>"
"<P>Click NEXT to Continue…</P>"

2. Determine if your passwords are secure using the four basic password rules presented in this chapter. W
3. Write down if your passwords were secure and the steps that you will take to make them secure.

Case Study. A real-world scenario to resolve using lessons learned in the chapter.

Case Study

Now that you have learned how to insert simple JavaScripts into web pages, with calls to document.write Has the site used any of the features you have learned about in this Lesson?

1. Import the appropriate Namespaces
2. Execute the Query/Instruction

Using a web design package, or just notepad and your web browser, create a front page for an Internet banking that uses document.write to display text within the <BODY> section of the page. A link should be created to the login page, which will be examined in the next chapter.

- The Computer Security Institute: http://www.gocsi.com/
- The Computer Security Clearing House http://csrc.nist.gov/
- The Computer Emergency Response Team http://www.cert.org/

http://www

This icon appears in the margin wherever additional information or links to downloads can be found at the series companion Web site, **www.prenhall.com/security**

Preface

Computer Security Fundamentals is designed as a gateway book: a general introduction to the field of information security. It explains how hackers target a system, obtain information, and use it to crack systems. Students will learn how to safeguard their systems, using passwords and network-scanning utilities. While it does explain security breaches in some detail, this book is not a cookbook for hackers. Explanations, definitions, and examples are designed to reinforce the importance of securing data, computers, and networks. They are always followed by the steps that should be taken to protect valuable information.

Finally, this book looks at security primarily from a Windows perspective. While the concepts covered apply to virtually any system, Windows was chosen because it is so widely used and has been a frequent target of attacks.

Audience

This book is a primer for students who want a solid introduction to the field. Although this book is introductory, the content assumes the readers are competent computer users -- meaning they have used a computer at work or at home, are comfortable with e-mail and Web browsers, and know what terms such as RAM and USB mean. Readers should have a basic understanding of PCs, but need not have taken formal computer courses.

People outside the typical computer science and computer information systems departments may also find this book useful, particularly law enforcement officers, criminal justice majors, and business majors.

Overview of the Book

Computer Security Fundamentals opens with an overview of cyber crime and security. Chapter 1, Introduction to Cyber Crime and Security, details just how serious cyber crime is and why learning how to protect systems from attack is so important. The chapter introduces some basics of computer security—types of threats, common attacks, terminology, and paradigms—and frames security efforts in a legal context. Finally, Chapter 1 describes some readily available security resources and directs students to explore these tools in the end of lesson exercises and projects.

Chapter 2, Networks and the Internet, reveals one of the most important elements of successful network security: a strong working knowledge of network operations. Some readers with more computer experience will be well-versed in the material presented here and may just need to skim the chapter as a refresher. However, readers with less experience will learn about the basic model of a network and how it works. Hands-on IPConfig, tracert, and ping exercises at the end of the chapter reinforce how understanding a network and its operations can help protect it.

Chapter 3, Assessing a System, highlights some of the tools hackers use to assess the vulnerability of a target system—and explains how network security managers can use these same tools to assess the safety of their systems so they never become targets. Several In Practice features walk students through some of the most popular port scanners and end-of-chapter exercises let students explore these tools further.

Chapters 4 and 5 delve into the specific types of attacks that hackers may launch. Chapter 4, Denial of Service Attacks, examines SYN flood, Smurf and Distributed Denial of Service attacks in particular. This chapter includes some real-world examples of Denial of Service attacks to demonstrate how damaging they can be and describes how best to protect against them. Chapter 5, Malware, describes viruses, Trojan horses, buffer overflow attacks, and spyware. Again, real-world examples are reviewed and specific tools for detecting and eradicating a malware problem are described and demonstrated including Norton and McAfee anti-virus software.

At this point in the book, readers will have been exposed to various threats to systems and some specific measures to prevent, detect, and eradicate these dangers. Chapter 6, Basics of Assessing and Securing a System, and Chapter 7, Encryption, shift away from specific attacks and defenses and take a more comprehensive look at computer security management. In Chapter 6, readers will learn some security fundamentals: probing for vulnerabilities, setting policies, evaluating consultants, securing individual workstations and servers, and safely surfing the Web. Chapter 7 introduces readers to encryption, covering the history of the field and modern cryptography methods. These chapters provide a wide angle lens view of the security management field, giving students enough information to at least 'ask the right questions' and preparing them for more in-depth study of the ideas in future coursework.

Chapters 8, 9 and 10 cover different types of crime perpetrated via the Internet. Chapter 8, Internet Fraud and Cyber Crime, discusses identity theft and cyber stalking, Chapter 9 explains industrial espionage in cyberspace, and Chapter 10 examines cyber terrorism and information warfare. Chapter 11, Cyber Detective, continues the vein of the three previous chapters, looking at how hackers exploit information on the Internet to perpetrate their crimes and contends that understanding these methods of exploitation are key to protecting against cyber crime. In each chapter, real-world examples show how the methods described in the first part of the book have been used to damage people and property, reinforcing the importance of network security.

Chapter 12, Computer Security Hardware and Software, turns to the more technical side of computer security, examining hardware and software, some of which was briefly mentioned in previous chapters. This chapter is intended to give readers a more detailed understanding of virus scanners, firewalls, intrusion detection systems, and anti-spyware. The practical information in this chapter will be particularly useful for students who will be moving forward into a career in computer security.

Finally, several appendices offer additional resources for instructors and students, including a list of links to useful Web sites, sample checklists, a glossary, and a list of references used in writing this book.

Conventions Used in This Book

To help you get the most from the text, we've used a few conventions throughout the book.

IN PRACTICE: About In Practice

These show readers how to take concepts from the book and apply them in the workplace.

FYI: About FYIs

These boxes offer additional information on topics that go beyond the scope of the book.

Caution

About Cautions

Cautions appear in the margins of the text. They flag critical, not-to-be forgotten information that is directly relevant to the surrounding text.

Snippets and blocks of code are boxed and numbered, and can be downloaded from the companion Web site (**www.prenhall.com/security**).

New key terms appear in ***bold italics***.

This icon appears in the margin wherever more information can be found at the series companion Web site, **www.prenhall.com/security**.

Instructor and Student Resources

Instructor's Resource Center on CD-ROM

The Instructor's Resource Center on CD-ROM (IRC on CD) is distributed to instructors only and is an interactive library of assets and links. It includes:

- Instructor's Manual. Provides instructional tips, an introduction to each chapter, teaching objectives, teaching suggestions, and answers to end-of-chapter questions and problems.
- PowerPoint Slide Presentations. Provides a chapter-by-chapter review of the book content for use in the classroom.
- Test Bank. This TestGen-compatible test bank file can be used with Prentice Hall's TestGen software (available as a free download at **www.prenhall.com/testgen**). TestGen is a test generator that lets you view and easily edit test bank questions, transfer them to tests, and print in a variety of formats suitable to your teaching situation. The program also offers many options for organizing and displaying test banks and tests. A built-in random number and text generator makes it ideal for creating multiple versions of tests that involve calculations and provides more possible test items than test bank questions. Powerful search and sort functions let you easily locate questions and arrange them in the order you prefer.

Companion Web Site

The Companion Web site (**www.prenhall.com/security**) is a Pearson learning tool that provides students and instructors with online support. Here you will find:

- Interactive Study Guide, a Web-based interactive quiz designed to provide students with a convenient online mechanism for self-testing their comprehension of the book material.
- Additional Web projects and resources to put into practice the concepts taught in each chapter.
- Information on certification (from Appendix A), links to useful Web resources (from Appendix B) and sample policy and checklists (from Appendix C).

About the Author

Chuck Easttom spent many years in the IT industry, followed by three years teaching computer science at a technical college, including courses in computer security. He left academia to return to industry as the IT manager for a company in Dallas, TX. Among his other duties there, he is responsible for system security. He has authored seven other books on programming, Web development, and Linux. Chuck holds over 20 different industry certifications including CIW Security Analyst, MCSE, MCSA, MCDBA, MCAD, Server+, and more. He has served as a subject matter expert for the Computer Technology Industry Association (CompTIA) in the development or revision of four of their certification tests, including the initial creation of their Security+ certification. Chuck still works part-time as an adjunct teacher for a Dallas area college teaching a variety of courses, including computer security. He also does computer security consulting work from time to time.

Chuck is a frequent guest speaker for computer groups, discussing computer security. You can reach Chuck at his Web site (**www.chuckeasttom.com**) or by e-mail at chuckeasttom@yahoo.com.

Quality Assurance

We would like to extend our thanks to the Quality Assurance team for their attention to detail and their efforts to make sure that we got it right.

Technical Editors

David Easton
Information Systems
Waubonsee Community College

David Parker
Computer Science
St. Charles Community College

Reviewers

Charles R. Esparza
Business Information Technology
Glendale Community College

Charles Hamby
Computer Systems Technology
Matanuska-Susitna College

Suresh C. Sonkavelly
Information Technology
Gibbs College

Chapter 1

Introduction to Cyber Crime and Security

Chapter Objectives

After reading this chapter and completing the exercises, you will be able to do the following:

- Identify the top threats to a computer network: intrusion, Denial of Service attacks, and malware.
- Assess the likelihood of an attack on your personal computer and network.
- Define key terms such as cracker, sneaker, firewall, and authentication.
- Compare and contrast perimeter and layered approaches to network security.
- Use online resources to secure your network.

Introduction

It's hard to find a facet of modern life that does not involve a computer system on some level. The following are just a few examples that illustrate this point.

- Financial transactions—including online banking, ATMs, and debit cards— are a pervasive part of modern commerce.
- Some retailers are using computerized automatic checkout.
- You may be taking this class online, or perhaps you registered for it online. You may have purchased this book online.
- There is even widespread discussion of eventually voting online.

Because so much of our business is transacted online, a great deal of personal information is stored in computers. Medical records, tax records, school records, and more are all stored in computer databases. Whether this level of technology in our daily lives is to our advantage or not is a question that is beyond the scope of this book. The fact is that our lives are inextricably intertwined with computer systems. This leads to several important questions:

- How is information safeguarded?
- What are the vulnerabilities to these systems?
- What steps are taken to ensure that these systems and data are safe?

FYI: Online Banking

A recent study found that 28% of U.S. consumers access their primary banking institution by phone, the Internet, or at branches at least three times per week (Online Banking Report). These consumers use online banking to view statements and checks, pay bills, check balances, and transfer funds.

Recent news stories do not offer encouraging answers to these questions. The media often gives a great deal of attention to dramatic virus attacks, hackers, and other interesting Internet phenomena. News of virus attacks, such as MyDoom, often become lead stories on national networks. Even the most technically naïve person cannot go more than a few weeks without hearing of some new virus or hacking incident, such as the dramatic attack in February 2003 when a hacker was able to get 5.6 million credit card numbers (CNN/Technology, 2003). Part of this article can be seen in Figure 1.1.

In spite of daily horror stories, however, many people (including some law enforcement professionals and trained computer professionals) lack an adequate understanding of the reality of these threats. Attention is often focused on the most dramatic computer security breaches (intrusions), which

FYI: Online Shopping

The U.S. Department of Commerce's reports show a rapid increase in online retail sales in just a few years. Since the year 2000, when sales were approximately $27.3 million, online sales increased by nearly 325% to approximately $88.2 million in 2004. At the time of this writing, sales for 2005 were projected to be approximately $109.4 million.

CNN.com/TECHNOLOGY

SEARCH The Web CNN.com Search Powered by YAHOO! search

Home Page
World
U.S.
Weather
Business at CNNMoney
Sports at SI.com
Politics
Law
Technology
Science & Space
Health
Entertainment
Travel
Education
Special Reports

SERVICES
Video
E-mail Newsletters
CNNtoGO
SEARCH
Web CNN.com
Search Powered by YAHOO! search

advertisement

Hacker accesses 5.6 million credit cards

Visa: No accounts have been used fraudulently

From Fred Katayama
CNNfn
Tuesday, February 18, 2003 Posted: 12:16 PM EST (1716 GMT)

NEW YORK (CNN) -- The hacker who breached a security system to get into credit card information had access to about 5.6 million Visa and Mastercard accounts, far more than originally announced, the two card associations told CNN Tuesday.

Monday, Visa and Mastercard said the hacker could look at as many as 2.2 million accounts after breaching the security system of a company that processes credit card transactions on behalf of merchants.

None of the original set of compromised Visa cards had been used fraudulently, Visa spokesman John Abrams said Monday. A Mastercard spokeswoman could not say whether any of their cards had been used fraudulently.

The affected accounts make up almost 1 percent of the 574 million Visa and Mastercard cards in the United States. Spokesmen for the two associations said Monday they promptly notified the banks that issued the affected cards.

Both card companies have zero-liability policies, which protect cardholders from responsibility for any unauthorized or fraudulent charges.

Story Tools
SAVE THIS E-MAIL THIS
PRINT THIS MOST POPULAR

VIDEO MORE VIDEO
Visa says none of its accounts have been used fraudulently after a hacker gained access to as many as 2.2 million Visa and MasterCard accounts. CNNfn's Fred Katayama reports (February 17)
PLAY VIDEO

FIGURE 1.1 CNN report of a cyber attack.

do not necessarily give an accurate picture of the most plausible threat scenarios. Clearly, many people are aware of the attacks that can be executed against a target system. Unfortunately, they are often not familiar with the attack's mechanism, its actual danger level, or how to prevent it.

This chapter outlines current dangers, describes the most common types of attacks on your personal computer and network, teaches you how to speak the lingo of both hackers and security professionals, and outlines the broad strokes of what is necessary to secure your computer and your network. All of these topics are explored more fully in subsequent chapters.

How Seriously Should You Take Threats to Network Security?

The first step in understanding computer and network security is to formulate a realistic assessment of the threats to those systems. The general population tends to have two extreme attitudes about computer security. The first group assumes there is no real threat. Subscribers to this theory believe that there is little real danger to computer systems and that much of the negative news is simply unwarranted panic. They often think that taking only minimal security precautions should ensure the safety of their systems. The prevailing sentiment of these individuals is, "If our computer/organization has not been attacked so far, we must be secure." They tend to have a ***reactive*** approach to security. They will wait until after an incident occurs to address security issues—the proverbial "closing the barn door after the horse has already gotten out." If you are fortunate, the incident will have only minor impact on you or your organization and will serve as a much needed wakeup call. If you are unfortunate, then your organization may face serious and possible catastrophic consequences. For example there are organizations that did not have an effective network security system in place when the MyDoom virus attacked their systems. One of those companies estimated that lost productivity through downtime of the systems cost over $100,000.

The second extreme attitude toward the dangers to computer and network security is one that tends to overestimate the dangers. The people in this group are prone to assume that talented hackers exist in great numbers and all are imminent threats to your system. They may believe that any teenager with a laptop can traverse highly secure systems at will. This viewpoint has, unfortunately, been fostered by a number of movies that depict computer hacking in a somewhat glamorous light. Such a world view makes excellent movie plots, but it is simply unrealistic. The reality is that many people who call themselves hackers are less knowledgeable than they think. They have ascertained a few buzzwords from the Internet and are convinced of their own digital supremacy, but they are not able to affect any real compromises to even a moderately secure system.

Both extremes of attitudes regarding the dangers to computer systems are inaccurate. It is certainly true that there are people who have both the comprehension of computer systems and the skills to compromise the security of many, if not most, systems. However, it is also true that many who call themselves hackers are not as skilled as they claim. As with any field of human endeavor, the majority of hackers are, by definition, mediocre. Often, the people who most loudly declare their cyber prowess are usually those with the least actual skill. The truly talented hacker is no more common than the truly talented concert pianist. Consider how many people take piano lessons at some point in their lives; then consider how many of those ever truly become virtuosos. The same is true of computer hackers. Keep in mind that even those who do possess the requisite skill also need the motivation to expend the time and effort to compromise your system. This does not mean that unskilled hackers are no threat at all, but rather they are much less of a threat than administrators, and the hackers themselves, might think. Additionally, the greatest threat to any system is not hackers, but rather virus attacks and Denial of Service attacks. (These are discussed in more detail below.)

A more balanced view and, therefore, a better way to assess the threat level to your system is to weigh the attractiveness of your system to potential intruders against the security measures in place. One method of making this assessment is discussed in the following In Practice. More details on assessing system security will be given in Chapter 6.

IN PRACTICE: Assessing Your Own System

Unfortunately, assessing your system is not a science. There is no mathematical formula to apply. Therefore, I have developed a crude, but effective method you might use.

1. Start by giving a numerical weight to two areas of your system: profile and value. In other words, on a scale of 1 to 10, determine how high a profile your system might have for potential hackers. A little-known finance company might receive a 3, whereas a well-known government site or site of a popular company might receive a 9. Then give a similar numerical number to the value of the information your system holds. A system containing credit card information might receive a 7, sensitive nuclear research might receive a 10, and a home business Web site with no personal or credit card data might receive a 2.
2. Add these two numbers together to obtain a value between 2 and 20.
3. Now, rate your current security on a scale of 1 to 10. If you have a dedicated security staff, multiple firewalls, intrusion detection systems, antivirus software, anti-spyware, good security polices, and so on, you might receive an 8. A bare system would receive a 1.
4. Now, subtract the second number from the first. Your final number should be between –8 (indicating a highly secure system that has no valuable data and a low profile) to 18 (indicating a system with no security, but sensitive national security information and a high profile). The lower the number, the better position your system is in.

This method is clearly subjective, but it provides a working method for you to begin to assess your systems' security levels. More details on assessing a system can be found in Chapter 6.

Identifying Types of Threats

Most attacks can be categorized as one of three broad classes:

- **Malware.** Malware is a generic term for software that has a malicious purpose. It includes virus attacks, Trojan horses, and spyware. This is the most prevalent danger to your system.
- **Intrusions.** This group of attacks includes any attempt to gain unauthorized access to your system.
- **Denial of Service (DoS) attacks.** These are designed to prevent legitimate access to your system.

This section offers a broad description of each type of attack. Later chapters will involve greater detail with each specific attack, how it is accomplished, and how to avoid it.

Malware

Malware is a generic term for software that has a malicious purpose. This section discusses three types of malware: viruses, Trojan horses, and spyware. Trojan horses and viruses are the most widely encountered.

According to Symantec (makers of Norton AntiVirus and other software products), a ***virus*** is "a small program that replicates and hides itself inside other programs, usually without your knowledge" (Symantec, 2003). This is the definition used throughout this book. A computer virus is similar to a biological virus in that both replicate and spread. The most common method for spreading a virus is using the victim's e-mail account to spread the virus to everyone in their address book. Some viruses do not actually harm the system itself, but *all* of them cause network slowdowns or shutdowns due to the heavy network traffic caused by the virus replication.

The ***Trojan horse*** receives its name from an ancient tale. In this tale, the city of Troy was besieged for an extended period of time, but the attackers could not gain entrance. Therefore, they constructed a huge wooden horse and left it in front of the gates to Troy one night. The next morning, the residents of Troy saw the horse and assumed it to be a gift, consequently

FYI: The Bagle Virus

The Bagle virus was a mass-mailing virus. Some companies were flooded by this virus to the point that several servers went completely offline. This is just one example of a virus that has no malicious payload but, by its simple volume, crashes systems.

rolling the wooden horse into the city. Unbeknownst to them, several soldiers where hidden inside the horse. That evening, the soldiers left the horse, opened the city gates, and let their fellow attackers into the city. An electronic Trojan horse works in the same manner, appearing to be benign software but secretly downloading a virus or some other type of malware onto your computer from within. How Trojan horses operate in general is discussed in Chapter 9 and the basics of how to secure protection against them are covered in Chapter 4. Specific Trojan horses (specific attacks) are detailed in Chapter 5.

Another category of malware currently on the rise is spyware. ***Spyware*** is simply software that literally spies on what you do on your computer. Spyware can be as simple as a ***cookie***—a text file that your browser creates and stores on your hard drive. Cookies are downloaded on to your machine by Web sites you visit. This text file is then used to recognize you when you return to the same site. That file can enable you to access pages more quickly and save you from having to enter your information multiple times on pages that you visit frequently. However, in order to do this, that file must be read by the Web site; this means that it can also be read by other Web sites. Any data that the file saves can be retrieved by any Web site, so your entire Internet browsing history can be tracked.

Another form of spyware, called a ***key logger***, records all of your keystrokes. Some key loggers also take periodic screen shots of your computer. Data is then either stored for later retrieval by the person who installed the key logger or is sent immediately back via e-mail. This action can have a legitimate purpose, such as an employer who wants to track the computer activities of their employees, but it can also be used for illegal/unethical purposes. Spyware, including key loggers, are discussed in depth in Chapter 5, and anti-spyware software is discussed throughout this text.

Compromising System Security

We will now look at attacks that breach your system's security. This activity is commonly referred to as ***hacking***, although that is not the term hackers themselves use. We will delve into appropriate terminology shortly; however, it should be noted at this point that ***cracking*** is the appropriate word for intruding onto a system without permission, usually with malevolent intent. Any attack that is designed to breach your security, either via some operating system flaw or any other means, can be classified as cracking. Simply put, hacking may or may not be for malevolent purposes. Cracking is hacking conducted for such malicious purposes.

Social engineering, which will be discussed in greater detail in Chapter 3, is a technique for breaching a system's security by exploiting human nature rather than technology. Social engineering uses standard con artist techniques to get users to offer up the information needed to gain access to a target system (Lemos, 2000). The way this method works is rather

FYI: Kevin Mitnick, A Social Engineer

Social engineering was the path that the famous hacker, Kevin Mitnick, most often used. Kevin Mitnick wrote a book on this subject titled *The Art of Deception: Controlling the Human Element of Security*. You may find this book to be a good resource for further information on social engineering. Mitnick, who now runs his own security company, is clearly one of the foremost experts on that topic.

simple. The perpetrator obtains preliminary information about a target organization and leverages it to gain additional information from the system's users.

Following is an example of social engineering in action. Armed with the name of a system administrator, you might call someone in the accounting department of a business and claim to be one of the company's technical support personnel. Mentioning the system administrator's name would help validate that claim, allowing you to ask questions in an attempt to ascertain more details about the system's specifications. A savvy intruder might even get the accounting person to say a username and password. As you can see, this method is based on how well the prospective intruder can manipulate people and actually has little to do with computer skills.

The growing popularity of wireless networks gives rise to new kinds of attacks. The most obvious and dangerous activity is ***war-driving***. This type of attack is an offshoot of war-dialing. With ***war-dialing***, a hacker sets up a computer to call phone numbers in sequence until another computer answers to try to gain entry to its system. War-driving, using much the same concept, is applied to locating vulnerable wireless networks. In this scenario, the hacker simply drives around trying to locate wireless networks (Poulsen, 2001). Many people forget that their wireless network signal often extends as much as 100 feet (thus, past walls). At the 2003 DefCon convention for hackers, there was a war-driving contest in which contestants drove around the city trying to locate as many vulnerable wireless networks as they could (DefCon II, 2003). While we will not discuss the mechanics of war-driving in this text, this kind of activity emphasizes the need for everyone, regardless of the size of their network, to be vigilant in their computer security.

Denial of Service Attacks

In addition to the various forms of malware and cracking attacks, there are attacks that prevent legitimate users from accessing their own systems. One such type of attack is called ***Denial of Service (DoS)***. In this type of attack, the attacker does not actually access the system, but rather simply blocks access from legitimate users. One common way to prevent legitimate service is to flood the targeted system with so many false connection requests that the system cannot respond to legitimate requests. DoS is an extremely common attack, second only to malware.

Common Attacks on Your Network

Now that we have examined the three broad classes of attack, it is an appropriate time to ask: What are the most likely attacks, and what are your vulnerabilities? This section covers the basics of what threats are possible and which are most likely to cause you or your organization problems. Chapters 4 and 5 answer these questions in greater detail.

The most likely threat to individuals and large organizations is the computer virus. In the first nine days of September 2003, the F-Secure security information Web site listed 20 new viruses (F-Secure, 2003). This is a fairly common monthly statistic. In any given month, several new virus outbreaks will be documented. New viruses are constantly being created, and old ones are still out there. As of this writing, all the major antivirus software vendors have released protection for the SoBig virus; today alone I received 18 e-mails with that virus as an attachment. Therefore, even when a virus is known and there is protection against it, it can continue to thrive because many people do not update their protection or clean their systems regularly.

Following viruses, the most common attack is unauthorized usage of computer systems. Unauthorized usage includes everything from Denial of Service attacks to outright intrusion of your system. It also includes internal employees misusing system resources. A recent survey by the Computer

FYI: Misusing System Resources

This has become a somewhat controversial topic. What, exactly, constitutes misuse of system resources? This can range from using business software to produce items for personal use to misuse of the Internet. It is important to realize that your work computer, software, and Internet connection are the property of your employer. Every minute spent idly surfing the Web is a minute of lost productivity to the employer and, ultimately, lost revenue. Wasting time at work is, in effect, stealing. This might not be a popular opinion with many employees, but it is one that most employers would heartily agree with.

Security Institute of 223 computer professionals showed over $445 million in losses due to computer security breaches. In 75% of the cases, an Internet connection was the point of attack, while 33% of professionals cited the location as their internal systems. A rather astonishing 78% of those surveyed detected employee abuse of systems/Internet (Computer Security Institute, 2002). This statistic means that, in any organization, one of the chief dangers might be its own employees.

In addition to the negative effects of employees misusing system resources, you need to also consider the possibility of an outright attack by an employee. An "insider" attack can cause considerably more damage than your typical Internet-based attack because the employee has more familiarity with the organization as a whole.

Basic Security Terminology

The security and hacking terms in this section are merely an introduction to computer security terminology, but they are an excellent starting point to help you prepare for learning more about computer security. Additional terms will be introduced throughout the text and listed in the Glossary at the end of this book.

The world of computer security takes its vocabulary from both the professional security community and the hacker community. As we explore these terms, you will see that there is a great deal of overlap. However, most hacker terminology is concerned with the activity (phreaking) or the person performing the activity (sneaker). In contrast, security professionals' terminology describes defensive barrier devices, procedures, and policies. This is quite logical because hacking is an offensive activity centered around attackers and attack methodologies, whereas security is a defensive activity concerning itself with defensive barriers and procedures.

People

There are many titles used for those individuals who set their sites on breaching computer security systems. In this section we describe some of the most common names. These are the terms that we will use throughout this text.

Hackers You probably have heard the term ***hacker*** used in movies and news broadcasts. Most people use it to describe any person who breaks into a computer system. In the hacking community, however, a hacker is an expert on a particular system or systems who wants to learn more about the system. Hackers feel that looking at a system's flaws is the best way to learn about that system. For example, someone well-versed in the Linux operating system who works to understand that system by learning its weaknesses and flaws would be a hacker.

This process does indeed often mean seeing whether a flaw can be exploited to gain access to a system. This "exploiting" part of the process is where hackers differentiate themselves into three groups:

- ***White hat hackers***, upon finding a vulnerability in a system, will report the vulnerability to the vendor of that system. For example, if they discovered some flaw in Red Hat Linuxtm, they would then e-mail the Red Hat company (probably anonymously) and explain exactly what the flaw is and how it was exploited.
- ***Black hat hackers*** are the people normally depicted in the media. Once they gain access to a system, their goal is to cause some type of harm. They might steal data, erase files, or deface Web sites. Black hat hackers are sometimes referred to as ***crackers***.
- ***Gray hat hackers*** are typically law-abiding citizens, but in some cases will venture into illegal activities. They may do so for a wide variety of reasons. Commonly, gray hat hackers conduct illegal activities for reasons they feel are ethical, such as hacking into a system belonging to a corporation that the hacker feels is engaged in unethical activities. Note that this term is not found in many textbooks, but is very common in the hacking community itself.

Regardless of how hackers view themselves, intruding on any system without permission is illegal. This means that, technically speaking, all hackers, regardless of the color of the metaphorical hat they may wear, are in violation of the law. However, many people feel that white hat hackers actually perform a service by finding flaws and informing vendors before those flaws are exploited by less ethically inclined individuals.

Script Kiddies So what is the term for someone who calls themselves a hacker, but lacks the expertise? The most common term for this sort of person is ***script kiddy*** (Glossary of Hacker Terminology, 1993). The name comes from the fact that the Internet is full of utilities and scripts that one can download to perform some hacking tasks. Someone who downloads such a tool without really understanding the target system would be considered a script kiddy.

Ethical Hackers: Sneakers When and why would someone give permission to another party to hack his system? The most common answer is in order to assess their systems' vulnerabilities. This employee, commonly called a ***sneaker***, legally breaks into a system in order to assess security deficiencies. In 1992, Robert Redford, Dan Aykroyd, and Sydney Poitier starred in a movie about this very subject. There are consultants who perform work of this type, and you can even find firms that specialize in this very activity as more and more companies are soliciting these services to assess their vulnerabilities.

Caution

Using Sneakers

It is amazing how few organizations employ sneakers to test their network defenses. While more employers are beginning to use these services, there are still a great many companies that do not. Perhaps your company uses internal employees or outside consultants to test its systems. Even so, it is my opinion that you also absolutely should have sneakers test your network defenses at least once per year. Although few organizations employ sneakers, it is crucial for your company to test its defenses by using actual hacking techniques.

Anyone hired to assess the vulnerabilities of a system should be both technically proficient and ethical. It is best to run a criminal background check and avoid those people with problem pasts. There are plenty of legitimate security professionals available who know and understand hacker skills, but have never committed security crimes. If you take the argument that hiring convicted hackers means hiring talented people to its logical conclusion, you would surmise that, obviously, the person in question is not as good a hacker as they would like to think because they where caught. Most importantly, giving a person with a criminal background access to your systems is on par with hiring a person with multiple DWI convictions to be your driver. In both cases, you are inviting problems and perhaps assuming significant civil liabilities.

Also, some review of their qualifications is clearly in order. Just as there are people who claim to be highly skilled hackers but are not, there are those who will claim to be skilled sneakers who lack the skills truly needed. You would not want to inadvertently hire a script kiddy who thinks she is a sneaker. Such a person might then pronounce your system to be sound, when in fact it was simply a lack of skills that prevented the script kiddy from successfully breaching your security. Later in this book we discuss the basics of assessing a target system. In that chapter, we also discuss the qualifications you should seek in any consultant you might hire for this purpose.

Security Devices

In addition to knowing the titles used for the people involved in breaching security, it would also be beneficial for you to start with a basic understanding of the security devices involved in stopping these individuals. You are probably familiar with some of these, and most of them will be discussed at much greater length in subsequent chapters.

Firewall The most basic security device is the ***firewall***. A firewall is a barrier between a network and the outside world. Sometimes a firewall takes the form of a stand-alone server, sometimes a router, and sometimes software running on a machine. Whatever its physical form, a firewall filters traffic entering and exiting the network. Chapter 12 will discuss firewalls in greater depth.

Proxy Server A ***proxy server*** is often used with a firewall to hide the internal network's IP (Internet Protocol) address and present a single IP address (its own) to the outside world. (For those readers not familiar with IP addresses, this topic and other network concepts will be discussed thoroughly in Chapter 2.) A proxy server is a server that sits between a client application, such as a Web browser, and a real server. It intercepts all requests to the real server to see whether it can fulfill the requests itself. If not, it forwards the request to the real server. Proxy servers have two main purposes: to improve performance and filter requests (Webopedia, 2004).

Intrusion Detection System (IDS) Firewalls and proxy servers guard the perimeter, but they do not interfere with network traffic. These two safeguards are often augmented by an ***Intrusion Detection System (IDS)***. An IDS simply monitors traffic, looking for suspicious activity that might indicate an attempted intrusion. For example, if you detect that some person has been scanning all the ports on your system to find out which ones are open, this might indicate that they are planning an attempt to breach your security. Chapters 3 and 12 discuss this in more detail.

Activities

The last set of terms that you need to be familiar with, before delving deeper into the topic of security, are the names given to the activities involved in either breaching security or preventing a security breach. Like the other terms defined in this introductory chapter, these terms will also be used throughout the text.

Phreaking One type of specialty hacking involves breaking into telephone systems. This sub-specialty of hacking is referred to as ***phreaking***. The *New Hacker's Dictionary* actually defines phreaking as "The action of using mischievous and mostly illegal ways in order to not pay for some sort of telecommunications bill, order, transfer, or other service" (Raymond, 2003). Phreaking requires a rather significant knowledge of telecommunications, and many phreakers have some professional experience working for a phone company or other telecommunications business. This type of activity is often dependent upon specific technology required to compromise phone systems more than simply knowing certain techniques. For example, there are certain devices used to compromise phone systems. Phone systems are often dependent on frequencies. (If you have a touchtone phone, you will notice that, as you press the keys, each has a different frequency.) Machines that record and duplicate certain frequencies are often essential to phone phreaking.

Authentication In addition to the security devices discussed above, there are specific security activities. ***Authentication*** is the most basic security activity. It is merely the process of determining whether the credentials given by a user or another system (such as a username and password) are authorized to access the network resource in question. When you log in with your username and password, the system will attempt to authenticate that username and password. If authenticated, you will be granted access.

Auditing Another crucial safeguard is ***auditing***, which is the process of reviewing logs, records, and procedures to determine whether these items meet standards. This activity will be mentioned in many places throughout this book and will be a definite focus in several chapters.

Network Security Paradigms

The approach you take toward security influences all subsequent security decisions and sets the tone for the entire organization's network security infrastructure. Network security paradigms can be classified by either the scope of security measures taken (perimeter, layered) or how proactive the system is.

Perimeter Security

In a ***perimeter security approach***, the bulk of security efforts are focused on the perimeter of the network. This focus might include firewalls, proxy servers, password policies (*note:* password policies will be discussed throughout this book, but are given more thorough treatment in Chapter 6), or any technology or procedure to make unauthorized access of the network less likely. Little or no effort is put into securing the systems within the network. In this approach, the perimeter is secured, but the various systems within that perimeter are often vulnerable.

The perimeter approach is clearly flawed. So why do some companies use it? A small organization might use the perimeter approach if they have budget constraints or inexperienced network administrators. This method might be adequate for small organizations that do not store sensitive data, but it rarely works in a larger corporate setting.

Layered Security

A ***layered security approach*** is one in which not only is the perimeter secured, but individual systems within the network are also secured. All servers, workstations, routers, and hubs within the network are secure. One way to accomplish this is to divide the network into segments and secure each segment as if it were a separate network so that, if perimeter security is compromised, not all internal systems are affected. Layered security is the preferred method whenever possible.

Proactive Versus Reactive

You should also measure your security approach by how proactive and/or reactive it is. This is done by gauging how much of the system's security infrastructure and policies are dedicated to preventive measures as opposed to how much are devoted to simply responding to an attack after it has occurred. A passive security approach takes few or no steps to prevent an attack. A dynamic or proactive defense is one in which steps are taken to prevent attacks before they occur.

One example of a proactive defense is the use of an IDS, which works to detect attempts to circumvent security measures. These systems can tell a system administrator that an attempt to breach security has been made, even if that attempt is not successful. An IDS can also be used to detect various techniques that intruders use to assess a target system, thus alerting a network administrator to the potential for an attempted breach before the attempt is even initiated.

Hybrid Security Methods

In the real world, network security is usually a combination of approaches and not focused completely in one paradigm or another. The two categories also combine. One can have a network that is predominantly passive, but layered, or one that is primarily perimeter, but proactive. It can be helpful to consider approaches to computer security along a Cartesian coordinate system, with the *x* axis representing the level of passive–active approaches and the *y* axis depicting the range from perimeter to layered defense. This system is shown in Figure 1.2.

The most desirable hybrid approach is a layered paradigm that is dynamic, which would be located in the upper right-hand quadrant of the figure. In this system, there would be perimeter security as well as layered internal security. Adding intrusion detection would give the system a level of dynamic activity that would make a much more complete security solution.

FIGURE 1.2 A security approach guide.

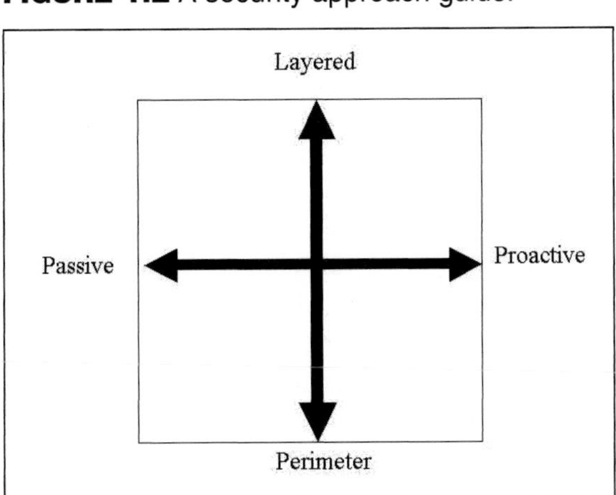

How Do Legal Issues Impact Network Security?

An increasing number of legal issues affect how one approaches computer security. If your organization is a publicly traded company, a government agency, or does business with either, there may be legal constraints regarding your network security. Even if your network is not legally bound to these security guidelines, it is useful to understand the various laws impacting computer security. You may choose to apply them to your own security standards.

One of the oldest pieces of legislation in the United States that affects computer security is the *Computer Security Act of 1987* (100th Congress, 1987). It requires government agencies to identify sensitive systems, conduct computer security training, and develop computer security plans. This law was a vague mandate ordering federal agencies in the United States to establish security measures, but it does not specify any standards.

This legislation established a legal mandate to enact specific standards, paving the way for future guidelines and regulations. It also helped define terms, such as what information is considered "sensitive." This quote is found in the legislation itself.

> *The term 'sensitive information' means any information, the loss, misuse, or unauthorized access to or modification of which could adversely affect the national interest or the conduct of Federal programs, or the privacy to which individuals are entitled under section 552a of title 5, United States Code (the Privacy Act), but which has not been specifically authorized under criteria established by an Executive order or an Act of Congress to be kept secret in the interest of national defense or foreign policy (100th Congress, 1987).*

Caution

Privacy Laws

It is also critical to keep in mind that any law that governs privacy (such as the Health Insurance Portability and Accountability Act of 1996, HIPAA) also has a direct impact on computer security. If your system is compromised and, thus, data that is covered under any privacy statute is compromised, you may need to prove that you exercised due diligence in protecting that data. If it can be shown that you did not take proper precautions, you might be found civilly liable.

This definition should be kept in mind, for it is not just social security information or medical history that must be secured. When considering what information needs to be secure, simply ask the question: Would the unauthorized access or modification of this information adversely affect your organization? If the answer is yes, then you must consider that information sensitive and in need of security precautions.

Another more specific federal law that applied to mandated security for government systems is *OMB Circular A-130* (specifically, Appendix III). This document requires that federal agencies establish security programs containing specified elements. It also describes requirements for developing standards for computer systems and for records held by government agencies.

Most states have specific laws regarding computer security, such as legislation like the *Computer Crimes Act of Florida,* the *Computer Crime Act of Alabama,* and the *Computer Crimes Act of Oklahoma.* If you are responsible for network security, you might find yourself part of a criminal investigation. This could be an investigation into a hacking incident or employee misuse of computer resources. A list of computer crime laws (organized by state) can be found at **www.alw.nih.gov/Security/FIRST/papers/legal/statelaw.txt.** This government list is from the Advanced Laboratory Workstation (ALW), National Institutes for Health (NIH), and Center for Information Technology (CIT).

Online Security Resources

As you read this book and when you move out into the professional world, you will have frequent need for additional security resources. Appendix B includes a more complete list of resources, but this section highlights a few of the most important ones and those you may find useful now.

CERT

CERT (**www.cert.org**) stands for Computer Emergency Response Team. This group is sponsored by Carnegie-Mellon University. CERT was the first computer incident–response team and is still one of the most respected in the industry. Anyone interested in network security should visit the site routinely. On the Web site, shown in Figure 1.3, you will find a wealth of documentation including guidelines for security policies, cutting-edge security research, and more.

FIGURE 1.3 CERT Web site.

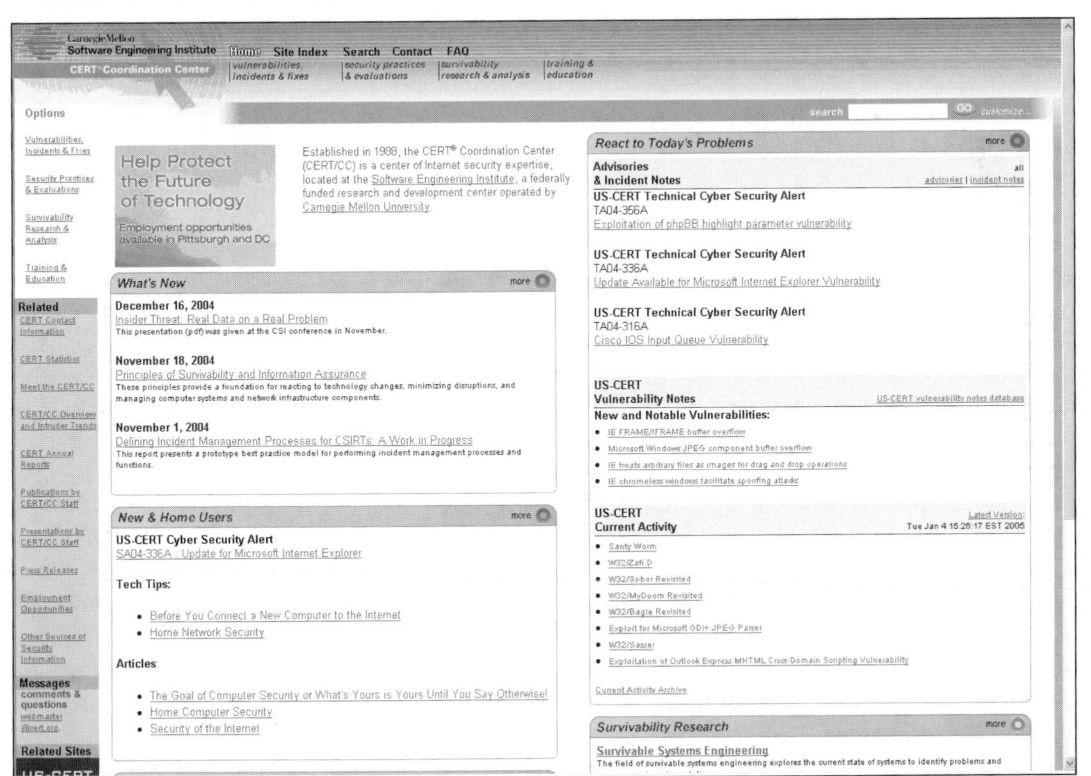

Microsoft Security Advisor

Because so many computers today run Microsoft operating systems, another good resource is the Microsoft Security Advisor Web site: **www.microsoft.com/security/default.mspx**. This site, shown in Figure 1.4, is a portal to all Microsoft security information, tools, and updates. If you use any Microsoft software, then it is advised that you visit this Web site regularly.

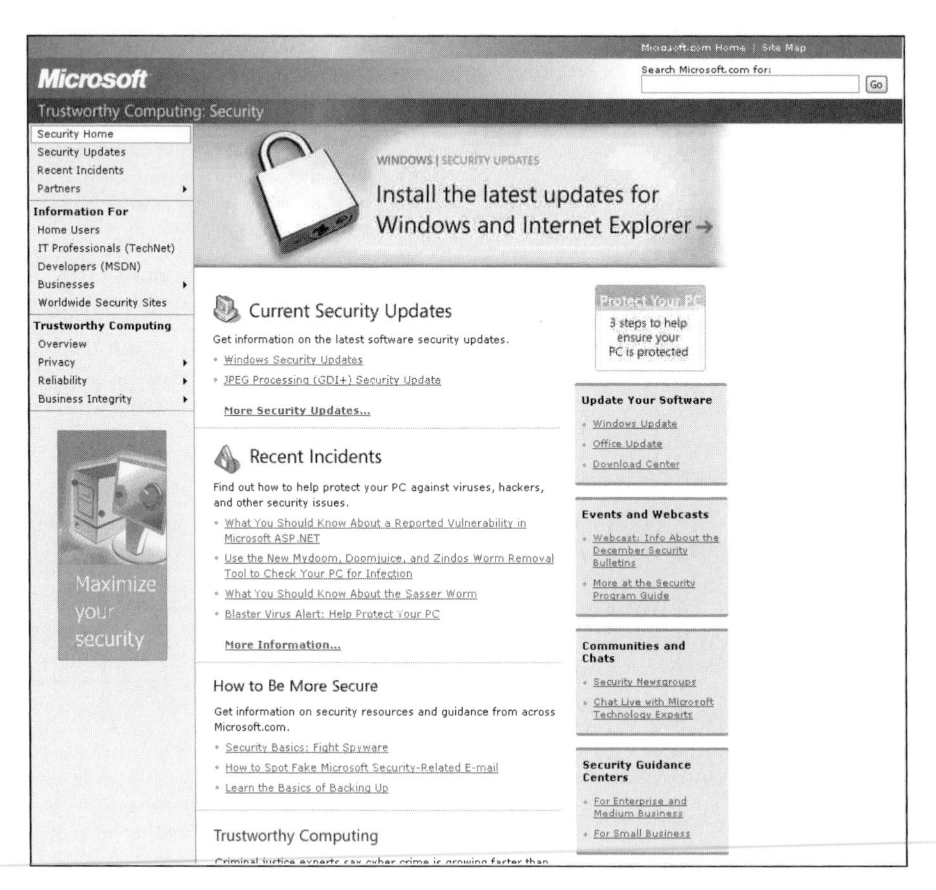

FIGURE 1.4 Microsoft Security Advisor Web site.

F-Secure

The F-Secure corporation maintains a Web site at **www.f-secure.com/** as shown in Figure 1.5. This site is, among other things, a repository for detailed information on virus outbreaks. Here you will not only find notifications about a particular virus, but you will also find detailed information about the virus. This information includes how the virus spreads; ways to recognize the virus; and, frequently, specific tools for cleaning an infected system of a particular virus.

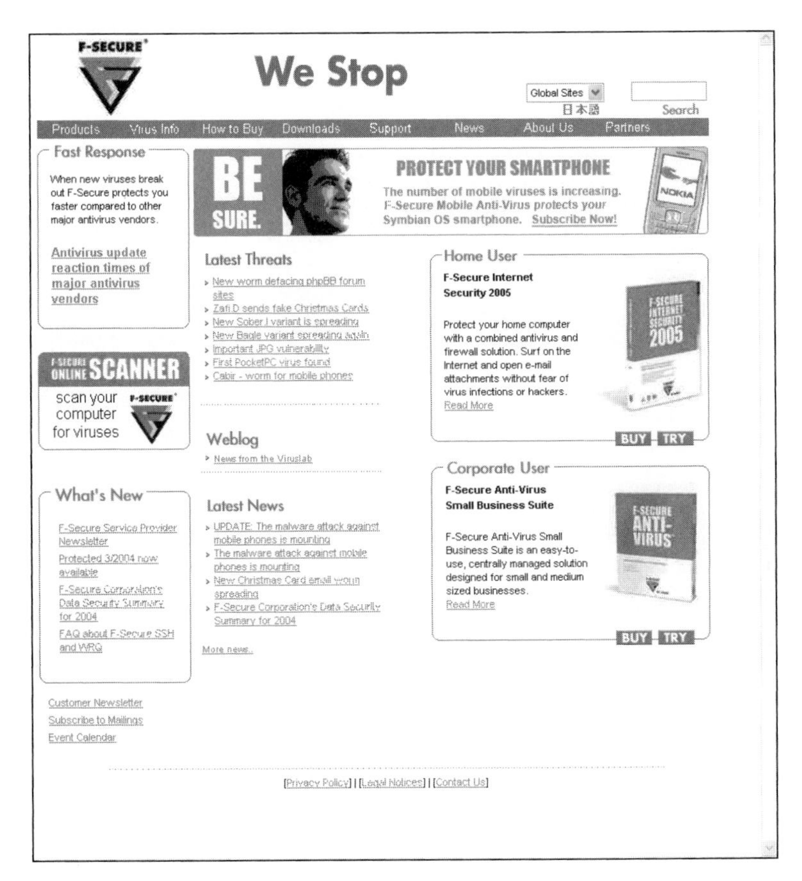

FIGURE 1.5 F-Secure Web site.

SANS Institute

The SANS Institute Web site (**www.sans.org/**) is a vast repository of security-related documentation. On this site, shown in Figure 1.6 on page 20, you will find detailed documentation on virtually every aspect of computer security you can imagine. The SANS Institute also sponsors a number of security research projects and publishes information about those projects on their Web site.

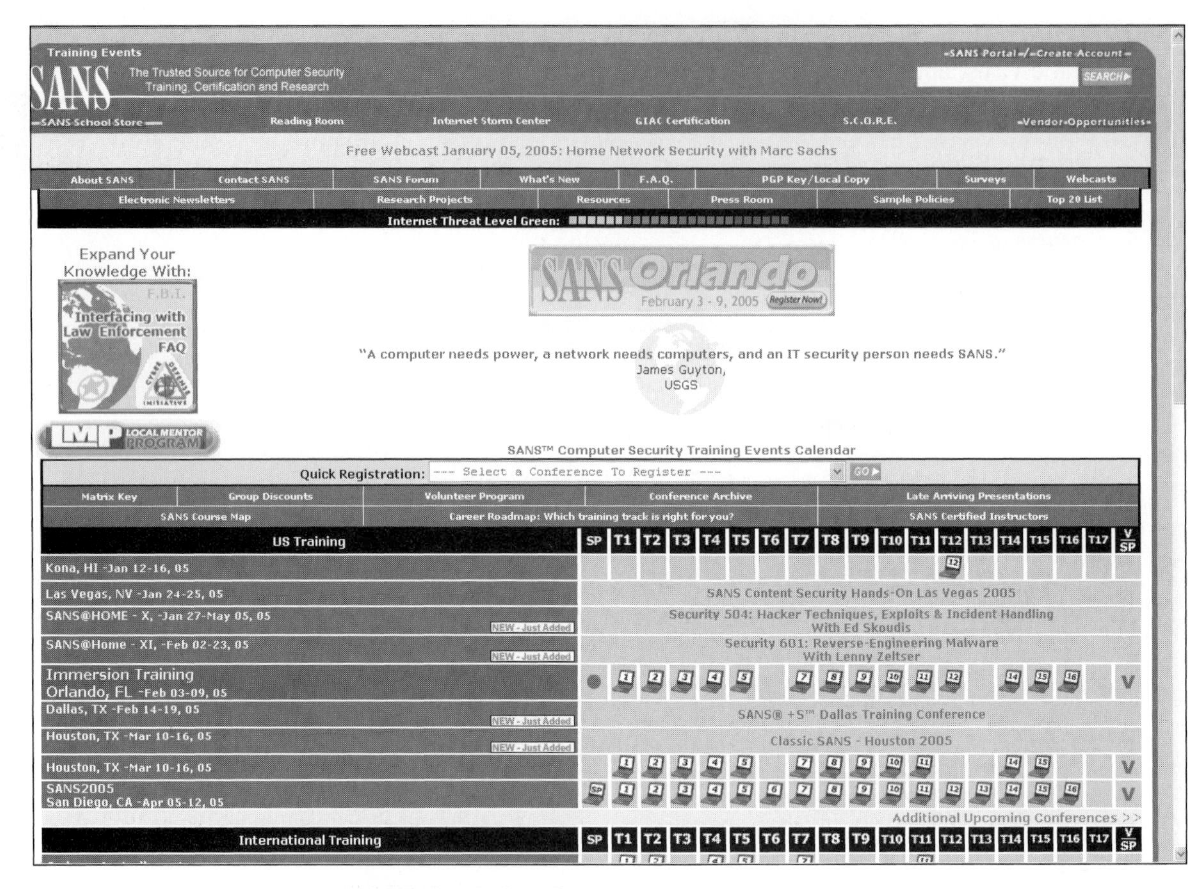

FIGURE 1.6 SANS Institute Web site.

Summary

Network security is a complex and constantly evolving field. Practitioners must stay on top of new threats and solutions and be proactive in assessing risk and protecting their networks. The first step to understanding network security is to become acquainted with the actual threats posed to a network. Without a realistic idea of what threats might affect your systems, you will be unable to effectively protect them. It is also critical that you acquire a basic understanding of the techniques used by both security professionals and those who would seek to compromise your network's security.

Test Your Skills

MULTIPLE CHOICE QUESTIONS

1. One extreme viewpoint about computer security is:
   A. the federal government will handle security.
   B. Microsoft will handle security.
   C. there are no imminent dangers to your system.
   D. there is no danger if you use Linux.

2. Before you can formulate a defense for a network, you will need:
   A. appropriate security certifications.
   B. a clear picture of the dangers to be defended against.
   C. to finish this textbook.
   D. the help of an outside consultant.

3. Which of the following is not one of the three major classes of threats?
   A. attempts to intrude on the system
   B. online auction fraud
   C. Denial of Service attacks
   D. a computer virus

4. A computer virus is any:
   A. program that is downloaded to your system without your permission.
   B. malicious program that self-replicates.
   C. program that causes harm to your system.
   D. program that can change your Windows registry.

5. Spyware is:
   A. any software that monitors your system.
   B. only software that logs keystrokes.
   C. any software used to gather intelligence.
   D. only software that monitors what Web sites you visit.

6. What is malware?
   A. software that has some malicious purpose
   B. software that is not functioning properly
   C. software that damages your system
   D. software that is not properly configured for your system

7. When a hacking technique uses persuasion and deception to get a person to provide information to help them compromise security, this is referred to as:
   A. social engineering.
   B. conning.
   C. human intel.
   D. soft hacking.

8. What is the most common threat on the Internet?
   A. auction fraud
   B. hackers
   C. computer viruses
   D. illegal software

9. According to a 2002 survey of 223 computer professionals prepared by the Computer Security Institute, which of the following was cited as an issue by more of the respondents?
   A. internal systems
   B. employee abuse
   C. routers
   D. Internet connection

10. What is the second most common attack on computer systems?
    A. Trojan horses
    B. unauthorized usage of the computer system
    C. illegal software
    D. sneakers

11. What is a sneaker?
    A. a person who hacks a system without being caught
    B. a person who hacks a system by faking a legitimate password
    C. a person who hacks a system to test its vulnerabilities
    D. a person who is an amateur hacker

12. What is the term for hacking a phone system?
    A. telco-hacking
    B. hacking
    C. cracking
    D. phreaking
13. An intrusion detection system is an example of:
    A. proactive security.
    B. perimeter security.
    C. hybrid security.
    D. good security practices.
14. Which of the following is the most basic security activity?
    A. authentication
    B. firewalls
    C. password protection
    D. auditing
15. The three approaches to security are:
    A. perimeter, layered, hybrid.
    B. high security, medium security, low security.
    C. internal, external, hybrid.
    D. perimeter, complete, none.
16. The most desirable approach to security is one that is:
    A. perimeter and dynamic.
    B. layered and dynamic.
    C. perimeter and static.
    D. layered and static.
17. The following type of privacy law affects computer security:
    A. any state privacy law.
    B. any privacy law applicable to your organization.
    C. any privacy law.
    D. any federal privacy law.

18. Which of the following is the best definition of "sensitive information?"
    A. any information that has impact on national security
    B. any information that is worth more than $1,000
    C. any information that, if accessed by unauthorized personnel, could damage your organization in any way
    D. any information that is protected by any privacy laws

19. The first computer incident–response team is affiliated with what university?
    A. Massachusetts Institute of Technology
    B. Carnegie-Mellon University
    C. Harvard University
    D. California Technical University

20. A major resource for detailed information on a computer virus is the:
    A. MIT Virus Library
    B. Microsoft Virus Library
    C. F-Secure Virus Library
    D. National Virus Repository

EXERCISES

Exercise 1.1: How Many Virus Attacks Have Occurred this Month?

1. Using a Web site resource, such as **www.f-secure.com**, look up recent computer virus outbreaks.
2. Write down how many virus outbreaks have occurred in the past seven days.
3. Write down how many outbreaks there have been in the past 30 days, 90 days, and one year.
4. Are virus attacks increasing in frequency?

Exercise 1.2: Learning About Cookies as Spyware

1. Perform some online research to get an idea of what kind of information cookies store. You might find the following Web sites helpful:

http://computercops.biz/article3911.html

www.ctc-solutions.co.uk/internet_security_2.html

www.howstuffworks.com/cookie1.htm

2. Write a brief essay explaining in what way cookies can invade privacy.

Exercise 1.3: Hacker Terminology

1. Use the *Hacker's Dictionary* at **www.hack.gr/jargon/** to define the following hacker terms:

alpha geek	grok
Red Book	wank

Exercise 1.4: Learning About the Law

1. Using the Web, journals, books, or other resources, find out whether your state or territory has any laws specific to computer security. You might find the following Web sites helpful:

   www.usdoj.gov/criminal/cybercrime/cclaws.html

   www.pbs.org/wgbh/pages/frontline/shows/hackers/blame/crimelaws.html

   www.ncsl.org/programs/lis/cip/viruslaws.htm

   www.cybercrime.gov/

2. List three laws that you find, with a brief description of each. The list can be a simple one, noting the pertinent laws in your region. Describe each one with one or two sentences.

Exercise 1.5: Using Security Resources

1. Using one of the preferred Web resources listed in this chapter, find three policy or procedure documents from that resource that you think are important to your school or organization's security.
2. List the documents you selected.
3. Write a brief essay explaining why those particular documents are important to your organization's security.

PROJECTS

Project 1.1: Learning About a Virus

1. Using Web resources from Appendix B and sites such as **www.f-secure.com**, find a virus that has been released in the last six months.

2. Research how the virus spread and what damage it caused.

3. Write a brief (1/2–1 page) paper on this virus. Tell how the virus worked, how it spread, and any other essential information you can find.

Project 1.2: Considering the Law (a group project)

Write a description of a computer law that you would like to have passed, along with specifications as to its implementation, enforcement, and justification.

Project 1.3: Recommending Security

1. Using the Web, journals, or books, locate security recommendations from any reputable source, such as the SANS Institute. Any of the sites mentioned in the resources section of this chapter would be a good choice.

2. List five of those recommendations.

3. Explain why you agree or disagree with each one.

Case Study

Consider the job of a network administrator for a small, family-oriented video store. The store is not part of a chain of stores and has a very limited security budget. It has five machines for employees to use to check out movies and one server on which to keep centralized records. That server is in the manager's office. The administrator takes the following security precautions:

1. Each machine is upgraded to Windows XP, with the personal firewall turned on.
2. Antivirus software was installed on all machines.
3. A tape backup is added to the server, and tapes are kept in a locked file cabinet in the manager's office.
4. Internet access to employee machines is removed.

Now consider these questions:

1. What did these actions accomplish?
2. What additional actions might you recommend?

Chapter 2

Networks and the Internet

Chapter Objectives

After reading this chapter and completing the exercises, you will be able to do the following:

- Describe the OSI model of network communication.
- Explain the use of MAC addresses.
- Identify each of the major protocols used in network communication (for example, FTP and Telnet) and what use you can make of each.
- Understand the various connection methods and speeds used on networks.
- Compare and contrast a hub and switch.
- Identify what a router is and its use.
- Understand how data is transmitted over a network.
- Explain how the Internet works and the use of IP addresses and URLs.
- Use network utilities such as these: ping, IPConfig, and tracert.
- Explain the use of firewalls and proxy servers.

Introduction

To manage network security, you will need knowledge of how computer networks operate. Those readers who already have a strong working knowledge of network operations may choose to skim this chapter or perhaps give it a quick read as a review. For other readers new to computer networking, studying this chapter will give you a basic introduction to how networks and the Internet work. This understanding of networks and the Internet will be crucial to your comprehension of later topics presented in this book.

In this chapter, we will examine the basic model of a network and the underlying technologies that allow networks to communicate. This information will be the foundation on which all of the other materials in this course are built. In the exercises at the end of the chapter, you will be able to practice using some utilities such as IPConfig, tracert, and ping.

The OSI Model

Let's begin with the ***OSI model*** or Open Systems Interconnect model. This model is a description of how networks communicate. It describes the various protocols and activities, and it delineates how the protocols and activities relate to each other. This model is divided into seven layers, as shown in Table 2.1. It

TABLE 2.1 The OSI model.

Layer	Description	Protocols
Application	This layer interfaces directly to the application and performs common application services for the application processes.	None
Presentation	The presentation layer relieves the application layer of concern regarding syntactical differences in data representation within the end-user systems.	POP, SMTP, DNS, FTP, Telnet, ARP
Session	The session layer provides the mechanism for managing the dialogue between end-user application processes.	NetBIOS
Transport	This layer provides end-to-end communication control.	TCP
Network	This layer routes the information in the network.	IP, ICMP
Data Link	This layer describes the logical organization of data bits transmitted on a particular medium. Data Link is divided into two sublayers: the Media Access Control layer (MAC) and the Logical Link Control layer (LLC).	SLIP, PPP
Physical	This layer describes the physical properties of the various communications media, as well as the electrical properties and interpretation of the exchanged signals. In other words, the physical layer is the actual NIC, Ethernet cable, and so forth.	None

was originally developed by the International Standards Organization (ISO) in the 1980s.

Many networking students memorize this model. It is good to at least memorize the names of the seven layers and in general understand what they each do. From a security perspective, the more you understand about network communications, the more sophisticated your defense can be. The most important thing for you to understand is that this model describes a hierarchy of communication. One layer will only communicate with the layer directly above it or below it.

Network Basics

Getting two or more computers to communicate and transmit data is a process that is simple in concept, but complex in application. Consider all the factors involved. First, you will need to physically connect the computers. This connection requires either a cable that plugs into your computer or is accomplished by infrared light. The cable is then plugged either directly into another computer or is plugged into a router switch or a hub that will, in turn, connect to several other computers. (Routers and hubs are connective devices that will be explained in detail later in this chapter.)

There is a card in most modern computers called a ***Network Interface Card*** or simply a ***NIC***. If the connection is through a cable, the part of the NIC that is external to the computer has a connection slot that looks like a telephone jack, only slightly bigger. Of course, wireless networks, which are being used with greater frequency, also use a NIC but, rather than having a slot for a cable to connect to, the wireless network simply uses infrared signals to transmit to a nearby wireless router or hub.

Media Access Control (MAC) Addresses

MAC addresses are an interesting topic. (You might notice that MAC is also a sublayer of the data link layer of the OSI model.) A MAC address is a unique address for a NIC. Every NIC in the world has a unique address that

> **FYI: IP Address**
>
> An IP address is an identifier for a computer or device on a TCP/IP network. In these types of networks, messages are routed based on the IP address of the destination. The format of an IP address is a 32-bit numeric address written as four numbers separated by periods. Each number can be zero to 255. More information on IP addresses and TCP/IP will be given later in this chapter.

is represented by a six-byte hexadecimal number. There is a protocol that is used to convert IP addresses to MAC addresses. This protocol is the Address Resolution Protocol or ARP. Therefore, when you type in a Web address, the DNS (Domain Name Server) protocol is used to translate that into an IP address. The ARP protocol will then translate that IP address into a specific MAC address of an individual NIC.

DNS Servers

How does a URL get translated into an IP address? How does the computer know what IP goes with what URL? There are servers set up just to do this task. They are called ***DNS servers***. ***DNS*** stands for ***Domain Name Server*** (or System or Service). DNS translates domain names (**www.example.com**) into IP addresses (198.203.167.9). Domain names are easy to remember because they are alphabetic, but the Internet is really based on IP addresses. Thus, every time you use a domain name, a DNS server must translate the name into the corresponding IP address. If you are on a corporate network, you probably have a DNS server on your network. If not, then your ISP has one. These servers maintain a table of IP-to-URL entries.

From time to time there are transfers of DNS data, called ***zone transfers***, that allow one DNS server to send its changes to another. Across the Internet, there are root DNS servers that are maintained with centralized data for all registered URL/IP addresses. The DNS system is, in fact, its own network. If one DNS server does not know how to translate a particular domain name, it asks another one, and so on, until the correct IP address is returned.

Primary DNS is the name given to the server or service that holds the authoritative information for a domain. Actually, a DNS server (the computer/software) is not specifically "primary" or "secondary." A DNS server can be primary for one zone (domain) and secondary for another. By definition, a primary DNS server holds the master copy of the data for a zone, and secondary servers have copies of this data that they synchronize with the primary server through zone transfers at intervals or when prompted by the primary server.

The Physical Connection: Local Networks

As mentioned, cables are one of the ways that computers are connected to each other. The cable connection used with hard-wired NICs is an RJ 45 connection. (RJ is short for "Registered Jack," which is an international industry standard.) In contrast to the computer's RJ 45 jacks, standard telephone lines use RJ 11 jacks. The biggest difference between jacks involves the number of wires in the connector, also called the terminator. Phone lines have four wires, whereas RJ 45 connectors have eight. Figure 2.1 shows an example of an RJ 45 connector.

FIGURE 2.1 RJ 45 connector.

If you look on the back of most computers or the connection area of a laptop, you will probably find three ports that, at first glance, look like phone jacks. Two of the three ports are probably for a traditional modem and telephone and accept a standard RJ 11 jack. The other port is larger and accepts an RJ 45 jack. Not all computers come with a NIC, but most modern computers do. Additionally, many modern computers no longer contain an internal modem, in which case there would not be an RJ 11 jack.

This standard connector jack must be crimped on the end of the cable. The cable used in most networks today is a category 5 cable—or CAT-5, as it is commonly known. (Note that CAT-6 cable is becoming more prevalent with high-speed networks.) Table 2.2 summarizes the various categories of cable and their uses.

TABLE 2.2 Cable types and uses.

Category	Specifications	Uses
1	Low-speed analog (less than 1 MHz)	Telephone, doorbell
2	Analog line (less than 10 MHz)	Telephone
3	Up to 16 MHz or 10 Mbps (megabits per second)	Voice transmissions
4	Up to 20 MHz/16 Mbps	Data lines, Ethernet networks
5	100 MHz/100 Mbps	Most common type of network cable
6	250 MHz/1,000 Mbps	Very high-speed networks

The type of cable used in connecting computers is also often referred to as unshielded twisted pair cable (UTP). In UTP, the wires in the cable are in pairs, twisted together without any additional shielding. As you can see in Table 2.2, each subsequent category of cable is somewhat faster and more robust than the last. It should be noted that, although CAT-4 can be used for networks, it is almost never used for that purpose simply because it is slower, less reliable, and older technology. You will usually see CAT-5 cable and, increasingly, CAT-6.

Notice the speeds listed in Table 2.2, such as Mbps. This speed stands for megabits per second. Ultimately, everything in the computer is stored in a binary format using a 1 or a 0. These units are called bits. It takes eight bits, or one byte, to represent a single character such as a letter, number, or carriage return. It follows, then, that CAT-5 cable can transmit up to 100,000,000 bits per second. This is known as the bandwidth of the cable. Remember, though, that this is the maximum that can be transmitted "across the wire" at any given second. If multiple users are on a network and all of them are sending data, the traffic generated is going to quickly use up all of the bandwidth. Any pictures transmitted also use a great deal of bandwidth. Simple scanned-in photos can easily reach two megabytes (2 million bytes or 16 million bits) or much more. Streaming media, such as video, is perhaps the most demanding on bandwidth.

If you simply want to connect two computers to each other, you can have the cable go directly from one computer to the other. But what do you do if you wish to connect more than one computer? What if 100 computers need to be connected on a network? There are three devices that can help you accomplish this task: the hub, the switch, and the router. These devices each use CAT-5 or CAT-6 cable with RJ 45 connectors and are explained in the following sections.

FYI: Cable Speed

Category 6 cable is for the new gigabit Ethernet. CAT-5 cable works at speeds of up to 100 megabits per second (Mbps), whereas CAT-6 works at 1,000 Mbps. CAT-6 has been widely available for several years. However, for CAT-6 to truly function properly, you need hubs/switches (explained below) and NICs that also transmit at gigabit speeds. For this reason, the spread of gigabit Ethernet has been much slower than many analysts expected.

The Hub The simplest connection device is the ***hub***. A hub is a small, box-shaped electronic device into which you can plug network cables. It will have four or more (commonly up to 24) RJ 45 jacks, each called a ***port***. A hub can connect as many computers as it has ports. (For example, an eight-port hub can connect eight computers). You can also connect one hub to another; this strategy is referred to as "stacking" hubs. Hubs are quite inexpensive and simple to set up—just plug in the cable. However, hubs have a downside. If you send a packet from one computer to another, a copy of that packet is actually sent out from every port on the hub. (A packet is the unit of data transmission and will be examined later in this chapter.) All of these copies lead to a great deal of unnecessary network traffic. This occurs because the hub, being a very simple device, has no way of knowing where a packet is supposed to go. Therefore, it simply sends copies of the packet out of all of its ports.

In the context of the OSI model, a hub is a layer 1 device.

The Switch The next connection device option is the ***switch***. A switch is basically an intelligent hub. However, a switch does not work in the same way as a hub. When a switch receives a packet, it will send that packet only out the port for the computer to which it needs to go. A switch builds a table based on MAC addresses and uses that to determine where a packet is being sent. How this determination is made is explained in the *Data Transmission* section below.

In the context of the OSI model, a switch is a layer 2 device.

The Router Finally, if you wish to connect two or more networks together, you use a ***router***. A router is similar in concept to a hub or switch, as it does relay packets; yet, it is far more sophisticated. You can program most routers and control how they relay packets. The specifics of how you program the router are different from vendor to vendor. There are entire books written specifically on just programming routers. It is not possible to cover specific router programming techniques in this book; however, you should be aware that most routers are programmable, allowing you to change how they route traffic. Also, unlike using a hub or switch, the two networks connected by a router are still separate networks. In summary, the three basic connection devices are the hub, switch, and router, all of which connect category 5 or category 6 cable using RJ 45 connectors.

The Physical Connection: Internet

The explanation above covers the connections between computers on a local network, but what connection methods are used for the Internet? Your Internet service provider or the company for which you work probably use one of the fast Internet connections described in Table 2.3. This table summarizes the most common Internet connection types and their speeds.

TABLE 2.3 Internet connection types.

Connection Type	Speed	Details
DS0	64 kilobits per second	1/24 of a T1 line or one T1 channel
ISDN	128 kilobits per second	2 DS0 lines working together to provide a high-speed data connection
T1	1.54 megabits per second	24 DS0 lines working as one, with 23 carrying data and one carrying information about the other lines. This type of connection has become common for schools and businesses.
T3	43.2 megabits per second	672 DS0 lines working together. This method is the equivalent of 28 T1 lines.
OC3	155 megabits per second	All OC lines are optical and do not use traditional phone lines. OC3 lines are quite fast, very expensive, and are often found at telecommunications companies.
OC12	622 megabits per second	The equivalent of 336 T1 lines or 8064 phone lines.
OC48	2.5 gigabits per second	The equivalent of 4 OC12 lines.

It is common to find T1 connection lines in many locations. A cable modem can sometimes achieve speeds comparable to a T1 line. Note that cable modems were not listed in Table 2.3 simply because their actual speeds vary greatly depending on a variety of circumstances, including how many people in your immediate vicinity are using the same cable modem provider. You are not likely to encounter the OC lines unless you work in telecommunications.

Data Transmission

We have briefly seen the physical connection methods, but how is data actually transmitted? To transmit data, a packet is sent. The basic purpose of a cable is to transmit packets from one machine to another. It does not matter whether that packet is a part of a document, video, image, or just some internal signal from the computer. This fact begs the question: What, exactly, is a packet? As we discussed earlier, everything in a computer is ultimately stored as 1s and 0s, called bits, which are grouped into sets of eight, called a byte. A ***packet***, also referred to as a ***datagram***, is a certain number of bytes divided into a header and a body. The header is a 20-byte section at the beginning of the packet. The header tells you where the packet is coming from, where it is going, and more. The body contains the actual data, in binary format, that you wish to send. The aforementioned routers and switches work by reading the header portion of any packets that come to them. This process is how they determine where the packet should be sent.

Protocols There are different types of network communications for different purposes. The different types of network communications are called ***protocols***. A protocol is essentially an agreed-upon method of communication. In fact, this definition is exactly how the word "protocol" is used in standard, non-computer usage. Each protocol has a specific purpose and normally operates on a certain logical port. (Ports are discussed in more detail below.)

Some of the most significant protocols that are currently used include TCP, IP, UDP, and ICMP. ***TCP*** (***Transmission Control Protocol***) enables two host computers to establish a connection and exchange data. It guarantees the delivery of data in the proper order. ***IP*** (***Internet Protocol***) specifies the format of the packets and the addressing scheme. Most networks combine IP with the higher-level TCP to form the protocol suite known as ***TCP/IP*** (***Transmission Control Protocol/Internet Protocol***), which establishes a virtual connection between a destination and a source. IP by itself is something similar to the postal system. It allows you to address a package and drop it in the system, but there is no direct link between you and the recipient. TCP/IP, on the other hand, establishes a connection between two hosts so that they can send messages back and forth for a period of time (Webopedia, 2004).

UDP (***User Datagram Protocol***) is a connectionless protocol, meaning that it is a network protocol in which a host can send a message without establishing a connection with the recipient. UDP runs on top of IP networks (referred to as UDP/IP) and, unlike TCP/IP, it provides very few error recovery services. Instead, it offers a direct way to send and receive datagrams (packets) over an IP network. Its primary use is broadcasting messages over a network, but it does not guarantee the delivery of packets.

ICMP (***Internet Control Message Protocol***) is an extension of IP. It supports packets containing error, informational, and control messages. The ping command (explored later in this chapter), for example, uses ICMP to test an Internet connection.

Some of the most important and commonly used application-layer protocols are listed in Table 2.4.

Each of these protocols will be explained in more detail, as needed, in later chapters of this book. You should also note that this list is not complete. There are dozens of other protocols, but for now these will suffice. The most important thing for you to realize is that all communication on networks takes place via packets, and those packets are transmitted according to certain protocols depending on the type of communication that is occurring.

Ports You may be wondering what a port is. Do not confuse this type of port with the connection locations on the back of your computer such as a serial port, parallel port, or RJ-45 and RJ-11 ports (physical ports) we discussed earlier. A ***port***, in networking terms, is a handle—a connection point. It is a numeric designation for a particular pathway of communications. All network communication, regardless of the port used, comes into your computer via the connection on your Network Interface Card.

The picture we have drawn of networks, to this point, is one of machines connected to each other via cables and perhaps to hubs/switches/routers. Networks transmit binary information in packets using certain protocols and ports.

How the Internet Works

Now that you have a basic idea of how computers communicate with each other over a network, it is time to discuss how the Internet works. The Internet is essentially just a large number of networks connected to each other. Therefore, the Internet works exactly the same way as your local network. It sends the same sort of data packets using the same protocols. These various networks are simply connected into main transmission lines called ***backbones***. The points where backbones connect to each other are called ***Network Access Points (NAP)***. When you log on to the Internet, you probably use an ***Internet Service Provider (ISP)***. That ISP has a connection either to the Internet backbone or to yet another provider that has a backbone. Thus, logging on to the Internet is a process of connecting your computer to your ISP's network, which is, in turn, connected to one of the backbones on the Internet.

IP Addresses

With tens of thousands of networks and millions of individual computers communicating and sending data, a predictable problem arises. That problem is ensuring that the data packets go to the correct computer. This task is accomplished in much the same way as traditional letter mail is delivered to the right person: via an address. With network communications, this

TABLE 2.4 Application layer protocols.

Protocol	Purpose	Port
FTP (File Transfer Protocol)	For transferring files between computers	20, 21
tFTP (Trivial File Transfer Protocol)	A quicker, but less reliable, form of FTP	69
Telnet	Used to remotely log on to a system. You can then use a command prompt or shell to execute commands on that system. Popular with network administrators.	23
SMTP (Simple Mail Transfer Protocol)	Sends e-mail	25
WhoIS	Command that queries a target IP address for information	43
DNS (Domain Name Service)	Translates URLs into Web addresses	53
HTTP (Hypertext Transfer Protocol)	Displays Web pages	80
POP3 (Post Office Protocol Version 3)	Retrieves e-mail	110
NNTP (Network News Transfer Protocol)	Used for network news groups (usenet newsgroups). You can access these groups over the Web via **www.google.com** by selecting the "groups" tab.	119
NetBIOS	An older Microsoft protocol used for naming systems on a local network	137, 138, 139
IRC (Internet Relay Chat)	Used for chat rooms	194
ICMP (Internet Control Message Protocol)	These are simply packets that contain error messages, informational messages, and control messages.	No specific port

address is a special one, referred to as an IP address. An ***IP address*** is an address used to uniquely identify a device on an IP network. It is a unique number ID assigned to one host or interface in a network. The address consists of four 3-digit numbers separated by periods. (An example would be

107.22.98.198.) Each of the three-digit numbers must be between 0 and 255. This rule stems from the fact that IP addresses are actually four binary numbers; you just see them in decimal format. Recall that a byte is eight bits (1s and 0s), and an eight-bit binary number converted to decimal format will be between 0 and 255.

IN PRACTICE: Converting Binary Numbers

For those readers not familiar with converting binary numbers to decimal, there are several methods. We will discuss one of these methods here. You should be aware that the computer will do this for you in the case of IP addresses, but some readers may wish to know how this is done. While there are many methods, perhaps the simplest is:

divide repeatedly by 2,

using "remainders" rather than decimal places, until you get down to 1. For example, convert decimal 31 to binary:

31/2 = 15 Remainder 1
15/2 = 7 Remainder 1
7/2 = 3 Remainder 1
3/2 = 1 Remainder 1
1/2 = 0 Remainder 1

Now read the remainders from bottom to top: the binary equivalent is 00011111. (Note that you complete the octet by filling in the leading spaces with "0"s to make an 8 bit numeral.)

While you can step through the math to convert a decimal number to a binary number, you may find it easier to use a converter. There are many converters available on the Internet that can be found by searching for the keywords "binary converter". Figures 2.2 and 2.3 show two examples of converters that are readily available.

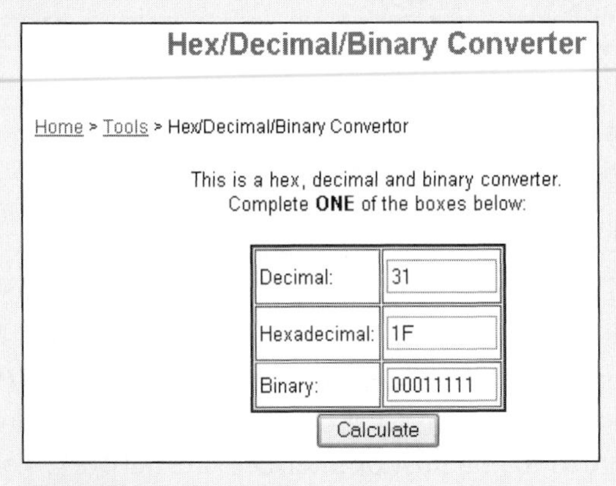

FIGURE 2.2 Example binary converter

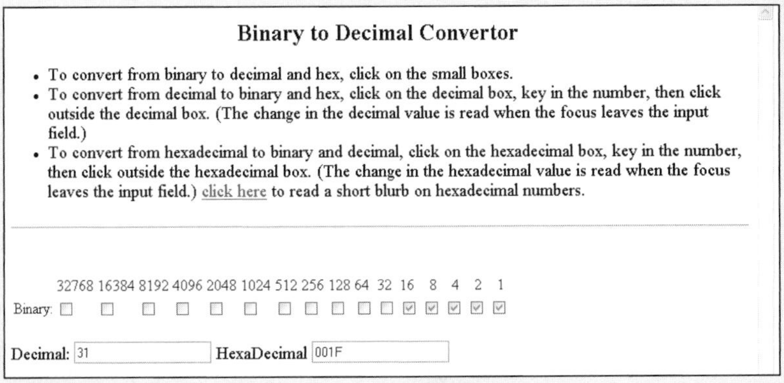

FIGURE 2.3 Example binary converter

Public versus Private IP addresses come in two groups: public and private. Public IP addresses are for computers connected to the Internet. No two public IP address can be the same. However, a private IP address, such as one on a private company network, only has to be unique within that network. Within an isolated network, you can assign IP addresses at random as long as each one is unique. It does not matter whether other computers throughout the world have the same IP address because this computer is never connected to those other worldwide computers. However, connecting a private network to the Internet requires using registered IP addresses (called Internet addresses) to avoid duplicates. Often, network administrators use private IP addresses that begin with a 10, such as 10.102.230.17.

It should also be pointed out that an ISP will often buy a pool of public IP addresses and assign them to you when you log on. Therefore, an ISP might own 1,000 public IP addresses and have 10,000 customers. Because all 10,000 customers will not be online at the same time, the ISP simply assigns an IP address to a customer when he logs on, and the ISP unassigns the IP address when the customer logs off.

Classes The address of a computer tells you a great deal about that computer. The first byte (or first decimal number) in an address tells you to what class of network that machine belongs. Table 2.5 summarizes the five network classes.

The four numbers in an IP address are used in different ways to identify a particular network and host on that network. There are four regional Internet registries (ARIN, RIPE NCC, LACNIC, APNIC) that assign Internet addresses from the A, B, and C classes.

These five classes of networks will become more important later in this book (or should you decide to study networking on a deeper level). Observe Table 2.5 carefully, and you probably will discover that the IP range of

TABLE 2.5 Network classes.

Class	IP Range for the First Byte	Use
A	0–126	Extremely large networks. All Class A network IP addresses have been used and none are left.
B	128–191	Large corporate and government networks. All Class B network IP addresses have been used.
C	192–223	The most common group of IP addresses. Your ISP probably has a Class C address.
D	224–247	These are reserved for multicasting. *Note:* Multicasting is transmitting the same data to multiple (but not all) destinations.
E	248–255	Reserved for experimental use.

127 was not listed. This omission is because that range is reserved for testing. The IP address of 127.0.0.1 designates the machine you are on, regardless of that machine's assigned IP address. This address is often referred to as the ***loop back address***. That address will be used often in testing your machine and your NIC. We will examine its use a bit later in this chapter in the section on *Basic Network Utilities*.

Availablity of Addresses If you do the math, you will find that our current addressing method means there are a total of over 4.2 billion possible IP addresses. That seems like a very large number but, in reality, the number of unassigned Internet addresses is running out. You should not be concerned, however, as methods are already in place to extend the use of addresses. The new addressing system will be a classless scheme called CIDR (Classless Inter-Domain Routing), and it is tied to the replacement of IP V4 with IP V6.

The entire discussion of IP addresses up to this point is based on IP V4 (version 4.0), the current standard. IP V6 (version 6.0), however, is likely to be implemented in the future. Rather than 32-bit addresses (four 8-bit numbers), the IP V6 uses 128-bit addresses. IP V6 is configured for backward compatibility, which means that to use the new IP V6, there will fortunately not be a need to change every IP address in the world. Keep in mind that, when we discuss the packet structure of an IP packet, we are talking about both the IP V4 and IP V6 packets. In comparison to IP V4 packets, IP V6 packets have longer header segments and the header is structured a little differently.

With CIDR, a single IP address can be used to designate many different and unique IP addresses. In contrast to an IP address, a CIDR IP address ends with a slash followed by a number, called the ***IP network prefix***. An example of a CIDR IP address is 156.201.10.10/12. The IP network prefix specifies how many addresses are covered by the CIDR address. Lower numbers specify more addresses. In addition to providing more addresses within organizations, CIDR addresses also reduce the size of routing tables.

Subnet A ***subnet*** is a portion of a network that shares a particular subnet address (a common address component). On a TCP/IP network, subnets are defined as all devices whose IP addresses have the same prefix. For example, all devices with an IP address that starts with 200.200.200. would be part of the same subnet. Dividing a network into subnets is useful for both security and performance reasons. Subnetting enables the network administrator to further divide the host part of the address into two or more subnets. In this case, a part of the host address is reserved to identify the particular subnet. IP networks are divided using a subnet mask.

Subnet Mask As we discussed earlier, an IP address is made up of 32 binary bits. These bits can be divided into two components: the network address and the host address. A ***subnet mask*** is a 32-bit combination used to describe which portion of an address refers to the subnet (network) and which part refers to the host. This mask is used to determine what subnet an IP address belongs to. For example, in the IP address 185.201.20.2 (assuming this is part of a Class B network), the first two numbers (185.201) represent the Class B network address, and the second two numbers (20.2) identify a particular host on this network.

Uniform Resource Locators

After you connect to your ISP you will, of course, want to visit some Web sites. You probably type names into your browser's address bar rather than IP addresses. For example, you might type in **www.chuckeasttom.com** to go my Web site. Your computer or your ISP must translate the name you typed (called a ***Uniform Resource Locator (URL)***) into an IP address. The DNS protocol, mentioned in the Table 2.4, handles this translation process. You are typing in a name that makes sense to humans, but your computer is using a corresponding IP address to connect. If that address is found, your browser sends a packet (using the HTTP protocol) to port 80. If that target computer has software that listens and responds to such requests (like Web-server software such as Apache or Microsoft Internet Information Server), then the target computer will respond to your browser's request and communication will be established. This method is how Web pages are viewed.

If you have ever received an Error 404: File Not Found message, what you are seeing is that your browser received back a packet (from the Web server) with error code 404, denoting that the Web page you requested could not be found. There are a series of error messages that the Web server can send back to your Web browser, indicating different problems. Many of these problems can be handled by the browser itself and you never see the error message. All error messages in the 400 series are ***client errors***. This term means that something is wrong on your side, not the Web server. Messages in the 500 series are ***server errors***, which mean that there is a problem on the Web server. The 100-series messages are simply informational; 200-series messages indicate success (you usually do not see these, for the browser simply processes them); 300-series messages are re-directional, meaning the Web page you are seeking has moved and your browser is then directed to the new location.

E-mail works the same way as visiting Web sites. Your e-mail client (the software you use to manage your e-mail account) will seek out the address of your e-mail server. Your e-mail client will then use either POP3 to retrieve your incoming e-mail or SMTP to send your outgoing e-mail. Your e-mail server (probably at your ISP or company) will then try to resolve the address you are sending to. If you send something to **chuckeasttom@yahoo.com**, your e-mail server will translate that e-mail address into an IP address for the e-mail server at **yahoo.com**; your server will then send your e-mail there. Note that there are newer e-mail protocols available, but POP3 is still the most commonly used.

Many readers are probably familiar with chat rooms. A chat room, like the other methods of communication we have discussed, works with packets. You first find the address of the chat room and then you connect. The difference here is that your computer's chat software is constantly sending packets back and forth, which is unlike e-mail, which only sends and receives when you tell it to or on a predetermined time interval.

Remember that a packet has a header section. That header section contains your IP address and the destination IP address that you are going to, as well as other information. This packet structure will become an important concept for you to know in subsequent chapters.

Basic Network Utilities

Later in this book, you will use information and techniques that are based, in part, on certain techniques anyone can perform on her machine. There are network utilities that you can execute from a command prompt (Windows) or from a shell (Unix/Linux). Many readers are already familiar with Windows, so the text's discussion will execute the commands and discuss them from the Windows command-prompt perspective. However, it must be stressed that these utilities are available in all operating systems. In this section, you will read about IPConfig, ping, and tracert utilities.

IPConfig

When beginning to study networks, the first thing you will want to do is to get information about your own system. To accomplish this fact-finding mission, you will need to get to a command prompt. In Windows XP or Windows 2000, you can open the command prompt by performing the following steps:

1. Open the Start menu
2. Select Run.
3. In the dialog box that opens, type cmd and click OK.
4. Type **ipconfig**. (You could input the same command in Unix or Linux by typing in ifconfig once inside the shell.)
5. Press the Enter key. You should see something much like what is shown in Figure 2.4.

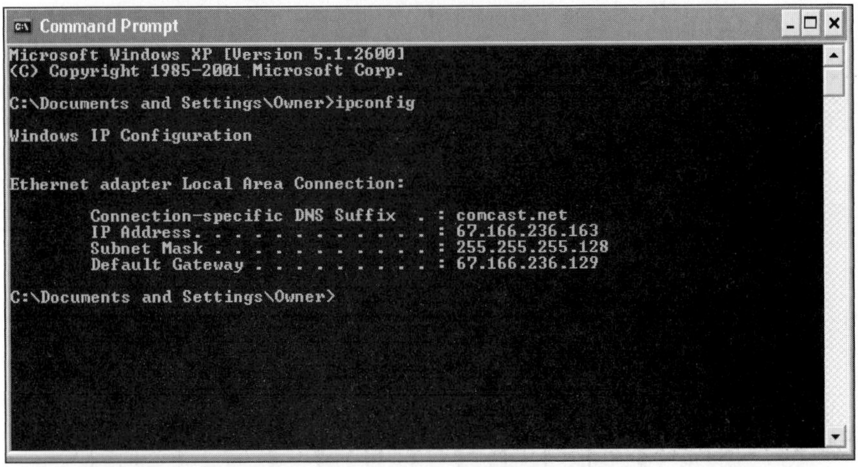

```
Command Prompt
Microsoft Windows XP [Version 5.1.2600]
(C) Copyright 1985-2001 Microsoft Corp.

C:\Documents and Settings\Owner>ipconfig

Windows IP Configuration


Ethernet adapter Local Area Connection:

        Connection-specific DNS Suffix  . : comcast.net
        IP Address. . . . . . . . . . . . : 67.166.236.163
        Subnet Mask . . . . . . . . . . . : 255.255.255.128
        Default Gateway . . . . . . . . . : 67.166.236.129

C:\Documents and Settings\Owner>
```

FIGURE 2.4 IPConfig.

This command gives you some information about your connection to a network (or to the Internet). Most importantly, you find out your own IP address. The command also has the IP address for your default gateway, which is your connection to the outside world. Running the ***IPConfig*** command is a first step in determining your system's network configuration. Most commands that this text will mention, including IPConfig, have a number of parameters, or flags, that can be passed to the commands to make the computer behave in a certain way. You can find out what these commands are by typing in the command, followed by a space, and then typing in hyphen question mark, -?. Figure 2.5 shows the results of this method for the IPConfig command.

FIGURE 2.5 IPConfig help.

```
Command Prompt

C:\Documents and Settings\Owner>ipconfig -?

USAGE:
    ipconfig [/? | /all | /renew [adapter] | /release [adapter] |
              /flushdns | /displaydns | /registerdns |
              /showclassid adapter |
              /setclassid adapter [classid] ]

where
    adapter         Connection name
                   (wildcard characters * and ? allowed, see examples)

    Options:
       /?           Display this help message
       /all         Display full configuration information.
       /release     Release the IP address for the specified adapter.
       /renew       Renew the IP address for the specified adapter.
       /flushdns    Purges the DNS Resolver cache.
       /registerdns Refreshes all DHCP leases and re-registers DNS names
       /displaydns  Display the contents of the DNS Resolver Cache.
       /showclassid Displays all the dhcp class IDs allowed for adapter.
       /setclassid  Modifies the dhcp class id.

The default is to display only the IP address, subnet mask and
default gateway for each adapter bound to TCP/IP.

For Release and Renew, if no adapter name is specified, then the IP address
leases for all adapters bound to TCP/IP will be released or renewed.

For Setclassid, if no ClassId is specified, then the ClassId is removed.

Examples:
    > ipconfig                   ... Show information.
    > ipconfig /all              ... Show detailed information
    > ipconfig /renew            ... renew all adapters
    > ipconfig /renew EL*        ... renew any connection that has its
                                     name starting with EL
    > ipconfig /release *Con*    ... release all matching connections,
                                     eg. "Local Area Connection 1" or
                                         "Local Area Connection 2"
```

FIGURE 2.6 IPConfig/all.

```
Command Prompt

C:\Documents and Settings\Owner>ipconfig /all

Windows IP Configuration

        Host Name . . . . . . . . . . . . : HAL9000
        Primary Dns Suffix  . . . . . . . :
        Node Type . . . . . . . . . . . . : Hybrid
        IP Routing Enabled. . . . . . . . : No
        WINS Proxy Enabled. . . . . . . . : No

Ethernet adapter Local Area Connection:

        Connection-specific DNS Suffix  . : comcast.net
        Description . . . . . . . . . . . : Realtek RTL8139 Family PCI Fast Ethe
rnet NIC
        Physical Address. . . . . . . . . : 00-40-CA-47-BF-23
        Dhcp Enabled. . . . . . . . . . . : Yes
        Autoconfiguration Enabled . . . . : Yes
        IP Address. . . . . . . . . . . . : 67.166.236.163
        Subnet Mask . . . . . . . . . . . : 255.255.255.128
        Default Gateway . . . . . . . . . : 67.166.236.129
        DHCP Server . . . . . . . . . . . : 12.242.18.34
        DNS Servers . . . . . . . . . . . : 63.240.76.198
                                            204.127.199.8
        Lease Obtained. . . . . . . . . . : Sunday, November 23, 2003 1:31:43 AM

        Lease Expires . . . . . . . . . . : Thursday, November 27, 2003 1:31:43
AM

C:\Documents and Settings\Owner>
```

As you can see in Figure 2.5, there are a number of options you might use to find out different details about your computer's configuration. The most commonly used method would probably be the IPConfig/all, shown in Figure 2.6. You can see that this option gives you much more information.

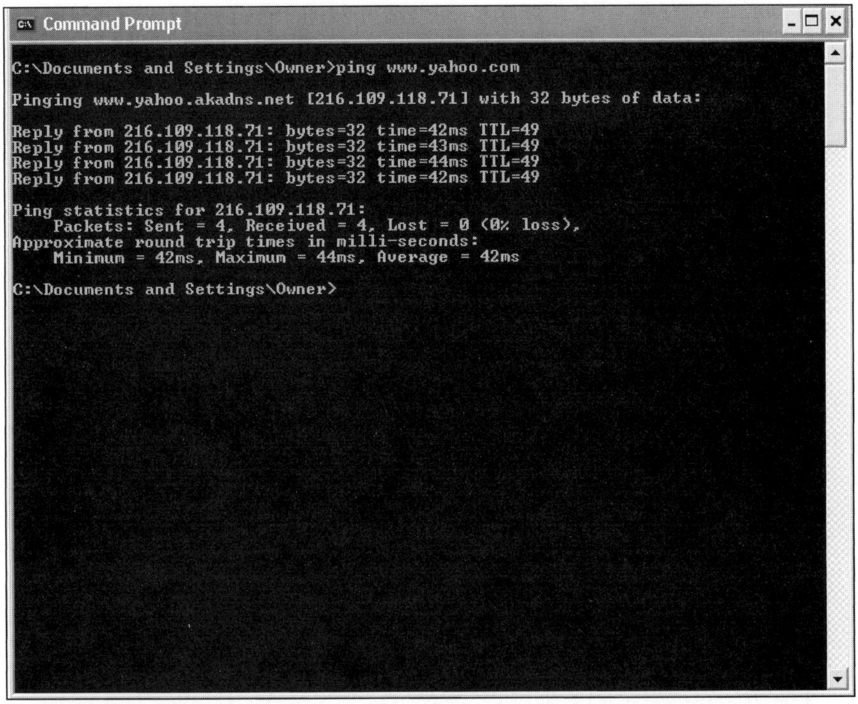

```
Command Prompt

C:\Documents and Settings\Owner>ping www.yahoo.com

Pinging www.yahoo.akadns.net [216.109.118.71] with 32 bytes of data:

Reply from 216.109.118.71: bytes=32 time=42ms TTL=49
Reply from 216.109.118.71: bytes=32 time=43ms TTL=49
Reply from 216.109.118.71: bytes=32 time=44ms TTL=49
Reply from 216.109.118.71: bytes=32 time=42ms TTL=49

Ping statistics for 216.109.118.71:
    Packets: Sent = 4, Received = 4, Lost = 0 (0% loss),
Approximate round trip times in milli-seconds:
    Minimum = 42ms, Maximum = 44ms, Average = 42ms

C:\Documents and Settings\Owner>
```

FIGURE 2.7 Ping.

For example, IPConfig/all gives the name of your computer, when your computer obtained its IP address, and more.

Ping

Another commonly used command is ***ping***. Ping is used to send a test packet, or echo packet, to a machine to find out whether the machine is reachable and how long the packet takes to reach the machine. This useful diagnostic tool can be employed in elementary hacking techniques (discussed in later chapters). In Figure 2.7, you see a ping command executed on **www.yahoo.com**.

This figure tells you that a 32-byte echo packet was sent to the destination and returned. The ttl item means "time to live." That time unit is how many intermediary steps, or hops, the packet should take to the destination before giving up. Remember that the Internet is a vast conglomerate of interconnected networks. Your packet probably will not go straight to its destination, but will have to take several hops to get there. As with IPConfig, you can type in ping -? to find out various ways you can refine your ping.

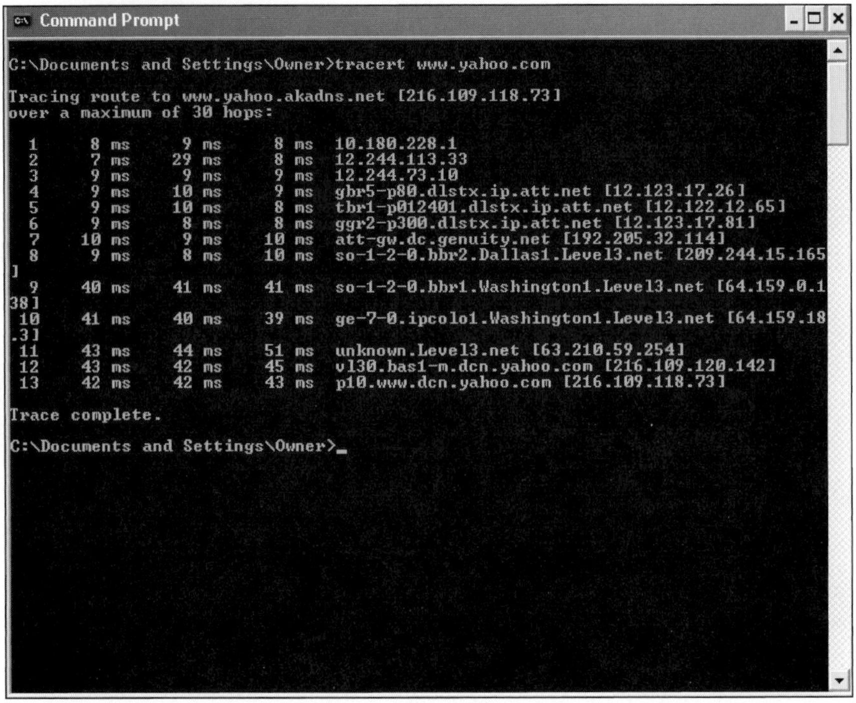

FIGURE 2.8 Tracert.

```
Command Prompt

C:\Documents and Settings\Owner>tracert www.yahoo.com

Tracing route to www.yahoo.akadns.net [216.109.118.73]
over a maximum of 30 hops:

  1     8 ms     9 ms     8 ms  10.180.228.1
  2     7 ms    29 ms     8 ms  12.244.113.33
  3     9 ms     9 ms     9 ms  12.244.73.10
  4     9 ms    10 ms     9 ms  gbr5-p80.dlstx.ip.att.net [12.123.17.26]
  5     9 ms    10 ms     8 ms  tbr1-p012401.dlstx.ip.att.net [12.122.12.65]
  6     9 ms     8 ms     8 ms  ggr2-p300.dlstx.ip.att.net [12.123.17.81]
  7    10 ms     9 ms    10 ms  att-gw.dc.genuity.net [192.205.32.114]
  8     9 ms     8 ms    10 ms  so-1-2-0.bbr2.Dallas1.Level3.net [209.244.15.165
]
  9    40 ms    41 ms    41 ms  so-1-2-0.bbr1.Washington1.Level3.net [64.159.0.1
38]
 10    41 ms    40 ms    39 ms  ge-7-0.ipcolo1.Washington1.Level3.net [64.159.18
.3]
 11    43 ms    44 ms    51 ms  unknown.Level3.net [63.210.59.254]
 12    43 ms    42 ms    45 ms  v130.bas1-m.dcn.yahoo.com [216.109.120.142]
 13    42 ms    42 ms    43 ms  p10.www.dcn.yahoo.com [216.109.118.73]

Trace complete.

C:\Documents and Settings\Owner>_
```

Tracert

The final command we will examine in this chapter is the ***tracert***. This command is basically a "ping deluxe." Tracert not only tells you whether the packet got to its destination and how long it took, but also tells you all the intermediate hops it took to get there. This utility will prove very useful to you later in this book. Figure 2.8 illustrates a tracert to **www.yahoo.com**. (This same command can be executed in Linux or Unix, but there it is called "traceroute" rather than "tracert.")

With tracert, you can see (in milliseconds) the IP addresses of each intermediate step listed and how long it took to get to that step. Knowing the steps required to reach a destination can be very important, as you will find later in this book.

Certainly, there are other utilities that can be of use to you when working with network communications. However, the three we just examined are the core utilities. These three (IPConfig, ping, tracert) are absolutely essential to any network administrator, and you should commit them to memory.

Other Network Devices

There are other devices involved in networking that work to protect your computer from the outside world. Some of these devices were briefly mentioned in Chapter 1. We will now review a few of them in more detail. The two most common devices in this category are the firewall and the proxy server. A ***firewall*** is essentially a barrier between your network and the rest of the Internet. A personal computer (pc) can be used as a firewall or, in many cases, a special router can function as a firewall. Firewalls, which can be hardware, software, or a combination of both, use different techniques to protect your network, but the most common strategy is packet filtering. In a packet-filtering firewall, each incoming packet is examined. Only those packets that match the criteria you set are allowed through. (Commonly, only packets using certain types of protocols are allowed through.) Many operating systems, such as Windows XP and many Linux distributions, include basic packet-filtering software with the operating system.

The second common type of defensive device is a ***proxy server***. A proxy server will almost always be another computer. You might see the same machine used as both a proxy server and a firewall. A proxy server's purpose is quite simple: it hides your entire network from the outside world. People trying to investigate your network from the outside will see only the proxy server. They will not see the actual machines on your network. When packets go out of your network, their headers are changed so that the packets have the return address of the proxy server. Conversely, the only way you can access the outside world is via the proxy server. A proxy server combined with a firewall is basic network security. It would frankly be negligent to ever run a network that did not have a firewall and proxy server. In a later chapter, we will examine firewalls in more detail.

Summary

This chapter cannot make you a networking expert. However, you should now have a basic understanding of the structure of networks, how they work, and knowledge of network utilities and devices. You should also have an understanding of the Internet as a network. This material will be critical in later chapters. If you are new to this material, you should thoroughly study this chapter before continuing. In the exercises at the end of this chapter, you will be able to practice using IPConfig, tracert, and ping.

Test Your Skills

MULTIPLE CHOICE QUESTIONS

1. The TCP protocol operates at what layer of the OSI model?
   A. Transport
   B. Application
   C. Network
   D. DataLink
2. The layer of the OSI model that is divided into two sublayers is the:
   A. DataLink.
   B. Network.
   C. Presentation.
   D. Session.
3. A unique hexadecimal number that identifies your network card is called a:
   A. NIC address.
   B. MAC address.
   C. NIC ID.
   D. MAC ID.
4. What is a NIC?
   A. Network Interface Card
   B. Network Interaction Card
   C. Network Interface Connector
   D. Network Interaction Connector
5. A protocol that translates Web addresses into IP addresses is called:
   A. DNS.
   B. TFTP.
   C. DHCP.
   D. SMTP.
6. The connector used with network cables is called:
   A. RJ 11.
   B. RJ 85.
   C. RJ 12.
   D. RJ 45.

7. What type of cable do most networks use?
   A. net cable
   B. category 3 cable
   C. phone cable
   D. category 5 cable

8. The cable used in networks is also referred to as:
   A. unshielded twisted pair.
   B. shielded twisted pair.
   C. unshielded untwisted pair.
   D. shielded untwisted pair.

9. The simplest device for connecting computers is called a(n):
   A. NIC.
   B. interface.
   C. hub.
   D. router.

10. A device used to connect two or more networks together is a:
    A. switch.
    B. router.
    C. hub.
    D. NIC.

11. A T1 line sends data at what speed?
    A. 100 Mbps
    B. 1.54 Mbps
    C. 155 Mbps
    D. 56.6 Kbps

12. How big is a TCP packet header?
    A. The size is dependent on the data being sent.
    B. The size is always 20 bytes.
    C. The size is dependent on the protocol being used.
    D. The size is always 40 bytes.

13. What protocol is used to send e-mail, and on what port does it work?

    A. SMTP port 110

    B. POP3 port 25

    C. SMTP port 25

    D. POP3 port 110

14. What protocol is used for remotely logging on to a computer?

    A. Telnet

    B. HTTP

    C. DNS

    D. SMTP

15. What protocol is used for Web pages, and what port does it work on?

    A. HTTP port 21

    B. HTTP port 80

    C. DHCP port 80

    D. DHCP port 21

16. The point where the backbones of the Internet connect is called:

    A. connectors.

    B. routers.

    C. network access points.

    D. switches.

17. The IP address of 193.44.34.12 would be in what class?

    A. A

    B. B

    C. C

    D. D

18. The IP address of 127.0.0.1 always refers to your:

    A. nearest router.

    B. ISP.

    C. computer.

    D. nearest NAP.

19. Internet addresses in the form of **www.chuckeasttom.com** are called:

    A. user-friendly web addresses.

    B. iniform resource locators.

    C. user-accessible web addresses.

    D. uniform address identifiers.

20. The utility that gives you information about your machine's network configuration is:

    A. ping.

    B. IPConfig.

    C. tracert.

    D. MyConfig.

EXERCISES

Exercise 2.1: Using IPConfig

1. Open your command prompt or DOS prompt. (Go to Start > Run and type **cmd** ([DOS prompt in Windows 98]).
2. Type **ipconfig**.
3. Use the IPConfig to find out information about your computer.
4. Write down your computer's IP address, default gateway, and subnet mask.

Exercise 2.2: Using Tracert

1. Open your command prompt or DOS prompt.
2. Type **tracert www.chuckeasttom.com**.
3. Note what hops your computer takes to get to **www.chuckeasttom.com**.
4. Try the same process with **www.whitehouse.gov** and **www.prenhall.com**.
5. Did you notice that the first few hops are the same? Write down what hops are taken to reach each destination and what hops are the same. Then briefly describe why you think some of the intermediate steps are the same for different destinations.

Exercise 2.3: NSLOOKUP

The command NSLOOKUP is not mentioned in this chapter. Yet, if you are comfortable with ping, tracert, and IPConfig, this command will be easy to learn.

1. Go to the command prompt.
2. Type **nslookup www.chuckeasttom.com**.
3. Note that this command gives you the actual name of the server, as per the hosting company's naming conventions; its IP address; and any aliases under which that server operates.

Exercise 2.4: More About IPConfig

1. Open your command prompt or DOS prompt.
2. Use the -? flag on the IPConfig command to find out what other options you have with these commands. You should notice a number of options, including /all, /renew, and others.
3. Now try ipconfig/all. What do you see now that you didn't see when you simply used ipconfig in Exercise 2.1?

Exercise 2.5: More About Ping

1. Open your command prompt or DOS prompt.
2. Use the -? flag on the ping command and find out what other options you have with these commands. You should notice several additional options such as -w, -t, -n, and -i.
3. Try a simple ping of **www.chuckeasttom.com**.
4. Try the option ping -n 2 **www.chuckeasttom.com**, then try ping -n 7 **www. chuckeasttom.com**. What differences do you notice?

PROJECTS

Project 2.1: Learning About DNS

1. Using Web resources, look up the DNS protocol. You may find the following Web sites to be of help:

   www.freesoft.org/CIE/Topics/75.htm

   www.dns.net/dnsrd/docs/whatis.html

   www.webfavor.com/tips/DNS.html

2. Look up these facts: Who invented this protocol? What is its purpose? How is it used?

3. Write a brief paper describing what the protocol does. Mention a bit of information about who invented it, when, and how it works.

Project 2.2: Learning About Your System

1. Find out whether your organization (for example, your school or business) uses switches, hubs, or both. Why does your group use these? You can find out by simply asking the network administrator or the help desk. Make sure you tell them that you are seeking this information for a class project.

2. Write a brief paper explaining your findings, including any changes you would make if you could. For example, if your organization uses only hubs, would you change that method? If so, why?

Project 2.3: Learning About NetStat

The NetStat command is used to display the status of network connections on either TCP, UDP, RAW, or UNIX. It displays network protocol statistics and information.

1. At the command prompt, type **netstat**. Notice the information it provides. You should be seeing any IP addresses or server names that are currently connected to your computer. (If you are using a home computer, you will need to log on to your Internet service provider in order to see anything.)

2. Now type **netstat -?** to see options with this command. You should see -a, -e, and others.

3. Now type **netstat -a** and note the information you see.

4. Finally, try **netstat -e**. What do you see now?

Caution

Stopping NetStat

Note that, with many versions of Windows, for the next steps you will need to use the control-break key combination to stop NetStat before starting it again with a new option.

Case Study

You have been hired by the owner of a new technical writing business. Your task is to establish a network of computers for the six employees who will need to communicate with each other, share files, and also be able to access the Internet in order to send and receive e-mail and perform research. Eventually, they will also need to host a Web site for the company. Create an outline or detail in some other format exactly how you intend to set up the network. How they will connect to each other and to the Internet? What firewalls will be used?

Chapter 3

Assessing a Target System

Chapter Objectives

After reading this chapter and completing the exercises, you will be able to do the following:

- Understand and be able to conduct basic system reconnaissance.
- Describe and use several port scanners.
- Understand how to derive useful information about a Web site from internic or the Netcraft Web site.
- Know how to locate information about a system or organization from Internet newsgroup postings.
- Understand the use of vulnerability scanners.
- Use port monitoring utilities.

Caution

Assessing Vulnerabilities Legally

In this chapter, we will walk through various utilities. Two things should be noted. The first is that this information is designed to help you identify vulnerabilities in your network and not for you to attempt to gain information about other networks. It is important you remember that unauthorized access of systems is a crime under U.S. federal law, various state laws, and many international laws.

Introduction

Ultimately, every hacker wishes to compromise a target system and gain access to that system. This goal is the same for any hacker, regardless of the hacker's "hat" (his or her ideology or motivation). Before a hacker can attempt to compromise a target system, he must know a great deal about the target system. There are a number of network utilities, Web sites, and programs that a hacker can use to find out about a target system. We will discuss these strategies in depth in this chapter. Learning these methods will help you for two reasons. First, you should know exactly what tools crackers have at their disposal to assess your system's vulnerabilities. Second, many security-savvy network administrators will frequently use these tools to assess their own systems. Another term for assessing your own system (or a client's) is ***auditing***. When a hacker or cracker is examining a potential target system, this assessment is called ***footprinting***. If you can find vulnerabilities, you have the chance to fix them before someone else exploits them.

Recall the discussion from Chapter 1 of the rather tedious process hackers have to use in order to enter a target system. The first stage of this process is learning about the system. It is important to know about the operating system, any software running on it, what security measures are in effect, and as much about the network as possible. This legwork is very similar to a robber "casing" a bank before attempting the crime. The thief needs to know all about alarm systems, work schedules, and guards. The same is true for a person planning to break into a computer system. The hacker's first step is to gather information about that system. To assess your own system, therefore, needs to be your first step also.

In this chapter, you will learn to use some common tools and techniques to assess a system. In the exercises at the end of this chapter, you will then have the chance to use tools, such as Netcop, NetBrute, Netcraft, tracert, and Netstat, to perform additional assessments.

FYI: Finding Utilities

You will find that some utilities will work only on some operating systems. In some cases, a utility might work in Windows 2000 but not Windows XP, or vice versa. For this reason, Appendix B is full of alternative sites to obtain similar utilities.

Basic Reconnaissance

On any system, you must first start finding out some general information. This task—commonly referred to as reconnaissance—is particularly easy with Web servers. A Web server, by definition, must communicate with Web clients. That activity means that a certain amount of information is easily accessible in the public domain. In the past, security managers had to use some rather arcane-looking commands from either a command prompt or a Linux/Unix shell to gather this information. But today, you can get the information in just a few simple steps by using some readily available utilities. These tools are used by both security managers as well as crackers.

The ways in which information is obtained by a cracker can vary greatly. Although there are many tools available, the ways listed below are the most likely initial reconnaissance methods used for Windows platforms:

- Nslookup
- Whois
- ARIN (This is available via any Internet browser client.)

- Web-based tools (Hundreds if not thousands of sites offer various reconnaissance tools.)
- Target Web site (The client's Web site often reveals too much information.)
- Social engineering (People are an organization's greatest asset as well as their greatest risk.)

In the following sections, we will explore a few of the many Web-based tools available for obtaining basic information on a target system.

Netcraft

The first stop on our journey is the Netcraft Web site. This Web site gathers information about Web servers—information that you can use in assessing a target system. It provides an online utility that will tell you what Web server software it is running, what operating system it is using, and other important and interesting information.

1. Open your browser and key **www.netcraft.com**.
2. Click the link titled "What's that site running," which is found on the left side of the page.
3. Key **www.chuckeasttom.com** into the "What's that site running?" text box.
4. Press Enter. As you see in Figure 3.1, you will find a great deal of important information.

You can see that the server is running the FreeBSD operating system, a Unix variant. You can also see the IP address of the machine. This step is your first in learning about the target system. In many cases, with other addresses, you would also find out what Web server the target system is running. You can then scan the Internet looking for any known flaws with either the operating system or the Web server software. This step gives you a starting place to find out about the system and what weaknesses you might be able to exploit. In this case, you would simply go to your favorite search engine (Google, Yahoo, Lycos, and so forth) and key in something such as "FreeBSD security flaws." You would be surprised how many Web sites will provide you with details on specific flaws in a system. Some sites even have step-by-step instructions on how to exploit these weaknesses.

The fact that this information is so readily available should be enough to alarm any system administrator. As software vendors become aware of flaws, they usually write corrections to their code, known as patches or updates. If you are not regularly updating your system's patches, then you are leaving your system open to attack.

Besides strengths and weaknesses of that software, sometimes just knowing the operating system and the Web server software is enough information in and of itself. For example, if a target system is running Windows

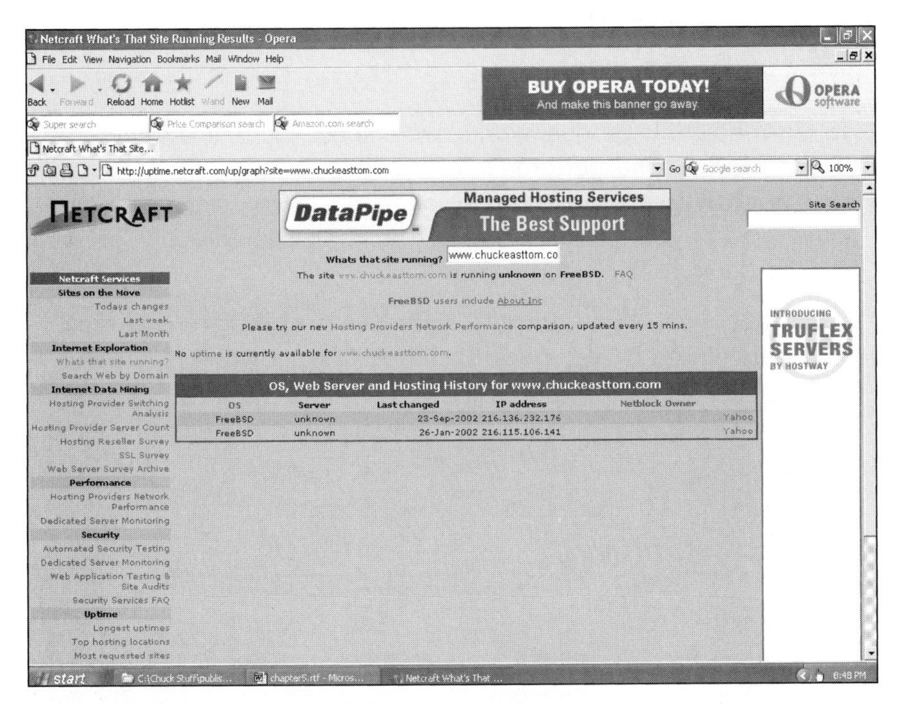

FIGURE 3.1 Running netcraft.com utilities.

NT 4.0, what would this fact tell a hacker? Because Microsoft has long ago released Windows 2000, Windows XP, and the Windows 2003 Server, the hacker can deduce that this target system does not frequently update its software. This could denote a company that is on a very tight budget or one that simply is not particularly computer-savvy. In either case, this lack of updating software means that this system probably does not employ the latest security devices and techniques.

Tracing the IP Address

The next piece of information you will want concerns the various connections between you and the target system. When you visit a Web site, the packets bouncing back and forth between you and the target site do not take a direct route from you to there. They usually bounce around the Internet, going through various Internet service providers and routers. The obvious way to obtain this information is to use the traceroute or tracert utility (discussed in Chapter 2). You can then write down the IP address of each step in the journey. However, this task can be very tedious. An easier process is offered through the Visualware Inc. Web site. Visualware offers some very interesting products, along with free online Web demos. These products automate network utilities, such as tracert and Whois, in a rich graphical interface. I find Visualware's product, VisualRoute, to be particularly useful and remarkably easy to employ.

IN PRACTICE: Using VisualRoute

To learn how this product works, we will use the online free demo of the product and perform a visual trace route on the Web site **www.chuckeasttom.com**. Note that, to try the demo, you must register your e-mail address. The Web site will only let you use the demo for a limited time.

1. Open your browser and enter **www.visualware.com**. You will see a Web page similar to that shown in Figure 3.2.

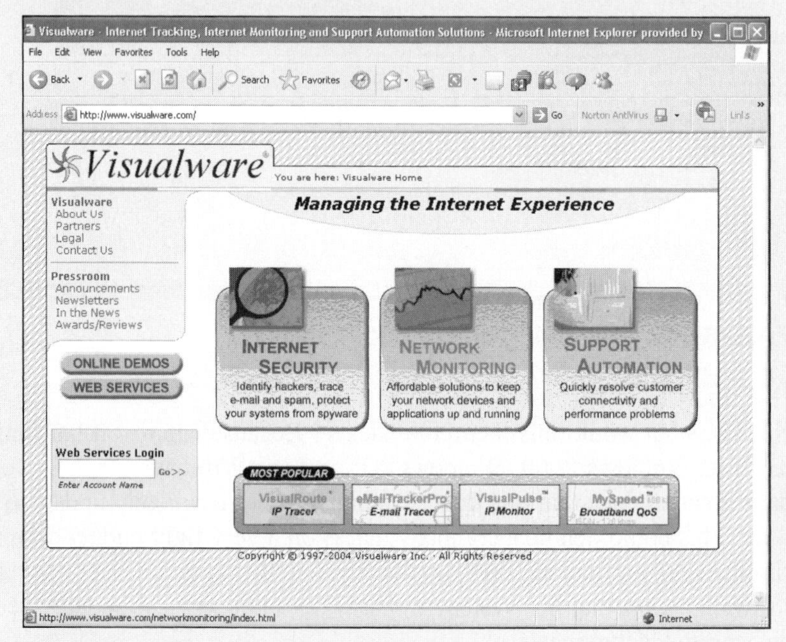

FIGURE 3.2 Visualware Web site.

2. Click the link to VisualRoute. You will see a Web page similar to that shown in Figure 3.3.
3. Click Live Demo on the left side of the page. This opens a page where you can select the starting location and enter your e-mail address in the Login/Quick Registration box, as shown in Figure 3.4.
4. Enter your e-mail address and click Go!. Within seconds (depending upon the speed of your Internet connection), you will receive an e-mail from Visualware Inc. with your login PIN number.

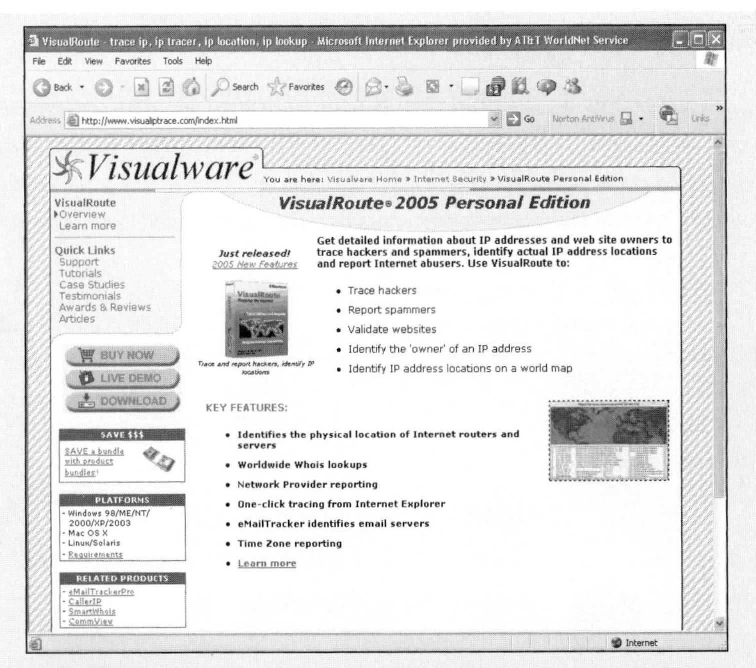

FIGURE 3.3 VisualRoute Web page.

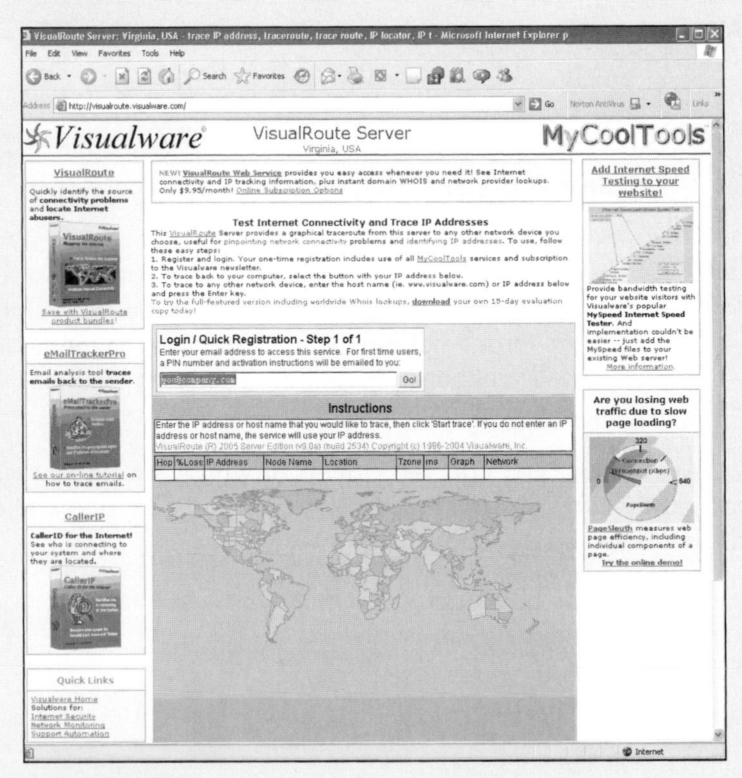

FIGURE 3.4 Live Demo login page.

CONTINUED ON NEXT PAGE

CONTINUED

5. Click the link within the e-mail or return to your browser and enter your PIN number. The VisualRoute Server page appears in your browser, as shown in Figure 3.5.

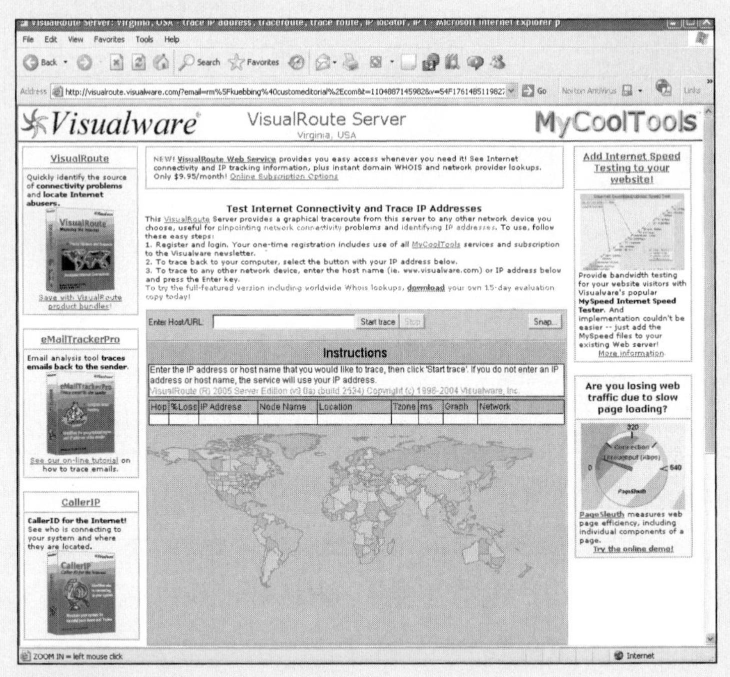

FIGURE 3.5 Visual Route Server page.

6. Enter **www.chuckeasttom.com** in the Enter Host/URL text box. You will actually be tracing the route from that location to the target, not from your location. With the full version, you will, of course, trace from your own location.
7. Click Start trace.

As a result, you can see a map of where the packet went around the world, as well as information on every single IP address it bounced through as shown in Figure 3.6.

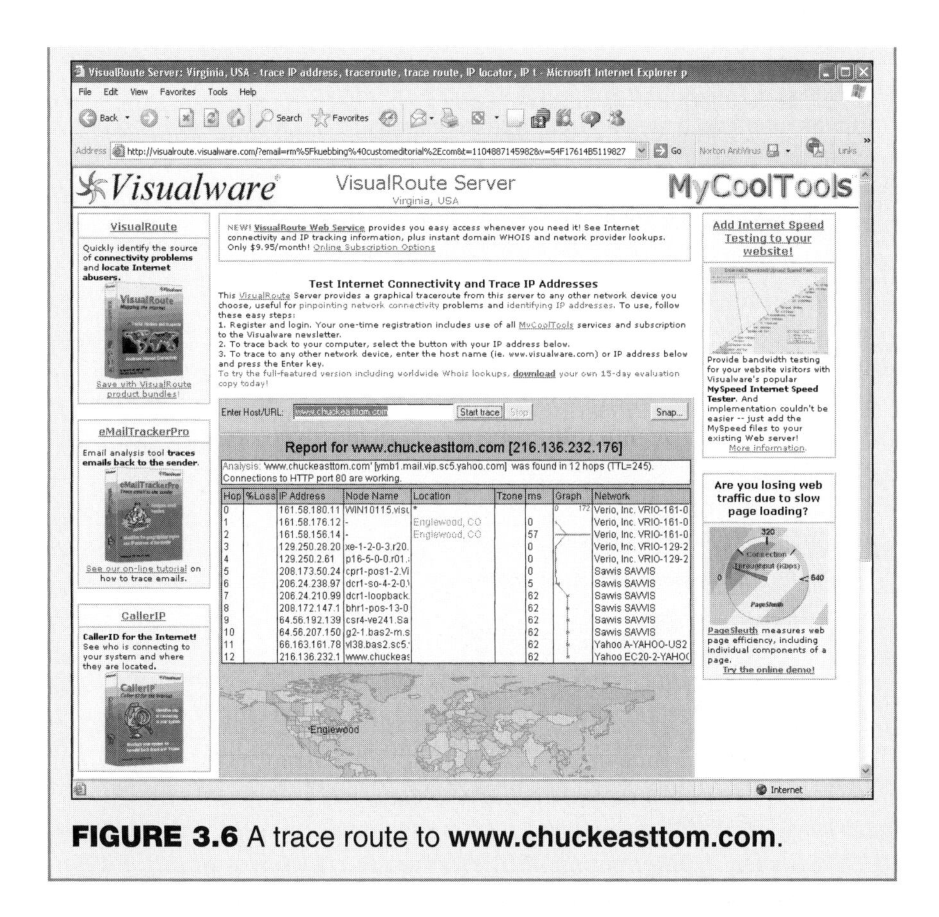

FIGURE 3.6 A trace route to **www.chuckeasttom.com**.

This information can be very useful. For example, let's say that you start a trace from different locations, and the trace always goes through the same IP address just before reaching the target. In that case, then, that IP is probably a router, gateway, or the target's ISP. With the full version of this product, you can do something even more interesting. You can double-click on any of the links and obtain a great deal of information about that IP address. You see, to register an IP on the Internet, you have to register a physical location, a person to contact (usually the network administrator), and other information. VisualRoute provides all of that information at the click of your mouse. The same information is available to you through **www.internic.net**, (see Figure 3.7) where you can look up any IP address.

Using IP Registration Information

The information gained with these utilities can be used in a variety of ways. For example, you can take the e-mail address of the administrator and do a Google "groups" search for that address. Google now provides a gateway,

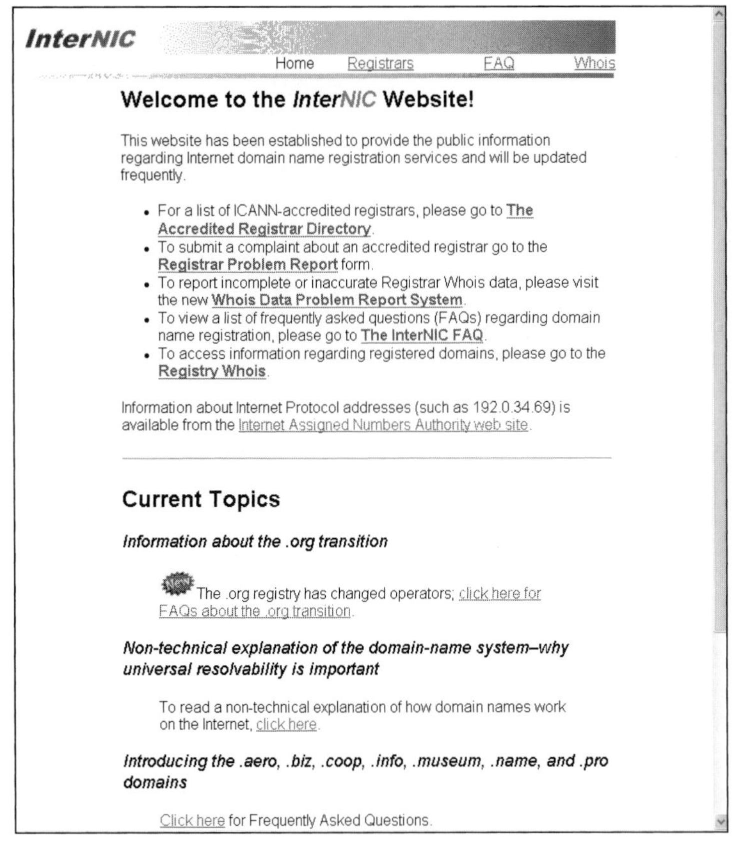

FIGURE 3.7 InterNIC Web page.

via its "groups" tab, to Usenet newsgroups. These groups are basically global bulletin boards where people can engage in discussions on a wide range of topics. Network administrators sometimes post questions in specific newsgroups hoping to get advice from their colleagues. If the network administrator of the target machine has posted, he or she may have given away more information about her network than is wise. In one case, a network administrator actually posted a link to a diagram showing his entire network, the servers, IP addresses, type of firewall, and so on. This information could have been easily exploited.

That is not to say that administrators must avoid using the Internet as an information source. That is certainly not the case. But when administrators do use newsgroups, they should not use their real name, their company's name, or any information that might facilitate tracking them back to their company. In this way, information that they discuss about their firm's network cannot readily be applied.

Social Engineering

One of the most common applications for using the information gained from reconnaissance work is social engineering, mentioned in Chapter 1. Social engineering is a non-technical way of intruding on a system. This can range from dumpster diving to trying to get employees to unwittingly compromise the system.

When ***dumpster diving***, someone trying to obtain information will go through trash cans or dumpsters looking for garbage that contains information such as an IP address, password, or even a map of the network. This technique can be very messy, but also quite effective.

The most common tactic is to try to get an authorized user of a system to give you her password. This task may sound impossible, but it is actually quite easy. For example, if a hacker has discovered the name of the system administrator and knows that the company is rather large with a big Information Technology (IT) department, she can use this name to her advantage. Assume a scenario in which a hacker finds out that the network administrator for a certain firm is named Jane Smith. She can get Jane's office location, e-mail address, and phone number from internic or from using VisualRoute software. She can now call a remote office and speak to a secretary. The plan could work extremely well if that secretary (let's call him Eric) is new to the company. The hacker tells Eric that she is a new intern working for Jane Smith and that Jane has instructed her to check all the PCs to ensure that they have proper virus-scanning software. The hacker tells Eric that she cannot get on to his computer remotely without his username and password, so could Eric please give these to her? It is amazing how often the person will indeed give a username and password to a caller. With this information, the hacker does not need to use any technical skills at all. She can simply use Eric's legitimate username and password and log on to the target system.

Note that schemes such as this one are exactly why all employees in any organization need to be familiar with basic computer security. No matter how secure your system is or how much time and money you invest in security, it is all for naught if your employees are easily duped into compromising security.

There are entire volumes written on social engineering. As with all topics in this book, the goal is to acquaint you with the basics, not to make you a master of any of the topics. If you wish more information on this topic, the following links may be of interest to you:

- www.securityfocus.com/cgi-bin/sfonline/infocus.pl?id=1527
- cybercrimes.net/Property/Hacking/Social%20Engineering/SocialEngineering.html
- www.sans.org/rr/catindex.php?cat_id=51

Scanning

Once you have used VisualRoute or perhaps simply used the traceroute utility and manually looked up information on **www.internic.net**, you are now ready to move to the next phase in gathering information about a target system. This phase is completed by scanning.

The process of scanning can involve many tools and a variety of techniques. The basic goal of scanning is to identify security holes and vulnerabilities in a target host or network. Scanning is based in science, but is considered an art by many because a skilled attacker is patient and has a knack for knowing (usually based on experience) precisely where and how to scan target devices.

There are a number of utilities freely available on the Internet for performing scans. Some of the more common tools are:

- Nmap (Powerful tool available for Unix or Windows that finds ports and services available via IP)
- Hping2 (Powerful Unix-based tool used to gain important information about a network.)
- Netcat (Others have quoted this application as the "Swiss Army knife" of network utilities)
- Ping (Available on most every platform and operating system to test for IP connectivity)
- Traceroute (Maps out the hops of the network to the target device or system)

Of these, Nmap ("Network Mapper") is probably the best known and most flexible scanning tool available today. It uses IP packets in a novel way to determine what hosts are available on a network, what operating systems are running, and what firewalls are in use. It also provides options for fragmentation, use of decoy IP addresses, spoofing, stealth scans, and a number of other features. Nmap is the most widely used tool by both crackers and security professionals for the purpose of port scanning and operating system identification. Formerly, this was only a Unix-based utility, however, it has recently been extended for use with Windows systems. If you have access to or will be working on a Unix system or care to obtain the newer Windows-based Nmap, this is a utility with which you should certainly become familiar.

Network mapping is a process in which you discover information about the topology of the network. This can include gateways, routers, and servers. The first step is to "sweep" for a live system. To find live hosts, hackers ping them by sending ICMP packets. If a system is live, it will send an ICMP echo reply. ICMP messages can be blocked, so an alternative is to send a TCP or UDP packet to a port, such as 80 (http), that is frequently open, and live machines will send a SYN-ACK (acknowledgment) packet in response. Once the live system is known, utilities such traceroute or the others already discussed can provide additional information about the network by discovering the paths taken by packets to each host. This provides information about the routers and gateways in the network and the general layout of the network.

In the following sections, we will examine some methods for performing port scans. Fortunately, there are a number of utilities freely available on the Internet for doing port scanning. We will also discuss network mapping and vulnerability scanning.

FYI: Scanning Utilities

You can find a list of additional URLs for port scanning software in Appendix B of this book. You can also search the Internet using the keywords "port scanning."

Port Scanning

Once the IP address of a target system is known, the next step is ***port scanning*** and ***network scanning***. Such scanning is the process of sending packets to each port on a target system to see what ports it has open (in the LISTEN state). A system has 65,535 port numbers, with one TCP port and one UDP port for each number. Each of these port numbers is a potential way to enter a system. Each port has an associated service that may be exploitable or contain vulnerabilities. Thus, viewing the ports tells you what sort of software is running. If someone has port 80 open, then he or she is probably running a Web server. If you see that all the default ports are open, that discovery probably indicates a network administrator who is not particularly security conscious and may have left all default settings on all of his or her systems. This deduction gives you valuable clues as to the kind of target you are examining. In the following sections, we will experiment with a few port scanning utilities.

IN PRACTICE: Using NetCop

We will start with NetCop, available as a free download from **www.cotse.com/pscan.htm**. (Note that this site lists other port scanners that we will work with as well.) When you download NetCop, you will get a simple, self-extracting executable that

CONTINUED ON NEXT PAGE

CONTINUED

will install the program on your machine and will even put a shortcut in your program menu.

1. Launch NetCop. It has an intuitive screen, as shown in Figure 3.8.

Notice that the default, "Starting host," is the IP address reserved for your own machine.

2. Key in a single IP address and click Scan Now.

You will see Netcop checking each and every port. This activity is shown in Figure 3.9; it is a very methodical task and, hence, a bit slow. But the simplicity of this tool makes it particularly useful for network administrators who wish to check for open ports on their network.

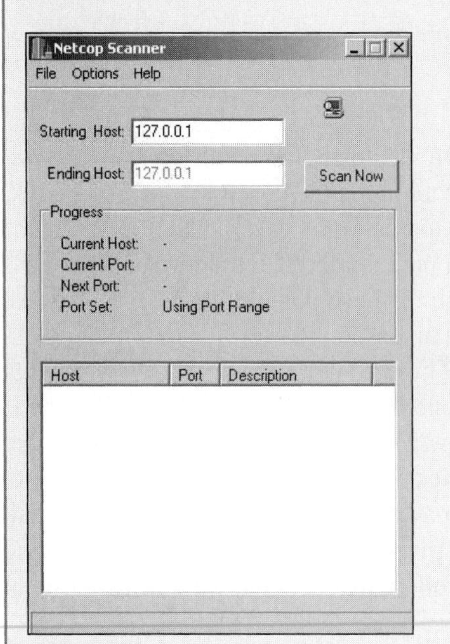

FIGURE 3.8 NetCop port scanner.

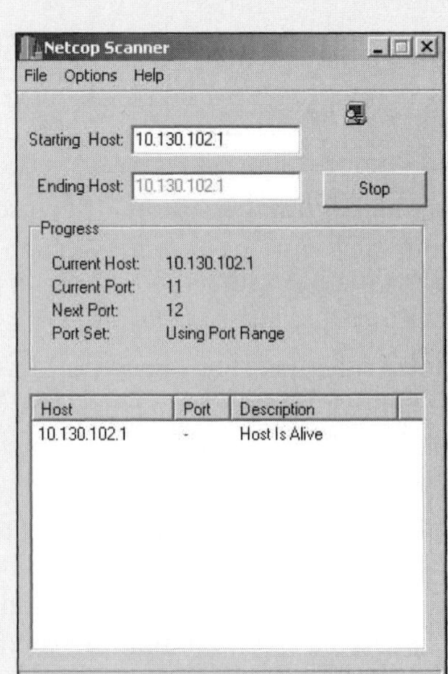

FIGURE 3.9 Scanning an IP address with NetCop.

You can, of course, stop the scan if you wish to do so; however, if you let the scan run through all of the ports, you will then see something similar to what is shown in Figure 3.10. Of course, different machines you examine will have different ports open.

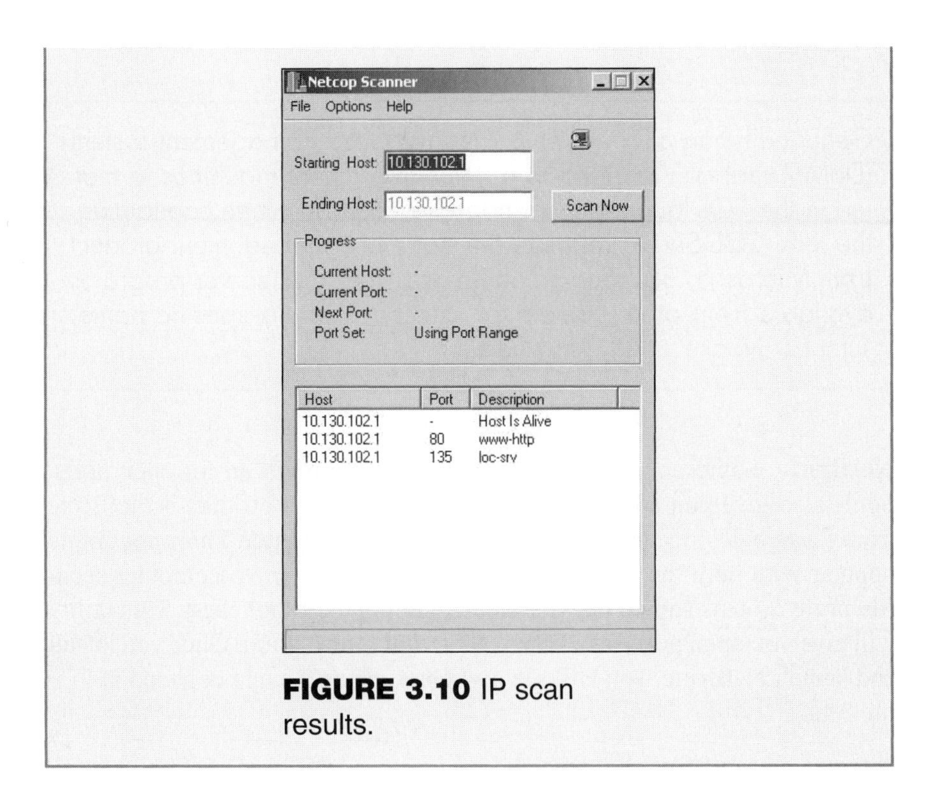

FIGURE 3.10 IP scan results.

Now that you have a tool for finding out what ports are open on a target machine, what can you do with that information? As we already mentioned, an open port can tell you a great deal about a system. Recall that, in Chapter 2, we briefly reviewed a number of well-known ports. That list was not exhaustive, but the list should give you an idea. The following Web sites list all well-known ports.

- www.networksorcery.com/enp/protocol/ip/ports00000.htm
- www.iana.org/assignments/port-numbers
- www.techadvice.com/tech/T/TCP_well_known_ports.htm

Using this information about well-known ports, you should be able to tell whether a system is using NetBIOS because such a system will have ports 137, 138, and 139 open. If a system is running an SQL server, then it may have port 118 open. This information can then be used by a hacker to begin to explore possible flaws or vulnerabilities in the service running on a given port number. Therefore, this information is quite important from a security perspective. If you are scanning your own machine and see ports that are open (ones that you do not use), then close them. All firewalls give you the option of blocking ports. That function is the most essential purpose of any firewall. A basic rule of thumb in security is that any port that you are not actively using should be blocked.

FYI: SQL Server

Generically, an SQL server is any database management system (DBMS) that can respond to queries from client machines formatted in the SQL language (Webopedia, 2004). When capitalized, the term SQL Server refers to the database management product from Microsoft: *SQL Server*. There are other SQL server programs available from other companies and each has a specific name, such as Sybase's *SQL Anywhere*.

NetBrute Some port scanners do more than simply scan for open ports. Some also give you additional information. One such product is NetBrute from RawLogic, located at **www.rawlogic.com/netbrute/**. This one is quite popular with both the security and hacker community. No computer security professionals should be without this item in their tool chest. This utility will give you open ports, as well as other vital information. Once you install and launch NetBrute, you will see a screen such as the one depicted in Figure 3.11.

FIGURE 3.11 NetBrute main screen.

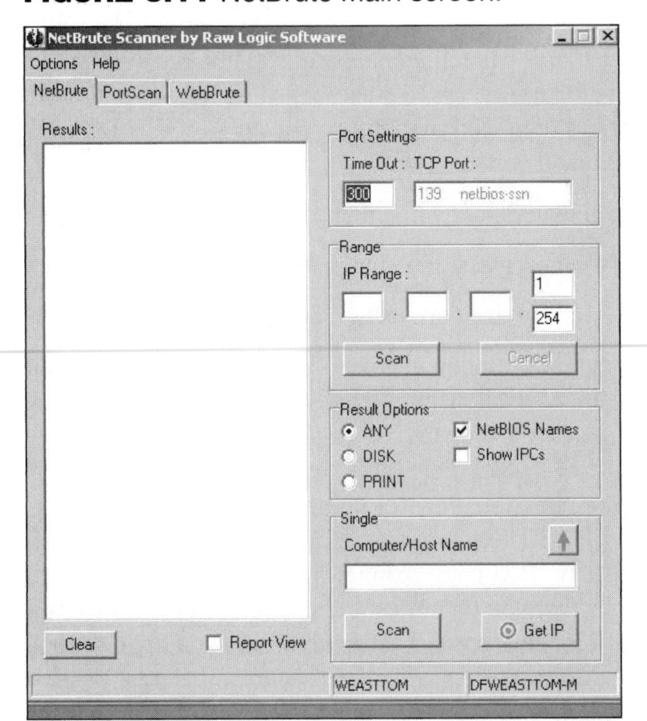

As you can see in the figure, there are three tabs. We will concentrate on the NetBrute tab first. You can elect to scan a range of IP addresses (perfect for network administrators assessing the vulnerability of their own systems), or you can choose to target an individual IP. When you are done, it will show you all the shared drives on that computer, as you see in Figure 3.12.

With the PortScan tab, you can find ports. It works exactly like the first tab except that, instead of giving you a list of shared folders/drives, it gives you a list of open ports. Thus, with NetBrute, you get a port scanner *and* a shared folder scanner. The WebBrute tab allows you to scan a target Web site and obtain information similar to what you would get from Netcraft. This scan gives you information such as the target system's operating system and Web server software. Shared folders and drives are important to security because they provide one possible way for a hacker to get into a system. If the hacker can gain access to that shared folder, she can use that area to upload a Trojan horse, virus, key logger, or other device.

Cerberus Internet Scanner Perhaps one of the most popular scanning utilities is the Cerberus Internet Scanner (a number of download locations are listed in Appendix B). This tool is remarkably simple to use and very informative. When you launch this tool, you will see a screen similar to the one shown in Figure 3.13.

FIGURE 3.12 Shared drives.

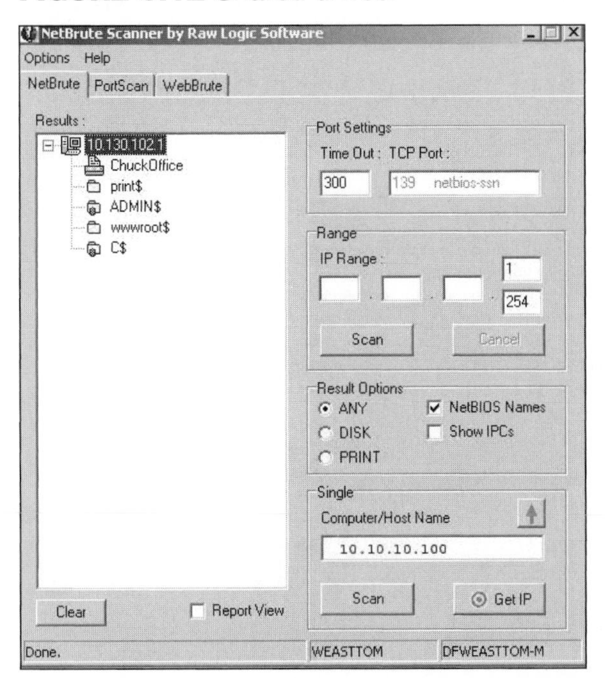

FIGURE 3.13 The Cerberus Internet Scanner.

From this screen, you can click the button on the far left that has an icon of a house, or you can go to "File" and select "Host." You then simply key in either the URL or the IP address of the machine that you wish to scan. Click either the button with the "S" on it or go to "File" and select "Start Scan." Cerberus will then scan that machine and give you back a wealth of information. You can see all the various categories of information that you receive from this scan in Figure 3.14.

FIGURE 3.14 Cerberus scan results.

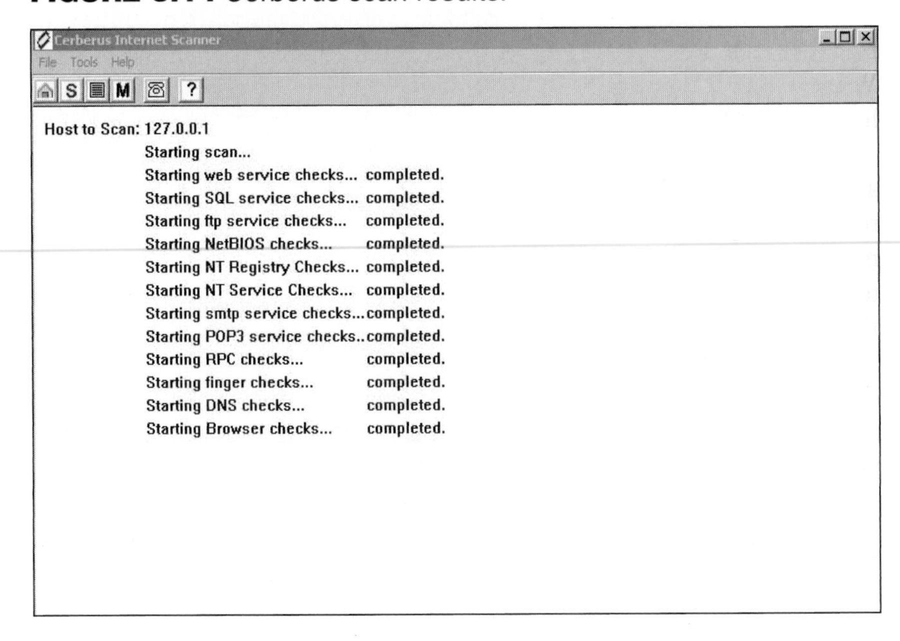

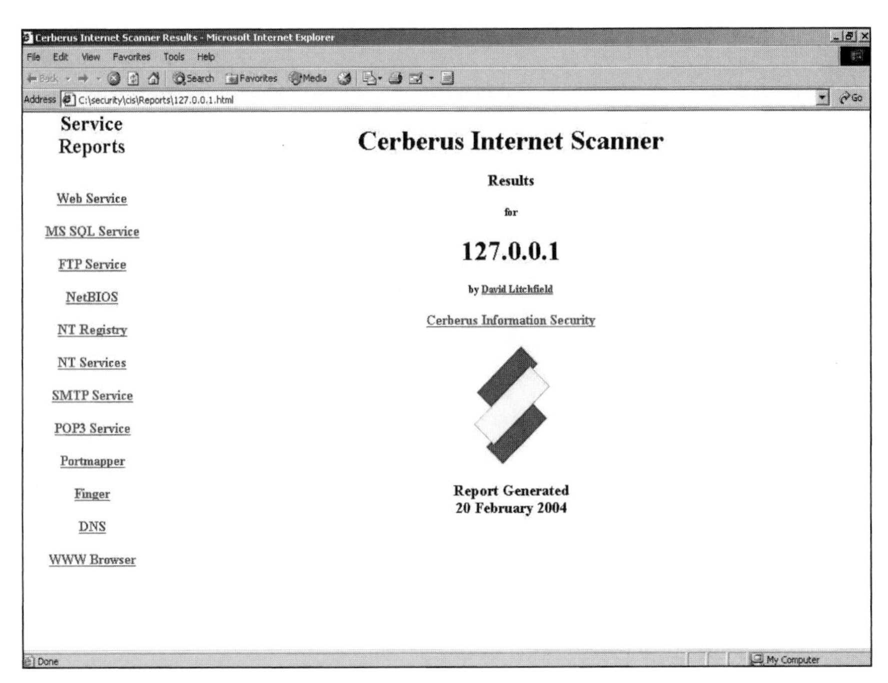

FIGURE 3.15 The Cerberus report.

Click on the third button to review the report. The report will launch a Hypertext Markup Language (html) document (thus the document is easy to save for future reference) with links to each category. (This document is shown in Figure 3.15.) Click on the category you wish to view.

One of the most interesting sections to review, particularly for a security administrator, is the NT Registry report. This report will examine the Windows Registry and inform you of any security flaws found there and how to correct them. This report is shown in Figure 3.16.

This list shows specific Windows Registry settings, why those settings are not particularly secure, and what you can do to secure them. For obvious reasons, this tool is very popular with hackers. Cerberus can provide a great map of all of a system's potential vulnerabilities including, but not limited to, shared drives, insecure registry settings, services running, and known flaws in the operating system.

All of these tools (and others we have not examined) have one thing in common: They provide information to anyone who wants it. Information is a powerful tool, but it is also a two-edged sword. Any information that a network administrator can use to secure his network, a cracker can also use to break into the network. It is imperative that all network administrators be comfortable with the various scanning tools that are available. It is a good idea to make a routine habit of scanning your own systems to search for vulnerabilities—and then close these vulnerabilities.

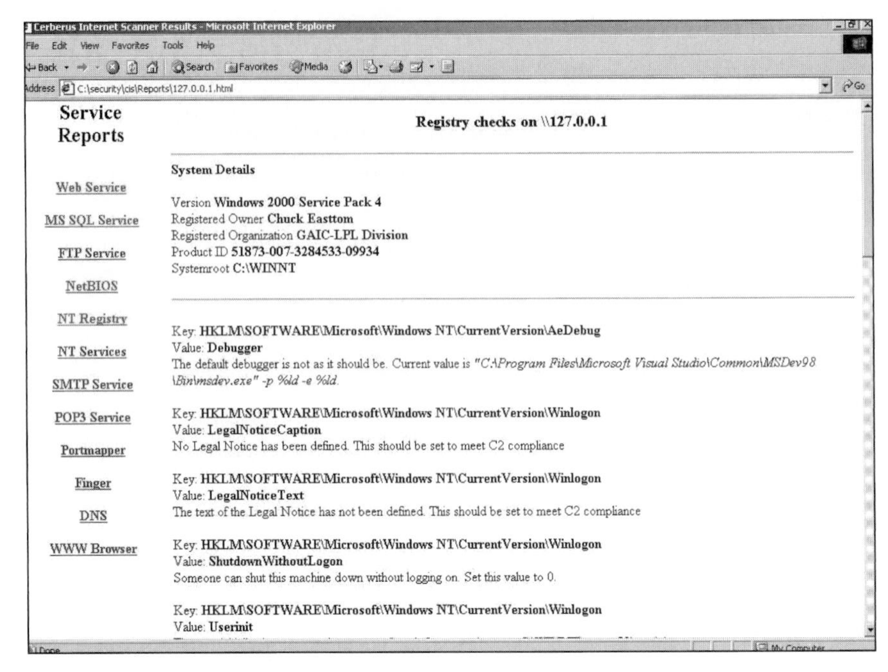

FIGURE 3.16 The NT Registry report.

FYI: Finding Utilities

There are other tools you can find for free on the Internet that will scan your computer. If you are interested in finding out more about these tools, then it is suggested that you consult the links in Appendix B. You might also consider simply using your favorite search engine to search for computer security utilities.

Port Scanner for Unix: SATAN One tool that has been popular with Unix administrators for years (as well as hackers) is SATAN. This tool is not some diabolical supernatural entity, but rather an acronym for Security Administrator Tool for Analyzing Networks. It can be downloaded for free from any number of Web sites. Many of those sites are listed at **www.fish. com/satan/mirrors.html** as shown in Figure 3.17. This tool is strictly for Unix and will not work in Windows. For that reason, we will not be discussing it here, but it is important that you be aware of it. If you intend to work with Unix or Linux, you should definitely get this utility.

FIGURE 3.17 List of SATAN mirror sites.

Vulnerability Scanning

In addition to the utilities and scanners we have already discussed, another essential type of tool for any attacker or defender is the vulnerability scanner. A vulnerability scanner, or security scanner, will remotely audit a network and determine whether someone (or something, such as a worm) may break into it or misuse it in some way. These tools allow the attacker to connect to a target system and check for such vulnerabilities as configuration errors, default configuration settings that allow attackers access, and the most recently reported system vulnerabilities. As with port scanners, there are both commercial as well as free open-source versions of vulnerability scanners. We will discuss two vulnerability scanners here, but there are many others available.

SAINT SAINT is a network vulnerability assessment scanner that takes a preventative approach to securing computer networks. It scans a system and finds security weaknesses. It prioritizes critical vulnerabilities in the network and recommends safeguards for your data. SAINT can benefit you in several ways:

- Prioritized vulnerabilities let you focus your resources on the most critical security issues.
- Fast assessment results help you identify problems quickly.
- Highly configurable scans increase the efficiency of your network security program.

Nessus Nessus, or the "Nessus Project" as it is also known, is another extremely powerful network scanner. It is one of the most up-to-date and easy-to-use remote security scanners currently available. It is fast, reliable, and has a modular architecture that allows you to configure it to your needs. Nessus works on Unix-like systems (MacOS X, FreeBSD, Linux, Solaris, and more) and also has a Windows version called NeWT.

Additionally, Nessus includes a variety of plug-ins that can be enabled depending on the type of security checks you want to perform. These plug-ins work cooperatively with each test specifying what is needed to proceed with the test. For example, if a certain test requires a remote ftp server and a previous test showed that none exists, that test will not be performed. Not performing futile tests speeds up the scanning process. These plug-ins are updated daily and are available from the Nessus Web site.

The output from a Nessus scan of a system is incredibly detailed, and there are multiple formats available for the reports. These reports give information about security holes, warnings, and notes. Nessus does not attempt to fix any security holes that it finds. It simply reports them and gives suggestions on how to make the vulnerable system more secure.

FYI: All-In-One Reconnaissance

In addition to the number of different tools mentioned in this chapter, there are also several "all-in-one" reconnaissance tools. One such tool is Sam Spade, which can make performing initial site recon much easier on Windows. Sam Spade is a versatile network query tool with extra utilities built in to handle spam mail. It includes the typical utilities such as ping, traceroute, whois, and finger.

Port Monitoring and Managing

Using the tools we have already outlined in this chapter, you have access to a great deal of information about the ports in use on a system. There are, however, some additional tools that allow you to obtain more specific information about ports in use and their state, as well as about the flow of information in and out of those ports. Some of these tools also allow you to link a listening port to its application.

NetStat Live

One of the most popular protocol monitors is NetStat, which ships free with Microsoft Windows. A version of this, NetStat Live (NSL), which is freely available on the Internet, is a small, easy-to-use TCP/IP protocol monitor that can be used to see the exact throughput on both incoming and outgoing data whether you are using a modem, cable modem, DSL, or even a local network. It allows you see the speed at which your data goes from your computer to another computer on the Internet. It will even tell you how many other computers your data must go through to get to its destination. NSL also graphs the CPU usage of a system. This can be especially useful if, for example, you are experiencing slowed connection speeds. It can identify whether your computer is the reason for the slow down or if it is your Internet connection.

After you download and install the program, you simply run it. When the program launches, you will see a screen similar to Figure 3.18 (in this case, a distribution from AnalogX).

FIGURE 3.18
NetStat Live display.

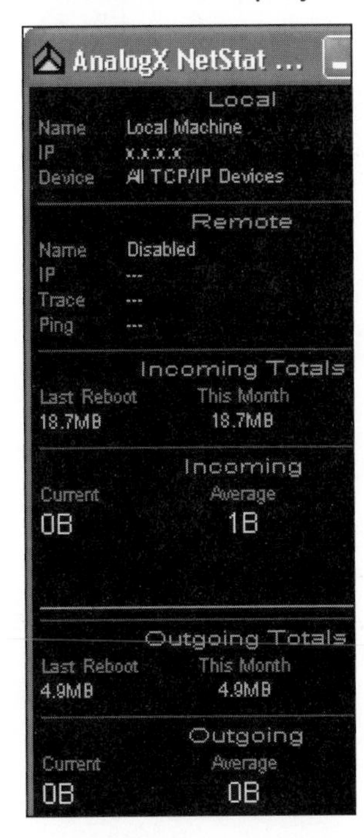

This display shows the last 60 seconds of data throughput. It displays the average datarate, the total amount of data sent since last reboot, and the maximum datarate. It tracks these for all incoming and outgoing messages. Figure 3.18 shows the default display window, but this window can be customized to show exactly what you want. To enable or disable a pane, simply right-click on the window, choose Statistics, and then place a check next to any statistics that you would like to see. Your choices are:

- Local Machine. The current machine name, IP address, and network interface being monitored
- Remote Machine. The remote machine, including average ping time and number of hops
- Incoming Data. Data on the incoming (download) channel
- Incoming Totals. Totals for the incoming data
- Outgoing Data. Data on the outgoing (upload) channel
- Outgoing Totals. Totals for the outgoing data

- System Threads. Total number of threads currently running in the system
- CPU Usage. Graphs the CPU load

Notice that the Remote section has a machine listed and some information pertaining to it. You can easily change the server for which you are gathering information. Simply open your Web browser, go to a Web page, and copy the URL (including the http://) into the clipboard (by using Ctrl+C). When you return to viewing NSL, you will see that the server has been replaced with information on the site to which you browsed.

In addition to adjusting the display, NSL can also be configured to operate in several different ways from the Configure dialog box. To access the Configure options, right-click on the NSL display and choose Configure. You will see the Configure dialog box as shown in Figure 3.19.

From this dialog box, you can configure the program in many ways. Your configuration options are:

- Auto Minimize. If enabled, when NSL starts up, it will automatically show up in the system tray instead of as a window on the screen.
- Auto Start. If enabled, NSL will automatically run every time you reboot your machine. (This is good to use with the Auto Minimize option.)
- Always on Top. If enabled, the NSL dialog box will always be on top of other windows. This allows you to see the information no matter what else is on the screen.
- URL ClipCap. If enabled, NetStat will scan the Windows clipboard for URLs and, if it finds one, will automatically ping/traceroute it.
- Close Minimizes. If enabled, pressing the Close button does not actually close NSL, but rather minimizes it to the system tray.
- TCP/IP Interface. This drop-down list allows you to select from the TCP/IP interfaces currently available or to monitor All available interfaces. (If a specific interface cannot be found, it defaults back to All.)

FIGURE 3.19 NetStat Live Configure dialog box.

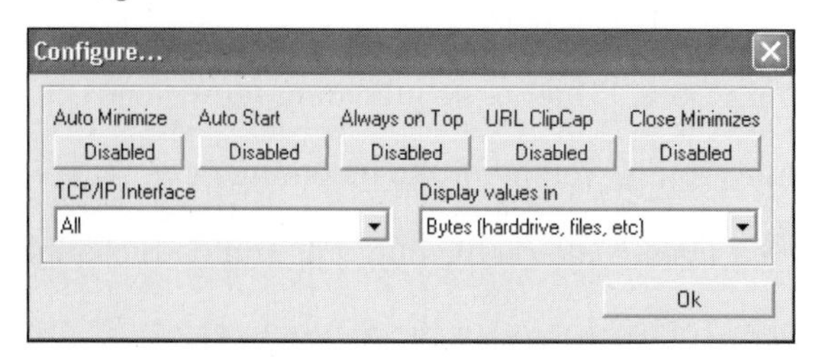

- Display values in. This drop-down list allows you to select whether or not the values are displayed in bits or bytes (the default).

NetStat Live tracks all network activity. This means that you can see how quickly data moves across the local network (as long as you are using TCP/IP) as well as to and from remote sites. Additionally, this means that, when used on a modem connection, you will see the actual throughput and not just what the dial-up networking adapter or modem says it is doing. This allows you to see exactly what kind of performance you are getting while you are browsing around Web pages.

Active Ports

Active Ports is another easy-to-use tool for Windows. This program enables you to monitor all open TCP and UDP ports on the local computer. Active Ports maps ports to the owning application so that you can watch which process has opened which port. It also displays a local and remote IP address for each connection and allows you to terminate the owning process. Active Ports can help you detect Trojan horses and other malicious programs. Figure 3.20 shows the Active Ports interface.

Like so many of these types of programs, Active Ports is available as a free download from many sites on the Internet.

Fport

Like Active Ports, fport reports all open TCP/IP and UDP ports and maps them to the owning application. Additionally, it maps those ports to running processes. Fport can be used to quickly identify unknown open ports and their associated applications.

FIGURE 3.20 Active Ports user interface.

Active Ports

File Options ?

Process	P.	Local IP	Local Port	Remote IP	Remote Port
UDP svchost.exe	460	192.168.0.105	1900		
TCP svchost.exe	1572	0.0.0.0	135		
UDP inetinfo.exe	1872	0.0.0.0	3456		
TCP inetinfo.exe	1872	0.0.0.0	1028		
TCP inetinfo.exe	1872	0.0.0.0	443		
TCP inetinfo.exe	1872	0.0.0.0	80		
TCP inetinfo.exe	1872	0.0.0.0	25		
UDP svchost.exe	1928	192.168.0.105	123		
UDP svchost.exe	2032	0.0.0.0	1619		
UDP svchost.exe	2032	0.0.0.0	1027		
TCP alg.exe	2544	127.0.0.1	1030		
UDP WINWORD.E...	2612	127.0.0.1	1132		
TCP ccApp.exe	2708	127.0.0.1	1036		

Terminate Process | Query Names | Exit

TCPView

TCPView is a Windows program that will show you detailed listings of all TCP and UDP endpoints on your system, including the remote address and the state of TCP connections. TCPView provides a conveniently presented subset of the Netstat program.

In-Depth Searches

Port scanners and other types of scanners can only tell you so much about a target system. At some point, you will probably have to take your investigation to a deeper level. For example, if you find out that a particular server is running IIS 5.0, that discovery probably means the company has Windows 2000. If you then uncover default shared folders and default registry settings, you know that the system is probably entirely set up with default settings. It is also less likely that this system is routinely patched and updated because a security-conscious administrator would not have left default settings in the first place. Your next step is to scan the Internet using various search engines (e.g., **www.yahoo.com**, **www.google.com**, **www.lycos.com**) to find out whether there are any known vulnerabilities with the target system and its configuration. There is a good chance that someone has actually documented the specific vulnerabilities and how these faults can be exploited. Once you have studied the potential vulnerabilities in a target system, you can take one of several actions, depending on your role in the investigation.

- If you are a system administrator, you must correct those vulnerabilities promptly.
- If you are a "sneaker" (or an "ethical" white hat hacker), you would document what you have found to then report to your client.
- If you are a cracker, you can use this information to select the most appropriate way to compromise the target system. However, be aware that such activities are illegal and can culminate in severe civil penalties, including as prison sentences.

Web searches and newsgroup searches (you can use Google's "groups" tab for this task) can also provide other interesting information about a site. You will often be able to find details about a company, such as its key personnel and ISP. There are several ways to use this information. For example, if you find that a company has a high turnover in its systems department (for example, you see the same job posted frequently, indicating rapid turnover), then it is less likely that the system is as secure as it should be. Or, if you see that one company is being bought out by another, this event might lead to some confusion in the two companies' IT departments as they try to merge. This information can help you identify other vulnerabilities in a target system.

Summary

Information is the key to compromising security. If someone can gain enough information about your systems and organization, then she has a much better chance of compromising the firm's security. It is imperative that you assess your own organization's vulnerabilities in this regard.

In this chapter, we have examined a variety of port scanners as well as vulnerability scanners. Having a port scanner and routinely examining your own system for vulnerabilities is a must for any security-conscious network administrator. These scanners are the same tools that hackers will use to assess your system; therefore, it is critical that you also use them.

Test Your Skills

MULTIPLE CHOICE QUESTIONS

1. When a hacker reviews a network's potential vulnerabilities, this assessment is referred to as:
   A. scanning.
   B. assessing.
   C. checking.
   D. footprinting.
2. To learn what operating system a Web server is running, what utility would you use?
   A. NetBrute
   B. NetCop
   C. www.netcraft.com
   D. www.netcheck.com
3. If you find a target Web server running Windows NT 4.0, what might this fact tell you about that system?
   A. It is a stable system that does not change often, and it is probably quite secure.
   B. The system, and possibly the administrator, have been around quite a long time and are therefore probably secure.
   C. The system is not updated frequently and may not be secure.
   D. The system is using an unproven version of Windows and therefore may not be secure.

4. Which of the following utilities will help you trace an IP address?
   A. tracert
   B. IPConfig
   C. NetCop
   D. NetBrute

5. If you trace to a destination IP from multiple-source IPs and if you see that the final few steps are always the same, what does this fact tell you?
   A. that there is an error in your trace
   B. that those final IPs could be the target's ISP or a router
   C. that those final IPs are within the target organization
   D. that those final IPs represent switches

6. What is the most common goal in social engineering?
   A. to get the phone number and e-mail address for the system administrator
   B. to get the username and password of an authorized user
   C. to get the open ports on a system
   D. to get the IP address of the e-mail server

7. What is port scanning?
   A. scanning a target to see what operating system it is running
   B. scanning a target to see what Web server it is running
   C. scanning a target to see what ports are open
   D. scanning a target to see what software is installed

8. Which of the following best describes the value of knowing what ports are open?
   A. It can reveal details about the operating system and software running.
   B. It can reveal details about the encryption of data transmission.
   C. It can reveal details about what Web server the firm is using.
   D. It can reveal details about system security.

9. If a scan determines that all default services are running, what might this finding indicate?
   A. that the system is set up with factory defaults and is therefore very secure
   B. that the system administrator is using a standard configuration
   C. that the system administrator is using a custom configuration
   D. that the system is set up with factory defaults and is therefore not very secure

10. What feature of NetCop makes it particularly useful?
    A. You can scan a single IP or multiple IPs.
    B. You can find out what ports are open.
    C. You can find out what operating system is running.
    D. You can scan multiple domains.

11. What application would you guess might be running on a Windows system that had port 118 open?
    A. Internet Information Server
    B. Windows XP
    C. Windows 2003
    D. SQL Server

12. What information do you get from the NetBrute tab of NetBrute?
    A. shared drives and folders on the target
    B. operating system on which the target is running
    C. open ports on the target
    D. Web server the target is using

13. Which scanner will give you information regarding Windows Registry settings?
    A. Cerberus Internet Scanner
    B. NetBrute
    C. NetCop
    D. Security Commander

14. Which of the following utilities gives you the most information?
    A. Cerberus Internet Scanner
    B. NetBrute
    C. NetCop
    D. Security Commander

Caution

Scanning and Intrusion Detection

In the following exercises and projects, if you use any of these port scanners on a machine that has an intrusion detection system, they will detect your port scan. For this reason, you are advised not to simply port scan random machines. You must have permission to scan a system.

15. What should a system administrator do about vulnerabilities that are found on their system?
    A. immediately correct them
    B. document them
    C. discuss the corrections with upper management
    D. change software to avoid them

EXERCISES

Exercise 3.1: Using NetCop

1. Use NetCop to scan a target machine (either your own or one that your instructor sets up for this purpose).
2. Identify any open ports, paying particular attention to open ports that your system does not require.
3. Shut down the services that use those ports.

Exercise 3.2: Using NetBrute

1. Use NetBrute to scan a target machine (either your own or one that your instructor sets up for this purpose).
2. Identify any open ports and shared drives.
3. If you have administrative rights in Windows, you can cause a shared drive or folder to no longer be shared.

Exercise 3.3: Using Netcraft

1. Use Netcraft to scan a Web site. You can use a Web site that your instructor designates, or you can select **www.chuckeasttom.com**.
2. Identify what operating system is employed and what Web server is running.

Exercise 3.4: Using Tracert and Netcraft

1. Use the tracert utility to trace any given IP address on the Internet. You can trace either the IP address or the URL (such as **www.prenticehall.com**).

2. Then use Netcraft to find information about the IP address just prior to your target.

3. Write a brief paper describing how that information might be useful to a hacker.

Exercise 3.5: Using Netstat

1. Use Netstat to determine the current statistics for the system you are using.

2. Use Ctrl+C to copy an URL from your browser window and establish that IP as the remote system.

3. Identify the speed at which data is moving across your local network as well as to the chosen remote IP address.

PROJECTS

Project 3.1: Using Cerberus Internet Scanner

1. Use Cerberus to scan a target machine that your instructor designates.

2. Note that Cerberus, in addition to port/service information, gives you information regarding insecure registry settings, shared drives, and even security flaws in database software.

3. Write a paper identifying all of the security flaws you find.

Project 3.2: Performing a Complete Scan of a System

1. Using all the utilities discussed in this chapter, scan a target system as designated by your instructor.

2. Note all deficiencies you find including open ports, insecure registry settings, shared folders, and so forth.

3. Write a paper discussing the different results you obtained from the different scanners. Did one scanner find flaws that another missed?

Project 3.3: Tracking Down Information

1. Gather information regarding a target's operating system and Web server. (You can use information derived from one of the previous exercises or projects.)
2. Then scan the Internet looking for known flaws in that version of that operating system. Simply using **www.google.com** or **www.yahoo.com** and searching for something such as "security flaws in Windows 98" should yield many results.
3. Write a brief paper on one of those flaws.

Case Study

A network administrator named Juanita works for a small company that has a limited IT budget. Juanita has several years of network administration experience, but she is new to network security. To assess her system, she downloads NetCop and scans her system for open ports. She is able to identify several ports/services that are open that do not need to be, and she closes them. Given this scenario, consider the following questions:

- What did Juanita accomplish by closing the ports?
- What vulnerabilities might she have missed with this course of action?
- Considering what you have learned in this chapter, what further course of action would you recommend to Juanita?

Chapter 4

Denial of Service Attacks

Chapter Objectives

After reading this chapter and completing the exercises, you will be able to do the following:

- Understand how Denial of Service (DoS) attacks are accomplished.
- Know how certain DoS attacks work, such as SYN flood, Smurf, and DDoS.
- Take specific measures to protect against DoS attacks.
- Know how to defend against specific DoS attacks.

Introduction

By now you are aware, in a general way, of the dangers of the Internet and have also explored a few basic rules for protection on the Internet. In Chapter 3, you explored ways to investigate a target system and to learn a great deal about it. It is now time to become more specific about how attacks on systems are conducted. In this chapter, you will examine one category of attack that might be used to cause harm to a target computer system. This chapter will describe for you, in depth, the workings of the ***Denial of Service (DoS)*** attack. This threat is one of the most common attacks on the Internet, so it is prudent for you to understand how it works and how to defend yourself against it. Further, in the exercises at the end of the book, you will practice stopping a DoS. In information security, the old adage that "knowledge is power" is not only good advice, but also an axiom upon which to build your entire security outlook.

Overview

As was said in the introduction, one of the most common and simplest forms of attack on a system is a Denial of Service (DoS). This attack does not even attempt to intrude on your system or to obtain sensitive information; it simply aims to prevent legitimate users from accessing the system. This type of attack is fairly easy to execute. The basic concept requires a minimum of technical skill. It is based on the fact that any device has operational limits. For example, a truck can only carry a finite load or travel a finite distance. Computers are no different than any other machine; they, too, have limits. Any computer system, Web server, or network can only handle a finite load. A workload for a computer system may be defined by the number of simultaneous users, the size of files, the speed of data transmission, or the amount of data stored. If you exceed any of those limits, the excess load will stop the system from responding. For example, if you can flood a Web server with more requests than it can process, it will be overloaded and will no longer be able to respond to further requests (Webopedia, 2004). This reality underlies the DoS attack. Simply overload the system with requests, and it will no longer be able to respond to legitimate users attempting to access the Web server.

IN PRACTICE: Illustrating an Attack

One simple way to illustrate this attack, especially in a classroom setting, involves the use of the ping command discussed in Chapter 2.

1. Start a Web server service running on one machine (you can use Apache, IIS, or any Web server).
2. Ask several people to open their browsers and key the IP address of that machine in the address bar. They should then be viewing the default Web site for that Web server.

Now you can do a rather primitive DoS attack on the system. Recall from Chapter 2 that typing in ping /h will show you all the options for the ping command. The –l option changes the size of the packet you can send. Remember from Chapter 2 that a TCP packet can be only of a finite size. Thus, you are going to set these packets to be almost as large as you can send. The –w option determines how many milliseconds the ping utility will wait for a response from the target. You are going to use –0 so that the ping utility does not wait at all. Then the –t instructs the ping utility to keep sending packets until explicitly told to stop.

3. Open the command prompt in Windows 2000/XP (that is the DOS prompt in Windows 98 and the Shell in Unix/Linux).

4. Key **ping <address of target machine goes here> –l 65000 –w 0 –t**. You will then see something very much like what is shown in Figure 4.1. Note that, in the figure, I am pinging the loop-back address for my own machine. You will want to substitute the address of the machine on which you are running the Web server.

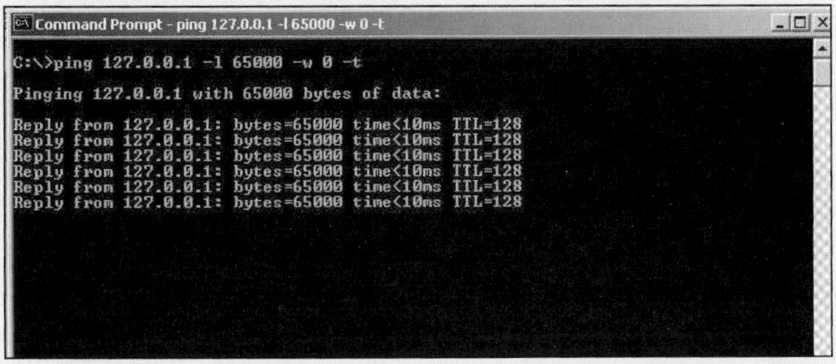

```
Command Prompt - ping 127.0.0.1 -l 65000 -w 0 -t

C:\>ping 127.0.0.1 -l 65000 -w 0 -t

Pinging 127.0.0.1 with 65000 bytes of data:

Reply from 127.0.0.1: bytes=65000 time<10ms TTL=128
Reply from 127.0.0.1: bytes=65000 time<10ms TTL=128
Reply from 127.0.0.1: bytes=65000 time<10ms TTL=128
Reply from 127.0.0.1: bytes=65000 time<10ms TTL=128
Reply from 127.0.0.1: bytes=65000 time<10ms TTL=128
Reply from 127.0.0.1: bytes=65000 time<10ms TTL=128
```

FIGURE 4.1 Ping from the command prompt.

What is happening at this point is that this single machine is continually pinging away at the target machine. Of course, just one machine in your classroom or lab that is simply pinging on your Web server is not going to adversely affect the Web server. However, you can now, one by one, get other machines in the classroom pinging the server in the same way. After each batch of three or four machines you add, try to go to the Web server's default Web page. After a certain threshold (certain number of machines pinging the server), it will stop responding to requests, and you will no longer be able to see the Web page.

How many machines it will take to deny service depends on the Web server you are using. In order to see this denial happen with as few machines involved as possible, you could use a very low-capacity PC as your Web server. For example, running an Apache Web server on a simple Pentium III laptop running Windows 98, it can take about 15 machines simultaneously pinging to cause a Web server to stop responding to legitimate requests. This strategy is, of course, counter to what you would normally select for a Web server—no real Web server would be running on a simple laptop with Windows 98. Likewise, actual DoS attacks use much more sophisticated methods. This simple exercise, however, should demonstrate for you the basic principle behind the DoS attack: Simply flood the target machine with so many packets that it can no longer respond to legitimate requests.

FYI: Buffer Overflows

A Denial of Service attack is "one of the most common" attacks on a system. Another extremely common type of attack is the buffer overflow. Which of these is the leading form of attack is subject to debate among the experts. Regardless, understanding DoS attacks and how to thwart them is clearly an important component of system security.

Generally, the methods used for DoS attacks are significantly more sophisticated than the illustration. For example, a hacker might develop a small virus whose sole purpose is to initiate a ping flood against a predetermined target. Once the virus has spread, the various machines that are infected with that virus then begin their ping flood of the target system. This sort of DoS is easy to do, and it can be hard to stop. A DoS that is launched from several different machines is called a Distributed Denial of Service (DDoS).

Common Tools Used for DoS

As with any of the security issues discussed in this book, you will find that hackers have at their disposal a vast array of tools with which to work. The DoS arena is no different. While it is certainly well beyond the scope of this book to begin to categorize or discuss all of these tools, a brief introduction to just a few of them will prove useful. The two tools discussed here, TFN and Stacheldraht, are typical of the types of tools that someone wishing to perform a DoS attack would utilize.

TFN and TFN2K TFN, also known as Tribal Flood Network, and TFN2K are not viruses, but rather attack tools that can be used to perform a DDoS. TFN2K is a newer version of TFN that supports both Windows NT and Unix platforms (and can easily be ported to additional platforms). It has some features that make detection more difficult than its predecessor,

FYI: What Is DoS?

The name for DoS attacks comes from the fact that such attempts literally deny legitimate users the service provided by the site in question. These attacks began to become widely known in 1995 when the simple Ping of Death DoS attack (discussed later in this chapter) began to be used frequently.

including sending decoy information to avoid being traced. Experts at using TFN2K can use the resources of a number of agents to coordinate an attack against one or more targets. Additionally, TFN and TFN2K can perform various attacks such as UDP flood attacks, ICMP flood attacks, and TCP SYN flood attacks (all discussed later in this chapter).

TFN2K works on two fronts. First, there is a command-driven client on the master system. Second, there is a daemon process operating on an agent system. The attack works like this:

1. The master instructs its agents to attack a list of designated targets.
2. The agents respond by flooding the targets with a barrage of packets.

With this tool, multiple agents, coordinated by the master, can work together during the attack to disrupt access to the target. Additionally, there are a number of "safety" features for the attacker that significantly complicates development of effective and efficient countermeasures for TFN2K.

- Master-to-agent communications are encrypted and may be mixed with any number of decoy packets.
- Both master-to-agent communications and the attacks themselves can be sent via randomized TCP, UDP, and ICMP packets.
- The master can falsify its IP address (spoof).

Stacheldraht Stacheldraht, which is German for "barbed wire," is a DDoS attack tool that combines features of the Trinoo DDoS tool (another common tool) with the source code from the TFN DDoS attack tool. Like TFN2K, it adds encryption of communication between the attacker and the Stacheldraht masters. It also adds an automatic updating of the agents.

Stacheldraht can perform a variety of attacks including UDP flood, ICMP flood, TCP SYN flood, and Smurf attacks. It also detects and automatically enables source address forgery.

DoS Weaknesses

The weakness in any DoS attack, from the attacker's point of view, is that the flood of packets must be sustained. As soon as the packets stop sending, the target system is back up. A DoS/DDoS attack, however, is very often used in conjunction with another form of attack, such as disabling one side of a connection in TCP hijacking or preventing authentication or logging between servers.

If the hacker is using a distributed attack, as soon as the administrators or owners of the infected machines realize their machine is infected, they will take steps to remove the virus and thus stop the attack. If a hacker attempts to launch an attack from her own machine, she must be aware that each packet has the potential to be traced back to its source. This fact means that a single hacker using a DoS will almost certainly be caught by the authorities. For this reason, the DDoS is quickly becoming the most common type of DoS attack. The specifics of DDoS attacks will be discussed later in this chapter.

DoS Attacks

As you can see, the basic concept for perpetrating a DoS attack is not complicated. The real problem for the attacker is performing the attack without being caught. The next few sections of this chapter will examine some specific types of DoS attacks and look at specific case studies. This information should help you gain a deeper understanding of this particular Internet threat.

TCP SYN Flood Attack

One popular version of the DoS attack is the ***SYN flood***. This particular attack depends on the hacker's knowledge of how connections are made to a server. When a session is initiated between the client and server in a network using the TCP protocol, a small buffer space in memory is set aside on the server to handle the "hand-shaking" exchange of messages that sets up the session. The session-establishing packets include a SYN field that identifies the sequence in the message exchange. An attacker can send a number of connection requests very rapidly and then fail to respond to the reply that is sent back by the server, or he can supply a spoofed (forged) IP address. In other words, he requests connections and then never follows through with the rest of the connection sequence. This process has the effect of leaving connections on the server half open, and the buffer memory allocated for them is reserved and not available to other applications. Although the packet in the buffer is dropped after a certain period of time (usually about three minutes) without a reply, the effect of many of these false connection requests is to make it difficult for legitimate requests for a session to get established.

There have been a number of well-known SYN flood attacks on Web servers. The reason for the popularity of this attack type is that any machine

> **FYI: Flood Attacks**
>
> In a ***flood attack***, the attacker overwhelms a target system by sending a continuous flood of traffic designed to consume resources at the targeted server (CPU cycles, memory) and/or in the network (bandwidth, packet buffers). The goal of these attacks is to degrade service or completely shut down a site.

that engages in TCP communication is vulnerable to it—and all machines connected to the Internet engage in TCP communications. Such communication is obviously the entire reason for Web servers. There are, however, several methods and techniques you can implement to protect against these attacks. The basic defensive techniques are:

- SYN cookies
- RST cookies
- stack tweaking

Some of these methods require more technical sophistication than others. These methods will be discussed in general here. When you are entrusted with defending a system against these forms of attacks, you can select the methods most appropriate for your network environment and your level of expertise and examine it further at that time. The specifics of how to implement any of these methods will depend on the operating system that your Web server is using. You will need to consult your operating system's documentation, or appropriate Web sites, in order to find explicit instruction on how to implement methods.

SYN Cookies As the name ***SYN cookies*** suggests, this method uses cookies, not unlike the standard cookies used on many Web sites. With this method, the system does not immediately create a buffer space in memory for the hand-shaking process. Rather, it first sends a ***SYNACK*** (the acknowledgment signal that begins the hand-shaking process). The SYNACK contains a carefully constructed cookie, generated as a hash that contains the IP address, port number, and other information from the client machine requesting the connection. When the client responds with a normal ACK (acknowledgement), the information from that cookie will be included, which the server then verifies. Thus, the system does not fully allocate any memory until the third stage of the hand-shaking process as illustrated in Figure 4.2. This enables the system to continue to operate normally; typically, the only effect seen is the disabling of large windows. However, the cryptographic hashing used in SYN cookies is fairly resource intensive, so system administrators that expect a great deal of incoming connections may choose not to use this defensive technique.

FIGURE 4.2 Hand-shaking process.

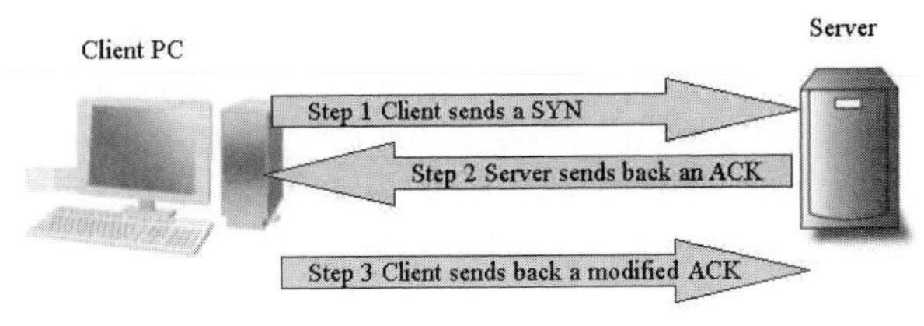

FYI: Hashing

A hash value is a number generated from a string of text. The hash is significantly smaller than the text itself and is generated by a formula in such a way that it is extremely unlikely that some other text will produce the same hash value. Hashing plays a role in security when it is used to ensure that transmitted messages have not been tampered with. To do this, the sending machine generates a hash of the message, encrypts it, and sends it with the message itself. The receiving machine then decrypts both the message and the hash, produces another hash from the received message, and compares the two hashes. If they are the same, there is a very high probability that the message was transmitted intact.

RST Cookies Another cookie method that is easier to implement than SYN cookies is the ***RST cookie***. In this method, the server sends a wrong SYNACK back to the client. The client should then generate an RST packet telling the server that something is wrong. Because the client sent back a packet notifying the server of the error, the server now knows the client request is legitimate and can now accept incoming connections from that client in the normal fashion. This method has two disadvantages. It might cause problems with Windows 95 machines and/or machines that are communicating from behind firewalls.

Stack Tweaking The method of ***stack tweaking*** involves altering the TCP stack on the server so that it will take less time to timeout when a SYN connection is left incomplete. Unfortunately, this protective method will just make executing a SYN flood against that target more difficult; to a determined hacker, the attack is still possible.

FYI: Stack Tweaking

The process of stack tweaking is often quite complicated, depending on the operating system. Some operating systems' documentation provides no help on this subject. For these reasons, this method is usually only used by very advanced network administrators and is not recommended unless you have a very solid knowledge of the operating system with which you are working.

Smurf IP Attack

The Smurf attack is a very popular version of the DoS attack. An ICMP (Internet Control Message Protocol) packet is sent out to the broadcast address of the network. Since it is broadcast, it responds by echoing the packet out to all hosts on the network, who then send it to the spoofed source address. Also, the spoofed source address can be anywhere on the Internet, not just on the local subnet. If the hacker can continually send such packets, she will cause the network itself to perform a DoS attack on one or more of its member servers. This attack is clever and rather simple. The only problem for the hacker is getting the packets started on the target network. This task can be accomplished via some software, such as a virus or Trojan horse, that will begin sending the packets.

In a Smurf attack, there are three people/systems involved: the attacker, the intermediary (who can also be a victim), and the victim. The attacker first sends an ICMP echo request packet to the intermediary's IP broadcast addresses. Since this is sent to the IP broadcast address, many of the machines on the intermediary's network will receive this request packet and will send an ICMP echo reply packet back. If all the machines on a network are responding to this request, the network becomes congested and there can be outages.

The attacker impacts the third party—the intended victim—by creating forged packets that contain the spoofed source address of the victim. Therefore, when all the machines on the intermediary's network start replying to the echo request, those replies will flood the victim's network. Thus, another network becomes congested and could become unusable.

The Smurf attack is an example of the creativity that some malicious parties can employ. It is sometimes viewed as the digital equivalent of the biological process in an auto-immune disorder. With such disorders, the immune system attacks the patient's own body. In a Smurf attack, the network performs a DoS attack on one of its own systems. This method's cleverness illustrates why it is important that you attempt to work creatively and in a forward-thinking manner if you are responsible for system security in your network. The perpetrators of computer attacks are inventive and always coming up with new techniques. If your defense is less creative and clever than the attackers' defense, then it is simply a matter of time before your system is compromised.

There are several ways to protect your system against this problem. One is to guard against Trojan horses. More will be said about the Trojan horse attack in later chapters; however, having policies prohibiting employees from downloading applications will help. Also, having adequate virus scanners can go a long way in protecting your system from a Trojan horse and, thus, a Smurf attack. It is also imperative that you use a proxy server, which was discussed in Chapter 2. If the internal IP addresses of your network are not known, then it is more difficult to target one in a

Smurf attack. Probably the best way to protect your system is to combine these defenses along with prohibiting directed broadcasts and patching the hosts to refuse to reply to any directed broadcasts.

UDP Flood Attack

UDP, as you will recall from Chapter 2, is a connectionless protocol that does not require any connection setup procedure prior to transferring data. In a ***UDP flood attack***, the attacker sends a UDP packet to a random port on a target system. When the target system receives a UDP packet, it automatically determines what application is waiting on the destination port. In this case, since there is no application waiting on the port, the target system will generate an ICMP packet of "destination unreachable" and attempt to send it back to the forged source address. If enough UDP packets are delivered to ports on the target, the system will become overloaded trying to determine awaiting applications (which do not exist) and then generating and sending packets back.

ICMP Flood Attack

There are two basic types of ***ICMP flood attacks***: floods and nukes. An ICMP flood is usually accomplished by broadcasting a large number of either pings or UDP packets. Like other flood attacks, the idea is to send so much data to the target system that it slows down. If it can be forced to slow down enough, the target will time out (not send replies fast enough) and be disconnected from the Internet. ICMP nukes exploit known bugs in specific operating systems. The attacker sends a packet of information that he knows the operating system on the target system cannot handle. In many cases, this will cause the target system to lock up completely.

The Ping of Death (PoD)

Recall from Chapter 2 that TCP packets are of limited size. In some cases, simply sending a packet that is too large can shut down a target machine.

FYI: Logic or Software Attacks

DoS attacks can also be of a logic or software type. In this type of attack a small number of malformed packets are sent to a target system. These packets are designed specifically to exploit known software bugs on the target system. Software attacks are relatively easy to counter. It is usually just a matter of installing a software patch that eliminates the vulnerabilities or adding specialized firewall rules to filter out the malformed packets before they reach the target system.

This action is referred to as the ***Ping of Death (PoD)***. It works simply by overloading the target system. The hacker sends merely a single ping, but he does so with a very large packet and thus can shut down some machines.

This attack is quite similar to the classroom example discussed earlier in this chapter. The aim in both cases is to overload the target system and cause it to quit responding. PoD works to compromise systems that cannot deal with extremely large packet sizes. If successful, the server will actually shut down completely. It can, of course be rebooted.

The only real safeguard against PoD is to ensure that all operating systems and software are routinely patched. This attack relies on vulnerabilities in the way a particular operating system (or application) handles abnormally large TCP packets. When such vulnerabilities are discovered, it is customary for the vendor to release a patch. The possibility of PoD is one reason, among many, why you must keep patches updated on all of your systems.

Teardrop Attack

In a ***teardrop attack***, the attacker sends a fragmented message. The two fragments overlap in ways that make it impossible to reassemble them properly without destroying the individual packet headers. Therefore, when the victim attempts to reconstruct the message, the message is destroyed. This causes the target system to halt or crash. There are a number of variations on the basic teardrop attack that are available such as TearDrop2, Boink, targa, Nestea Boink, NewTear, and SYNdrop.

Land Attack

A ***land attack*** is probably the simplest in concept. The attacker sends a forged packet with the same source IP address and destination IP address (the target's IP address). The method is to drive the target system "crazy" by having it attempt to send messages to and from itself. The victim system will often be confused and will crash or reboot.

Echo/Chargen Attack

The character generator (chargen) service was designed primarily for testing purposes. It simply generates a stream of characters. In an ***echo/chargen attack***, this service is abused by attackers who exhaust the target system's resources. The attacker accomplishes this by creating a spoofed network session that appears to come from that local system's echo service and which is pointed at the chargen service to form a "loop." This session will cause huge amounts of data to be passed in an endless loop. This constant looping causes a heavy load to the system. Alternately, if the spoofed session is pointed at a system's echo service, it will cause heavy network traffic that slows down the target's network.

FYI: Man-in-the-Middle Attack

One form of attack, known as the man-in-the-middle attack, sometimes requires the use of a Denial of Service attack. In the man-in-the-middle attack, the attacker intercepts one side of an Internet conversation by using a packet sniffer at some point between the two end points. The attacker then pretends to be one end of the connection. For example the attacker might intercept traffic between a client PC and an e-commerce site. The attacker responds as if she were the intended server, therefore the client continues to send information that the attacker then retrieves. In some cases a Denial of Service is first used on the server the attacker wishes to impersonate to shut it down before the attacker attempts to 'hijack' the communication with clients.

The famous (or infamous, depending on your perspective) hacker Kevin Mitnick is alleged to have used this technique to gain passwords and login information that he later used to break into a number of major systems such as Digital Equipment Corporation (DEC), Santa Cruz Operation (SCO), and even the United States Defense Department.

Distributed Denial of Service (DDoS)

Another form of trickery is the ***Distributed Denial of Service*** attack (***DDoS***). As with all such denial attacks, it is accomplished by the hacker getting a number of machines to attack the target. However, this attack works a bit differently then other DoS attacks. Rather than getting computers to attack the target, one of the ways the hacker accomplishes a DDoS is to trick Internet routers into attacking a target. Another form of DDoS relies on compromised (zombie) hosts to simultaneously attack a given target with a large number of packets.

Recall from the discussion of ports in Chapter 2, that many of the routers on the Internet backbone communicate on port 179 (Gibson, 2002). This attack exploits that communication line and gets routers to attack a target system. What makes this attack particularly wicked is that it does not require the routers in question to be compromised in any way. Instead, the hacker sends a stream of packets to the various routers requesting a connection. The packets have been altered so that they appear to come from the target system's IP address. The routers respond by initiating connections with the target system. What occurs then is a flood of connections from multiple routers, all hitting the same target system. This flood has the effect of rendering the system unreachable.

Real-World Examples

A good deal of time has been spent discussing the basics of how various DoS attacks are conducted. By now, you should have a firm grasp of what a DoS attack is and have a basic understanding of how it works. It is now time to begin discussing specific, real-world, examples of such attacks. This section will take the theoretical knowledge you have gained and give you real-world examples of its application.

MyDoom

One of the most well publicized DoS attacks was the MyDoom attack. This threat was a classically distributed DoS attack. The virus/worm would e-mail itself to everyone in your address book and then, at a preset time, all infected machines would begin a coordinated attack on **www.sco.com** (Delio, 2004). Estimates put the number of infected machines between 500,000 and 1 million. This attack was successful and promptly shut down the SCO Web site. It should be noted that well before the day that the DoS attack was actually executed, network administrators and home users were well aware of what MyDoom would do. There were also several tools available free of charge on the Internet for removing the virus/worm. However, it appears that many people did not take the steps necessary to clean their machines of this virus/worm.

What makes this attack so interesting is that it is clearly an example of domestic cyber terrorism (although it is certain that the creators of MyDoom would probably see it differently). (Cyber terrorism will be discussed further in Chapter 10.) For those readers who do not know the story, it will be examined here briefly. Santa Cruz Operations (SCO) makes a version of the Unix operating system. Like most Unix versions, their version is copyright protected. Several months before this attack, SCO began accusing certain Linux distributions of containing segments of SCO Unix code. SCO sent demand letters to many Linux users demanding license fees. Many

> **FYI: Virus or Worm?**
>
> Definitions of the terms virus and worm are widely debated among the experts. And, depending upon the definition, what some would call a virus, others would call a worm. One general distinction that is accepted by many is that worms do not require direct human interaction to propagate, whereas viruses do. If you accept this definition, then both MyDoom and Slammer are worms. To avoid confusion on this issue, however, the term "virus/worm" will be used.

people in the Linux community viewed this request as simply an attempt to undermine the growing popularity of Linux, an open-source operating system. SCO went even further and filed suit against major companies that were distributing Linux (SCO./Linux, 2003). This claim by SCO seemed unfounded to many legal and technology analysts. It was also viewed with great suspicion because SCO had close ties to Microsoft, which had been trying desperately to stop the growing popularity of Linux.

Many analysts feel that the MyDoom virus/worm was created by some individual (or group of individuals) who felt that the Santa Cruz Operations tactics were unacceptable. The hackers wished to cause economic harm to SCO and damage its public image. This probable motive makes this case clearly one of domestic economic terrorism: One group attacks the technological assets of another group based on an ideological difference. Prior to this virus/worm, there were numerous Web site defacements and other small-scale attacks that were part of ideological conflicts. However, this virus/worm was the first such attack to be so widespread and successful. This incident began a new trend in information warfare. As technology becomes less expensive and the tactics more readily available, you can expect to see an increase in this sort of attack in the coming years.

Slammer

Another virus/worm responsible for DoS attacks was the Slammer virus/worm. Some experts rate Slammer as the fastest-spreading virus/worm to ever hit the Internet (Moore, 2004). This virus/worm achieved its DoS simply by spreading so fast that it clogged up networks. It began spreading on January 25th, 2003. It would scan a network for any computers running the Microsoft SQL Server Desktop Engine. It then used a flaw in that application to infect the target machine. It would continually scan every computer connected to the infected machine, seeking one with Microsoft SQL Server Desktop Engine. At its peak, it performed millions of scans per second. This activity resulted in a tremendous number of packets going across infected networks. That flood of scanning packets brought many systems down.

This particular attack was interesting for two reasons. First, what defines this virus as also being a worm, is its method of propagation. It was able to spread without anyone downloading it or opening an attachment on an e-mail. Instead, it would randomly scan IP addresses, looking for any machine it could infect. This method meant that it spread much faster than many other virus/worm attacks had previously. The second interesting fact about this attack was that it was totally preventable. Microsoft had released a patch for this flaw weeks before the attack took place. This story should illustrate the critical need to frequently update your machine's software. You must make certain that you have all the latest patches installed on your machine.

How to Defend Against DoS Attacks

There is no guaranteed way to prevent all DoS attacks, just as there is no sure way to prevent any hacking attack. However, there are steps you can take to minimize the danger. Some methodologies, such as SYN cookies and RST cookies, have already been mentioned. In this section, a few of the steps you can take to make your system less susceptible to a DoS attack will be examined.

One of the first things for you to consider is how these attacks are perpetrated. They may be executed via ICMP packets that are used to send error messages on the Internet or are sent by the ping and traceroute utilities. If you have a firewall (and you absolutely should have one), then simply configuring it to refuse ICMP packets from outside your network will be a major step in protecting your network from DoS attacks. Since DoS/DDoS attacks can be executed via a wide variety of protocols, you can also configure your firewall to disallow any incoming traffic at all, regardless of what protocol or port it occurs on. This step may seem radical, but it is certainly a secure one.

It is also possible to detect some threats from certain DoS tools, such as TFN2K, by using information tools like NetStat. Many of these tools can be configured to look for the SYN_RECEIVED state, which could indicate a SYN flood attack.

FYI: Blocking ICMP Packets

There are very few legitimate reasons (and, some would argue, no good reasons) for an ICMP packet from outside your network to enter your network. Thus, blocking such packets is very often used as one part of the strategy to defend against DoS attacks.

If your network is large enough to have internal routers, then you can configure those routers to disallow any traffic that does not originate with your network. In that way, should packets make it past your firewall, they will not be propagated throughout the network. You should also consider disabling directed IP broadcasts on all routers. This strategy will prevent the router from sending broadcast packets to all machines on the network, thus stopping many DoS attacks. Additionally, you can install a filter on the router to verify that external packets actually have external IP addresses and that internal IPs have internal IP addresses.

Because many distributed DoS attacks depend on "unwitting" computers being used as launch points, one way to reduce such attacks is to protect your computer against virus attacks and Trojan horses. This problem will be discussed in more detail in a later chapter, but for now, it is important that you remember three things:

- Always use virus-scanning software and keep it updated.
- Always keep operating system and software patches updated.
- Have an organizational policy stating that employees cannot download anything onto their machines unless the download has been cleared by the IT staff.

As previously stated, none of these steps will make your network totally secure from either being the victim of a DoS attack or being the launch point for one, but they will help reduce the chances of either occurring. A good resource for this topic is the SANS Institute Web site, at **www.sans.org/dosstep/**. This site, shown in Figure 4.3, has some good tips on how to prevent DoS attacks.

FIGURE 4.3 SANS steps to defeat DoS attacks.

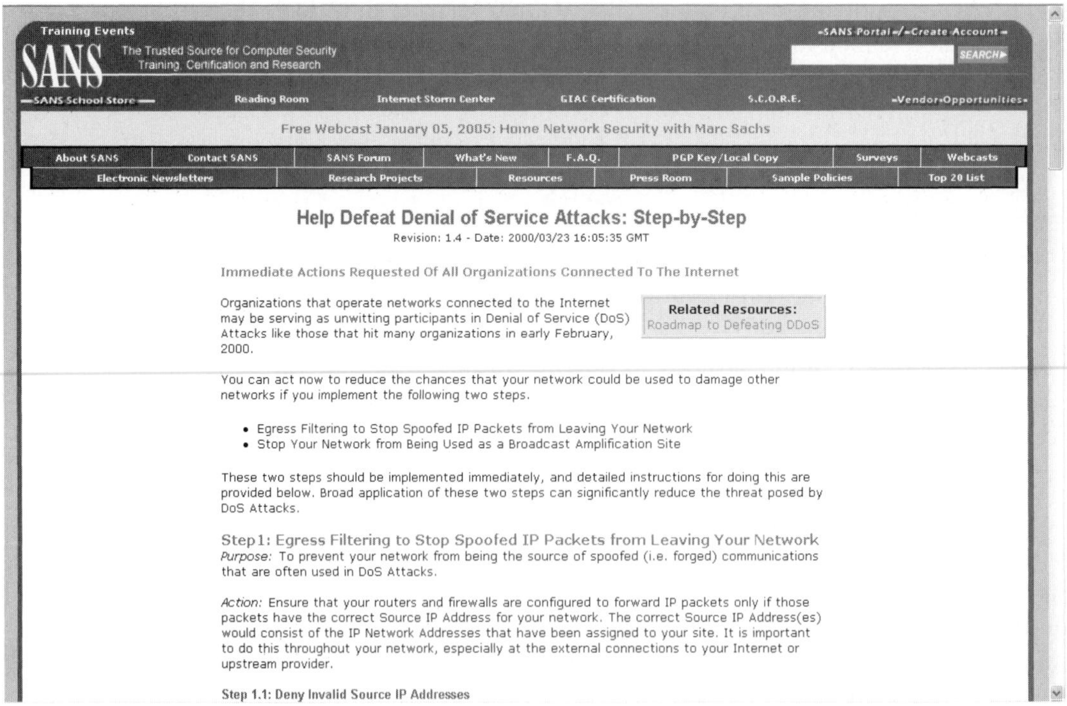

Summary

DoS attacks are among the most common attacks on the Internet. They are easy to perform, do not require a great deal of sophistication on the part of the perpetrator, and can have devastating effects on the target system. Only virus attacks are more common. (And, in some cases, the virus can be the source of the DoS attack.) In the exercises, you will practice stopping a DoS.

Test Your Skills

MULTIPLE CHOICE QUESTIONS

1. What is one of the most common and simplest attacks on a system?
   A. Denial of Service
   B. Buffer overflow
   C. Session hacking
   D. Password cracking
2. Which of the following is not a valid way to define a computer's workload?
   A. Number of simultaneous users
   B. Storage capacity
   C. Maximum voltage
   D. Speed of network connection
3. What do you call a DoS launched from several machines simultaneously?
   A. Wide-area attack.
   B. Smurf attack
   C. SYN flood
   D. DDoS attack
4. Leaving a connection half open is referred to as a:
   A. Smurf attack.
   B. Partial attack.
   C. SYN flood attack.
   D. DDoS attack.

5. What is the basic mechanism behind a DoS attack?
   A. Computers don't handle TCP packets well.
   B. Computers can only handle a finite load.
   C. Computers cannot handle large volumes of TCP traffic.
   D. Computers cannot handle large loads.

6. What is the most significant weakness in a DoS attack from the attacker's viewpoint?
   A. The attack is often unsuccessful.
   B. The attack is difficult to execute.
   C. The attack is easy to stop.
   D. The attack must be sustained.

7. What is the most common class of DoS attacks?
   A. Distributed Denial of Service
   B. Smurf attacks
   C. SYN floods
   D. Ping of Death

8. What are three methods for protecting against SYN flood attacks?
   A. SYN cookies, RST cookies, and stack tweaking
   B. SYN cookies, DoS cookies, and stack tweaking
   C. DoS cookies, RST cookies, and stack deletion
   D. DoS cookies, SYN cookies, and stack deletion

9. Which attack mentioned in this chapter causes a network to perform a DoS on one of its own servers?
   A. SYN flood
   B. Ping of Death
   C. Smurf attack
   D. DDoS

10. A defense that depends on a hash encryption being sent back to the requesting client is called:
    A. Stack tweaking
    B. RST cookies
    C. SYN cookies
    D. Hash tweaking

11. What type of defense depends on sending the client an incorrect SYNACK?
    A. Stack tweaking
    B. RST cookies
    C. SYN cookies
    D. Hash tweaking

12. What type of defense depends on changing the server so that unfinished hand-shaking times out sooner?
    A. Stack tweaking
    B. RST cookies
    C. SYN cookies
    D. Hash tweaking

13. What type of attack is dependent on sending packets too large for the server to handle?
    A. Ping of Death
    B. Smurf attack
    C. Slammer attack
    D. DDoS

14. What type of attack uses Internet routers to perform a DoS on the target?
    A. Ping of Death
    B. Smurf attack
    C. Slammer attack
    D. DDoS

15. Which of the following is an example of a DDoS attack?
    A. MyDoom virus
    B. Bagle virus
    C. DoS virus
    D. Smurf virus

16. How can securing internal routers help protect against DoS attacks?
    A. Attacks cannot occur if your internal router is secured.
    B. Because attacks originate outside your network, securing internal routers cannot help protect you against DoS.
    C. Securing the router will only stop router-based DoS attacks.
    D. It will prevent an attack from propagating across network segments.

17. What can you do to your internal network routers to help defend against DoS attacks?
    A. Disallow all traffic that is not encrypted
    B. Disallow all traffic that comes from outside the network
    C. Disallow all traffic that comes from inside the network
    D. Disallow all traffic that comes from untrusted sources

18. Which of the following was rated by many experts to be the fastest growing virus on the Internet?
    A. MyDoom virus
    B. Bagle virus
    C. Slammer virus
    D. Smurf virus

19. What can you do with your firewall to defend against DoS attacks?
    A. Block all incoming traffic
    B. Block all incoming TCP packets
    C. Block all incoming traffic on port 80
    D. Block all incoming ICMP packets

20. Why will protecting against Trojan horse attacks reduce DoS attacks?

    A. Because many DoS attacks are conducted using a Trojan horse to get an unsuspecting machine to execute the DoS.

    B. Because if you can stop a Trojan horse attack, you will also stop DoS attacks.

    C. Because a Trojan horse will often open ports allowing a DoS attack.

    D. Because a Trojan horse attacks in much the same way as a DoS attack.

EXERCISES

Exercise 4.1: Executing a DoS

Exercise 4.1 is best done in a laboratory setting where there are several machines available for this purpose.

1. Set up one machine (preferably a machine with very limited capacity) to run a small Web server. (You can download Apache for free for either Windows or Linux from **www.apache.org/**)
2. Use the ping utility with various other computers to attempt to perform a simple DoS on that Web server. This attempt is accomplished by getting other machines to begin a continuous ping of that target machine using the previously mentioned ping command of 'ping–l 65000 –w0 –t <insert target address here>.
3. You should add only one to three lab machines to the "attack" at a time (start with one, add on a few more, and then a few more).
4. As you add more machines, time how long it takes for another machine to bring up the home page of the target server. Also note the threshold (when that server quits responding completely).

Exercise 4.2: Stopping SYN Flood Attacks

Note that this exercise is advanced. Some students may wish to work in groups.

1. Search the Web or your operating system's documentation for instructions on implementing either the RST cookie or the SYN cookie.

2. Follow those implementation instructions on either your own machine or on a machine designated by your instructor. The following Web sites might be of help to you in this matter.

   Linux:

   www.liquifried.com/docs/security/scookies.html

   www.linuxjournal.com/article.php?sid=3554

   Windows:

   cr.yp.to/syncookies.html

   www.securityfocus.com/infocus/1729

   Both Linux and Windows:

   www.securiteam.com/tools/6D00K0K01O.html

Exercise 4.3: Using Firewall Settings

This exercise is only for students with access to a lab firewall.

1. Use your firewall's documentation to see how to block ICMP packets.
2. Set your firewall to block those packets.

Exercise 4.4: Using Router Settings

This exercise is only for students with access to a lab router.

1. Use your router's documentation to see how to block all traffic not originating on your own network.
2. Set your router to block that traffic.

PROJECTS

Project 4.1: Employing Alternative Defenses

1. Using the Web or another research tool, search for alternative means of defending against either general DoS attacks or a specific type of DoS attack. This means can be any defense other than the ones already mentioned in this chapter.

2. Write a brief paper concerning this defense technique.

Project 4.2: Defending Against Specific Denial of Service Attacks

1. Using the Web or other tools, find a DoS attack that has occurred in the last six months. You might find some resources at **www.f-secure.com**.
2. Note how that attack was conducted.
3. Write a brief explanation of how one might have defended against that specific attack.

Project 4.3: Hardening the TCP Stack Against DoS

Note that this project requires access to a lab machine. It is also a long project, requiring some research time on the part of the students.

1. Using manuals, vendor documentation, and other resources, find one method for altering TCP communications to help prevent DoS attacks. You may find the following Web sites helpful:

   support.microsoft.com/default.aspx?scid=kb;en-us;315669

   moat.nlanr.net/Software/TCPtune/

   www.anzio.com/support/whitepapers/tuning.htm
2. Using this information, implement one of these methods on your lab computer.

Case Study

Runa Singh is the network administrator in charge of network security for a medium-sized company. The firm already has a firewall, its network is divided into multiple segments separated by routers, and it has updated virus scanners on all machines. Runa wants to take extra precautions to prevent DoS attacks. She takes the following actions:

- She adjusts her firewall so that no incoming ICMP packets are allowed.
- She changes the Web server so that it uses SYN cookies.

Now consider the following questions:

- Are there problems with any of her precautions? If so, what are the problems?
- What additional steps would you recommend to Runa?

Chapter 5

Malware

Chapter Objectives

After reading this chapter and completing the exercises, you will be able to do the following:

- Understand viruses (worms) and how they propagate, including the Sobig and Sasser types.
- Have a working knowledge of several specific virus outbreaks.
- Understand how virus scanners operate.
- Understand what a Trojan horse is and how it operates.
- Have a working knowledge of several specific Trojan horse attacks.
- Grasp the concept behind the buffer overflow attack.
- Have a better understanding of spyware and how it enters a system.
- Defend against each of these attacks through sound practices, antivirus software, and anti-spyware software.

Introduction

In Chapter 4, we examined the Denial of Service attack. It is a very common attack and one that can easily be perpetrated. In this chapter, you will continue your examination of security threats by learning about several other types of attacks. First, you will learn about virus outbreaks. Our discussion will focus on crucial information about how and why virus attacks work, including their deployment through Trojan horses. This chapter is not a "how to create your own virus" tutorial, but rather an introduction to the concepts underlying these attacks as well as an examination of some specific case studies.

This chapter will also explore buffer overflow attacks, spyware, and several other forms of malware. Each of these brings a unique approach to an attack, and each needs to be considered when defending a system. Your ability to defend against such attacks will be enhanced by expanding your knowledge of how they work. In the exercises at the end of the chapter, you will have the opportunity to research preventative methods for viruses and to try out antivirus methods from McAffee and Norton.

Viruses

By definition, a computer ***virus*** is a program that self-replicates. Generally, a virus will also have some other unpleasant function, but the self-replication and rapid spread are the hallmarks of a virus. Often this growth, in and of itself, can be a problem for an infected network. The last chapter discussed the Slammer virus and the effects of its rapid, high-volume scanning. Any rapidly spreading virus can reduce the functionality and responsiveness of a network. Simply by exceeding the traffic load that a network was designed to carry, the network may be rendered temporarily non-functional.

How a Virus Spreads

A virus will usually spread primarily in one of two ways. The first is to simply scan your computer for connections to a network, then copy itself to other machines on the network to which your computer has access. This is actually the most efficient way for a virus to spread. However, this method requires more programming skill than other methods. The more common method is to read your e-mail address book and e-mail itself to everyone in your address book. Programming this is a trivial task, which explains why it is so common.

The latter method is, by far, the most common method for virus propagation, and Microsoft Outlook may be the one e-mail program most often hit with such virus attacks. The reason is not so much a security flaw in Outlook as it is the ease of working with Outlook. All Microsoft Office products are made so that a legitimate programmer who is writing software for a business can access many of the application's internal objects and thereby easily create applications that integrate the applications within the Microsoft Office suite. For example, a programmer could write an application that would access a Word document, import an Excel spreadsheet, and then use Outlook to automatically e-mail the resulting document to interested parties. Microsoft has done a good job of making this process very easy, for it usually takes a minimum amount of programming to accomplish these tasks. Using Outlook, it takes less than five lines of code to reference Outlook and send out an e-mail. This means a program can literally cause Outlook itself to send e-mails, unbeknownst to the user. There are numerous code examples on the Internet that show exactly how to do this, free for the taking. For this reason, it does not take a very skilled programmer to be able to access your Outlook address book and automatically send e-mails. Essentially, the ease of programming Outlook is why there are so many virus attacks that target Outlook.

While the overwhelming majority of virus attacks spread by attaching themselves to the victim's existing e-mail software, some recent virus outbreaks have used other methods for propagation, such as their own internal e-mail engine. Another virus propagation method is to simply copy itself across a network. Virus outbreaks that spread via multiple routes are becoming more common.

The method of delivering a payload can be rather simplistic and rely more on end-user negligence than on the skill of the virus writer. Enticing users to go to Web sites or open files they should not is a common method for delivering a virus and one that requires no programming skill at all. Regardless of the way a virus arrives at your doorstep, once it is on your system, it will attempt to spread and, in many cases, will also attempt to cause some harm to your system. Once a virus is on your system, it can do anything that any legitimate program can do. That means it could potentially delete files, change system settings, or cause other harm.

Recent Virus Examples

The threat from virus attacks cannot be overstated. While there are many Web pages that give virus information, in my opinion, there are only a handful of Web pages that consistently give the latest, most reliable, most detailed information on virus outbreaks. Any security professional will want to consult these sites on a regular basis. You can read more about any virus, past or current, at the following Web sites:

- www.f-secure.com/virus-info/virus-news/
- www.cert.org/nav/index_red.html
- securityresponse.symantec.com/
- vil.nai.com/vil/

The sections below will look at a few recent virus outbreaks and review how they operated and what they did.

The Sobig Virus The virus that received the most media attention and perhaps caused the most harm in 2003 was clearly the Sobig virus. The first interesting thing about this virus was how it spread. It spread utilizing a multi-modal approach to spreading. This means that it used more than one mechanism to spread and infect new machines. It would copy itself to any shared drives on your network *and* it would e-mail itself out to everyone in your address book. For these reasons, this virus was particularly virulent.

FYI: Virulent Virus

The term ***virulent*** means essentially the same thing in reference to a computer virus as it does to a biological virus. It is a measure of how rapidly the infection spreads and how easily it infects new targets.

In the case of Sobig, if one person on a network was unfortunate enough to open an e-mail containing the virus, not only would his machine be infected, but so would every shared drive on that network to which this person had access. However, Sobig, like most e-mail-distributed virus attacks, had tell-tale signs in the e-mail subject or title that could be used to identify the e-mail as one infected by a virus. The e-mail would have some enticing title such as "here is the sample" or "the document" to encourage you to be curious enough to open the attached file. The virus would then copy itself into the Windows system directory.

This particular virus spread so far and infected so many networks that the multiple copying of the virus alone was enough to bring some networks to a standstill. This virus did not destroy files or damage the system, but it generated a great deal of traffic that bogged down the networks infected by it. The virus itself was of moderate sophistication. Once it was out, however, many variants began to spring up, further complicating the situation. One of the effects of some variants of Sobig was to download a file from the Internet that would then cause printing problems. Some network printers would just start printing junk. The Sobig.E variant would even write to the Windows registry, causing itself to be in the computer startup (F-Secure, 2003). These complex characteristics indicate that the creator knew how to access the Windows registry, access shared drives, alter the Windows startup, and access Outlook.

This brings up the issue of virus variants and how they occur. In the case of a biological virus, mutations in the genetic code cause new virus strains to appear, and the pressures of natural selection allow some of these strains to evolve into entirely new species of viruses. Obviously, the biological method is not what occurs with a computer virus. With a computer virus, what occurs is that some intrepid programmer with malicious intent will get a copy of a virus (perhaps her own machine becomes infected) and will then reverse-engineer it. Since many virus attacks are in the form of a script attached to an e-mail, unlike traditionally compiled programs, the source code of these attacks is readily readable and alterable. The programmer in question then simply takes the original virus code and introduces some change, then re-releases the variant. Frequently, the people who are caught for virus creation are actually the developers of the variants who lacked the skill of the original virus writer and therefore were easily caught.

The Mimail Virus The Mimail virus did not receive as much media attention as Sobig, but it had its intriguing characteristics. This virus not only collected e-mail addresses from your address book, but also from other documents on your machine (Gudmundsson, 2004). Thus, if you had a Word document on your hard drive and an e-mail address was in that document, Mimail would find it. This strategy meant that Mimail would spread farther than many other viruses. Mimail had its own built-in e-mail engine, so it did not have to "piggy back" off your e-mail client. It could spread regardless of what e-mail software you used.

These two variations from most virus attacks made Mimail interesting to people who study computer viruses. There are a variety of techniques that allow one to programmatically open and process files on your computer; however, most virus attacks do not employ them. The scanning of the document for e-mail addresses indicates a certain level of skill and creativity on the part of the virus writer. In this author's opinion, Mimail was not the work of an amateur, but rather a person with professional-level programming skill.

The Bagle Virus Another virus that spread rapidly in the fourth quarter of 2003 was the Bagle virus. The e-mail it sent claimed to be from your system administrator. It would tell you that your e-mail account had been infected by a virus and that you should open the attached file to get instructions. Once you opened the attached file, your system was infected. This virus was particularly interesting for several reasons. To begin with, it spread both through e-mail and copying itself to shared folders. Secondly, it could also scan files on your PC looking for e-mail addresses. Finally, it would disable processes used by antivirus scanners. In biological terms, this virus took out your computers "immune system." The disabling of virus scanners is a new twist that indicates at least moderate programming skills on the part of the virus creator.

A Non-Virus Virus Another new type of virus has been gaining popularity in the past few years, and that is the "non-virus virus" or, put simply, a hoax. Rather than actually writing a virus, a hacker sends an e-mail to every address he has. The e-mail claims to be from some well known antivirus center and warns of a new virus that is circulating. The e-mail instructs people to delete some file from their computer to get rid of the virus. The file, however, is not really a virus but part of a computer's system. The jdbgmgr.exe virus hoax used this scheme (Vmyths.com, 2002). It encouraged the reader to delete a file that was actually needed by the system. Surprisingly, a number of people followed this advice and not only deleted the file, but promptly e-mailed their friends and colleagues to warn them to delete the file from their machines.

FYI: The Morris Internet Worm

The Morris worm was one of the first computer worms ever to be distributed over the Internet. And it was certainly the first to gain any significant media attention.

Robert Tappan Morris, Jr., then a student at Cornell University, wrote this worm and launched it from an MIT system on November 2, 1988. Morris did not actually intend to cause any damage with the worm. Instead, he wanted the worm to reveal bugs in the programs it exploited in order to spread. However, bugs in the code allowed an individual computer to be infected multiple times, and the worm became a menace. Each additional 'infection' spawned a new process on the infected computer. At a certain point the high number of processes running on an infected machine slowed down the computer to the point of being unusable. At least 6,000 Unix machines were infected with this worm.

Morris was convicted of violating the 1986 Computer Fraud and Abuse Act and was sentenced to a $10,000 fine, three years probation, and 400 hours of community service. But perhaps the greatest impact of this worm was that it led to the creation of the Computer Emergency Response Team (CERT).

Rules for Avoiding Viruses

You should notice a common theme with all virus attacks (except the hoax), which is that they want you to open some type of attachment. The most common way for a virus to spread is as an e-mail attachment. This realization leads to some simple rules that will drastically reduce the odds of becoming infected with a virus.

- Use a virus scanner. McAffee and Norton (explored in the exercises at the end of this chapter) are the two most widely accepted and used virus scanners. Each costs about $30 per year to keep your virus scanner updated. Do it.
- If you are not sure about an attachment, do not open it.
- You might even exchange a code word with friends and colleagues. Tell them that if they wish to send you an attachment, they should put the code word in the title of the message. Without seeing the code word, you will not open any attachment.
- Do not believe "security alerts" that are sent to you. Microsoft does not send out alerts in this manner. Check the Microsoft Web site regularly, as well as one of the antivirus Web sites previously mentioned.

These rules will not make your system 100% virus proof, but they will go a long way toward protecting your system.

Trojan Horses

Recall from earlier chapters that a ***Trojan horse*** is a term for a program that looks benign but actually has a malicious purpose. You might receive or download a program that appears to be a harmless business utility or game. More likely, the Trojan horse is just a script attached to a benign-looking e-mail. When you run the program or open the attachment, it does something else other than or in addition to what you thought it would. It might:

- Download harmful software from a Web site.
- Install a key logger or other spyware on your machine.
- Delete files.
- Open a backdoor for a hacker to use.

It is common to find combination virus plus Trojan horse attacks. In those scenarios, the Trojan horse spreads like a virus. The MyDoom virus opened a port on your machine that a later virus, doomjuice, would exploit, thus making MyDoom a combination virus and Trojan horse.

A Trojan horse could also be crafted especially for an individual. If a hacker wished to spy on a certain individual, such as the company accountant, she could craft a program specifically to attract that person's attention. For example, if she knew the accountant was an avid golfer, she could write a program that computed handicap and listed best golf courses. She would post that program on a free Web server. She would then e-mail a number of people, including the accountant, telling them about the free software. The software, once installed, could check the name of the currently logged-on person. If the logged-on name matched the accountant's name, the software could then go out, unknown to the user, and download a key logger or other monitoring application. If the software did not damage files or replicate itself, then it would probably go undetected for quite a long time.

FYI: Virus or Worm?

As noted in the previous chapter, there is disagreement among the experts as to the distinction between a virus and a worm. Some experts would call MyDoom (as well as Sasser, which will be discussed later) a worm because it spread without human intervention. For the purpose of this text, these malware will be referred to as viruses.

Such a program could be within the skill set of virtually any moderately competent programmer. This is one reason that many organizations have rules against downloading ANY software onto company machines. I am unaware of any actual incident of a Trojan horse being custom-tailored in this fashion. However, it is important to remember that those creating virus attacks tend to be innovative people.

Another scenario to consider is one that would be quite devastating. Without divulging programming details, the basic premise will be outlined here to illustrate the grave dangers of Trojan horses. Imagine a small application that displays a series of unflattering pictures of Osama Bin Laden. This application would probably be popular with many people in the United States, particularly people in the military, intelligence community, or defense-related industries. Now assume that this application simply sits dormant on the machine for a period of time. It need not replicate like a virus because the computer user will probably send it to many of his associates. On a certain date and time, the software connects to any drive it can, including network drives, and begins deleting all files. If such a Trojan horse were released "in the wild," within 30 days it would probably be shipped to thousands, perhaps millions, of people. Imagine the devastation when thousands of computers begin deleting files and folders.

This scenario is mentioned precisely to frighten you a little. Computer users, including professionals who should know better, routinely download all sorts of things from the Internet, such as amusing flash videos and cute games. Every time an employee downloads something of this nature, there is the chance of downloading a Trojan horse. One need not be a statistician to realize that if employees continue that practice long enough, they will eventually download a Trojan horse onto a company machine. If so, hopefully the virus will not be as vicious as the theoretical one just outlined here.

The Buffer Overflow Attack

You have become knowledgeable about a number of ways to attack a target system: Denial of Service, virus, and Trojan horse. While these attacks are probably the most common, they are not the only methods. Another method of attacking a system is called a ***buffer overflow*** (or buffer overrun) attack. A buffer overflow attack happens when one tries to put more data in a buffer than it was designed to hold (searchSecurity.com, 2004a). Any program that communicates with the Internet or a private network must take in some data. This data is stored, at least temporarily, in a space in memory called a *buffer*. If the programmer who wrote the application was careful, when you try to place too much information into a buffer, that information is then either simply truncated or outright rejected. Given the number of applications that might be running on a target system and the number of buffers in each application, the chances of having at least one buffer that was not written properly are significant enough to cause any prudent person some concern.

Someone who is moderately skilled in programming can write a program that purposefully writes more into the buffer than it can hold. For example, if the buffer can hold 1024 bytes of data and you try to fill it with 2048 bytes, the extra 1024 bytes is then simply loaded into memory. If that extra data is actually a malicious program, then it has just been loaded into memory and is thus now running on the target system. Or, perhaps the perpetrator simply wants to flood the target machine's memory, thus overwriting other items that are currently in memory and causing them to crash. Either way, the buffer overflow is a very serious attack.

Fortunately, buffer overflow attacks are a bit harder to execute than a DoS or simple Microsoft Outlook script virus. To create a buffer overflow attack, you must have a good working knowledge of some programming language (C or C++ is often chosen) and understand the target operating system/application well enough to know whether it has a buffer overflow weakness and how that weakness might be exploited.

The Sasser Virus/Buffer Overflow

It should be interesting to note that, while writing this book, several major new virus outbreaks took place—most notably, the Sasser virus. Sasser is a combination attack in that the virus (or worm) spreads by exploiting a buffer overrun.

The Sasser virus spreads by exploiting a known flaw in a Windows system program. Sasser copies itself to the Windows directory as avserve.exe and creates a registry key to load itself at startup. In that way, once your machine is infected, you will start the virus every time you start the machine. This virus scans random IP addresses, listening on successive TCP ports starting at 1068 for exploitable systems—that is, systems that have not been patched to fix this flaw. When one is found, the worm exploits the vulnerable system by overflowing a buffer in LSASS.EXE, which is a file that is part of the Windows operating system. That executable is a built-in system file and is part of Windows. Sasser also acts as an FTP server on TCP port 5554, and it creates a remote shell on TCP port 9996. Next, Sasser creates an FTP script named cmd.ftp on the remote host and executes that script. This FTP script instructs the target victim to download and execute the worm from the infected host. The infected host accepts this FTP traffic on TCP port 5554. The computer also creates a file named win.log on the C: drive. This file contains the IP address of the localhost. Copies of the virus are created in the Windows System directory as #_up.exe. Examples are shown here:

- c:\WINDOWS\system32\12553_up.exe
- c:\WINDOWS\system32\17923_up.exe
- c:\WINDOWS\system32\29679_up.exe

A side effect of this virus is that it causes your machine to reboot. A machine that is repeatedly rebooting without any other known cause may well be infected with the Sasser virus.

This is another case in which the infection can easily be prevented by several means. First, if you update your systems on a regular basis, your systems should not be vulnerable to this flaw. Secondly, if your network's routers or firewall block traffic on the ports mentioned (9996 and 5554), you will then prevent most of Sasser's damage. Your firewall should only allow in traffic on specified ports; all other ports should be shut down. In short, if you as the network administrator are aware of security issues and are taking prudent steps to protect the network, your network will be safe. The fact that so many networks were affected by this virus should indicate that not enough administrators are properly trained in computer security.

Spyware

In Chapter 1, ***spyware*** was mentioned as one of the threats to computer security. Using spyware, however, requires a great deal more technical knowledge on the part of the perpetrator than some other forms of malware. The perpetrator must be able to develop spyware for the particular situation or customize existing spyware for his needs. He must then be able to get the spyware on the target machine.

Spyware can be as simple as a cookie used by a Web site to record a few brief facts about your visit to that Web site, or spyware could be of a more insidious type, such as a key logger. Recall from Chapter 1 that key loggers are programs that record every keystroke you make on your keyboard; this spyware then logs your keystrokes to the spy's file. The most common use of a key logger is to capture usernames and passwords. However, this method can capture every username and password you enter and every document you type, as well as anything else you might type. This data can be stored in a small file hidden on your machine for later extraction or sent out in TCP packets to some predetermined address. In some cases, the software is even set to wait until after hours to upload this data to some server or to use your own e-mail software to send the data to an anonymous e-mail address. There are also some key loggers that take periodic screen shots from your machine, revealing anything that is open on your computer. Whatever the specific mode of operation, spyware is software that literally spies on your activities on a particular computer.

Legal Uses of Spyware

There are some perfectly legal uses for spyware. Some employers have embraced such spyware as a means of monitoring employee use of company technology. Many companies have elected to monitor phone, e-mail, or Web traffic within the organization. Keep in mind that the computer, network, and phone systems are the property of the company or organization, not of the employee. These technologies are supposedly only used for work purposes; therefore, company monitoring might not constitute any invasion of privacy. While courts have upheld this monitoring as a company's right, it is critical to consult an attorney before initiating this level of employee monitoring as well as to consider the potential negative impact on employee morale.

Parents can also elect to use this type of software on their home computer to monitor the activities of their children on the Internet. The goal is usually a laudable one—protecting their children from online predators. Yet, as with employees in a company, the practice may illicit a strong negative reaction from the parties being spied upon—namely, their children. Parents have to weigh the risk to their children versus what might be viewed as a breach of trust.

How Is Spyware Delivered to a Target System?

Clearly, spyware programs can track all activity on a computer, and that information can be retrieved by another party via a number of different methods. The real question is this: How does spyware get onto a computer system in the first place? The most common method is a Trojan horse. It is also possible that, when you visit a certain Web site, spyware may download in the background while you are simply perusing the Web site. Of course, if an employer (or parent) is installing the spyware, it can then be installed non-covertly in the same way that organization would install any other application.

Obtaining Spyware Software

Given the many other utilities and tools that have been mentioned as available from the Internet, you probably will not be surprised to learn that you can obtain many spyware products for free, or at very low cost, on the Internet. You can check the Counterexploitation (**www.cexx.org**) Web site, shown in Figure 5.1, for a lengthy list of known spyware products circulating on the Internet and for information about methods one can use to remove them. The Spyware Guide Web site (SpywareGuide, 2004) (**www.spywareguide.com**) lists spyware that you can get right off the Internet should you feel some compelling reason to spy on someone's computer activities. Figure 5.2 (on page 120) shows the categories of malware that are available from this site. Several key logger applications are listed on this site, as shown in Figure 5.3 (on page 120). These applications include well-known key loggers such as Absolute Keylogger, Tiny Keylogger, and TypO. Most can be downloaded for free or for a nominal charge from the Internet.

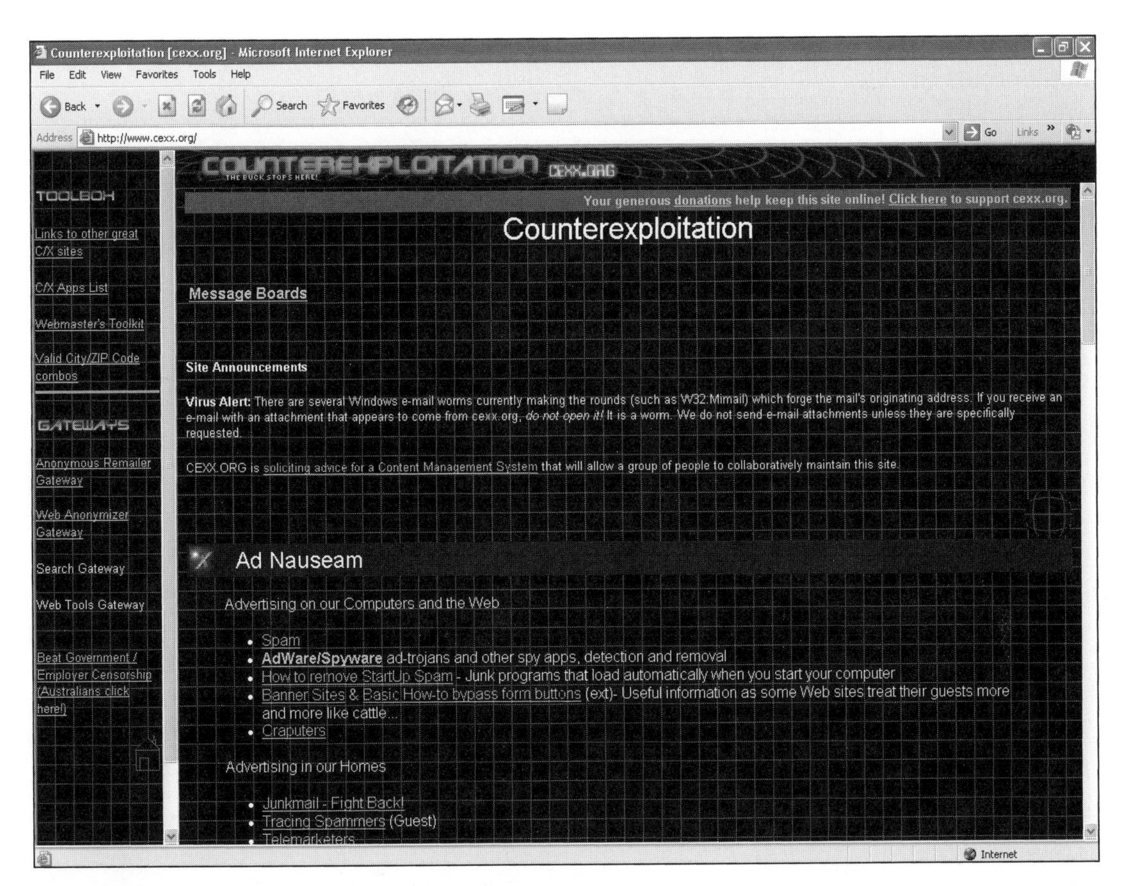

FIGURE 5.1 Counterexploitation Web site.

Some well-known Trojan horses are also listed at this site (as shown in Figure 5.4, on page 121), such as the 2nd Thought application that downloads to a person's personal computer (PC) and then blasts it with advertisements. This particular piece of spyware is one that downloads to your PC when you visit certain Web sites. It is benign in that it causes no direct harm to your system or files, nor does it gather sensitive information from your PC. However, it is incredibly annoying as it inundates your machine with unwanted ads. This sort of software is often referred to as ***adware***. Frequently, these ads cannot be stopped by normal protective pop-up blockers because the pop-up windows are not generated by a Web site that you visit, but rather by some rogue software running on your machine. Pop-up blockers only work to stop sites you visit from opening new windows. Web sites use well-known scripting techniques to cause your browser to open a window, and pop-up blockers recognize these techniques and prevent the ad window from opening. However, if the adware launches a new browser instance, it bypasses the pop-up blocker's function.

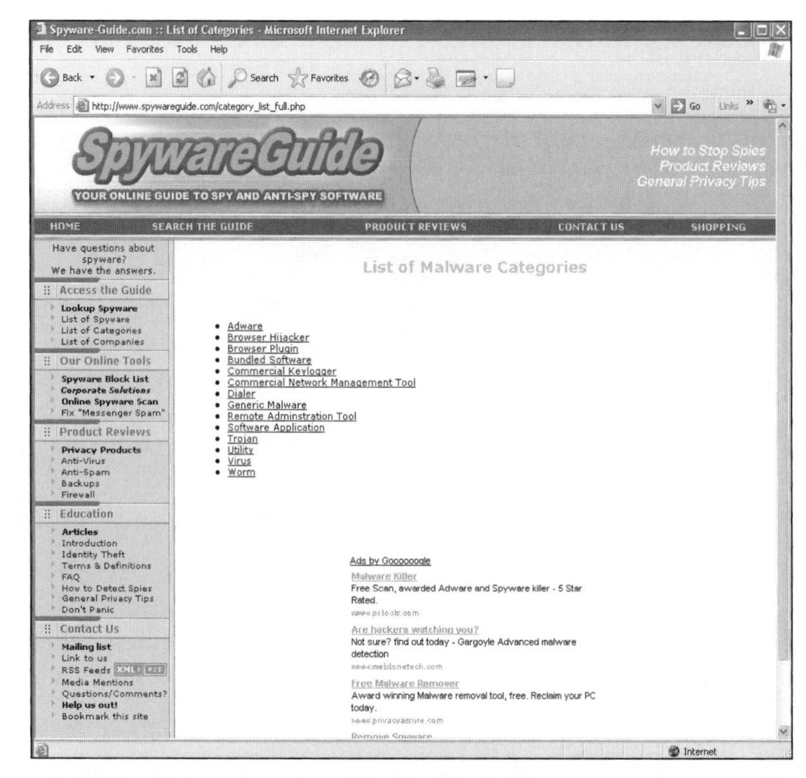

FIGURE 5.2 Malware categories at the Spyware Guide Web site.

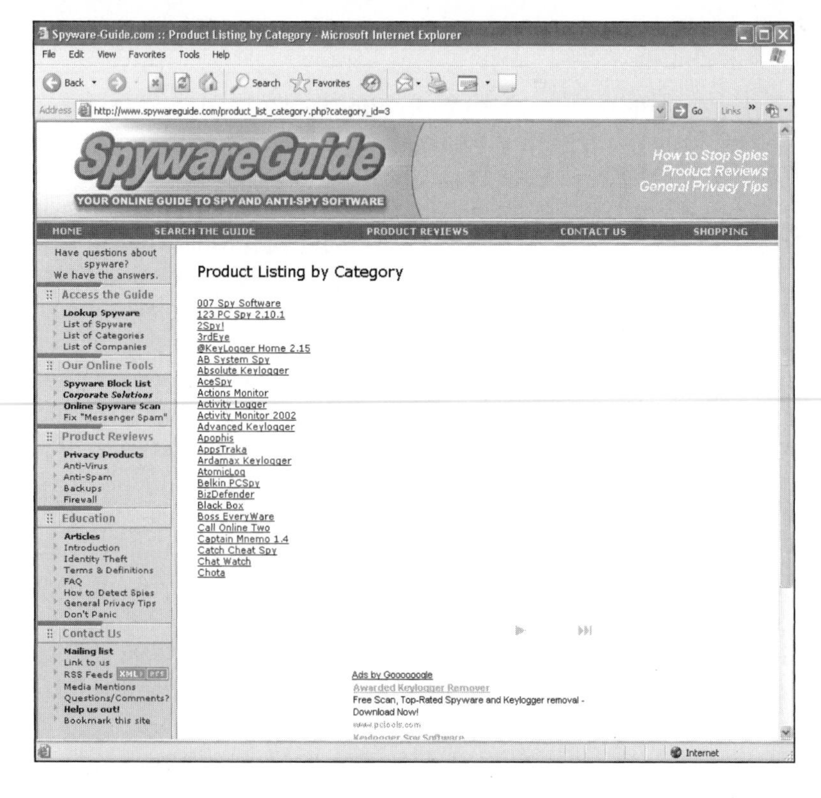

FIGURE 5.3 List of key loggers available through the Spyware Guide Web site.

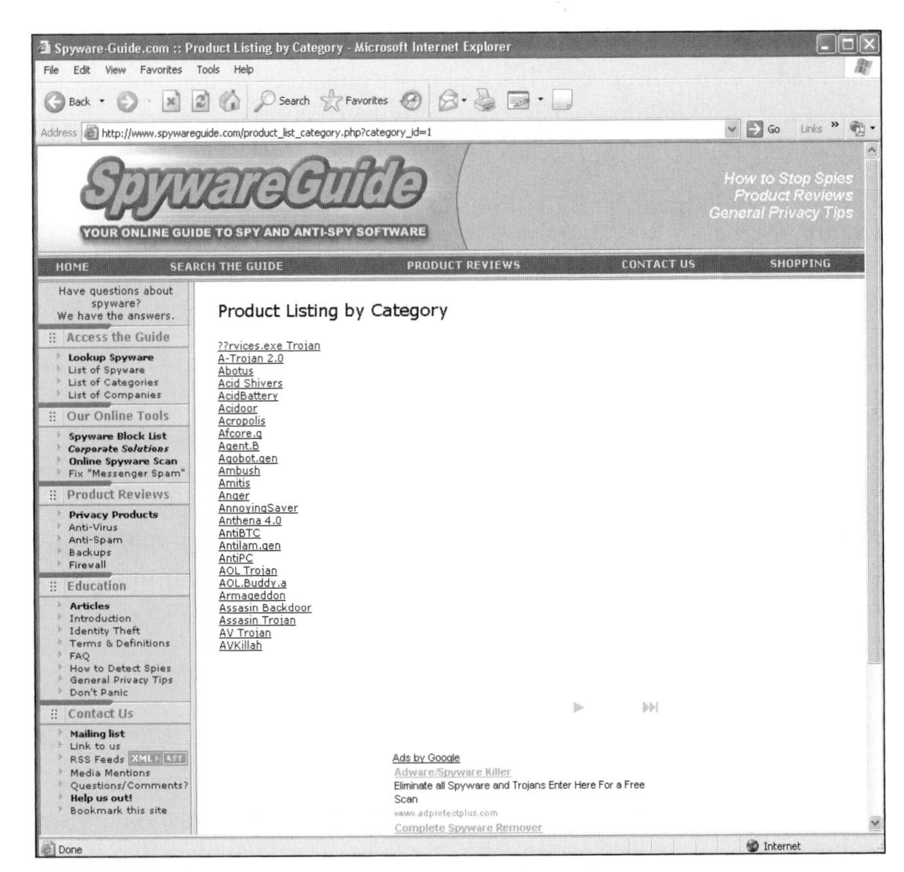

FIGURE 5.4 Trojan horses available at the Spyware Guide Web site.

Other Forms of Malware

In this and preceding chapters, the most prominent forms of malware have been discussed. There are, however, many other forms of attack. It is beyond the scope of this book to explore each of these, but you should be aware of the existence of these other forms of malware. Simply being aware can go a long way toward enabling you to defend your system efficiently. This section will touch upon just a few other forms of malware. You should reference the Web sites discussed in the end of chapter exercises and projects often so that you can stay up-to-date with all current forms of attack and defenses.

Rootkit

A rootkit is a collection of tools that a hacker uses to mask her intrusion and obtain administrator-level access to a computer or computer network. The intruder installs a rootkit on a computer after first obtaining user-level access, either by exploiting a known vulnerability or cracking a password. The rootkit then collects user IDs and passwords to other machines on the network, thus giving the hacker root or privileged access.

A rootkit may consist of utilities that also:

- monitor traffic and keystrokes
- create a "backdoor" into the system for the hacker's use
- alter log files
- attack other machines on the network
- alter existing system tools to circumvent detection

The presence of a rootkit on a network was first documented in the early 1990s. At that time, Sun and Linux operating systems were the primary targets for a hacker looking to install a rootkit. Today, rootkits are available for a number of operating systems and are increasingly difficult to detect on any network (searchSecurity.com, 2004b).

Malicious Web-Based Code

A malicious Web-based code, also known as a Web-based mobile code, simply refers to a code that is portable to all operating systems or platforms such as HTTP, Java, and so on. The "malicious" part implies that is it a virus, worm, Trojan horse, or some other form of malware. Simply put, the malicious code does not care what the operating system may be or what browser is in use. It infects them all blindly (Yakabovicz, 2003).

Where do these codes come from, and how are they spread? The first generation of the Internet was mostly indexed text files. However, as the Internet has grown into a graphical, multimedia user experience, programmers have created scripting languages and new application technologies to enable a more interactive experience. As with any new technology, programs written with scripting languages run the gamut from useful to poorly crafted to outright dangerous.

Technologies such as Java and ActiveX enable these buggy or untrustworthy programs to move to and execute on user workstations. (Other technologies that can enable malicious code are executables, JavaScript, Visual Basic Script, and plug-ins.) The Web acts to increase the mobility of code without differentiating between program quality, integrity, or reliability. Using available tools, it is quite simple to "drag and drop" code into documents that are subsequently placed on Web servers and made available to employees throughout the organization or individuals across the Internet. If this code is maliciously programmed or just improperly tested, it can cause serious damage.

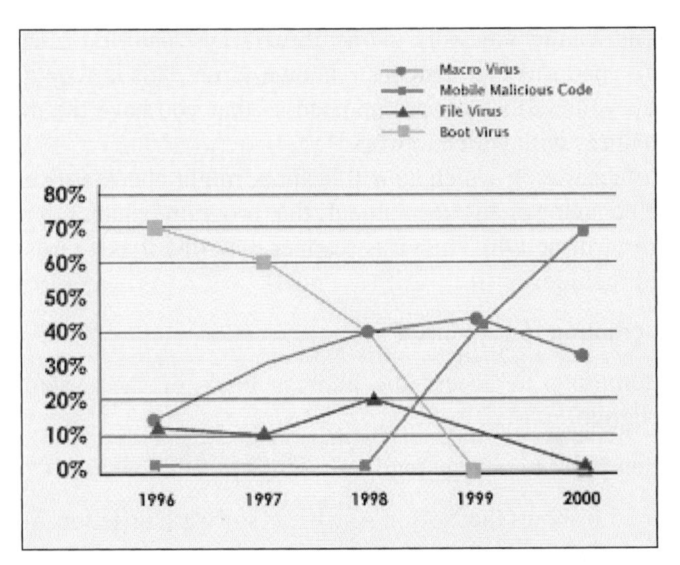

FIGURE 5.5 Growth of mobile malicious code.

Not surprisingly, hackers have used these very useful tools to steal, alter, and erase data files as well as gain unauthorized access to corporate networks. A malicious code attack can penetrate corporate networks and systems from a variety of access points including Web sites, HTML content in e-mail messages, or corporate intranets. Figure 5.5 shows the rapid growth of mobile malicious code in recent years versus viruses.

Today, with over 200 million Internet users, new malicious code attacks can spread almost instantly through corporations. The majority of damage caused by malicious code happens in the first hours after a first-strike attack occurs—before there is time for countermeasures. The costs of network downtime or theft of IP make malicious code a top priority (finjan software, 2004).

Detecting and Eliminating Viruses and Spyware

Antivirus Software

In this chapter and throughout this book, the need for running virus-scanning software has been discussed. It is prudent at this point to provide you with some details on how virus scanners work and information on the major virus-scanning software packages. This information should help you better understand how a virus scanner might help protect your system and help you make intelligent decisions regarding the purchase and deployment of some antivirus solution.

A virus scanner can work in one of two ways. The first is to look for a signature (or pattern) that matches a known virus. This is why it is important to keep your virus software updated so that you have the most recent list of signatures with which to work.

The other way in which a virus scanner might check a given PC is to look at the behavior of an executable. If that program behaves in a way consistent with virus activity, the virus scanner may flag it as a virus. Such activity could include:

- attempting to copy itself
- attempting to access the address book of the system's e-mail program
- attempting to change registry settings in Windows

Figure 5.6 shows the Norton AntiVirus software in action. You can see that the virus definitions are up-to-date, that the virus scanning is enabled, auto-protection is enabled, and the Internet worm protection is enabled as well. The other popular virus scanners have many of the same features.

Anti-Spyware Software

Fortunately, just as there are many different spyware applications available, there are likewise many different software applications on the market that are designed specifically to detect and remove spyware. These applications are also usually available at extremely low cost. You can often get a free trial

FIGURE 5.6 Norton AntiVirus interface.

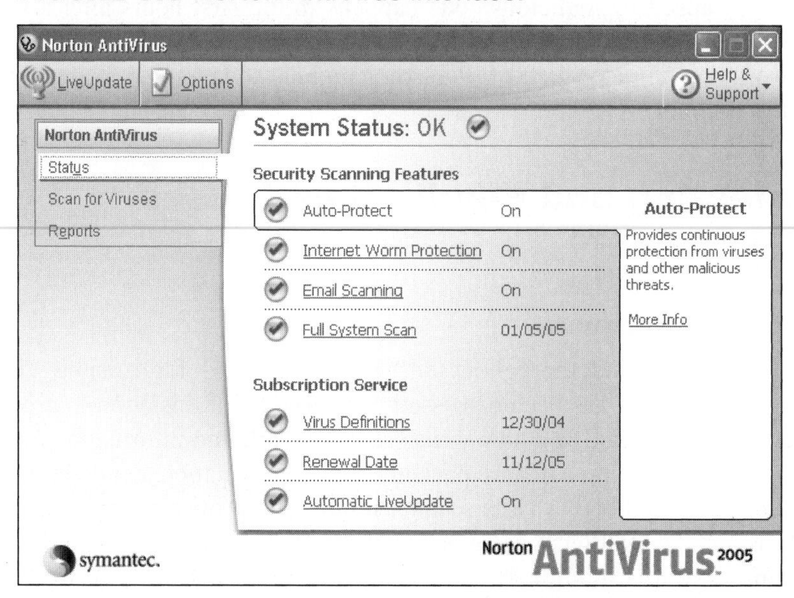

version to use for a limited time so you can make a more intelligent purchasing decision. Of course, the most prudent course of action you can take to avoid getting spyware on your machine is to never download anything from the Internet that does not come from a very well-known and trusted Web site. However, in an organizational environment, you cannot simply rely on your employees to do the right thing. It is prudent as the company's computer security expert to take steps yourself to prevent the employees from compromising your system security.

Some of the better known and more widely used anti-spyware applications include Spy Sweeper from **www.webroot.com**, Spy Killer from **www.spykiller.com**, Zero Spyware Removal from **www.zerospyware.com**, and Spector Pro from **www.spectorsoft.com**. All of these applications can be obtained for anywhere from $20 to $50, and many offer a free trial version.

Figure 5.7 shows the items found by running the WebRoot Spy Sweeper software on a system. These items can be selected for quarantine and removal.

Figure 5.8 shows the summary results after all of the items found have been quarantined. Note that the number of files scanned, the number of items removed, the date the full sweep was performed, as well as additional information is all detailed on this summary page. Each of the anti-spyware applications would provide similar results and each contain similar options for sweeping a system.

FIGURE 5.7 Items recommended for removal by Spy Sweeper.

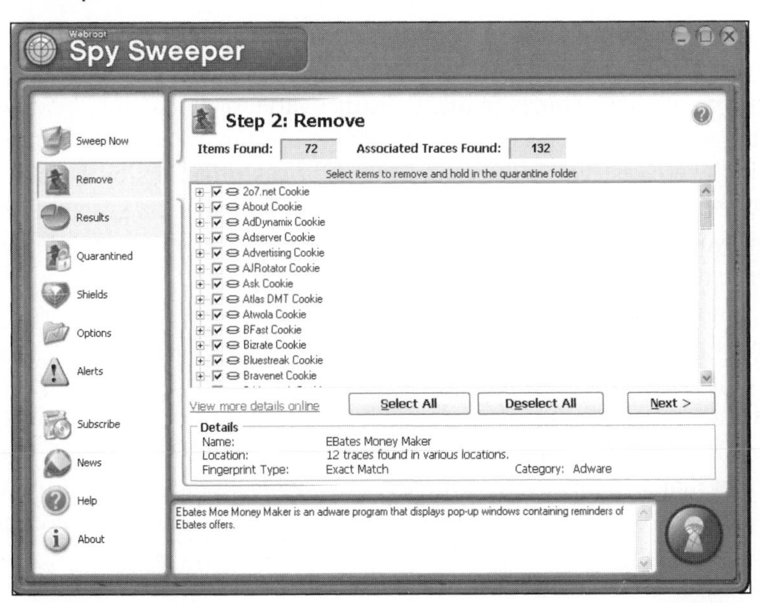

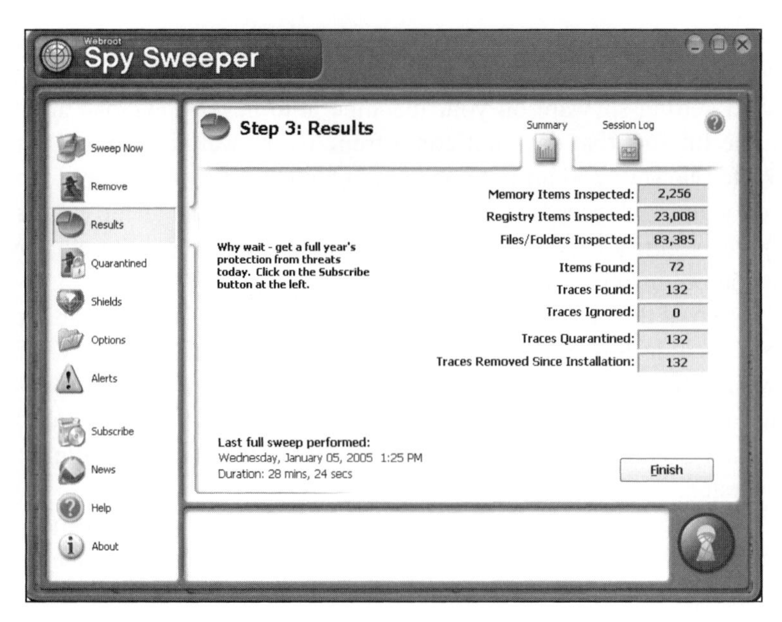

FIGURE 5.8 Summary results of a system sweep.

Summary

Clearly, there are a number of ways to attack a target system: by Denial of Service, virus/worm, Trojan horse, buffer overflow attacks, and spyware. Each type of attack comes in many distinct variations. It should be obvious by this point that securing your system is absolutely critical. In the upcoming exercises, you will try out the antivirus programs by Norton and McAffee. There are so many ways for a hacker to attack a system that securing your system can be a rather complex task. Chapter 6 will deal with specific methods whereby you can secure your system.

Another theme that is driven home throughout this chapter is that many, if not most, attacks are preventable. The exercises ahead will give you practice in figuring out how to prevent the Sasser and Sobig virus. In most cases, prompt and regular patching of the system, use of antivirus tools, and blocking unneeded ports would prevent the attack. The fact that so many systems do get infected is an indication of the very real problem of network professionals who are not skilled in computer security.

Test Your Skills

MULTIPLE CHOICE QUESTIONS

1. Which of the following is the best definition of virus?
   A. program that causes harm on your computer
   B. program used in a DoS attack
   C. program that slows down networks
   D. program that self-replicates

2. What is the most common damage caused by virus attacks?
   A. slowing down networks by the virus traffic
   B. deleting files
   C. changing the Windows registry
   D. corrupting the operating system

3. What is the most common way for a virus to spread?
   A. by copying to shared folders
   B. by e-mail attachment
   C. by FTP
   D. by downloading from a Web site

4. Which of the following is the primary reason that Microsoft Outlook is so often a target for virus attacks?
   A. Many hackers dislike Microsoft.
   B. Outlook copies virus files faster.
   C. It is easy to write programs that access Outlook's inner mechanisms.
   D. Outlook is more common than other e-mail systems.

5. Which of the following virus attacks used a multi-modal approach?
   A. Slammer virus
   B. Mimail virus
   C. Sobig virus
   D. Bagle virus

6. What factor about the Sobig virus made it most intriguing to security experts?
   A. It spread in multiple ways.
   B. It deleted critical system files.
   C. It was difficult to protect against.
   D. It was very sophisticated.

7. What was most interesting to security experts about the Mimail virus?
   A. It spread more rapidly than other virus attacks.
   B. It spread in multiple ways.
   C. It grabbed e-mail addresses from documents on the hard drive.
   D. It deleted critical system files.

8. Which of the following reasons most likely made the Bagle virus spread so rapidly?
   A. The e-mail containing it claimed to be from the system administrator.
   B. It copied itself across the network.
   C. It was a sophisticated virus.
   D. It was particularly virulent.

9. What made the Bagle virus so dangerous?
   A. It changed Windows registry settings.
   B. It disabled antivirus software.
   C. It deleted key system files.
   D. It corrupted the operating system.

10. Which of the following is a way that any person can use to protect against virus attacks?
    A. set up a firewall
    B. use encrypted transmissions
    C. use secure e-mail software
    D. never open unknown e-mail attachments

11. Which of the following is the safest way to send and receive attachments?
    A. use a code word indicating the attachment is legitimate
    B. only send spreadsheet attachments

C. use encryption

D. use virus scanners before opening attachments

12. Which of the following is true regarding e-mailed security alerts?

A. You must follow them.

B. Most companies do not send alerts via e-mail.

C. You can trust attachments on security alerts.

D. Most companies send alerts via e-mail.

13. Which of the following is something a Trojan horse might do?

A. open a back door for malicious software

B. change your memory configuration

C. change ports on your computer

D. alter your IP address

14. What is a buffer overflow attack?

A. overflowing a port with too many packets

B. putting more e-mail in an e-mail system than it can hold

C. overflowing the system

D. putting more data in a buffer than it can hold

15. What virus exploited buffer overflows?

A. Sobig virus

B. Mimail virus

C. Sasser virus

D. Bagle virus

16. What can you do with a firewall to help protect against virus attacks?

A. There is nothing you can do on the firewall to stop virus attacks

B. Shut down all unneeded ports

C. Close all incoming ports

D. None of the above

17. A key logger is what type of malware?

A. virus

B. buffer overflow

C. Trojan horse

D. spyware

18. Which of the following is a step that all computer users should take to protect against virus attacks?
    A. purchase and configure a firewall
    B. shut down all incoming ports
    C. use non-standard e-mail clients
    D. install and use antivirus software

19. What is the primary way a virus scanner works?
    A. by comparing files against a list of known virus profiles
    B. by blocking files that copy themselves
    C. by blocking all unknown files
    D. by looking at files for virus-like behavior

20. What other way can a virus scanner work?
    A. by comparing files against a list of known virus profiles
    B. by blocking files that copy themselves
    C. by blocking all unknown files
    D. by looking at files for virus-like behavior

EXERCISES

Exercise 5.1: Using Norton Anti-Virus

1. Go to the Norton antivirus Web site (**www.symantec.com/downloads**) and download the trial version of their software.
2. Install and run their software.
3. Carefully study the application, noting features that you like and dislike.

Exercise 5.2: Using McAffee Anti-virus

1. Go to the Mcaffee antivirus Web site (**us.mcafee.com/root/package.asp?pkgid=100&cid=9901**) anddownload the trial version of their software.
2. Install and run their software.
3. Carefully study the application, noting features you like and dislike.

Exercise 5.3: Preventing Sasser

1. Using resources on the Web or in journals, carefully research the Sasser virus. You may find that **www.f-secure.com** or Symantec's virus information center at **www.sarc.com/avcenter/** are helpful in this exercise.
2. Write a brief essay about how it spread, what damage it caused, and what steps could be taken to prevent it.

Exercise 5.4: Preventing Sobig

1. Using resources on the Web or in journals, carefully research the Sobig virus. You may find that **www.f-secure.com** or Symantec's virus information center at **www.sarc.com/avcenter/** are helpful in this exercise.
2. Write a brief essay about how it spread, what damage it caused, and what steps could be taken to prevent it.

Exercise 5.5: Learning about Current Virus Attacks

1. Using resources on the Web or in journals, find a virus that has been spreading in the last 90 days. You may find that **www.f-secure.com** or Symantec's virus information center at **www.sarc.com/avcenter/** are helpful in this exercise.
2. Write a brief essay about how it spread, what damage it caused, and what steps could be taken to prevent it.

Exercise 5.6: Using Anti-Spyware Software

1. Go to Spy Sweeper Web site (**www.webroot.com/downloads**) and download the trial version of the software.
2. Install and run the Spy Sweeper software.
3. Carefully study the application, exploring the options and noting features that you like and dislike.
4. Repeat this process to download and explore Adaware software (which is available from a variety of Web sites).
5. Assess which of these two anti-spyware applications would work best for your computer system.

PROJECTS

Project 5.1: Antivirus Policies

This activity can also work as a group project.

Considering what you have learned in this chapter and in previous chapters, as well as using outside resources, write an antivirus policy for a small business or school. Your policy should include technical recommendations as well as procedural guidelines. You may choose to consult existing antivirus policy guidelines that you find on the Web to give you some ideas. The following Web sites may be of some help to you in this project:

- www.sans.org/resources/policies/Anti-virus_Guidelines.pdf
- irmc.state.nc.us/documents/approvals/1_VirusPolicy.pdf

However, you should not simply copy their antivirus policies. Rather, you should come up with your own.

Project 5.2: The Worst Virus Attacks

Using resources on the Web, books, or journals, find a virus outbreak that you consider to have been the worst in history. Write a brief paper describing this attack, and explain why you think it is the worst. Was it widely spread? How quickly did it spread? What damage did it do?

Project 5.3: Why Write a Virus?

A number of hypotheses have been formed regarding why people write a virus. These hypotheses range from the frankly conspiratorial to the academically psychological. Taking whatever position you feel is most likely, write a paper explaining why you think people take the time and effort to write a virus.

Case Study

Chiao Chien manages IT security for a school. Given the wide range of people who use the school's computers, it is difficult for Chien to prevent virus attacks. Chien has a reasonably good budget and has installed antivirus software on every machine. He also has a firewall that has all unneeded ports blocked, and there is a school policy prohibiting the downloading of any software from the Web. Consider the following questions:

- How secure do you think Chien's network is from virus attacks?
- What areas has Chien not secured?
- What recommendations would you make to Chien?

Chapter 6

Basics of Assessing and Securing a System

Chapter Objectives

After reading this chapter and completing the exercises, you will be able to do the following:

- Probe a system for vulnerabilities.
- Understand how policies are set.
- Evaluate potential security consultants.
- Properly set security on an individual workstation.
- Properly secure a server.
- Establish general guidelines for network security.
- Safely surf the Web.

Introduction

At this point, it should be clear that it is necessary to assess any system periodically for vulnerabilities. The first part of this chapter will discuss the essential steps that you should follow in assessing a system for vulnerabilities. The purpose of this chapter is to get someone who is new to computer security to begin thinking about these issues. This chapter is not meant to be a comprehensive treatment of the subject, nor a substitute for getting an expert consultant. In fact, many of the topics, such as disaster recovery and policies, have had entire volumes written on them. However, it should give you a basic blueprint you can follow. Specific details will depend on your particular environment, budget, skills, and security needs.

In this book, you have thus far examined a number of threats to individual computers and networks. You have discussed specific defenses against each of these dangers. However, you have not yet looked at a comprehensive approach to security. In the second part of this chapter, you will learn many of the security procedures that can be implemented to provide your environment with more secure computing. Note that this chapter is about overall procedures that you need to perform in securing a system rather than specific step-by-step techniques.

Basics of Assessing a System

Disaster recovery, access rights, and appropriate policies are topics that are often overlooked by those new to security. To keep it simple and easy to remember, the stages of assessing a system's security can be separated into the "six p's":

- Patch
- Ports
- Protect
- Policies
- Probe
- Physical

Patch

The first rule of computer security is to check patches. This is true for networks, home computers, laptops—literally any computer. This means that the operating system, database management systems, development tools, Internet browsers, and so forth are all checked for patches. In a Microsoft

FYI: Patching and Applications

Whenever there is a patch to an operating system or application, there is also documentation (sometimes in a Read Me file, sometimes at the download site) that indicates what the patch is fixing. This documentation also lists any known adverse interactions with other applications. Therefore, you should always read this documentation before you install a patch. In most cases, the problems are minimal and often involve obscure situations. But it is always good to check first to make sure that a service or application upon which you are dependent is not adversely impacted.

FYI: Ports on Routers

One security flaw seen in many organizations that are otherwise security conscious is a failure to close ports on routers. This is particularly a problem for large organizations with wide area networks (WANs) spread over multiple locations. The router between each location should be filtered and too often is not.

environment, this should be easy, as the Microsoft Web site has a utility that will scan your system for any required patches to the browser, operating system, or Office products. It is a very basic tenet of security to ensure that all patches are up to date. This should be one of the first tasks when assessing a system.

Once you have ensured that all patches are up to date, the next step is to set up a system to ensure that they are kept up to date. One simple method is to initiate a periodic patch review where, at a scheduled time, all machines are checked for patches. There are also automated solutions that will patch all systems in your organization. It is imperative that all machines be patched, not just the servers.

Ports

As you learned in Chapter 2, all communication takes place via some port. Any port you do not explicitly need should be shut down. This means that those unused services on servers and individual workstations should be shut down. Both Windows XP and Linux have built-in port-filtering capability. Windows 2000 Professional also has port-filtering capability. Shutting down a service in Windows and port filtering are both discussed in more detail below.

You should also shut down any unused router ports in your network. If your network is part of a larger wide area network (WAN), then it is likely you have a router connecting you to that WAN. Every open port is a possible avenue of entry for a virus or intruder. Therefore, every port you can close is one less opportunity for such attacks to affect your system.

Caution

Don't Know—Don't Touch

Caution should be taken when shutting down services so you do not inadvertently shut down a service that you need. It is always a good idea to check with your operating system documentation. The rule of thumb is that if you are not sure, don't touch it.

IN PRACTICE: Shutting Down a Service in Windows

For an individual machine that is not running firewall software, you do not directly close ports; instead, you shut down the service using that port. For example, if you do not use an FTP service but you see that port is on, chances are that you unknowingly have an

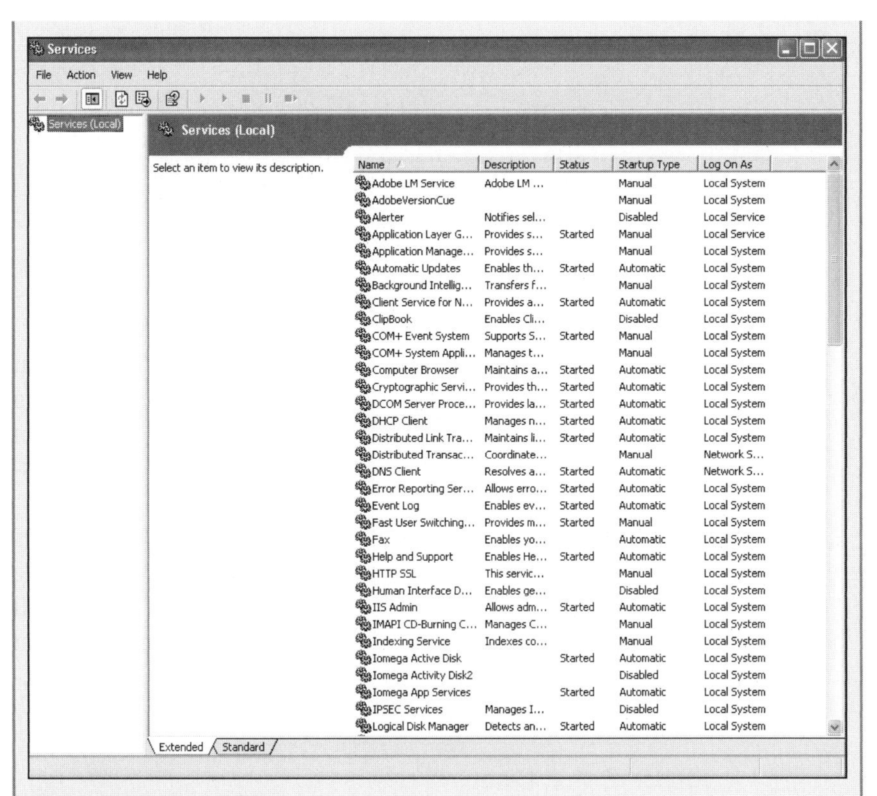

FIGURE 6.1 Services.

FTP service running on that machine. In Windows 2000 or Windows XP, if you have administrative privileges, the following three steps can be taken to shut down an unneeded service.

1. Go to Start, select Settings (in Windows 2000 only), and choose Control Panel. Double-click Administrative Tools.
2. Double-click Services. You should see a window similar to the one shown in Figure 6.1.

The window in Figure 6.1 shows all services installed on your machine, whether they are running or not. Notice that the window also displays information about whether a service is running, whether it starts up automatically, and so forth. In Windows XP, more information can be seen by selecting an individual service. When you double-click on an individual service in either Windows 2000 or Windows XP, you see a dialog box similar to Figure 6.2 that describes the details about that service.

CONTINUED ON NEXT PAGE

CONTINUED

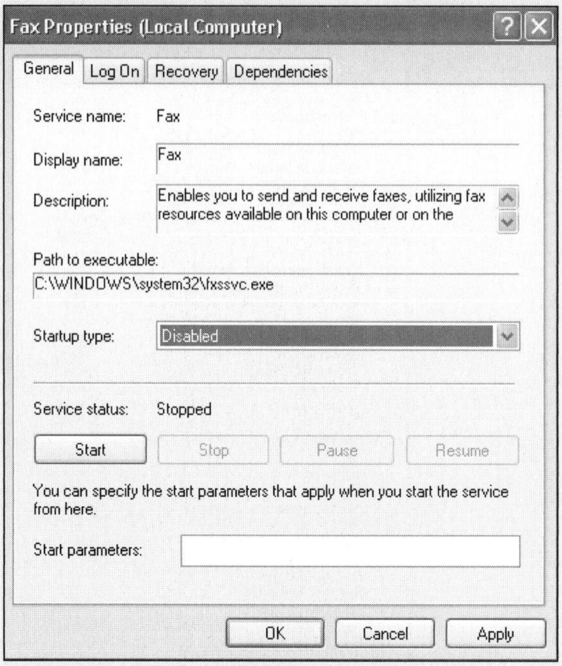

FIGURE 6.2 Disabled services.

In the example shown in Figure 6.1, you see a fax service on a machine that does not require it. To illustrate the procedure, this service is going to be disabled. Before you turn off any service, however, you need to check whether other services depend on the one you are about to shut off. If other services depend on the one you want to turn off and you proceed to turn it off, you will cause the other services to fail.

3. Click on the Dependencies tab. In our case, the fax service has no dependencies.
4. Click the General tab.
5. Change the Startup type to Disabled.
6. Click the Stop button in the Service status section, if necessary. Your dialog box should look similar to Figure 6.2. The fax service is now shut down.
7. Click OK to accept the edits made and close the Properties dialog box. Close the Services dialog box and the Administrative Tools dialog box.

Caution

Dependencies

Always check dependencies before shutting down a service. If other services depend on that service, you will then be causing them to malfunction by shutting it down.

Shutting down unneeded ports and services is an essential and very basic part of computer security. As mentioned above, every port open (and every service running) is a possible avenue for a hacker or virus to get to your machine. Therefore, the rule is: If you don't need it, shut it down and block it. NetCop, which was discussed in Chapter 3, is a tool that allows you to detect running ports. It is easy to use and effective, but is not the only tool available. In fact, there are many such tools, some of which are listed in Appendix B of this book. Or, you can simply conduct a Web search for *port scanner* to find a number of options, many of which are free.

IN PRACTICE: Port Filtering in Windows

Windows 2000 and Windows XP also have port-filtering services available. (Note that port filtering cannot be applied to adapters on an interface-by-interface basis. Anything you set will be applied universally to all adapters.)

1. Go to the Control Panel and double-click Network Connections. You will see a window similar to Figure 6.3.

FIGURE 6.3 Network connections.

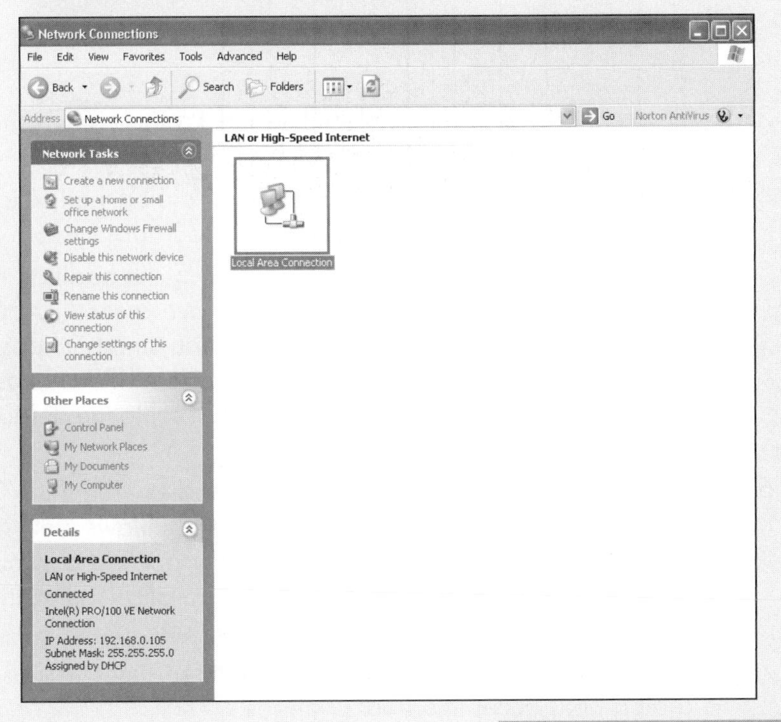

CONTINUED ON NEXT PAGE

CONTINUED

2. Right-click Local Area Connection and select Properties. You will see a dialog box similar to Figure 6.4.

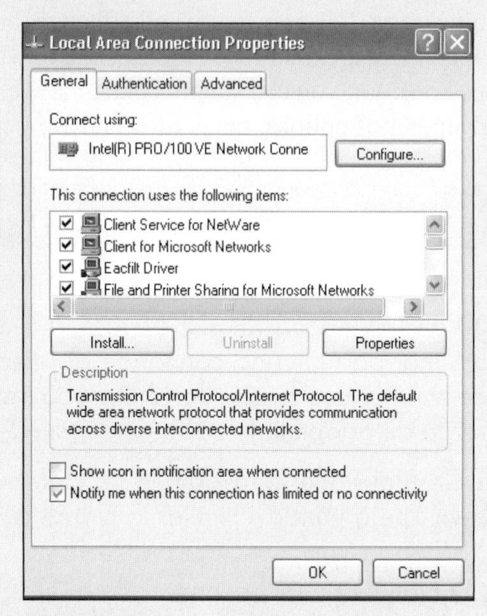

FIGURE 6.4 TCP/IP properties.

3. Scroll down, if necessary, select Internet Protocol (TCP/IP), and then click Properties.
4. In the Internet Protocol (TCP/IP) Properties dialog box, click Advanced. You will see a dialog box with four tabs.
5. Select the Options tab as shown in Figure 6.5. (In addition to the filtering option shown, you may also have a security option. The security option is rather simple. You simply choose whether to use IPSec or not. Because the topic of IPSec is beyond the scope of this chapter, just leave that set to the default setting.)
6. Select TCP/IP filtering and then click Properties. The TCP/IP Filtering dialog box, shown in Figure 6.6, allows you to choose whether to allow all packets or only packets communicating on certain ports. You can choose to allow all traffic or only traffic on ports or protocols that you set.
7. Make your selections and then click OK three times to close the dialog box, accepting your changes.

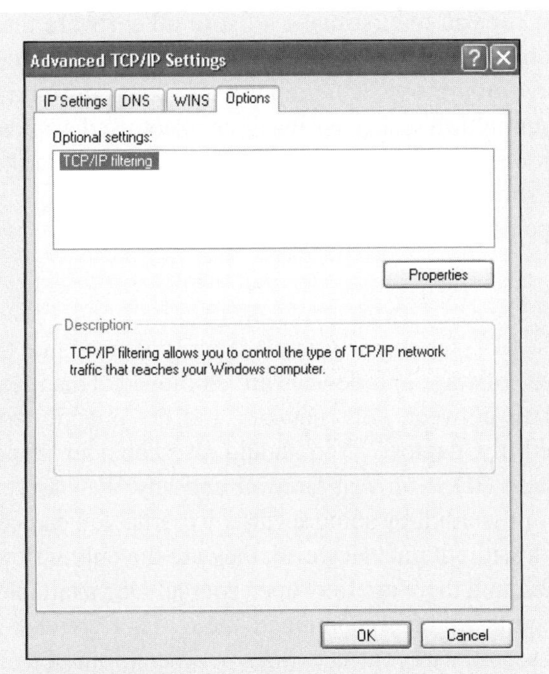

FIGURE 6.5 Options tab.

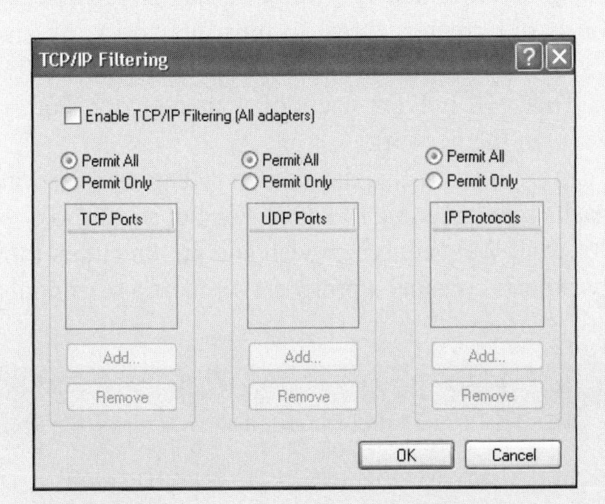

FIGURE 6.6 Filtering ports and protocols.

8. Click Close in the Local Area Connections Properties dialog box to accept any changes made.
9. Close the Network Connections window.

It is best for you to first make a list of all software that you are running. Then, look up the ports and protocols that you will need for that software and allow only those. It is important to keep in mind that these are ports for incoming traffic. If your machine is not used as a database server, Web server, or other type of server and if your machine is a stand-alone one, you can (and should) close all ports. Workstations on networks may need some ports open for network utilities.

Protect

The next phase of assessing a system's security is to ensure that all reasonable protective software and devices are employed. This means, at a minimum, a firewall between your network and the outside world. Firewalls were discussed in Chapter 2. You should also consider using an intrusion detection system (IDS) on that firewall and any Web servers. An IDS is considered non-essential by some security experts; you can certainly have a secure network without one. However, they are the only way to know of impending attacks, and there are free, open source IDSs available. For that reason, most experts highly recommend them. The firewall and IDS will provide basic security to your network's perimeter, but you also need virus scanning. Each and every machine, including servers, must have a virus scanner that is updated regularly. The point has already been made that a virus infection is the greatest threat to most networks. As also previously discussed, it is probably prudent to consider anti-spyware software on all of your systems. This will prevent users of your network from inadvertently running spyware on the network.

Finally, a proxy server, also discussed in Chapter 2, is a very good idea. It not only masks your internal IP addresses, but most proxy servers allow you to discover what Web sites users visit and put on filters for certain sites. Many security experts consider a proxy server to be as essential as a firewall.

IN PRACTICE: Finding a Firewall

When selecting a firewall to use, you have a number of options. You can purchase a very inexpensive router-based firewall for your high speed Internet connection. You can get a router that is separate from your DSL or cable router. Or you can get one that includes the functions of your cable or DSL router with the firewall. The Web sites listed below should be helpful to you in finding more information on these options and determining which will best suit your needs.

- Linksys: **www.linksys.com/products/product.asp?prid=20&grid=5**
- Home PC Firewall Guide: **www.firewallguide.com/**

- Broadband Guide: **www.firewallguide.com/broadband.htm**

In addition to the information on the firewall options available, you can also find many free or very inexpensive firewall packages on the Internet. Following is a list of some of the more popular firewalls available via the Internet.

- Firestarter: This is a free packet filtering application for Linux available at **www.fs-security.com**. This software is installed a Linux machine designed to be used as your network firewall.
- Norton Personal Firewall: This product is inexpensive and is available for multiple operating systems. A free trial download is available from **www.symantec.com**.
- McAffee Personal Firewall: This product is similar in price and basic function to Norton Personal Firewall. You can find out more about this product at **us.mcafee.com**.
- Outpost Firewall: This product is designed for the home or small office user. It has both a free version and an enhanced commercial version. You can find out more about this product at **www.agnitum.com/products/outpost/**.

For medium-sized or larger networks, with more flexible budgets, you might consider the options listed below.

- The company Teros offers an application gateway specifically tailored for Web servers. This solution is relatively inexpensive and can be ideal for companies whose primary function is to provide Web sites or Web services. Information is available at **www.teros.com/products/appliances/gateway/index.shtml**.
- The Firebox, from Watchguard Technologies (**www.watchguard.com/products/fireboxx.asp**), is an application gateway firewall that is router-based. It is relatively easy to setup and configure and is appropriate for medium sized networks.

And finally, for Linux users, you might consider the Wolverine product. Wolverine is a robust commercial firewall solution for Linux available from **www.coyotelinux.com**. Wolverine provides stateful packet inspection, built in VPN capabilities (VPNs will be discussed in detail in Chapter 7), several encryption methods (AES, DES, and more), and offers a Web-based administration utility. It is also very inexpensive. This is an excellent solution for any network using Linux.

Policies

It is absolutely essential that any organization have clearly written policies on computer security—and that those policies be strongly enforced by management. Those policies should cover acceptable use of organizational computers, the Internet, e-mail, and any other aspect of the system. Policies should prohibit the installation of any software on the systems. Only IT personnel should install software and only after they have verified its safety.

Policies should also advise users against opening unknown and/or unexpected attachments. Something that I recommend is for people within an organization or department use a codeword. If that codeword does not appear in the body of the e-mail (or in the subject line), then they do not open the attachment. Most virus attacks spread via e-mail attachments. The subject line and body of such e-mail messages are generated automatically by the virus itself. If all of your legitimate attachments have a codeword in the subject line, it is highly unlikely that this word would be in the subject line of an e-mail sent by a virus. This alone could prevent your users from inadvertently opening a virus.

Polices should also be in place that clearly delineate who has access to what data, how backups are performed, and what to do to recover data in the case of a disaster (commonly called a disaster recovery plan). Data access must be limited to only those personnel with an actual need to access the data. For example, not everyone in the human resources department needs access to disciplinary files on all employees. Does your organization have a plan for what to do if a fire destroys your servers with all their data? Where do you get new machines? Who gets them? Is there an offsite copy of the data backup? All of these questions must be addressed in a disaster recovery plan.

There should be a policy regarding passwords: acceptable minimum length, lifetime of a password, password history, and passwords to be avoided, such as any word that has a direct connection to the user. For example, a user who is a big fan of the Dallas Cowboys should not use a password that has any relation to that sports team. Also, passwords that relate to personal data, such as spouse's birthday, children's names, or pet's names, are poor choices. A password policy could also include recommendations or restrictions on a password.

Additionally, a password should not be kept for long periods of time. A 90- or 180-day password replacement schedule is good for most situations. This is referred to as ***password age***. (This, of course, must be weighed against the user's access to sensitive information or data. A company financial officer might change her password weekly; a nuclear arms engineer might change his password daily; and a mail clerk might need to change her password on a much less frequent basis.)You can set many systems (including Windows) to force the user to get a new password after a certain period of time. You should also make sure the person does not merely reuse old

FYI: Good Passwords

A good password is at least eight (preferably 15) characters long; contains letters, numbers, and characters; and combines upper- and lowercase. A good general practice is to select a word that has no personal meaning to you, a random sequence of numbers, and then various case letters and characters to further disguise the password. For example, you might use something such as $TrEe785. That password would be virtually impossible for anyone to guess and difficult for password-cracking software to break. It would, however, also be difficult to remember. For this reason, many people in the information security field are recommending the use of ***pass phrases*** instead of passwords. These create longer passwords that are even more difficult to break. An example would be: *My telephone # is 555-555-1234.* This is a 30-character password containing uppercase, lowercase, numbers, and special characters. It is also much easier to remember than $TrEe785.

passwords, referred to as ***password history*** and also referred to in some operating systems as uniqueness. A good rule of thumb is a history depth of five—meaning that the person cannot reuse any of their previous five passwords. Additionally, you may need to implement a minimum password age to prevent users from immediately changing their password five times to return to their current password. Generally, a minimum of one day is recommended.

FYI: How Extensive Should Policies Be?

This question frequently arises: How extensive should policies be? Should they be a few brief pages or a lengthy manual? Various computer security experts will have differing opinions. My opinion is that the policies should be lengthy enough to cover your organizational needs, but not so lengthy as to be unwieldy. In short, overly long policy manuals are likely to be left unread by employees and hence not be followed. If you absolutely must have a long policy manual, then create a few brief sub-manuals for specific employee groups so as to increase the chances of the policies being read and followed. It is probably a good idea to have new hires briefed on security polices by someone from the IT Security department.

FYI: Checklists and Policies

For your convenience and to assist in getting you started in securing your systems and establishing good policies, Appendix C contains a basic PC security checklist, a network security checklist, a list of home PC policy recommendations, a sample acceptable use policy, as well as a sample password policy. Each of these is also available electronically through the companion Web site for this text.

Finally, policies should include specific instructions on what to do in case of an employee termination. It is imperative that all of that person's login accounts be immediately disabled and any physical access they have to any part of the system be immediately discontinued. Unfortunately, many organizations fail to address this properly and give an opportunity to a disgruntled former employee to inflict retribution on his or her former employer.

Probe

An important step in assessing any network is to probe the network. In Chapter 3, several tools were mentioned that are freely available from the Internet that can be used to scan your network. Microsoft also has its own security analyzer tool that can scan one or a range of IP addresses. This tool is available from **support.microsoft.com/default.aspx?scid=kb%3Ben-us%3Bq320454**, or you can simply do a Web search in any search engine for it. A general recommendation is that any security assessment be comprised of at least three separate analysis tools to assess the network. For example, on a Microsoft network, you should use the Cerberus Internet Scanner, the Microsoft Security Analyzer, and one other tool, such as NetCop or SATAN.

The key is to periodically probe your own network for security flaws. This should be a regularly scheduled event—perhaps once a quarter. At a minimum, a complete audit of your security should be completed once per year. That would, of course, include probing your ports. However, a true security audit would also include a review of your security policies, your patching system, any security logs you maintain, personnel files of those in secure positions, and so forth.

Physical

Lastly, you cannot ignore physical security. The most robustly secure computer that is left sitting unattended in an unlocked room is not at all secure. You must have some policy or procedure governing the locking of rooms with computers as well as the handling of laptops, PDAs, and other mobile computer devices. Servers must be in a locked and secure room with as few people as is reasonably possible having access to them. Backup tapes should be stored in a fireproof safe. Documents and old backup tapes should be destroyed before disposal (e.g., by melting tapes, magnetizing hard disks, breaking CDs).

Physical access to routers and hubs should also be tightly controlled. Having the most hi-tech, professional information security on the planet but leaving your server in an unlocked room to which everyone has access is a recipe for disaster. One of the most common mistakes in the arena of physical security is co-locating a router or switch in a janitorial closet. This means that, in addition to your own security personnel and network administrators, the entire cleaning staff has access to your router or switch, and any one of them could leave the door unlocked for an extended period of time.

There are some basic rules you should follow regarding physical security:

- Server Rooms: The room where servers are kept should be the most fire-resistant room in your building. It should have a strong door with a strong lock, such as a deadbolt. Only those personnel who actually have a need to go in the room should have a key. You might also consider a server room log wherein each person logs in when they enter or exit the room. There are actually electronic locks that record who enters a room, when they enter, and when they leave. Consult local security vendors in your area for more details on price and availability.

- Workstations: All workstations should have an engraved identifying mark. You should also routinely inventory them. It is usually physically impossible to secure them as well as you secure servers, but you can take a few steps to improve their security.

- Miscellaneous equipment: Projectors, CD burners, laptops, and so forth should be kept under lock and key. Any employee that wishes to use one should be required to sign it out, and it should be checked to see that it is in proper working condition and that all parts are present when it is returned.

Securing Computer Systems

In this section, you will examine various security specifics for an individual workstation, a server, and a network. You should be aware, however, that you do not need to reinvent the wheel. A number of very reputable organizations have put together step-by-step guides, or security templates, that you can use in your network setting. These can be modified to fit your particular organization, or they can be used as a starting point for you in forming your own security strategy.

- The National Security Agency has a Web site with a number of specific network security guides: **www.nsa.gov/snac/**
- The Center for Internet Security offers a number of security guides and benchmarks: **www.cisecurity.com/**
- The SANS institute has a number of sample policies you can download and modify or use: **www.sans.org/resources/policies/**

There are also templates that can be applied to many operating systems and applications (such as Microsoft Windows and Microsoft Exchange) that will implement certain security precautions. These templates can be found for many products and then simply installed on the appropriate machine. Some security professionals prefer to handle the details of security themselves, but many administrators find these templates to be useful—and they can be invaluable for the beginner.

- Windows 2000 templates: **web.ukonline.co.uk/cook/sectemplate.htm**
- MS Exchange templates: **www.microsoft.com/exchange/default.mspx**
- A collection of Windows templates: **www.networkcert.net/security/templates.htm**

The use of these templates will at least give you a baseline of security on the applications to which they are applied.

Securing an Individual Workstation

There are a number of steps that any prudent individual can take to make their individual computer secure. These steps should be taken for both home computers and workstations on a network. In the former case, securing the individual computer is the only security option available. In the

FYI: Hardening a System

The process of securing a computer system against hackers, malware, and other intruders is sometimes referred to as ***hardening*** a system. You may see the terms "server hardening" or "router hardening" commonly used.

latter case, securing the individual computers as well as the perimeter allows for a layered approach to security. While some network administrators simply secure the perimeter via a firewall and/or proxy server, it is generally believed that you should also secure each and every machine in your organization. This is particularly vital in protecting against virus attacks and some of the Distributed Denial of Service attacks that you learned about in Chapter 4.

The first step with an individual computer is to ensure that all patches are appropriately applied. Microsoft's Web site has utilities that will scan your machine for needed patches for both Windows and Microsoft Office. It is critical that you do this on a regular basis—once per quarter as a minimum. You should also check your other software vendors to see whether they have some similar mechanism to update patches for their products. It is amazing how many virus outbreaks have been widespread despite patches being available to secure the flaws they exploited. Too many people simply do not ensure that patches are applied regularly. For a home computer, this is the most critical step in your security strategy and will protect you from a number of attacks designed to exploit security flaws. For a networked workstation, this is still a vital piece of the overall security strategy and cannot be ignored.

The second step in securing an individual computer is restricting the ability to install programs or alter the machine configuration. In a network environment, this would mean that most users do not have permissions to install software or change any system settings. Only network administrators and designated support staff should have that ability. In a home environment, this would mean that only a responsible party or parties (such as the parents) have access rights to install software.

One of the reasons for this particular precaution is to prevent users from accidentally installing a Trojan horse or other malware on their machine. If a person is prevented from installing any software, then there is no chance of inadvertently installing improper software such as a Trojan horse, adware, or other malware. Blocking users from altering the machine's configuration also prevents them from changing system security settings. Novice users may hear of some way to change some setting and will do so, not realizing the security risks they are exposing their system to.

A perfect example in which a novice might adversely alter security settings involves the Windows messenger service. This is not used for chat rooms or instant messaging, as many novices incorrectly assume. It is instead used for network administrators to send a broadcast message to all people on a network. Unfortunately, some adware programs also use that service to circumvent pop-up blockers and inundate you with ads. Thus, a security-conscious person might disable that service. You would not want an inexperienced person to turn it back on by thinking it is needed for instant messaging.

It is absolutely critical in any network environment that limits be placed on what the average user can do to a machine's configuration. Without such limits, even well-meaning employees could eventually compromise security. This particular step is often met with some resistance from the organization. If you are in charge of a system's security, it is your job to educate the decision makers as to why this step is so critical.

The next step has been discussed previously in this book. Each and every computer must have antivirus and anti-spyware software. You must also set it to routinely automatically update its virus definitions. Updated, running antivirus software is an integral part of any security solution. The two-pronged approach of anti-spyware and antivirus software should be a major component in your individual computer security strategy. Some analysts feel that anti-spyware is a nice extra, but not a critical component. Others contend that spyware is a rapidly growing problem and will probably eventually equal or surpass the dangers of virus attacks.

Of course, if your operating system has a built-in firewall, it is a good idea to configure it and have it turned on. Windows XP and Linux both come with built-in firewall features. Turn them on and configure them properly. The only significant problem you may encounter in implementing this step is that most networks require a certain amount of traffic between key servers (such as the DNS server) and individual computers. When you configure your firewall, make certain you are allowing appropriate traffic through. If you are at home, you can simply block all incoming traffic. If you are on a network, you must identify what traffic you need to allow.

Passwords and physical security, as discussed earlier in this chapter, are a critical part of computer security. You must ensure that all users utilize passwords that are at least eight characters long and consist of a combination of letters, numbers, and characters. In general, make sure that your password policy is complete and that all employees follow it. This will ensure that your physical security system is sound.

Caution

Completely Secure?

You should not be lulled into a false sense of security by employing these methods. The very best security will always be attentive and security-conscious computer users. The only totally secure computer is one that is not connected to any network or the Internet and never has any software installed on it. Unfortunately, that is also a useless computer.

Following these guidelines will not make your computer totally impervious to danger, but these guidelines will make your workstation as secure as it reasonably can be. Remember that, even in a network environment, it is critical to also secure each individual computer as well as the perimeter.

Securing a Server

The core of any network lies in its servers. This includes database servers, Web servers, DNS servers, file and print servers, and so on. These computers provide the resources for the rest of the network. Generally, your most critical data will be stored on these machines. This means that these computers are an especially attractive target for intruders and securing them is of paramount importance.

Essentially, to secure a server, you should apply the steps you would to any workstation and then add additional steps. There will not be a user on that machine routinely typing documents or using spreadsheets, so extra-tight restrictions are unlikely to cause the same difficulties for end users that they might on a workstation.

To begin with, you must follow the same steps you would for a workstation. Each and every server should have its software routinely patched. It should also have virus-scanning software and perhaps anti-spyware as well. It is critical that access to these machines, both via logging on and physical access, be limited to only those people with a clear need. There are, however, additional steps you should take with a server that you might not take with a standard workstation.

Most operating systems for servers (e.g., Windows 2000 Server edition, Linux) have the ability to log a variety of activities. These activities would include failed logon attempts, software installation, and other activities. You should make sure that logging is turned on and that all actions that might pose any security risk are logged. You then must make certain that those logs are checked on a periodic basis.

Remember that the data on a server is more valuable than the actual machine. For this reason, data must be backed up on a regular basis. A daily backup is usually preferred but, in some cases, a weekly backup might be adequate. The backup tapes should be kept in a secure offsite location (such as a bank safety deposit box) or in a fireproof safe. It is critical that you limit access to those backup tapes just as you would limit access to the servers themselves.

With any computer, you should shut down any service you do not need. However, with a server, you may wish to take the extra step of uninstalling any software or operating system components you do not need, meaning that anything not required for the server to function should be removed. But think carefully about this before proceeding. Clearly, games and office suites are not needed for a server. However, a browser might be necessary to update patches.

There is another step that should be taken with servers that is not necessary with workstations. Most server operating systems have built-in accounts. For example, Windows has built-in administrator, guest, and power user accounts. Any hacker who wants to try and guess passwords will begin by trying to guess the passwords that go with these standard users. In fact, there are utilities on the Web that will do this automatically for the would-be intruder. First, you should create your own accounts with names that do not reflect their level of permission. For example, disable the administrator account and create an account called basic_user. Set up basic_user as the administrator account, with appropriate permissions. (Of course, only give that username and password to those people you want to have administrator privileges.) If you do this, a

Caution

Windows Registry

A note of caution should be made: If you are not comfortable and experienced with the Windows registry, you should not make any changes. You can change things that can severely impact your computer's operation.

FYI: Handling Old Backup Media

Unfortunately, many network administrators simply throw old backup media in the trash. If a person with malicious intent retrieves this discarded media, they could restore it to their own machine. This could give them access to your older data without breaking in to your system or could give them very valuable clues as to your current security practices, depending on what is found on that media. Old media (e.g., tapes, CDs, hard disks) should be thoroughly destroyed. For a CD, this means physically breaking it. For a tape, this means partially or completely melting it. Hard disks should be magnetized with a powerful magnet.

hacker would not immediately guess that this account is the one that they want to crack. Remember, hackers ultimately want administrative privileges on a target system; concealing which accounts have those privileges is a vital step in preventing the hacker from breaching your security.

There are a variety of registry settings in any version of Windows that can be altered to increase your security. If you use a scanning tool, such as Cerberus, it returns a report stating the weaknesses in your registry settings. What items in the registry settings might cause a security problem? A few items that are commonly examined include:

- Logon: If your registry is set so that the logon screen shows the last user's name, you have done half of the hacker's work for her. Since she now has a username, she only needs to guess the password.
- Default Shares: Certain drives/folders are shared by default. Leaving them shared like this presents a security hazard.

These are just a few of the potential problems in the Windows registry. A tool such as Cerberus will not only tell you what the problems are, but will make recommendations for corrections. To edit your registry, go to Start, select Run, and then key regedit. This will start the registry editor.

Securing a Network

Obviously, the first step in securing a network is to secure all computers that take part in that network, including all workstations and servers. However, this is just one part of network security. By now it should be clear that using a firewall and proxy server are also critical elements in network security. Chapter 12 will provide more details on these devices. For now, it is important to realize that you need to have them. Most experts also recommend using an IDS. There are a number of such systems available—some are even free. These systems can detect things, such as port scanning, which might indicate that a person is preparing to attempt a breach of your security perimeter.

If your network is at all large, then you might consider partitioning it into smaller segments with a firewall-enabled router between segments. In this way, if one segment is compromised, the entire network will not be compromised. In this system, you might consider putting your most important servers (database, file) on a secure segment.

Since Web servers must be exposed to the outside world and are the most common point of attack, it then makes sense to separate them from the rest of the network. Many network administrators will put a second firewall between the Web server and the rest of the network. This means that, if a hacker exploits a flaw in your Web server and gains access to it, then he will not have access to your entire network. This brings up the issue of what should be on your Web server. The answer is: only what you need to post Web pages. No data, documents, or other information should be stored on that server, and certainly no extraneous software. The operating system and Web server software are all that are required. You may add a few other items (such as an IDS) if your situation requires it. Any other software running on that server is a potential security risk.

You must also have policies that guide users in how to use the system, as we discussed earlier in this chapter. The most robust security in the world will not be of much use if a careless user inadvertently compromises your security. Keep in mind that you must have policies in place that guide users in what is considered appropriate use of the system and what is not.

Just as you take steps to harden your servers (e.g., patching the operating system, shutting down unneeded services), you should also harden your router. The specifics of what needs to be done will be contingent on your particular router manufacturer and model, but a few general rules should be followed:

- Use good passwords: All routers are configurable. They can be programmed. Therefore, you must obey the same password policies on a router that you would use on any server including minimum password length and complexity, age of password, and password history. If your router allows you to encrypt the password (as Cisco and other vendors do), then do it.
- Use logging: Most routers allow for logging. You should turn this on and monitor it just as you would monitor server logs.
- Security Rules: Some basic router security rules should also be followed:

- Do not answer to Address Resolution Protocol (ARP) requests for hosts that are not on the user local area network (LAN).
- If no applications on your network use a given port, that port should be also shut down on the router.
- Packets not originating from inside your LAN should not be forwarded.

These rules are simply a beginning. You will need to consult your vendor's documentation for additional recommendations. You must absolutely pay as much attention to securing your router as you do to securing your servers. The following links might be helpful:

- Router security: **www.mavetju.org/networking/security.php**
- Cisco router hardening: **www.sans.org/rr/whitepapers/firewalls/794.php**

Safe Web Surfing

People like to surf the Web. It is one of the most common activities that people engage in on a computer. There are privacy and security settings within your browser software. Utilizing these tools is the first step to safe Web surfing. You should not even consider Web surfing without first setting the appropriate privacy and security settings for your browser.

Obviously, antivirus and anti-spyware software play a role in safe Web surfing. In fact, using the Internet without those two pieces of software is simply reckless. Likewise, you should not reveal any personal information online. That, too, is a critical part of Web surfing.

Are there other things you can do to surf the Web safely? Yes, there are. To begin with, the World Wide Web (WWW) is much like any city—there are good neighborhoods and bad neighborhoods. Some Web sites, often referred to as warez sites, offer the ability to download illegal copies of commercial software. In addition to the fact that this is both illegal and unethical, it should be noted that these sites are famous for virus infections. Visiting those sites is an open invitation to getting a virus or Trojan horse. Similarly, you should be extremely cautious in your use of bulletin boards and chat rooms. These sites can be magnets for potential hackers and other individuals whose intention it is to do you harm. In short, you should follow the same advice on the Web as you do in an unknown city: stick to the well-lit, populated, major streets.

You should also be wary of downloading anything from the Internet. Unless it comes from a well-known and reliable source, simply do not download it. It is often tempting to download free music, games, and so on. However, anytime you download anything from the Internet, there is a chance of downloading a virus or a Trojan horse.

Getting Professional Help

You may decide that you need outside help to set up and test your system's security. This option is one that most security professionals would highly recommend if at all possible, particularly if you are new to security. It can be extremely helpful to get a professional consultant to assist you in setting up your initial security strategy and policies and perhaps do a periodic audit of your security. As mentioned in Chapter 1, there are a number of people who claim to be hackers who are not. Frankly, there are also a number of self-proclaimed security experts who simply do not have the requisite skills. The question here is: How do you determine whether an individual is qualified? Following are some guidelines to consider in making this decision.

Experience is the most important factor when looking for a security professional. You want someone with a minimum of five years of IT experience, with two years related to security. Often, this will be a network administrator or programmer who has moved into security. Note that this is a minimum level of experience. More experience is always better. It is certainly possible that someone with less experience might have the requisite skill, but it is unlikely. Everyone needs a place to start, but you do not want your systems to be the place where someone is learning.

The quality of the person's experience is as important as the length of experience. Ask details about the person's experience. For example, exactly what role did she play in computer security? Did she simply set up policies, or did she actually do hands-on security work? What was the result? Was her system free from virus infections and hacker breaches or not? Can you contact her references? In short, simply because a person states that she was responsible for information security on her resume is not enough. You need to find out exactly what she did and what the results were.

Another important aspect of a security professional is education. Remember that computer security is a very broad subject. One needs an understanding of networks, protocols, programming, and more. It is entirely possible for a person with no formal education to have these skills, but it is less likely than if they had a formal education. Generally, these skills will most likely be found in a person with experience and a degree in a computer- or math-related field. That may sound somewhat intellectually snobbish, but it is a fact. There are many people in IT who are self-taught, such as people with history degrees that are network administrators or psychology majors that are now programmers. However, the more areas a person focuses in, the harder it is to obtain mastery. This is not to say that a person cannot be a security professional without a computer science, math, or engineering degree. The point is simply that this is one factor you should consider. If someone has an unrelated degree but meets or exceeds all other qualifications, you might still consider them. Some colleges are beginning

Caution

Free from Intrusion?

No matter how good a security system is most will eventually fail. When considering the qualifications of a security professional, you may start by asking: *Was your system free from virus infections and breaches?* It would not be surprising, nor necessary disqualifying, if the answer to this question was *No*. You would just need to follow up that question with: *How often was your system infected with a virus or breeched by a hacker?*

to offer security-specific curriculum, and a few even offer security degrees. Clearly, specific training in computer security would be the most preferable security background.

Certifications have become very controversial in the IT profession. Some people swear by them. You can easily find many job advertisements that demand certain certifications, such as the CNE (Certified Novel Engineer) or MCSE (Microsoft Certified Systems Engineer). On the other hand, you would have no problem finding some IT professionals who denigrate certifications and consider them utterly worthless. A more reasonable position is somewhat between the two extremes. A certification can be a good indicator of a candidate's knowledge of a specific product. For example, if you want someone to secure your Microsoft network, looking at people that are Microsoft-certified is not a bad idea. You should balance that, however, by keeping in mind that it is entirely possible for someone with a good memory to use the various study guides available on the Internet and pass a test they don't actually understand. That is where experience comes in. A certification coupled with appropriate experience is a good indicator of skill.

In addition to the certifications for network administrators, there are a number of security-related certifications. Some have more credibility than others. The Security+ exam from CompTIA and the CIW Security Analyst are both conceptual exams. This means that they test a candidate's knowledge of security concepts and not their ability to actually implement any security solution. This means that, by themselves, they may not indicate the skill level you need. But if, for example, you are securing a network using Novell, a candidate who is a CNE and has CIW Security Analyst or Security+ might be a good person to consider.

Microsoft also now offers a security track to their MCSE certification. If you have a Microsoft network you wish to secure, it might be a good idea to consider this. However, the most respected security certification is the CISSP (Certified Information Systems Security Professional). This test is a grueling six-hour exam and can only be taken if you first verify three years of security-related experience. CISSP holders are also required to submit a

FYI: Computer Security Education and Certifications

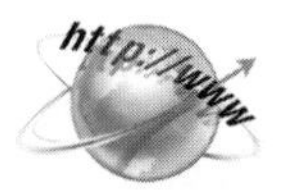

More detailed information on computer security education (both academic and corporate training) as well as professional certifications can be found in Appendix A. This appendix also contains useful information to consider should you need to hire a security professional.

recommendation from another CISSP or an officer of their company and to take continuing education credits to maintain the certification. This is probably the most respected security-related certification.

With all of that being said, you should never hire a person based solely on certifications. Those certifications should simply be one element that you consider.

Finally, you should consider personal background. A security consultant or full-time employee will, by definition, have access to confidential information. Any legitimate security professional will not mind giving you:

- References
- Permission to check their credit history
- Permission to check their criminal background

Anyone who seems reluctant to provide any of these items should be avoided. Therefore, an ideal security consultant might be a person with five or more years of experience, a degree in a computer-related discipline, a certification in your organization's operating systems as well as one of the major security certifications, and a completely clean background, with references. As a rule, you simply cannot be too careful in hiring a security consultant.

Unless you have a highly trained security expert on staff, you should consider bringing in a security consultant to assess your system at least once. In our current legal environment, liability for security breaches is still being hotly debated. Companies are being sued for failing to practice due diligence in computer security. It is simply a wise move, both from a computer industry perspective as well as from a legal perspective, to do everything reasonable to ensure the security of your systems.

Summary

This chapter has outlined some basic items to look for in any security assessment. You should periodically assess your network/system for security vulnerabilities. A general recommendation would be a quarterly assessment for non-critical/low-security sites and perhaps as frequently as a weekly assessment for high-security sites. In any case, what are outlined in this chapter are the basics of assessing the security of a network, and they should give you a start toward securing your own network.

Safe computing is a matter of securing your computer, your network, and your servers and using common sense on the Web. It is important to rigorously apply security practices and standards to all computers, whether they are home computers or part of an organizational network.

Test Your Skills

MULTIPLE CHOICE QUESTIONS

1. What are the six p's of security?
   A. patch, ports, personnel, privacy, protect, policies
   B. ports, patch, protect, probe, policies, physical
   C. physical, privacy, patch, ports, probe, protect
   D. ports, patch, probe, physical, privacy, policies
2. What is the most basic rule of computer security?
   A. Keep systems patched.
   B. Always use an IDS.
   C. Install a firewall.
   D. Always use anti-spyware.
3. How might you ensure that system patches are kept up to date?
   A. Use an automated patching system.
   B. Patch anytime you receive a vendor notification of a new patch.
   C. Patch whenever a new threat is announced.
   D. Use periodic scheduled patching.
4. What is the rule about ports?
   A. Block all incoming ports.
   B. Block ICMP packets.
   C. Block all unused ports.
   D. Block all non-standard ports.
5. Which of the following is a good reason to check dependencies before shutting down a service?
   A. to determine whether you will need to shut down other services as well
   B. to determine whether shutting down this service will affect other services
   C. to find out what this service does
   D. to find out whether this service is critical to system operations

6. If your machine is not used as a server and is not on a local network, what packet-filtering strategy should you use?
   A. Block all ports except 80.
   B. Do not block any ports.
   C. Block all ports.
   D. Do not block well-known ports.

7. Which of the following is the least essential device for protecting your network?
   A. firewall
   B. virus scanners on all machines
   C. IDS system
   D. proxy server

8. What is the rule of thumb on data access?
   A. Data must be available to the widest range of people possible.
   B. Only administrators and supervisors should access sensitive data.
   C. Only those with a need for the specific data should have access.
   D. All employees should have access to any data used in their department.

9. What is password age?
   A. how long a user has had a password
   B. the length the password history
   C. a reference to the sophistication (maturity) of the password
   D. a reference to a password's length

10. What is the minimum frequency for system probing and audits?
    A. once per month
    B. once per year
    C. every other year
    D. every other month

11. An audit should check what areas?
    A. System patching, review polices, check personnel records of all managers, and probe for flaws
    B. Only probe for flaws
    C. System patches, probe for flaws, check logs, and review policies
    D. Check all machines for illicit software, complete system virus scan, and review of firewall polices

12. Which of the following is true of the room in which the server is located?
    A. It should be in the most fire-resistant room in the building.
    B. It should have a strong lock with a strong door.
    C. It should be accessible only to those who have a need for access.
    D. All of the above

13. What would be most important to block end users from doing on their own machine?
    A. Running programs other than those installed by the IT staff
    B. Surfing the Web and using chat rooms
    C. Changing their screen saver and using chat rooms
    D. Installing software or changing system settings

14. What is the preferred method for storing back ups?
    A. Near the server for quick restore if needed
    B. Offsite in a secure location
    C. In the IT manager's office for security
    D. At the home of one of the IT staff

15. Which of the following is a step you would definitely take with any server, but might not be required for a workstation?
    A. Uninstall all unneeded programs/software.
    B. Shut down unneeded services.
    C. Turn off the screen saver.
    D. Block all Internet access.

16. Which of the following is a step you might take for large networks, but not for smaller networks?
    A. Use an IDS.
    B. Segment the network with firewalls between the segments.
    C. Use antivirus software on all machines on the network.
    D. Do criminal background checks for network administrators.

17. Which of the following is a common way to establish security between a Web server and a network?
    A. Block all traffic between the Web server and the network.
    B. Place virus scanning between the network and the Web server.
    C. Put a firewall between the Web server and the network.
    D. Do not connect your network to the Web server.

18. What is the rule on downloading from the Internet?
    A. Do not ever download anything.
    B. Only download if the download is free of charge.
    C. Only download from well-known, reputable sites.
    D. Never download executables. Only download graphics.

19. Which of the following certifications is the most prestigious?
    A. CISSP
    B. PE
    C. MCSA
    D. Security+

20. Which of the following set of credentials would be best for a security consultant?
    A. Ten years' IT experience, one year in security, CIW Security analyst, MBA
    B. Eight years' IT experience, three years in security, CISSP, BS in computer science
    C. Eleven years' IT experience, three years in security, MCSE and CISSP, MS in information systems
    D. Ten years' experience as a hacker and cracker, MCSE/CIW/ and Security +, Ph.D. in computer science

EXERCISES

Exercise 6.1: Patching Systems

1. Using a lab system, find and apply all operating system patches.
2. Check with all vendors of software installed on that machine and apply patches for those applications as well (if available).
3. Note the time taken to fully patch a machine. Consider how long it would take to patch a 100-machine network.

4. Write an essay that answers the following questions: Are there ways you could speed the process of patching a 100-machine network? How might you approach such a task?

Exercise 6.2: Learning About Policies

1. Using the resources given or other resources, find at least one sample security policy document.
2. Analyze that document.
3. Write a brief essay giving your opinion of that policy. Did it miss items? Did it include items you had not thought of?

Exercise 6.3: Learning About Disaster Recovery

1. Using the resources given, or other resources, find at least one sample disaster recovery plan.
2. Analyze that document.
3. Write a brief essay giving your opinion of that disaster recovery plan. Also note any changes you would recommend to that policy.

Exercise 6.4: Learning About Audits

1. Using the resources given or other resources, find at least one sample security audit plan.
2. Analyze that document.
3. Write a brief essay giving your opinion of that plan. Do you feel the audit plan is adequate? What changes might you recommend?

FYI: Helpful Resources

For Exercises 6.2, 6.3, and 6.4, you may find the following resources helpful:

- **www.cert.org/**
- **www.sans.org/**
- **csrc.nist.gov/fasp/**
- **www.information-security-policies-and-standards.com/**

Exercise 6.5: Securing Your Computer

Using either your home computer or a lab computer, follow the guidelines given in this chapter to secure that computer. Those steps should include:

- Scan for all patches and install them.
- Shut down all unneeded services.
- Install anti-virus software. (A demo version can be used for this exercise.)
- Install anti-spyware software. (A demo version can be used for this exercise.)
- Set appropriate password permissions.

Exercise 6.6: Secure Passwords

1. Using the Web or other resources, find out why longer passwords are harder to break.
2. Also find out what other things you should do to make a password harder to crack.
3. Write a brief essay describing what makes a perfect password.

Exercise 6.7: Securing a Server

Note: This exercise is for those students with access to a lab server.

Using the guidelines discussed in this chapter, secure a lab server. The steps taken should include:

- Scan for all patches and install them.
- Shut down all unneeded services.
- Remove unneeded software.
- Install anti-virus software. (A demo version can be used for this exercise.)
- Install anti-spyware software. (A demo version can be used for this exercise.)
- Set appropriate password permissions.
- Enable logging of any security violations. (Consult your operating system documentation for instructions.)

Exercise 6.8: Backups

Using the Web and other resources as a guide, develop a backup plan for a Web server. The plan should cover how frequently to back up and where to store the backup media.

Exercise 6.9: User Accounts

Note: This exercise is best done with a lab computer, not a machine actually in use.

1. Locate user accounts. (In Windows 2000 or Windows XP, this is done by going to Start > Control Panel > Administrative Tools > Computer Management and looking for Groups and Users.)
2. Disable all default accounts (Guest, Administrator).

PROJECTS

Project 6.1: Writing and Executing an Audit Plan

With the knowledge you have gained while studying six chapters of this text and in examining security policies in the preceding exercises, it is now time to devise your own audit plan. This plan should detail all the steps in an audit.

Note: The second part of this project is contingent upon getting permission from some organization to allow you to audit their security. It is also ideal for a group project.

Taking the audit plan you wrote, audit a network. This audit can be conducted for any sort of organization, but you should make your first audit one with a small network (less than 100 users).

Project 6.2: Forming a Disaster Recovery Plan

Using the knowledge you have gained thus far, create an IT disaster recovery plan for an organization. You may use a fictitious organization, but a real organization would be better.

Project 6.3: Writing a Security Policy Document

Note: This project is designed as a group project.

It is now time to bring all you have learned thus far together. Write a complete set of security policies for an organization. Again, you may use a fictitious company, but real organizations are better. This set of policies must cover user access, password policies, frequency of audits (both internal and external), minimum security requirements, guidelines for Web surfing, and so on.

Project 6.4: Secure Web Servers

Using the information in this chapter as well as other resources, come up with a strategy specifically for securing a Web server. This strategy should include the security of the server itself as well as securing the network from the server.

Project 6.5: Adding Your Own Guidelines

Note: This project is ideal for a group project.

This chapter has outlined some general procedures for security. Write an essay detailing your own additional guidelines. These can be guidelines for individual computers, servers, networks, or any combination thereof.

Case Study

Juan Garcia is the network administrator for a small company that also maintains its own Web server. He has taken the following precautions:

- All computers are patched, have antivirus software, and have unneeded services shut down.
- The network has a firewall with proxy server and IDS.
- The organization has a policy requiring passwords of ten characters in length, and they must be changed every 90 days.

Has Juan done enough to secure the network? What other actions would you recommend he take?

Chapter 7

Encryption

Chapter Objectives

After reading this chapter and completing the exercises, you will be able to do the following:

- Explain the basics of encryption.
- Discuss modern cryptography methods.
- Select appropriate cryptography for your organization.
- Understand the function and protocols of VPNs.

Introduction

There are many aspects of computer and information security. ***Encryption***, the process of scrambling a message or other information so that it cannot be easily read, is one of the most critical parts to the security puzzle. If you have the best firewall, very tight security policies, hardened operating systems, virus scanners, intrusion detection software, anti-spyware, and every other computer security angle covered but send your data in raw, plain text, then you simply are not secure.

In this chapter, you will obtain what can be termed a "manager's understanding" of ***cryptography***—the art of writing in or deciphering secret code. It is important to understand that this chapter will not make you a cryptographer. In fact, reading several volumes on encryption would not accomplish that lofty goal. Rather, this chapter is designed to give you a basic overview of what encryption is, some idea of how it works, and enough information so that you can make intelligent decisions about what sorts of encryption to incorporate in your organization. You will learn the basic history of encryption, the fundamental concepts, and, once you have completed the exercises at the end of the chapter, enough knowledge to at least be able to ask the right questions.

Cryptography Basics

The aim of cryptography is not to hide the existence of a message, but rather to hide its meaning—the process known as encryption. To make a message unintelligible, it is scrambled according to a particular algorithm, which is agreed upon beforehand between the sender and the intended recipient. Thus, the recipient can reverse the scrambling protocol and make the message comprehensible (Singh, 2001). This reversal of the scrambling is referred to as ***decryption***. The advantage of using encryption/decryption is that, without knowing the scrambling protocol, the message is difficult to re-create.

There are two basic types of cryptography: ***transposition*** and ***substitution***. Transposition involves simply rearranging the letters of a message, as is done in an anagram. Substitution, the type on which we will focus in this text, involves, at its root, replacing each letter in the alphabet with a different letter (or number).

Within the substitution branch of cryptography, there are two basic forms of encryption:

- Single key encryption / Symmetric key encryption
- Public key encryption / Asymmetric key encryption

We will discuss these two forms of encryption, along with a few popular examples, later in this chapter. But first, let's take a brief look at the history of encryption.

History of Encryption

The idea of encryption is probably as old as written communication. The basic concept is actually fairly simple. Messages must be changed in such a way that the message cannot be easily read by an enemy, but they can be easily decoded by the intended recipient. In this section, you will examine a few historical methods of encryption. It should be noted that these are very old methods, and they cannot be used for secure communication today. The methods discussed in this section would be easily cracked, even by an amateur. However, they are wonderful for conveying the concept of encryption without having to incorporate a great deal of math, which is required of the more complex encryption methods.

If you are interested in learning more about the history of cryptography than what we touch upon here, you may wish to read one of the many books written on the subject. Or, you might consult the following Web sites which are shown in Figure 7.1 and Figure 7.2:

- The Stanford University History of Cryptography Web site: **www-cs-education.stanford.edu/classes/sophomore-college/projects-97/cryptography/history.html**
- A Brief History of Cryptography from Cybercrimes.net: **www.cybercrimes.net/Cryptography/Articles/Hebert.html**

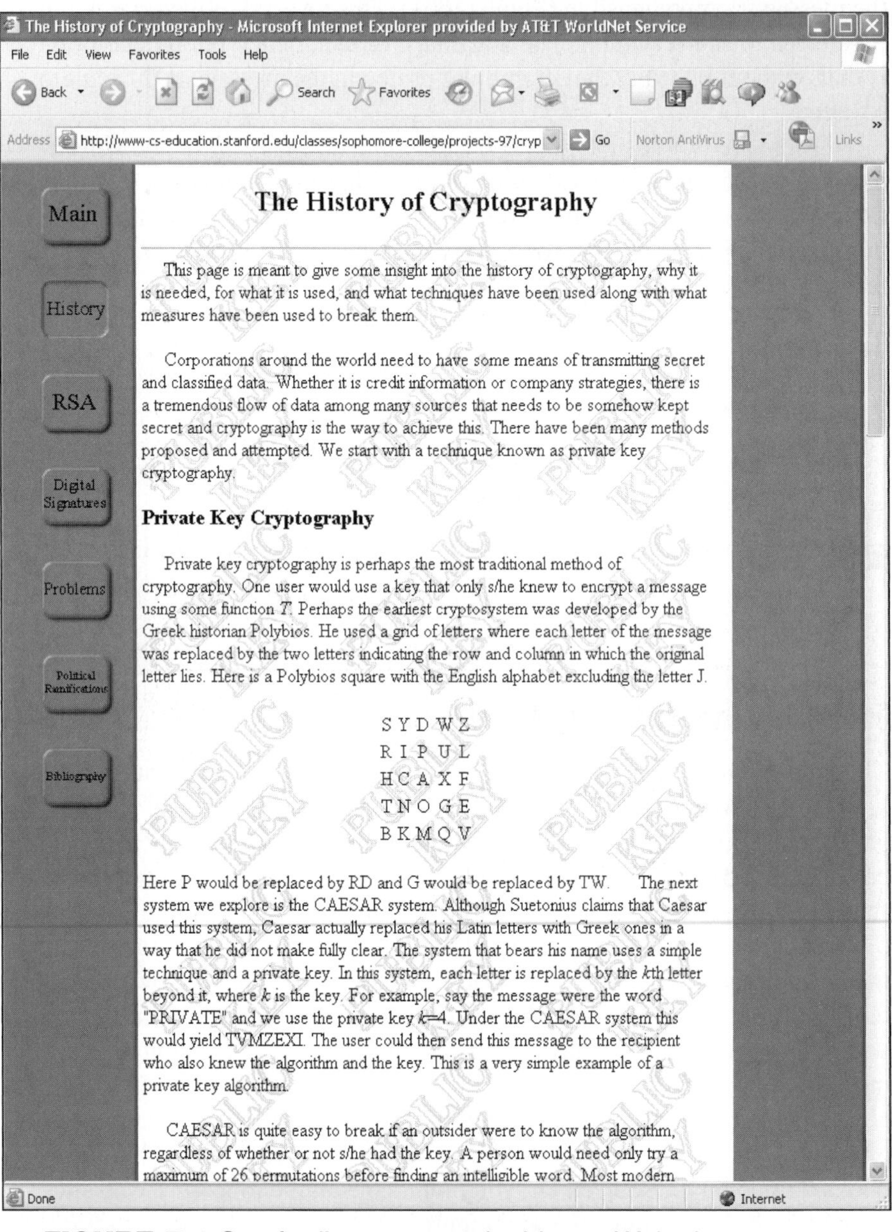

The History of Cryptography

This page is meant to give some insight into the history of cryptography, why it is needed, for what it is used, and what techniques have been used along with what measures have been used to break them.

Corporations around the world need to have some means of transmitting secret and classified data. Whether it is credit information or company strategies, there is a tremendous flow of data among many sources that needs to be somehow kept secret and cryptography is the way to achieve this. There have been many methods proposed and attempted. We start with a technique known as private key cryptography.

Private Key Cryptography

Private key cryptography is perhaps the most traditional method of cryptography. One user would use a key that only s/he knew to encrypt a message using some function *T*. Perhaps the earliest cryptosystem was developed by the Greek historian Polybios. He used a grid of letters where each letter of the message was replaced by the two letters indicating the row and column in which the original letter lies. Here is a Polybios square with the English alphabet excluding the letter J.

S Y D W Z
R I P U L
H C A X F
T N O G E
B K M Q V

Here P would be replaced by RD and G would be replaced by TW. The next system we explore is the CAESAR system. Although Suetonius claims that Caesar used this system, Caesar actually replaced his Latin letters with Greek ones in a way that he did not make fully clear. The system that bears his name uses a simple technique and a private key. In this system, each letter is replaced by the *k*th letter beyond it, where *k* is the key. For example, say the message were the word "PRIVATE" and we use the private key *k*=4. Under the CAESAR system this would yield TVMZEXI. The user could then send this message to the recipient who also knew the algorithm and the key. This is a very simple example of a private key algorithm.

CAESAR is quite easy to break if an outsider were to know the algorithm, regardless of whether or not s/he had the key. A person would need only try a maximum of 26 permutations before finding an intelligible word. Most modern

FIGURE 7.1 Stanford's cryptography history Web site.

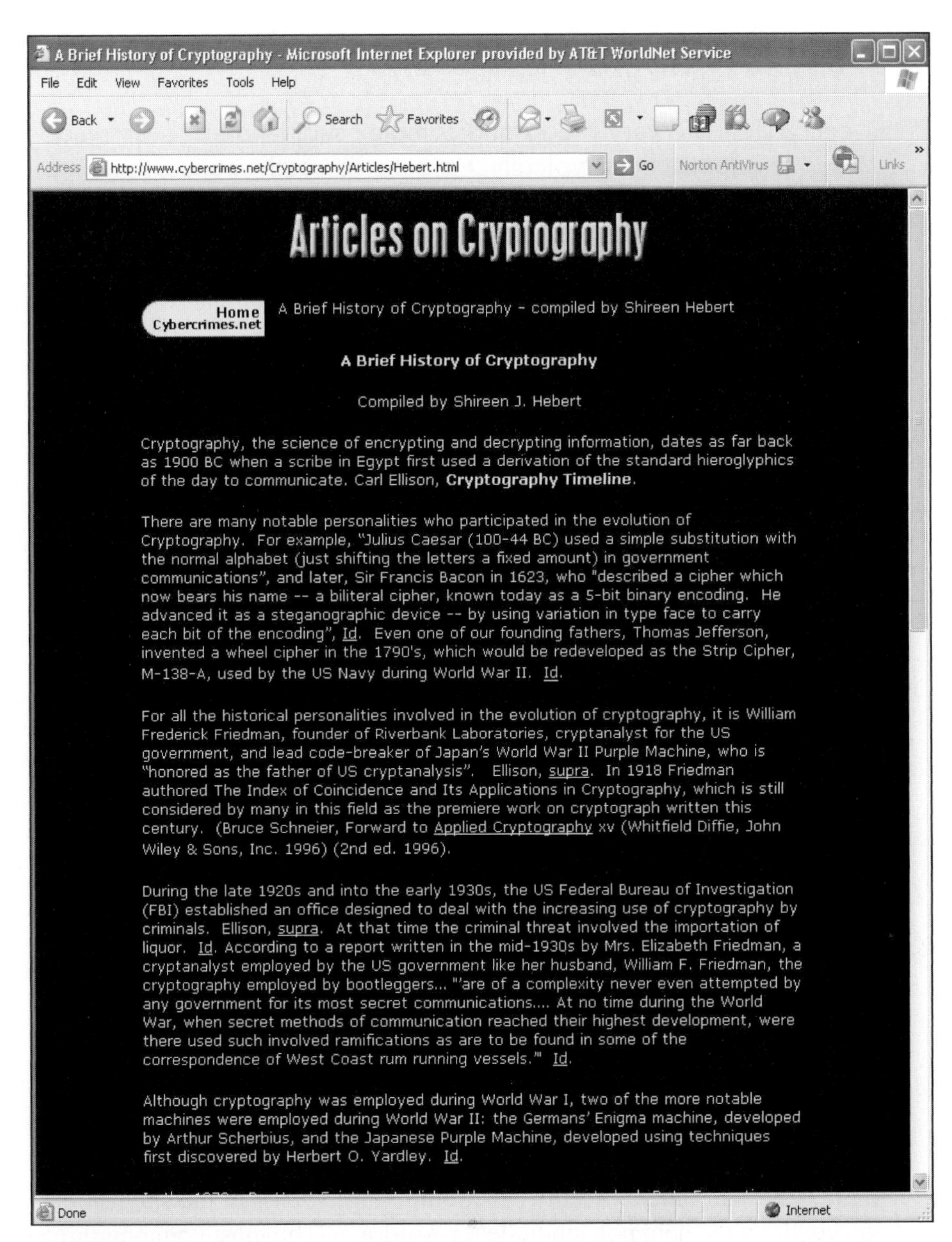
A Brief History of Cryptography - Microsoft Internet Explorer provided by AT&T WorldNet Service

http://www.cybercrimes.net/Cryptography/Articles/Hebert.html

Articles on Cryptography

Home Cybercrimes.net

A Brief History of Cryptography - compiled by Shireen Hebert

A Brief History of Cryptography

Compiled by Shireen J. Hebert

Cryptography, the science of encrypting and decrypting information, dates as far back as 1900 BC when a scribe in Egypt first used a derivation of the standard hieroglyphics of the day to communicate. Carl Ellison, **Cryptography Timeline**.

There are many notable personalities who participated in the evolution of Cryptography. For example, "Julius Caesar (100-44 BC) used a simple substitution with the normal alphabet (just shifting the letters a fixed amount) in government communications", and later, Sir Francis Bacon in 1623, who "described a cipher which now bears his name -- a biliteral cipher, known today as a 5-bit binary encoding. He advanced it as a steganographic device -- by using variation in type face to carry each bit of the encoding", Id. Even one of our founding fathers, Thomas Jefferson, invented a wheel cipher in the 1790's, which would be redeveloped as the Strip Cipher, M-138-A, used by the US Navy during World War II. Id.

For all the historical personalities involved in the evolution of cryptography, it is William Frederick Friedman, founder of Riverbank Laboratories, cryptanalyst for the US government, and lead code-breaker of Japan's World War II Purple Machine, who is "honored as the father of US cryptanalysis". Ellison, supra. In 1918 Friedman authored The Index of Coincidence and Its Applications in Cryptography, which is still considered by many in this field as the premiere work on cryptograph written this century. (Bruce Schneier, Forward to Applied Cryptography xv (Whitfield Diffie, John Wiley & Sons, Inc. 1996) (2nd ed. 1996).

During the late 1920s and into the early 1930s, the US Federal Bureau of Investigation (FBI) established an office designed to deal with the increasing use of cryptography by criminals. Ellison, supra. At that time the criminal threat involved the importation of liquor. Id. According to a report written in the mid-1930s by Mrs. Elizabeth Friedman, a cryptanalyst employed by the US government like her husband, William F. Friedman, the cryptography employed by bootleggers... "are of a complexity never even attempted by any government for its most secret communications.... At no time during the World War, when secret methods of communication reached their highest development, were there used such involved ramifications as are to be found in some of the correspondence of West Coast rum running vessels." Id.

Although cryptography was employed during World War I, two of the more notable machines were employed during World War II: the Germans' Enigma machine, developed by Arthur Scherbius, and the Japanese Purple Machine, developed using techniques first discovered by Herbert O. Yardley. Id.

FIGURE 7.2 Hebert's cryptography history Web site.

Understanding the simple methods described here and other methods listed on the aforementioned Web sites should give you a sense of how cryptography works as well as what is involved in encrypting a message. Regardless of whether you go on to study modern, sophisticated encryption methods, it is important for you to have some basic idea of how encryption

FYI: Cryptographers

Encryption is a very broad and complex subject area. Even amateur cryptographers typically have some mathematical training and have studied cryptographic methods for several years.

works at a conceptual level. Having a basic grasp of how encryption works, in principle, will make you better able to understand the concepts of any encryption method you encounter in the real world.

The Caesar Cipher

One of the oldest encryption methods is the ***Caesar cipher***. This method is purported to have been used by the ancient roman Caesars—thus the name. It is actually quite simple to do. You choose some number by which to shift each letter of a text. For example, if the text is:

```
A cat
```

And you choose to shift by two letters, then the message becomes:

```
C ecv
```

Or, if you choose to shift by three letters, it becomes:

```
D fdw
```

You can choose any shifting pattern you wish. You can shift either to the right or left by any number of spaces you like. Because this is a very simple method to understand, it makes a good place to start our study of encryption. It is, however, extremely easy to crack. You see, any language has a certain letter and word frequency, meaning that some letters are used more frequently than others (Security in Computing, 1988). In the English language, the most common single-letter word is *a*. The most common three-letter word is *the*. Those two rules alone could help you decrypt a Caesar cipher. For example, if you saw a string of seemingly nonsense letters and noticed that a three-letter word was frequently repeated in the message, you might easily surmise that this word was *the*—and the odds are highly in favor of this being correct. Furthermore, if you frequently noticed a single-letter word in the text, it is most likely the letter *a*. You now have found the substitution scheme for *a, t, h,* and *e*. You can now either translate all of those letters in the message and attempt to surmise the rest or simply analyze the substitute letters used for *a, t, h,* and *e* and derive the substitution cipher that was used for this message. Decrypting a message of this type does not even require a computer. It could be done in less than ten minutes using pen and paper by someone with no background in cryptography.

The substitution scheme you choose (e.g., +2, +1) is referred to as a ***substitution alphabet*** (i.e., b substitutes for a, u substitutes for t). Thus, the Caesar cipher is also referred to as a ***mono-alphabet substitution*** method, meaning that it uses a single substitution for the encryption.

The Caesar cipher, however, is not useless. Since most programming languages have some function to convert a character or number to its ASCII code, a programmer can write a simple function that loops through text converting each character to its ASCII code, then either adding or subtracting the appropriate number. Again, it must be stressed that this is not a secure method of encrypting messages, but an interesting exercise to begin introducing you to the basic concepts of encryption.

IN PRACTICE: Converting to ASCII Code

ASCII (American Standard Code for Information Interchange) is a standard code for every letter (upper- and lowercase), number, and key on your keyboard. It was proposed by ANSI (www.ansi.org) in 1963, and finalized in 1968. ASCII's purpose was to establish compatibility between the various types of data processing equipment. All key strokes can be converted to a numeric ASCII code.

ASCII, pronounced "ask-key," is the common code for microcomputer equipment. The standard ASCII character set consists of 128 decimal numbers ranging from zero through 127 assigned to letters, numbers, punctuation marks, and the most common special characters. The Extended ASCII Character Set also consists of 128 decimal numbers and ranges from 128 through 255 representing additional special, mathematical, graphic, and foreign characters. For example the capital A is ASCII code 65 and the return key is ASCII code 13.

As we discussed in Chapter 2, decimal numbers can be converted to binary numbers. So, as you can probably guess, there are binary equivalents (as well as hexadecimal equivalents) to each of these decimal values. Like the ASCII decimal values, there

CONTINUED ON NEXT PAGE

CONTINUED

TABLE 7.1 ASCII decimal values.

Decimal	Value
000	NUL (Null char.)
001	SOH (Start of Header)
002	STX (Start of Text)
003	ETX (End of Text)
004	EOT (End of Transmission)
005	ENQ (Enquiry)
006	ACK (Acknowledgment)
007	BEL (Bell)
008	BS (Backspace)
009	HT (Horizontal Tab)
010	LF (Line Feed)
011	VT (Vertical Tab)
012	FF (Form Feed)
013	CR (Carriage Return)
014	SO (Shift Out)
015	SI (Shift In)
016	DLE (Data Link Escape)
017	DC1 (XON) (Device Control 1)
018	DC2 (Device Control 2)
019	DC3 (XOFF) (Device Control 3)
020	DC4 (Device Control 4)
021	NAK (Negative Acknowledgement)
022	SYN (Synchronous Idle)
023	ETB (End of Trans. Block)
024	CAN (Cancel)
025	EM (End of Medium)
026	SUB (Substitute)
027	ESC (Escape)
028	FS (File Separator)
029	GS (Group Separator)
030	RS (Request to Send)(Record Separator)
031	US (Unit Separator)
032	SP (Space)
033	! (exclamation mark)
034	" (double quote)
035	# (number sign)
036	$ (dollar sign)
037	% (percent)
038	& (ampersand)
039	' (single quote)
040	((left/opening parenthesis)
041	) (right/closing parenthesis)
042	* (asterisk)
043	+ (plus)
044	, (comma)
045	- (minus or dash)
046	. (dot)
047	/ (forward slash)
048	0
049	1
050	2
051	3
052	4
053	5
054	6
055	7
056	8
057	9
058	: (colon)
059	; (semi-colon)
060	< (less than)

table continued

Decimal	Value	Decimal	Value
061	= (equal sign)	096	`
062	> (greater than)	097	a
063	? (question mark)	098	b
064	@ (AT symbol)	099	c
065	A	100	d
066	B	101	e
067	C	102	f
068	D	103	g
069	E	104	h
070	F	105	i
071	G	106	j
072	H	107	k
073	I	108	l
074	J	109	m
075	K	110	n
076	L	111	o
077	M	112	p
078	N	113	q
079	O	114	r
080	P	115	s
081	Q	116	t
082	R	117	u
083	S	118	v
084	T	119	w
085	U	120	x
086	V	121	y
087	W	122	z
088	X	123	{ (left/opening brace)
089	Y	124	| (vertical bar)
090	Z	125	} (right/closing brace)
091	[(left/opening bracket)	126	~ (tilde)
092	\ (back slash)	127	DEL (delete)
093	] (right/closing bracket)		
094	^ (caret/cirumflex)		
095	_ (underscore)		

CONTINUED ON NEXT PAGE

7

▸▸ CONTINUED

are tables available for determining either the binary or hexadecimal values. Table 7.2 is an example of a table for determining hexadecimal values.

TABLE 7.2 ASCII hexadecimal values.

*	0	1	2	3	4	5	6	7	8	9	A	B	C	D	E	F
0	NUL	SOH	STX	ETX	EOT	ENQ	ACK	BEL	BS	TAB	LF	VT	FF	CR	SO	SI
1	DLE	DC1	DC2	DC3	DC4	NAK	SYN	ETB	CAN	EM	SUB	ESC	FS	GS	RS	US
2		!	"	#	$	%	&	'	(	)	*	+	,	-	.	/
3	0	1	2	3	4	5	6	7	8	9	:	;	<	=	>	?
4	@	A	B	C	D	E	F	G	H	I	J	K	L	M	N	O
5	P	Q	R	S	T	U	V	W	X	Y	Z	[	\	]	^	_
6	`	a	b	c	d	e	f	g	h	i	j	k	l	m	n	o
7	p	q	r	s	t	u	v	w	x	y	z	{	|	}	~	

Like the conversion to binary numbers that we discussed in Chapter 2, there are many readily available converters that can make determining the ASCII equivalencies much easier than searching through tables. A simple search of the Internet will turn up many such converters. Figure 7.3 is an example of a converter found at **www.cplusplus.com/doc/papers/ascii.html**. This particular converter, given any one value, will generate the other three. In this illustration, the uppercase A was entered and the decimal, hexadecimal, and binary ("oct.") numbers were all generated.

FIGURE 7.3 ASCII converter.

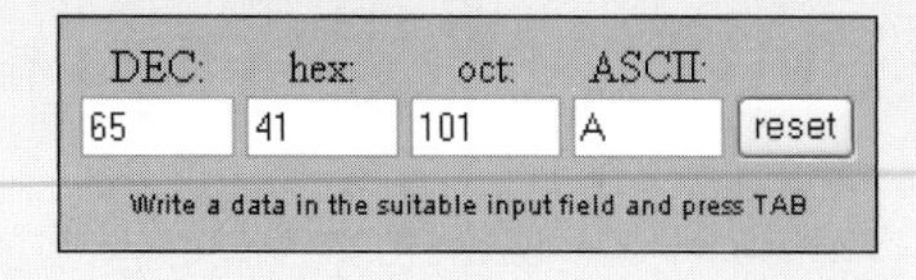

Multi-Alphabet Substitution

Eventually, a slight improvement on the Caesar cipher was developed, called ***multi-alphabet substitution***. In this scheme, you select multiple numbers by which to shift letters (i.e., multiple substitution alphabets). For example, if you select three substitution alphabets (+2, −2, +3), then

```
A CAT
```

becomes

```
C ADV
```

Notice that the fourth letter starts over with another +2, and you can see that the first A was transformed to C and the second A was transformed to D. This makes it more difficult to decipher the underlying text. While this is harder to decrypt than a Caesar cipher, it is not overly difficult. It can be done with simple pen and paper and a bit of effort. It can be cracked very quickly with a computer. In fact, no one would use such a method today to send any truly secure message, for this type of encryption is considered very weak.

Binary Operations

Various operations on ***binary numbers*** (numbers made of only zeroes and ones) are well known to programmers and programming students. But for those readers not familiar with them, a brief explanation follows. When working with binary numbers, there are three operations not found in normal math: AND, OR, and XOR operations. Each is illustrated below.

```
AND
```

To perform the AND operation, you take two binary numbers and compare them one place at a time. If both numbers have a one in both places, then the resultant number is a one. If not, then the resultant number is a zero, as you see here:

```
1 1 0 1

1 0 0 1

_______

1 0 0 1
```

```
OR
```

The OR operation checks to see whether there is a one in either or both numbers in a given place. If so, then the resultant number is one. If not, the resultant number is zero, as you see here:

```
1 1 0 1

1 0 0 1

_______

1 1 0 1
```

```
XOR
```

The XOR operation impacts your study of encryption the most. It checks to see whether there is a one in a number in a given place, but *not* in both numbers at that place. If it is in one number but not the other, then the resultant number is one. If not, the resultant number is zero, as you see here:

```
1 1 0 1
1 0 0 1
_______
0 1 0 0
```

XORing has a very interesting property in that it is reversible. If you XOR the resultant number with the second number, you get back the first number. And, if you XOR the resultant number with the first number, you get the second number.

```
0 1 0 0
1 0 0 1
_______
1 1 0 1
```

Binary encryption using the XOR operation opens the door for some rather simple encryption. Take any message and convert it to binary numbers and then XOR that with some key. Converting a message to a binary number is really a simple two-step process. First, convert a message to its ASCII code, then convert those codes to binary numbers. Each letter/number will generate an eight-bit binary number. Then you can use a random string of binary numbers of any given length as the key. Simply XOR your message with the key to get the encrypted text, then XOR it with the key again to retrieve the original message. This method is easy to use and great for computer science students; however, it does not work well for truly secure communications because the underlying letter and word frequency remains. This exposes valuable clues that even an amateur cryptographer can use to decrypt the message. Yet, it does provide a valuable introduction to the concept of ***single-key encryption***, which will be discussed in more detail in the next section. While simply XORing the text is not the method typically employed, single-key encryption methods are widely used today. For example, you could simply include a multi-alphabet substitution that was then XORed with some random bit stream—variations of which do exist in a few actual encryption methods currently used.

Modern Methods

Modern cryptography methods, as well as computers, make decryption a rather advanced science. Therefore, encryption must be equally sophisticated in order to have a chance of success.

What you have seen so far regarding encryption is simply for educational purposes. As has been noted several times, you would not have a truly secure system if you implemented any of the previously mentioned encryption schemes. You may feel that this has been overstated in this text. However, it is critical that you have an accurate view of what encryption methods do and do not work. It is now time to discuss a few methods that are actually in use today.

Single-Key (Symmetric) Encryption

Basically, single-key encryption means that the same key is used to both encrypt and decrypt a message. This is also referred to as symmetric key encryption.

Blowfish Blowfish is a symmetric block cipher. This means that it uses a single key to both encrypt and decrypt the message and works on "blocks" of the message at a time. It uses a variable-length key ranging from 32 to 448 bits (MyCrypto.net, 2004). This flexibility in key size allows you to use it in various situations. Blowfish was designed in 1993 by Bruce Schneier. It has been analyzed extensively by the cryptography community and has gained wide acceptance. It is also a non-commercial (i.e., free of charge) product, thus making it attractive to budget-conscious organizations.

Data Encryption Standard ***Data Encryption Standard***, or ***DES*** as it is often called, was developed by IBM in the early 1970s. DES uses a symmetric key system. The DES uses short keys and relies on complex procedures to protect its information. The actual DES algorithm is quite complex and beyond the scope of this text. The basic concept, however, is as follows: (Federal Information Processing Standards, 1993)

> **FYI: Block Ciphers and Stream Ciphers**
>
> When applying a key to plain text to encrypt it and produce the cipher text, you must also choose how to apply the key and the algorithm. In a block cipher, the key is applied to blocks (often 64 bits in size) at a time. This differs from a stream cipher that encrypts one bit at a time.

1. Data is divided into 64-bit blocks, and those blocks are then transposed.
2. Transposed data is then manipulated by 16 separate steps of encryption involving substitutions, bit-shifting, and logical operations using a 56-bit key.
3. Data is then further scrambled using a swapping algorithm.
4. Data is finally transposed one last time.

One advantage that DES offers is efficiency. Some implementations of DES offer data throughput rates on the order of hundreds of megabytes per second. In plain English, what this means is that it can encrypt a great deal of data very quickly. You might assume that 16 steps would cause encryption to be quite slow; however, that is not the case using modern computer equipment. The problem with DES is the same problem that all symmetric key algorithms have: How do you transmit the key without risking it becoming compromised? This issue led to the development of public key encryption.

Public Key (Asymmetric) Encryption

Public key encryption is essentially the opposite of single-key encryption. With any public key encryption algorithm, one key is used to encrypt a message (called the public key) and another is used to decrypt the message (called the private key). You can freely distribute your public key so that anyone can encrypt a message to send to you, but only you have the private key and only you can decrypt the message. The actual mathematics behind the creation and application of the keys is a bit complex and beyond the scope of this book. It should be pointed out, however, that many public key algorithms are dependent, to some extent, on large prime numbers, factoring, and number theory.

Many commonly used algorithms, such as PGP, use public key encryption. It is very easy to implement since the public key can be freely distributed to anyone and sometimes even put on a Web site for download.

Public key encryption is fast becoming the most widely used type of encryption because there are no issues to deal with concerning distribution of the keys. With symmetric key encryption, you must get a copy of the key to every person to whom you wish to send your encrypted messages. If that key were lost or copied, someone else might be able to decrypt all of your messages. With public key encryption, you can freely distribute your public key to the entire world, yet only you can decrypt messages encrypted with that public key.

Caution

Encryption Strength

Federal law prohibits the exportation of encryption beyond a certain strength. Currently, that exact limit is being contested in various court cases. It is recommended that you consult current federal guidelines before implementing encryption in your organization.

PGP ***PGP***, a public key system, stands for ***Pretty Good Privacy***. It is a widely used system that is considered very secure by most experts (International PGP, 2004). There are several software implementations available as

FYI: "Old" Encryption

PGP is more than ten years old. Some readers might wonder whether it is old and outdated. Cryptography is unlike other technological endeavors in this regard—older is better. It is usually unwise to use the "latest thing" in encryption for the simple reason that it is unproven. An older encryption method, provided it has not yet been broken, is usually a better choice because it has been subjected to years of examination by experts and to cracking attempts by both experts and less honorably motivated individuals. This is sometimes hard for computer professionals to understand since the newest technology is often preferred in the computer business.

freeware for most desktop operating systems. There are PGP plug-ins for Netscape Messenger, MSN Messenger, and many other popular communications software packages (McCune, 2004). A simple Yahoo or Google search for *PGP* will help you find many of these software products.

PGP was invented by Phil Zimmermann (Zimmermann, 2004). Before creating PGP, Mr. Zimmermann had been a software engineer for 20 years and had experience with existing forms of cryptography. A great deal of controversy surrounded the birth of PGP because it was created without an easy means for government intrusion and its encryption was considered too strong for export. This caused Mr. Zimmermann to be the target of a three-year government investigation. However, those legal matters are now resolved and PGP is one of the most widely used encryption methods available.

The important things to know about PGP are that it is:

- A public key encryption
- Considered quite secure
- Available free of charge

These facts make it well worth your time to investigate PGP as a possible solution for your organization's encryption needs.

RSA The ***RSA*** method is a very widely used encryption algorithm. You cannot discuss cryptography without at least some discussion of RSA. This is a public key method developed in 1977 by three mathematicians, Ron Rivest, Adi Shamir, and Len Adlema. The name RSA is derived from the first letter of each mathematician's last name (Burnett and Paine, 2001). This text will not delve too deeply into the mathematics; however, for those who are curious, the following paragraphs will give you a brief description of the essential math.

To start, two large prime numbers are selected and then multiplied together:

`n = p*q.`

You then let

`f(n) = (p − 1) (q − 1), and e>1`

such that

`greatest common denominator (e, f(n)) = 1`

Here *e* will have a large probability of being co-prime to *f(n)*, if *n* is large enough and *e* will be part of the encryption key. You solve the equation for *d*. (The actual equation is based on linear algebra and is not really critical for this discussion. You can reference details in the RSA Security's *Official Guide to Cryptography* if desired, or you can do a Web search and find details on several Web sites.) The pair of integers (*e, n*) is the public key, and (*d, n*) form the private key. Encryption of *M* can be accomplished by an equation using these integers for the keys. This method has become very popular.

Legitimate versus Fraudulent Encryption Methods

The encryption methods discussed above are just a few of the more widely used modern encryption methods. Dozens of other methods are released to the public for free or are patented and sold for profit every year. However, it is important to realize that this particular area of the computer industry is replete with frauds and charlatans. One need only scan any search engine searching for *encryption* to find a plethora of advertisements for the latest and greatest "unbreakable" encryption. If you are not knowledgeable about encryption, how do you separate legitimate encryption methods from frauds?

Matt Curtin has a Web site titled *Snake Oil Warning Signs* (Curtin, 1998) (**www.interhack.net/people/cmcurtin/snake-oil-faq.html**) that does a very good job of listing specific warning signs and also explaining some of the basics of cryptography. If you have an interest in cryptography, you should definitely visit his Web site and bookmark it for future reference. Below is a list of warning signs. You will notice that it is similar to Curtin's, with just a few differences.

- **Unbreakable:** Anyone with experience in cryptography knows that there is no such thing as an unbreakable code. There are codes that have not yet been broken. There are codes that are very hard to break. But when someone claims that their method is "completely unbreakable," you should be suspicious.

- **Certified:** Guess what? There is no recognized certification process for encryption methods. Therefore, any "certification" the company has is totally worthless.
- **Inexperienced people:** A company is marketing a new encryption method. What is the experience of the people working with it? Does the cryptographer have a background in math, encryption, or algorithms? If not, has he submitted their method to experts in peer-reviewed journals? Or, is he at least willing to disclose how their method works so that it can be fairly judged? Recall that PGP's inventor had decades of software engineering and encryption experience.

Some experts claim that you should only use widely known methods, such as Blowfish and PGP, although it is certainly possible to use less well-known, or even new, encryption methods and have a very secure system. Consider the fact that today's widely used methods were once new and untested. However, if you are using a less well-known method, you need to take extra precautions to ensure that you are not being misled.

Virtual Private Networks

A ***VPN*** is a ***virtual private network***. This is essentially a way to use the Internet to create a virtual connection between a remote user or site and a central location. The packets sent back and forth over this connection are encrypted, thus making it private. The VPN must emulate a direct network connection.

There are three different protocols that are used to create VPN's. They are:

- Point to Point Tunneling Protocol (PPTP)
- Layer 2 Tunneling Protocol (L2TP)
- Internet Protocol Security (IPSec)

These are each discussed in more depth in the following sections.

PPTP

Point-to-Point Tunneling Protocol (PPTP) is the oldest of the three protocols used in VPNs. It was originally designed as a secure extension to Point-to-Point Protocol (PPP). The Point-to-Point Tunneling Protocol was originally proposed as a standard in 1996 by the PPTP Forum—a group of companies that included Ascend Communications, ECI Telematics, Microsoft, 3Com, and U.S. Robotics. It adds the features of encrypting packets and authenticating users to the older PPP protocol. PPTP works at the data link layer of the OSI model (discussed in Chapter 2).

PPTP offers two different methods of authenticating the user: Extensible Authentication Protocol (EAP) and Challenge Handshake Authentication Protocol (CHAP). EAP was actually designed specifically for PPTP and is not proprietary. CHAP is a three-way process whereby the client sends a code to the server, the server authenticates it, and then the server responds to the client. CHAP also periodically re-authenticates a remote client, even after the connection is established.

PPTP uses Microsoft Point-to-Point Encryption (MPPE) to encrypt packets. MPPE is actually a version of DES. DES is still useful for many situations; however, newer versions of DES, such as DES 3, have been released.

L2TP

Layer 2 Tunneling Protocol (L2TP) was explicitly designed as an enhancement to PPTP. Like PPTP, it works at the data link layer of the OSI model. It has several improvements to PPTP. First, it offers more and varied methods for authentication—PPTP offers two, whereas L2TP offers five. In addition to CHAP and EAP, L2TP offers PAP, SPAP, and MS-CHAP.

- **PAP:** Password Authentication Protocol is the simplest form of authentication and the least secure. Usernames and passwords are sent unencrypted, in plain text.
- **SPAP:** Shiva Password Authentication Protocol is an extension to PAP that does encrypt the username and password that is sent over the Internet.
- **MS-CHAP** is a Microsoft-specific extension to CHAP.

In addition to more authentication protocols available for use, L2TP offers other enhancements. PPTP will only work over standard IP networks, whereas L2TP will work over X.25 networks (a common protocol in phone systems) and ATM (asynchronous transfer mode, a high-speed networking technology) systems. L2TP also uses IPSec for its encryption.

IPSEC

IPSec is short for ***Internet Protocol Security***. It is the latest of the three VPN protocols. One of the differences between IPSec and the other two methods is that it encrypts not only the packet data (recall the discussion of packets in Chapter 2), but also the header information. It also has protection against unauthorized retransmission of packets. This is important because one trick that a hacker can use is to simply grab the first packet from a transmission and use it to get their own transmissions to go through. Essentially, the first packet (or packets) has to contain the login data. If you simply re-send that packet (even if you cannot crack its encryption), you will be sending a valid logon and password that can then be followed with additional packets. Preventing unauthorized retransmission of packets prevents this from happening.

Summary

A basic element of computer security is encryption. Sending sensitive data that is not encrypted is simply foolish. This chapter provided the basic information on how cryptography works. The most important thing to remember is that, ultimately, it is not your computer or your network that will be compromised, but rather your data. Encrypting the data when transmitting it is an integral part of any security plan.

In the exercises at the end of this chapter, you will practice using different cipher methods and learn more about a number of encryption methods.

Test Your Skills

MULTIPLE CHOICE QUESTIONS

1. Which of the following most accurately defines encryption?
   A. changing a message so it can only be easily read by the intended recipient
   B. using complex mathematics to conceal a message
   C. changing a message using complex mathematics
   D. applying keys to a message to conceal it

2. Which of the following is the oldest encryption method discussed in this text?
   A. PGP
   B. multi-alphabet encryption
   C. Caesar cipher
   D. cryptic cipher

3. What is the main problem with simple substitution?
   A. It does not use complex mathematics.
   B. It is easily broken with modern computers.
   C. It is too simple.
   D. It maintains letter and word frequency.

4. Which of the following is an encryption method using two or more different shifts?
   A. Caesar cipher
   B. multi-alphabet encryption
   C. DES
   D. PGP

5. Which binary mathematical operation can be used for a simple encryption method?
   A. bit shift
   B. OR
   C. XOR
   D. bit swap

6. Why is binary mathematical encryption not secure?
   A. It does not change letter or word frequency.
   B. It leaves the message intact.
   C. It is too simple.
   D. The mathematics of it is flawed.

7. Which of the following is most true regarding binary operations and encryption?
   A. They are completely useless.
   B. They can form a part of viable encryption methods.
   C. They are only useful as a teaching method.
   D. They can provide secure encryption.

8. What is PGP?
   A. Pretty Good Privacy, a public key encryption method
   B. Pretty Good Protection, a public key encryption method
   C. Pretty Good Privacy, a symmetric key encryption method
   D. Pretty Good Protection, a symmetric key encryption method

9. Which of the following methods is available as an add-in for most e-mail clients?
   A. DES
   B. RSA
   C. Caesar cipher
   D. PGP

10. Which of the following is a symmetric key system using 64-bit blocks?
    A. RSA
    B. DES
    C. PGP
    D. Blowfish

11. What advantage does a symmetric key system using 64-bit blocks have?
    A. It is fast.
    B. It is unbreakable.
    C. It uses asymmetric keys.
    D. It is complex.

12. What size key does a DES system use?
    A. 64 bit
    B. 128 bit
    C. 56 bit
    D. 256 bit

13. What type of encryption uses different keys to encrypt and decrypt the message?
    A. private key
    B. public key
    C. symmetric
    D. secure

14. Which of the following methods uses a variable-length symmetric key?
    A. Blowfish
    B. Caesar
    C. DES
    D. RSA

15. What should you be most careful of when looking for an encryption method to use?
    A. complexity of the algorithm
    B. veracity of the vendor's claims
    C. speed of the algorithm
    D. how long the algorithm has been around

16. Which of the following is most likely to be true of an encryption method that is advertised as unbreakable?
    A. It is probably suitable for military use.
    B. It may be too expensive for your organization.
    C. It is likely to be exaggerated.
    D. It is probably one you want to use.

17. Which of the following is most true regarding certified encryption methods?
    A. These are the only methods you should use.
    B. It depends on the level of certification.
    C. It depends on the source of the certification.
    D. There is no such thing as certified encryption.

18. Which of the following is most true regarding new encryption methods?
    A. Never use them until they have been proven.
    B. You can use them, but you must be cautious.
    C. Only use them if they are certified.
    D. Only use them if they are rated unbreakable.

19. Which of the following is the oldest protocol used by VPN?
    A. PPTP
    B. L2TP
    C. IPSec
    D. SPAP

20. Which of the following is used by PPTP to encrypt packets?
    A. Microsoft Point-to-Point Encryption
    B. Layer 2 Tunneling Protocol
    C. Extensible Authentication Protocol
    D. Challenge Handshake Authentication Protocol

EXERCISES

Exercise 7.1: Using the Caesar Cipher

Note: This exercise is well suited for group or classroom exercises.

1. Write a sentence in normal text.
2. Use a Caesar cipher of your own design to encrypt it.
3. Pass it to another person in your group or class.
4. Time how long it takes that person to break the encryption.
5. (Optional) Compute the mean time for the class to break Caesar ciphers.

Exercise 7.2: Using Multi-Alphabet Ciphers

Note: This exercise also works well for group settings and is best used in conjunction with the preceding exercise.

1. Write a sentence in normal text.
2. Use a multi-alphabet cipher of your own design to encrypt it.
3. Pass it to another person in your group or class.
4. Time how long it takes that person to break the encryption.
5. (Optional) Compute the mean time for the class to break these, and compare that to the mean time required to break the Caesar ciphers.

Exercise 7.3: Using PGP

1. Download a PGP attachment for your favorite e-mail client. Doing a Web search for PGP and your e-mail client (i.e., PGP and Outlook or PGP and Euodora) should locate both modules and instructions.
2. Install and configure the PGP module.
3. Send encrypted messages to and from a classmate.

Exercise 7.4: Finding Good Encryption Solutions

1. Scan the Web for various commercial encryption algorithms.
2. Find one that you feel may be "snake oil."
3. Write a brief paper explaining your opinion.

Exercise 7.5: Learn More about VPN

1. Using the Web, journals, books, or other resources, find out more about VPN.
2. Write a brief essay describing how VPN could increase the security of your transmissions.

PROJECTS

Project 7.1: RSA Encryption

Using the Web or other resources, write a brief paper about RSA, its history, methodology, and where it is used. Students with a sufficient math background may choose to delve more deeply into the RSA algorithm's mathematical basis.

Project 7.2: Programming Caesar Cipher

Note: This project is for those students with some programming background.

Write a simple program in any language you prefer (or your instructor dictates) that can perform a Caesar cipher. In this chapter, you not only saw how this cipher works, but were also given some ideas on how to use ASCII codes to make this work in any standard programming language.

Project 7.3: Other Encryption Methods

Write a brief essay describing any encryption method not already mentioned in this chapter. In this paper, describe the history and origin of that algorithm. You should also provide some comparisons with other well-known algorithms.

Case Study

Jane Doe is responsible for selecting an encryption method that is suitable for her company, which sells insurance. The data they send is sensitive, but is not military or classified in nature. Jane is looking at a variety of methods. She ultimately selects a commercial implementation of RSA. Was this the best choice? Why or why not?

Chapter 8

Internet Fraud and Cyber Crime

Chapter Objectives

After reading this chapter and completing the exercises, you will be able to do the following:

- Explain the methods used in Internet investment scams and auction frauds, such as pump and dump and bid siphoning.
- Take specific steps to avoid fraud on the Internet.
- Know specific steps to avoid identity theft.
- Understand cyber stalking and relevant laws.
- Know some legal aspects that apply to computer crimes.
- Configure a Web browser's privacy settings.

Introduction

In every new frontier, a criminal element is bound to emerge. In times past, the high seas gave rise to pirates and America's Wild West produced gangs of outlaws. The Internet is no different than any other frontier; it has its share of outlaws. Besides hacking and virus creation, which where both mentioned earlier in this book, there are other dangers. Fraud is one of the most common dangers of the Internet. Fraud has been a part of life for as long as civilization has existed. In past centuries, "snake oil" salespeople roamed the country selling fake cures and elixirs. As more people use the Internet as a conduit for commerce, there arises a greater opportunity for fraud. In fact, many experts would consider fraud to be the most prevalent danger on the Internet.

There are multiple reasons for the popularity of Internet fraud among con artists. First, committing an Internet fraud does not require the technical expertise that hacking and virus creation require. Secondly, there are a great number of people engaging in various forms of online commerce, and this large amount of business creates a great many opportunities for fraud.

There are many avenues for fraud on the Internet. This chapter will explore what the various major types of fraud are, what the law says, and what you can do to protect yourself. Chapter exercises will give you a chance to try out setting browsers for privacy and using anti-spy methods. This chapter is not particularly technical simply because most Internet fraud does not rely on in-depth technological expertise. Internet fraud merely uses the computer as a venue for many of the same fraud schemes that have been perpetrated throughout history.

Internet Fraud

There are a variety of ways that a fraud can be perpetrated via the Internet. The Securities and Exchange Commission lists several types of Internet fraud on their Web site (U.S. Securities and Exchange Commission, 2001). Figure 8.1 shows part of the list from this Web site. This chapter briefly discusses each of the types listed, as well as others. However, it is not possible for this text to cover every variation of each fraud scheme that has been used on the Internet. Such an undertaking would not only fill an entire book, but possibly also several volumes. What this text can do is cover the more common scams and then extrapolate from these to form some general principles that you can apply. These should enable you to avoid most fraudulent schemes.

FYI: Investment Offers

Investment offers are nothing new. Some stockbrokers make their living by "cold calling," the process of simply calling people (perhaps from the phone book) and trying to get them to invest in a specific stock. This practice is employed by some legitimate firms, but it is also a favorite con game for perpetrators of fraud. The Internet has allowed investment offers, both genuine and fraudulent, to be more easily disseminated to the general public. Most readers are probably familiar with investment offers flooding their inbox on a daily basis. Some of these e-mail notifications entice you to become directly involved with a particular investment plan, while other e-mails offer seemingly unbiased information from investors, free of charge. Unfortunately, much of this advice is not as unbiased as it might appear to be. While legitimate online newsletters can help investors gather valuable information, keep in mind that some online newsletters are fraudulent.

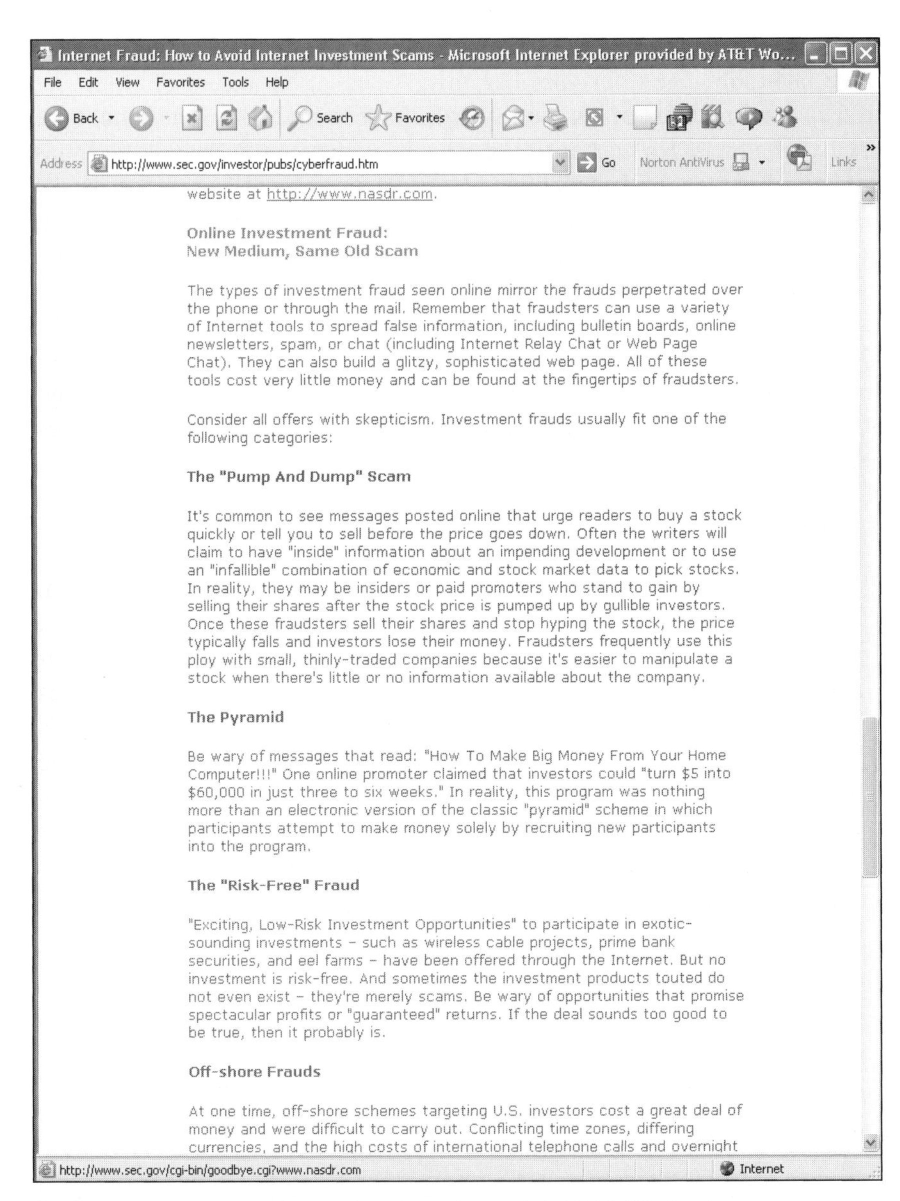

website at http://www.nasdr.com.

Online Investment Fraud:
New Medium, Same Old Scam

The types of investment fraud seen online mirror the frauds perpetrated over the phone or through the mail. Remember that fraudsters can use a variety of Internet tools to spread false information, including bulletin boards, online newsletters, spam, or chat (including Internet Relay Chat or Web Page Chat). They can also build a glitzy, sophisticated web page. All of these tools cost very little money and can be found at the fingertips of fraudsters.

Consider all offers with skepticism. Investment frauds usually fit one of the following categories:

The "Pump And Dump" Scam

It's common to see messages posted online that urge readers to buy a stock quickly or tell you to sell before the price goes down. Often the writers will claim to have "inside" information about an impending development or to use an "infallible" combination of economic and stock market data to pick stocks. In reality, they may be insiders or paid promoters who stand to gain by selling their shares after the stock price is pumped up by gullible investors. Once these fraudsters sell their shares and stop hyping the stock, the price typically falls and investors lose their money. Fraudsters frequently use this ploy with small, thinly-traded companies because it's easier to manipulate a stock when there's little or no information available about the company.

The Pyramid

Be wary of messages that read: "How To Make Big Money From Your Home Computer!!!" One online promoter claimed that investors could "turn $5 into $60,000 in just three to six weeks." In reality, this program was nothing more than an electronic version of the classic "pyramid" scheme in which participants attempt to make money solely by recruiting new participants into the program.

The "Risk-Free" Fraud

"Exciting, Low-Risk Investment Opportunities" to participate in exotic-sounding investments - such as wireless cable projects, prime bank securities, and eel farms - have been offered through the Internet. But no investment is risk-free. And sometimes the investment products touted do not even exist - they're merely scams. Be wary of opportunities that promise spectacular profits or "guaranteed" returns. If the deal sounds too good to be true, then it probably is.

Off-shore Frauds

At one time, off-shore schemes targeting U.S. investors cost a great deal of money and were difficult to carry out. Conflicting time zones, differing currencies, and the high costs of international telephone calls and overnight

FIGURE 8.1 List of Internet frauds at the SEC Web site.

Fraudulent Investment Offers

One of the more common investment offer schemes involves sending out an e-mail suggesting that you can make an outrageous sum of money with a very minimal investment. Perhaps the most famous of these schemes has been the Nigerian Fraud. In this scenario, an e-mail is sent to a number of random e-mail addresses. Each one contains a message purporting to be from a relative of some deceased Nigerian doctor or government official. The deceased person will be someone you would associate with significant social standing, thus increasing the likelihood that you would view the offer more favorably. The offer goes like this: A person has a sum of money he wishes to transfer out of his country and, for security reasons, he cannot use normal channels. He wishes to use your bank account to "park" the funds temporarily. If you will allow him access to your account, you will receive a hefty fee. If you agree to this arrangement, you will receive, via normal mail, a variety of very official-looking documents, enough to convince most casual observers that the arrangement is legitimate. You will then be asked to advance some money to cover items such as taxes and wire fees. Should you actually send any money, you will have lost the money you advanced and will never hear from these individuals again. The U.S. Secret Service has issued a bulletin detailing this particular fraud scheme (U.S. Secret Service, 2002).

Now consider this investment scam, and variations of it, from a logical point of view. If you had large sums of money you needed to transfer, would you send it to a person you had never met in a foreign country? Wouldn't you be worried that the recipient would cash out her account and take the next plane to Rio? If a person needs to transfer money internationally, why not just transfer the money to an account in the Bahamas? Or, cash out the account and send it via Federal Express or United Parcel Service to a storage facility in the United States? The point is that there are many ways a person could get money out of a country without trusting a stranger he has never met. That fact alone should indicate to you that this offer is simply not legitimate. This concept is the first general principle you should derive concerning fraud. In any offer, consider the point of view of the person offering it. Does it sound as if he is taking an inordinately large risk? Does the deal seem oddly biased in your favor? Put yourself in his position. Would you engage in the deal if you where in his position? If not, then this factor is a sign that the deal might not be what it seems.

FYI: Allowing Active Code

Any time you allow active code to run on your browser there is a risk that you may be opening the door to a Trojan horse or virus. Active code includes Active X components, Java Script, and other scripting languages. These items are often used by Web designers to add multimedia to a Web site. If you simply block all active code you will find that you cannot view some Web pages. On the other hand if you allow all active code, you will be endangering your system. The best route to take is to set your browser to prompt you for permission before executing any Active X or script code.

FYI: Prosecuting Cyber Crime

As mentioned in this chapter, many countries are developing specific laws to counteract cyber crime. One of the greatest challenges to prosecution of computer crime, however, is the difficulty of determining jurisdiction. This is especially true with the international usage of the Internet.

Fraudulent Investment Advice

Such fraudulent investment offer schemes are not the only investment pitfall on the Internet. Some companies pay the people who write online newsletters to recommend their stocks. While this activity is not actually illegal, U.S. federal securities laws do require the newsletters to disclose that they where paid to proffer this advice. Such laws are in place because, when the writers are recommending any product, their opinion might be swayed by the fact that compensation is being provided to them for that opinion. Despite the laws, many online investment newsletters do not disclose that they are actually being paid to recommend certain stocks. This situation means that the "unbiased" stock advice you are getting could actually be quite biased. Rather than getting the advice of an unbiased expert, you may be getting a paid advertisement. This pitfall is one of the most common traps of online investment advice and is more common than the blatant investment offer frauds.

Sometimes these online stock bulletins can be part of a wider scheme, often called a ***pump and dump***. A classic pump and dump is rather simple. The con artist takes a stock that is virtually worthless and purchases large amounts of the stock. She then artificially inflates ("pumps") its value in one or more ways (Fraud Bureau, 1999). One common method is to begin circulating rumors on various Internet bulletin boards and chat rooms that the stock is about to go up significantly. The trickster often suggests that the company has some new innovative product due out in the next few weeks. Another method is to simply push the stock on as many people as possible. The more people vying to buy a stock, the higher its price will rise. If both methods are combined, it is possible to take a worthless stock and temporarily double or triple its value. The perpetrator of the fraud has already purchased large volumes of the stock, at a very low price, before executing this scheme. When the stock goes as high as she thinks it can, she then "dumps" her stock and takes the money. In a short time, and certainly by the time the companies' next quarterly earnings report is released, the stock returns to its real value. This sort of scheme has been very popular in the past several decades. One should always be wary of such "insider" information. If a person is aware that Company X is about to release an innovative new product that will drive her stock value up, why would she share that information with total strangers?

The U.S. Securities and Exchange Commission (2000) lists several tips for avoiding such scams.

- Consider the source. If you are not well versed in the market, make sure you accept advice only from well-known and reputable stock analysts.
- Independently verify claims. Do not simply accept someone else's word about anything.
- Research. Read up on the company, the claims about the company, its stock history, and so forth.
- Beware of high-pressure tactics. Legitimate stock traders do not pressure customers into buying. They help customers pick stocks that customers want. If you are being pressured, that is an indication of potential problems.
- Be skeptical. A healthy dose of skepticism can save you a lot of money. Or, as the saying goes, "If it's too good to be true, it probably isn't true."

The truth is that these types of fraud depend on the greed of the victim. It is not my intent to blame victims of fraud, but it is important to realize that, if you allow avarice to do your thinking for you, you are a prime candidate to be a victim of fraud. Your 401K or IRA may not earn you exorbitant wealth overnight, but they are steady and relatively safe (no investment is completely safe). If you are seeking ways to make large sums of money with minimal time and effort, then you are an ideal target for perpetrators of fraud.

Auction Frauds

Online auctions, such as eBay, can be a wonderful way to find merchandise at very good prices. Many people routinely use such auctions to purchase goods. However, any auction site can be fraught with peril. Will you actually get the merchandise you ordered? Will it be "as advertised?" Most online auctions are legitimate and most auction Web sites take precautions to limit fraud on their Web site, but problems still occur. In fact, the U.S. Federal Trade Commission (FTC) lists the following four categories of online auction fraud (U.S. Federal Trade Commission, 2004):

- Failure to send the merchandise
- Sending something of lesser value than advertised
- Failure to deliver in a timely manner
- Failure to disclose all relevant information about a product or terms of the sale

IN PRACTICE: Handling Online Investments

Practically speaking, the recommended way to handle online investments is to only participate in them if you initiated the discussion with a reputable broker. This rule would mean you would never respond to (or participate in) any investment offer that was sent to you via e-mail, online ads, and so forth. You would only participate in investments that you initiated with well-known brokers. Usually, such brokers are from traditional investment firms with long-standing reputations that now simply offer their services online.

The first category, failure to deliver the merchandise, is the most clear-cut case of fraud and is fairly simple. Once you have paid for an item, no item arrives. The seller simply keeps your money. In organized fraud, the seller will simultaneously advertise several items for sale, collect money on all the auctions, and then disappear. If he has planned this well, the entire process was done with fake identification, using a rented mailbox and anonymous e-mail service. The person then walks away with the proceeds of the scam.

The second category of fraud, delivering an item of lesser value than the one advertised, can become a gray area. In some cases, it is outright fraud. The seller advertises something about the product that simply is not true. For example, the seller might advertise a signed copy of the first printing of a famous author's book, but then instead ships you a fourth printing with either no autograph or one that is unverified. However, in other cases of this type of problem, it can simply be that the seller is overzealous or frankly mistaken. The seller might claim his baseball was signed by a famous athlete, but not be aware himself that the autograph is a fraud.

This problem is closely related to the fourth item on the FTC list, failure to disclose all relevant facts about the item. For example, a book might be an authentic first printing and autographed, but be in such poor physical condition as to render it worthless. This fact may or may not be mentioned in advance by the seller. Failure to be forthcoming with all relevant facts about a particular item might be the result of outright fraud or simply the seller's ignorance.

The FTC also lists failure to deliver the product on time as a form of fraud. It is unclear whether this is considered fraud in many cases or merely woefully inadequate customer service.

The FTC also lists three other areas of bidding fraud that are growing in popularity on the Internet (U.S. Federal Trade Commission, 2004):

FYI: Phishing

Phishing is a growing problem that is plaguing Internet users. Phishing is the process of sending e-mails that claim to be from some legitimate source in an attempt to get the receiver to divulge sensitive data—in essence, electronic social engineering. This might include an e-mail that claims to be from your credit card company and is requesting your account details. If you do provide the information, it may be used to make purchases with your account or as part of an identity theft scam.

In 2003, there was a widespread phishing scam in which users were sent e-mails purporting to be from eBay claiming that the user's account was about to be suspended unless he clicked on the provided link and updated the credit card information. When users clicked on the link, they were taken to a spoofed site that was meant to look like eBay. All the information they entered was taken by the criminals perpetrating the scam.

- *Shill bidding,* whereby fraudulent sellers (or their "shills") bid on the seller's items to drive up the price.
- *Bid shielding,* whereby fraudulent buyers submit very high bids to discourage other bidders from competing for the same item. The fake buyers then retract their bids so that people they know can get the item at a lower price.
- *Bid siphoning,* whereby con artists lure bidders off legitimate auction sites by offering to sell the "same" item at a lower price. Their intent is to trick consumers into sending money without proffering the item. By going off-site, buyers lose any protections the original site may provide such as insurance, feedback forms, or guarantees.

All of these tactics have a common aim: to subvert the normal auction process. The normal auction process is an ideal blend of capitalism and democracy. Everyone has an equal chance to obtain the product in question if they are willing to outbid the other shoppers. The buyers themselves set the price of the product based on the value they perceive the product to have. Auctions are an excellent vehicle for commerce; however, unscrupulous individuals will always attempt to subvert the process for their own goals.

Shill Bidding ***Shill bidding*** is probably the most common of these three auction frauds. It is not very complex. If the perpetrator is selling an item at an auction site, she will also create several fake identities. She will use these fake identities to bid on the item and thus drive up the price. It is very difficult to detect whether such a scheme is in operation. However, a simple rule of thumb on auctions is to decide what your maximum price is before you start bidding. Then, under no circumstances, do you exceed that price by even one penny.

Bid Shielding While shill bidding may be difficult to combat, ***bid shielding*** can be addressed fairly easily by the proprietors of the auction site. Many major auction sites, such as eBay, have taken steps to prevent bid shielding. The most obvious is to revoke bidding privileges for bidders who back out after they have won an auction. If a person puts in a very high bid to keep others away and then at the last moment retracts his bid, he might lose his ability to return to that auction site.

Bid Siphoning ***Bid siphoning*** is a less common practice. In this scheme, the perpetrator places a legitimate item up for bid on an auction site. Yet, in the ad for that item, she provides links to sites that are not part of the auction site. The unwary buyer who follows these links might find himself on an alternative site that is a "setup" to perpetrate some sort of fraud.

Identity Theft

Identity theft is a growing problem—and a very troubling one. The concept is rather simple, although the process can be complex and the consequences for the victim can be quite severe. The idea is simply for one person to take on the identity of another. This con game is usually attempted to make purchases. However, identity theft can be done for other reasons, such as obtaining credit cards or even driver's licenses in the victim's name.

If the perpetrator obtains a credit card in someone else's name, he can then purchase products. The victim of this fraud is left with debts she was not aware of and did not authorize.

Getting a driver's license in the victim's name might be an attempt to shield the perpetrator from the consequences of his own poor driving record. For example, a person may have a very bad driving record and possibly have warrants out for immediate arrest. Should the person be stopped by law enforcement officers, he can then show the fake license. When the police officer checks the license, it is legitimate and has no outstanding warrants. However, the ticket the criminal receives will be going on your driving record because it is your information on the driver's license. It is also unlikely that the perpetrator of that fraud will actually pay the ticket, so at some point you—whose identity was stolen—will receive notification that your license has been revoked for failure to pay a ticket. Unless you can then prove, with witnesses, that you were not at the location at the time the ticket was given, you may have no recourse but to pay the ticket in order to re-establish your driving privileges.

The U.S. Department of Justice defines identity theft in this manner (U.S. Department of Justice, 2000):

> "*Identity theft* and *identity fraud* are terms used to refer to all types of crime in which someone wrongfully obtains and uses another person's personal data in some way that involves fraud or deception, typically for economic gain."

The advent of the Internet has made the process of stealing a person's identity even easier than previously. Many states now have court and motor vehicle records online. In some states, a person's social security number is used for the driver's license number. Therefore, if a criminal obtains a person's social security number, she can look up that person's driving record, perhaps get a duplicate of the person's license, find out about any court records concerning that person, and, on some Web sites, even run the person's credit history. Using the Internet as an investigative tool will be examined later in this book. Like any tool, it can be used for benign or malevolent purposes. The same tools you can use to do a background check on a prospective employee can be used to find out enough information to forge someone else's identity.

IN PRACTICE: Credit Card Security

There is a new method for conducting identity theft using a handheld scanner. A ring of criminals in the Dallas-Fort Worth area were working with waiters in restaurants. When the waiter took a patron's credit or debit card to pay for the meal, the waiter used a small handheld device (kept hidden in a pocket) to scan the patron's credit card information. The waiter gave this information to the identity theft ring, which could either make online purchases or use that information to produce fake credit cards with the patron's name and account data. This fraud is a new twist on identity theft. The only way to avoid this sort of danger is to never use your credit or debit card unless it is going to be processed right there in front of you. Do not let someone take your card out of your sight to process it.

Most people trust a waiter or waitress with important credit card information without even giving it a thought. But many of those same people are leery of using their credit card numbers online. In truth, if the site uses encryption and your Web protocol has changed to https: you are just as safe on the Web as if you watched the credit card processed in front of you at the restaurant.

Cyber Stalking

Stalking in general has received a great deal of attention in the past few years. The primary reason for this awareness is that stalking has often been a prelude to violent acts, including sexual assault and homicide. For this reason, many states have passed a variety of anti-stalking laws. However, this stalking problem has recently been expanded into cyberspace. What is ***cyber stalking***? It is using the Internet to harass another person or, as the U.S. Department of Justice puts it (U.S. Department of Justice, 2003):

> "Although there is no universally accepted definition of *cyber stalking*, the term is used in this report to refer to the use of the Internet, e-mail, or other electronic communications devices to stalk another person. Stalking generally involves harassing or threatening behavior that an individual engages in repeatedly, such as following a person, appearing at a person's home or place of business, making harassing phone calls, leaving written messages or objects, or vandalizing a person's property. Most stalking laws require that the perpetrator make a credible threat of violence against the victim; others include threats against the victim's immediate family; and still others require only that the alleged stalker's course of conduct constitute an implied threat. While some conduct involving annoying or menacing behavior might fall short of illegal stalking, such behavior may be a prelude to stalking and violence and should be treated seriously."

If someone uses the Internet to harass, threaten, or intimidate another person, then the perpetrator is guilty of cyber stalking. The most obvious example is the sending of threatening e-mail. The guidelines on what is considered "threatening" can vary a great deal from jurisdiction to jurisdiction. But a good rule of thumb is that, if the e-mail's content would be considered threatening in normal speech, then it will probably be considered a threat if sent electronically. *Black's Law Dictionary* (2000) defines *harassment* as:

> "A course of conduct directed at a specific person that causes substantial emotional distress in such person and serves no legitimate purpose."

> "Words, gestures, and actions that tend to annoy, alarm, and abuse (verbally) another person."

Other examples of cyber stalking are less clear. If you request that someone quit e-mailing you, yet he continues to do so, is that a crime? Unfortunately, there is no clear answer on that issue. The truth is that it may or may not be considered a crime depending on such factors as the content of the e-mails, the frequency, and the prior relationship between you and the sender, as well as your jurisdiction. Usually, law enforcement officials will need some credible threat of harm in order to pursue harassment complaints. In simple terms, this situation means that if you are in an anonymous chat room and someone utters some obscenity, that act probably will not be considered harassment. However, if you receive specific threats via e-mail, those threats would probably be considered harassment.

The following three cases from a 1999 report by the Department of Justice illustrate episodes of cyber stalking (U.S. Department of Justice, 2003). Examining the facts in these cases might help you get an idea of what legally constitutes cyber stalking.

- In the first successful prosecution under California's new cyber stalking law, prosecutors in the Los Angeles District Attorney's Office obtained a guilty plea from a 50-year-old former security guard who used the Internet to solicit the rape of a woman who rejected his romantic advances. The defendant terrorized his 28-year-old victim by impersonating her in various Internet chat rooms and online bulletin boards, where he posted, along with her telephone number and address, messages that she fantasized being raped. On at least six occasions, sometimes in the middle of the night, men knocked on the woman's door saying they wanted to rape her. The former security guard pleaded guilty in April 1999 to one count of stalking and three counts of solicitation of sexual assault. He faces up to six years in prison.
- A local prosecutor's office in Massachusetts charged a man who, using anonymous re-mailers (a computer service which privatizes your e-mail), allegedly engaged in a systematic pattern of harassment of a co-worker that culminated in an attempt to extort sexual favors from the victim under threat of disclosing past sexual activities to the victim's new husband.
- An honors graduate from the University of San Diego terrorized five female university students over the Internet for more than a year. The victims received hundreds of violent and threatening e-mails, sometimes receiving four or five messages a day. The graduate student, who has entered a guilty plea and faces up to six years in prison, told police he committed the crimes because he thought the women were laughing at him and causing others to ridicule him. In fact, the victims had never met him.

The entire 1999 report, of which these three cases were a small part, is available at the Department of Justice Web site (**www.usdoj.gov/criminal/cybercrime/cyberstalking.htm**). A portion of this report is shown in Figure 8.2.

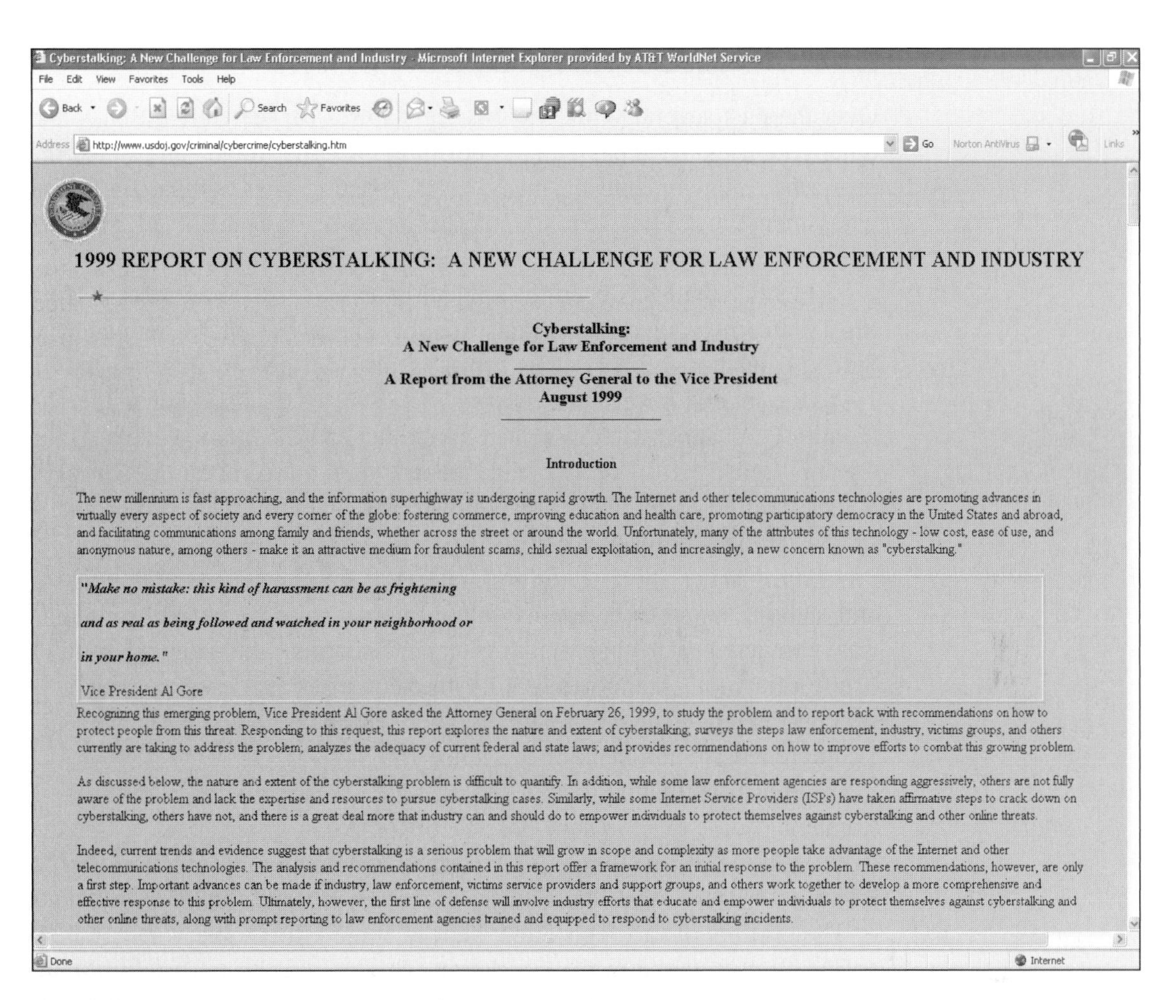

Cyberstalking: A New Challenge for Law Enforcement and Industry - Microsoft Internet Explorer provided by AT&T WorldNet Service

http://www.usdoj.gov/criminal/cybercrime/cyberstalking.htm

1999 REPORT ON CYBERSTALKING: A NEW CHALLENGE FOR LAW ENFORCEMENT AND INDUSTRY

Cyberstalking:
A New Challenge for Law Enforcement and Industry

A Report from the Attorney General to the Vice President
August 1999

Introduction

The new millennium is fast approaching, and the information superhighway is undergoing rapid growth. The Internet and other telecommunications technologies are promoting advances in virtually every aspect of society and every corner of the globe: fostering commerce, improving education and health care, promoting participatory democracy in the United States and abroad, and facilitating communications among family and friends, whether across the street or around the world. Unfortunately, many of the attributes of this technology - low cost, ease of use, and anonymous nature, among others - make it an attractive medium for fraudulent scams, child sexual exploitation, and increasingly, a new concern known as "cyberstalking."

"Make no mistake: this kind of harassment can be as frightening and as real as being followed and watched in your neighborhood or in your home."

Vice President Al Gore

Recognizing this emerging problem, Vice President Al Gore asked the Attorney General on February 26, 1999, to study the problem and to report back with recommendations on how to protect people from this threat. Responding to this request, this report explores the nature and extent of cyberstalking; surveys the steps law enforcement, industry, victims groups, and others currently are taking to address the problem; analyzes the adequacy of current federal and state laws; and provides recommendations on how to improve efforts to combat this growing problem.

As discussed below, the nature and extent of the cyberstalking problem is difficult to quantify. In addition, while some law enforcement agencies are responding aggressively, others are not fully aware of the problem and lack the expertise and resources to pursue cyberstalking cases. Similarly, while some Internet Service Providers (ISPs) have taken affirmative steps to crack down on cyberstalking, others have not, and there is a great deal more that industry can and should do to empower individuals to protect themselves against cyberstalking and other online threats.

Indeed, current trends and evidence suggest that cyberstalking is a serious problem that will grow in scope and complexity as more people take advantage of the Internet and other telecommunications technologies. The analysis and recommendations contained in this report offer a framework for an initial response to the problem. These recommendations, however, are only a first step. Important advances can be made if industry, law enforcement, victims service providers and support groups, and others work together to develop a more comprehensive and effective response to this problem. Ultimately, however, the first line of defense will involve industry efforts that educate and empower individuals to protect themselves against cyberstalking and other online threats, along with prompt reporting to law enforcement agencies trained and equipped to respond to cyberstalking incidents.

FIGURE 8.2 A 1999 report from the Attorney General to the Vice President.

Clearly, using the Internet to harass people is just as serious a crime as harassing them in person. This problem has even extended to workplace issues. For example, court cases have upheld that unwanted e-mail pornography can be construed as sexual harassment. If an employee complains about unwanted e-mail, the employer has a duty to at least attempt to ameliorate the situation. This attempt can be as simple as installing a very inexpensive spam blocker (software that tries to limit or eradicate unwanted e-mail). However, if the employer takes no steps whatsoever to correct the problem, that reticence may be seen by a court as contributing to a hostile work environment.

Laws Concerning Cyber Crime

Over the past several years, various legislatures (in the United States and other countries) have passed laws defining "Internet fraud" and stated the proscribed punishments. In many cases, existing laws against fraud and harassment are applicable to the Internet as well; however, some legislators felt that cyber crime warranted its own distinct legislation.

Identity theft has been the subject of various state and federal laws. Most states now have laws against identity theft (National Conference of State Legislatures, 2004). This crime is also covered by federal law. In 1998, the federal government passed 18 U.S.C. 1028, also known as "The Identity Theft and Assumption Deterrence Act of 1998" (U.S. Federal Trade Commission, 1998). This law made identity theft a federal crime. Throughout the United States, federal law now covers identity theft and, in many states, identity theft is also covered by state law.

Many states specifically prohibit cyber stalking; in general, existing anti-stalking laws can be applied to the Internet. In 2001, a California man was convicted of cyber stalking under existing anti-stalking statutes (California Youth Authority, 2000). Other countries also have existing anti-stalking laws that can be applied to cyber stalking as well. Canada has had a comprehensive anti-stalking law since 1993.

One nation that has decided to crack down hard on cyber criminals is Romania. Some experts have described Romanian cyber crime law as the strictest in the world (Romanian Information Technology Initiative, 2002). However, what is most interesting about Romanian law is how specific it is. The crafters of this legislation went to some effort to very specifically define all terms used in the legislation. This specificity is very important in order to avoid defendants finding loopholes in laws. Unfortunately, the Romanian government only took such measures after media sources around the world identified their country as a "Citadel for Cyber Crime." The country's reactive approach to cyber crime is probably not the best solution.

Susan Brenner, a renowned cyber crime scholar and a Professor of Law at the University of Dayton School of Law, has an entire Web site devoted to cyber crime. This site (**www.cybercrimes.net**), shown in Figure 8.3, has some rather extensive links on cyber crime, cyber stalking, and other Internet-based crimes. As the twenty-first century moves forward, one can expect to see more law schools with courses dedicated to cyber crime. An interesting phenomenon has begun in the past few years: the emergence of attorneys who specialize in cyber crime cases. The fact that lawyers specialize in this area of law is a strong indicator that Internet crime is becoming a growing problem in modern society.

FIGURE 8.3 Brenner's cyber crime Web site.

Protecting Yourself against Cyber Crime

Now that you know about various frauds that are prevalent on the Internet and have looked at the relevant laws, you might be wondering what you can do to protect yourself. There are several steps you can take to minimize the chances of being the victim of Internet crime. There are also some clear guidelines on how you should handle the situation if should you become a victim.

Protecting Against Investment Fraud

To protect yourself against investment fraud, follow these guidelines:

- Only invest with well-known, reputable brokers.
- If it sounds too good to be true, then avoid it.
- Ask yourself why this person is informing you of this great investment deal. Why would a complete stranger decide to share some incredible investment opportunity with you?
- Remember that even legitimate investment involves risk, so never invest money that you cannot afford to lose.

Protecting Against Auction Fraud

Dealing with auction fraud involves a different set of precautions. Here are four good ideas.

- Only use reputable auction sites. The most well-known site is eBay, but any widely known, reputable site will be a safer gamble. Such auction sites tend to take precautions to prevent fraud and abuse.
- If it sounds too good to be true, do not bid.
- Some sites actually allow you to read feedback that other buyers have provided on a given seller. Read the feedback and only work with reputable sellers.
- When possible, use a separate credit card with a low limit for online auctions. In that way, your liability is limited should your credit card be compromised. Using your debit card is simply inviting trouble.

Online auctions can be a very good way to obtain valuable merchandise at low prices. However, one must exercise some degree of caution when using these services.

Protecting Against Identity Theft

When the issue is identity theft, your steps are clear:

- Do not provide your personal information to anyone if it is not absolutely necessary. This rule means that, when communicating on the Internet with anyone you do not personally know, do not reveal anything about yourself—not your age, occupation, or real name. Reveal nothing.
- Destroy documents that have personal information on them. If you simply throw away bank statements and credit card bills, then someone rummaging through your trash can get a great deal of personal data. You can obtain a paper shredder from an office supply store or many retail department stores for less than $20. Shred these documents before disposing of them. This rule may not seem related to computer security, but information gathered through nontechnical means can be used in conjunction with the Internet to perpetrate identity theft.
- Check your credit frequently. Many Web sites, including **www.qspace.com**, allow you to check your credit and even get your beacon score for a nominal fee. It is good practice to check your credit twice per year. If you see any items you did not authorize, that is a clear indication that you might be a victim of identity theft.
- If your state has online driving records, then check yours once per year. If you see driving infractions that you did not commit, this evidence is a clear sign that your identity is being used by someone else. Chapter 11 will explore, in detail, how to obtain such records online, often for less than $5.

Another part of protecting your identity is protecting your privacy in general. That task means preventing others from gaining information about you that you do not explicitly provide them. That preventative method includes keeping Web sites from gathering information about you without your knowledge. Many Web sites store information about you and your visit to their site in small files called cookies. These cookie files are stored on your machine. The problem with cookies is that any Web site can read any cookie on your machine, even ones that the Web site you are currently visiting did not create. Thus, if you visit one Web site and it stores items, such as your name, the site you visited, and the time you where there, then another Web site could potentially read that cookie and know where you have been on the Internet. One of the best ways to stop cookies you do not want is anti-spyware software. You can also change your Internet settings to help reduce exposures to your privacy.

IN PRACTICE: Securing Browser Settings for Microsoft Internet Explorer

1. Open Microsoft Internet Explorer.
2. Select Tools on the menu bar, and then select Internet Options. You will see a screen much like the one shown in Figure 8.4.

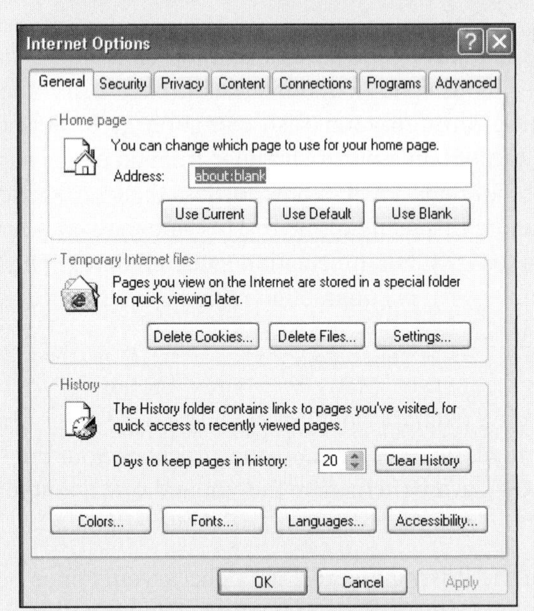

FIGURE 8.4 Internet Explorer options.

3. Select the Privacy tab. You will see the screen shown in Figure 8.5.

FIGURE 8.5 Internet Explorer privacy options.

4. Notice the sliding bar on the left that lets you select various levels of general protection against cookies. Select medium high as your level.
5. Note the Advanced button in the lower half of the screen. This button allows you to block or allow individual Web sites from creating cookies on your computer's hard drive. Altering cookie settings on your machine is just one part of protecting your privacy, but it is an important part.
6. Click OK to close the Advanced Privacy Settings dialog box if necessary and then click OK to close the Internet Options dialog box.

IN PRACTICE: Securing Browser Settings for Netscape Navigator

1. Open Netscape Navigator.
2. Select Edit on the menu bar and then select Preferences. You will see the screen shown in Figure 8.6.

FIGURE 8.6 Netscape preferences.

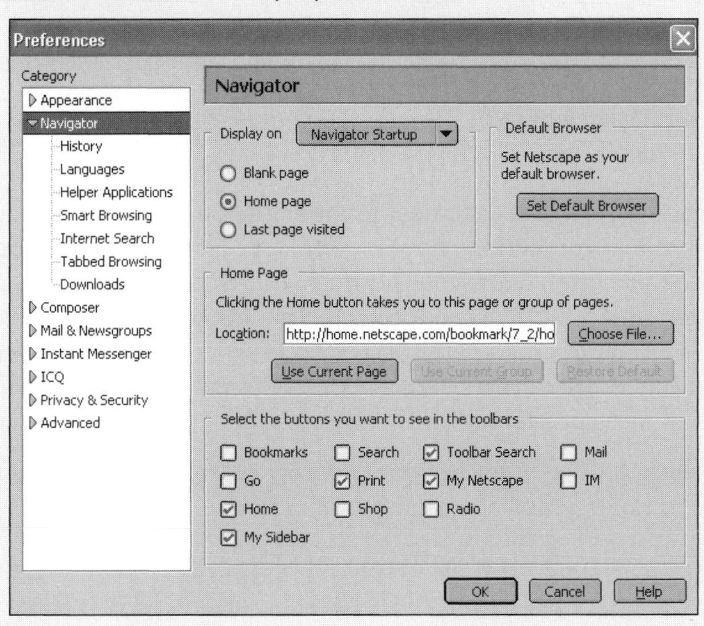

CONTINUED ON NEXT PAGE

CONTINUED

3. Notice the Privacy and Security option near the bottom of the Category panel. Double-click on that option. It will expand, giving you several options.
4. Select cookies from the expanded options. The panel on the right side of the dialog box will appear as shown in Figure 8.7.

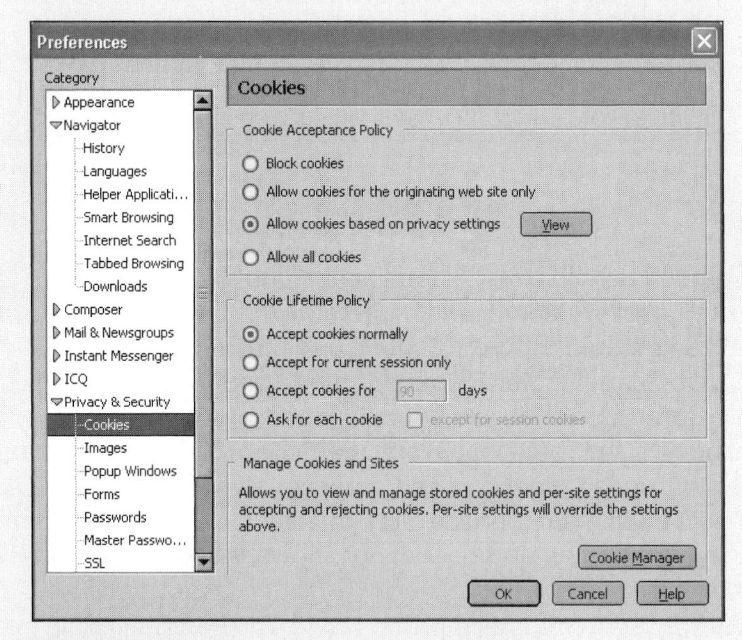

FIGURE 8.7 Netscape cookie settings.

You can use the Cookie Manager button to access a dialog box that lets you choose how to handle cookies as well as delete all cookies currently on your hard drive. If you use Netscape, it is recommended that you periodically visit this screen and delete all cookies on your computer. It is a good idea to limit the life of cookies to ten days or less. That limit significantly reduces the likelihood of another site getting much data about your Internet travels.

5. Click on the View button in order to fine-tune your settings. The Privacy Settings dialog box is shown in Figure 8.8.

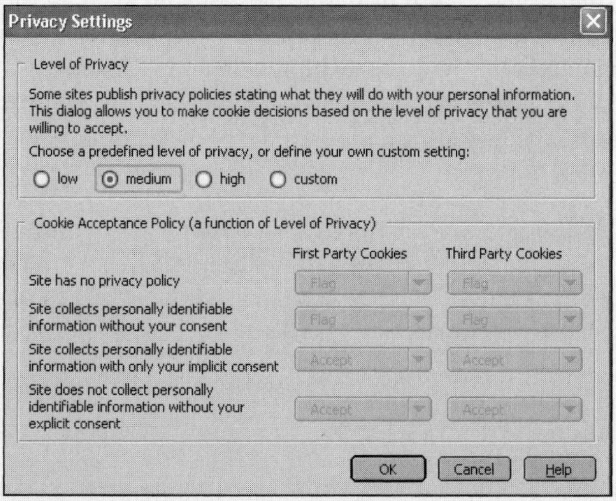

FIGURE 8.8 Netscape Privacy Settings.

You should select high security or custom. If you select custom, you can then choose specifically how to handle first-party and third-party cookies. It is safest to only allow first-party cookies. Third-party cookies are notorious for behaving in ways that violate user privacy. These simple steps can go a long way toward helping to secure your privacy.

Protecting Against Cyber Stalking

Protecting yourself from online harassment also has its own guidelines:

- If you use chat rooms, discussion boards, and so forth, do not use your real name. Set up a separate e-mail account with an anonymous service, such as Yahoo or Hotmail. Use that account and a fake name online. This strategy makes it very hard for an online stalker to trace a path back to you personally.

FYI: Netscape Navigator

It is important that anyone in the security business be familiar with alternative software and not simply be familiar with one vendor in a given product line. If you do not have Netscape Navigator, it can be downloaded for free from **channels.netscape.com/ns/browsers/default.jsp.**

8

- If you are the victim of online harassment, keep all of the e-mails in both digital and printed format. Use some of the investigative techniques that will be explored later in Chapter 11 to try and identify the perpetrator. If you are successful, you can then take the e-mails and information on the perpetrator to law enforcement officials.
- Do not, in any case, ignore cyber stalking. According to the Working to Halt Online Abuse Web site (2004) (**www.haltabuse.org**) shown in Figure 8.9, 19% of cyber stalking cases escalate to stalking in the real world.

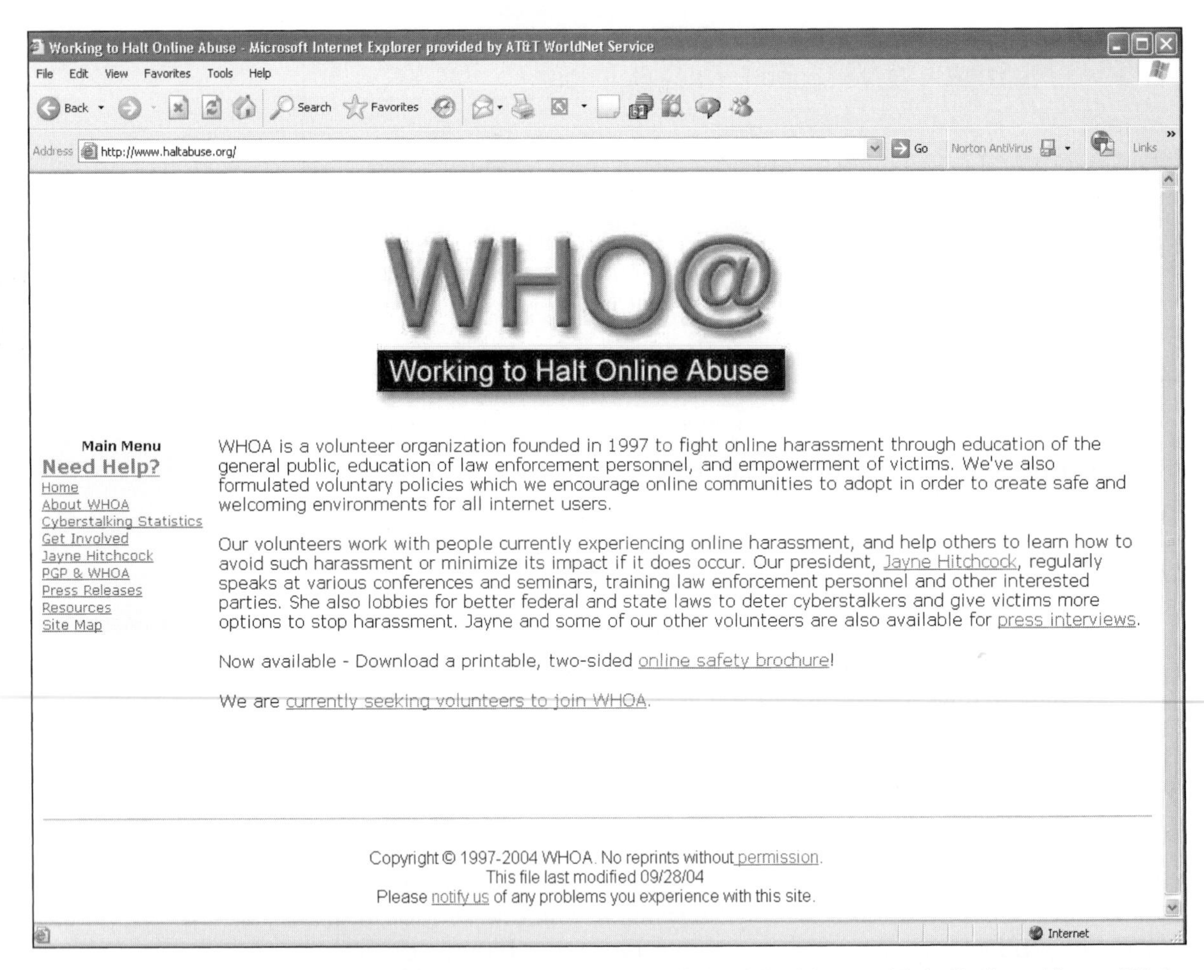

FIGURE 8.9 Home page of the Working to Halt Online Abuse Web site.

Summary

Clearly, fraud and identity theft are very real and growing problems. It is not the intent of this chapter or this book to make you frightened about using the Internet. Millions of people routinely use the Internet for entertainment, commerce, and informational purposes. You simply need to exercise some caution when using the Internet.

In our modern age of instant access to information and online purchasing, it is critical that all people take steps to protect themselves against this problem. Individuals must work to protect their privacy using steps outlined in this chapter. In the exercises at the end of this chapter, you will have a chance to try out various protection methods.

Test Your Skills

MULTIPLE CHOICE QUESTIONS

1. A common Internet investment fraud is known as the:
   A. Nigerian Fraud
   B. Manhattan Fraud
   C. pump and dump
   D. bait and switch

2. What is the most likely problem with unsolicited investment advice?
   A. You might not earn as much as claimed.
   B. The advice might not be truly unbiased.
   C. The advice might not be from a legitimate firm.
   D. You might lose money.

3. Artificially inflating a stock in order to sell it at a higher value is referred to as:
   A. bait and switch
   B. the Nigerian Fraud
   C. pump and dump
   D. the Wall Street Fraud

4. What are the four categories of auction fraud?
   A. failure to send, failure to disclose, sending to wrong address, failure to deliver in a timely manner
   B. failure to send, failure to disclose, sending something of lesser value, failure to deliver in a timely manner
   C. failure to disclose, sending something of greater value, failure to send, failure to deliver in a timely manner
   D. failure to disclose, sending something of lesser value, failure to send, sending something of greater value

5. A seller bidding on her own item to drive up the price is referred to as:
   A. bid siphoning
   B. bid shielding
   C. shill bidding
   D. ghost bidding

6. Submitting a fake but very high bid to deter other bidders is referred to as:
   A. bid siphoning
   B. bid shielding
   C. shill bidding
   D. ghost bidding

7. Identity theft is most often attempted in order to accomplish what goal?
   A. make illegal purchases
   B. discredit the victim
   C. avoid criminal prosecution
   D. invade privacy

8. According to the U.S. Department of Justice, identity theft is generally motivated by:
   A. malicious intent
   B. personal hostility toward the victim
   C. economic gain
   D. thrill-seeking

9. Why is cyber stalking a serious crime?
   A. It is frightening to the victim.
   B. It can be a prelude to violent crime.
   C. It is using interstate communication.
   D. It can be a prelude to identity theft.

10. What is cyber stalking?
    A. any use of the Internet to send or post threats
    B. any use of electronic communications to stalk a person
    C. only use of e-mail to send threats
    D. only use of e-mail to stalk a person

11. What will law enforcement officials usually require of the victim in order to pursue harassment allegations?
    A. verifiable threat of death or serious injury
    B. credible threat of death or serious injury
    C. verifiable threat of harm
    D. credible threat of harm

12. What must exist in order for cyber stalking to be illegal in a state or territory?
    A. specific laws against cyber stalking in that state or territory
    B. specific laws against cyber stalking in that nation
    C. nothing; existing stalking laws can apply
    D. nothing; existing international cyber stalking laws apply

13. What is the top rule for avoiding Internet fraud?
    A. If it seems too good to be true, it probably is.
    B. Never use your bank account numbers.
    C. Only work with people who have verifiable e-mail addresses.
    D. Do not invest in foreign deals.

14. Which of the following is not one of the Security and Exchange Commission's tips for avoiding investment fraud?
    A. Do not invest online.
    B. Consider the source of the offer.
    C. Always be skeptical.
    D. Always research the investment.

15. Which of the following is not an efficient method of protecting yourself from auction fraud?
    A. Only use auctions for inexpensive items.
    B. Only use reputable auction sites.
    C. Only work with well-rated sellers.
    D. Only bid on items that seem realistic.
16. What is the first step in protecting yourself from identity theft?
    A. Never provide any personal data about yourself unless absolutely necessary.
    B. Routinely check your records for signs of identity theft.
    C. Never use your real name on the Internet.
    D. Routinely check for spyware on your computer.
17. Why is it useful to have a separate credit card dedicated to online purchases?
    A. If the credit card number is used illegally, you will limit your financial liability.
    B. You can keep better track of your auction activities.
    C. If you are defrauded, you can possibly get the credit card company to handle the problem.
    D. You can easily cancel that single card if you need to do so.
18. What can you do on your local computer to protect your privacy?
    A. install a virus scanner
    B. install a firewall
    C. set your browser's security settings
    D. set your computer's filter settings
19. What percentage of cyber stalking cases escalates to real-world violence?
    A. less than 1%
    B. 25%
    C. 90% or more
    D. approximately 19%
20. What is the top way to protect yourself from cyber stalking?
    A. Do not use your real identity online.
    B. Always use a firewall.
    C. Always use a virus scanner.
    D. Do not give out e-mail addresses.

EXERCISES

Exercise 8.1: Setting Web Browser Privacy in Internet Explorer

This exercise gives you practice in setting Web browser privacy. You may also want to review the description in the chapter of this process where you can see detail and screen images.

1. Select Tools from the menu bar in Internet Explorer.
2. Choose Internet Options.
3. Select the Privacy tab.
4. Click the Advanced button.
5. Set your browser to accept first-party cookies; to prompt for third-party cookies; and to accept session cookies.
6. Click OK twice to close the dialog boxes. Close the browser.

Exercise 8.2: Setting Web Browser Privacy in Netscape Navigator

This exercise provides practice in setting the Web browser privacy options in Netscape Navigator. You may also want to review the description in the chapter of this process where you can see detail and screen images.

1. Select Edit from the menu bar in Netscape Navigator
2. Choose Preferences.
3. Double-click Privacy and Security—the second option from the bottom—to expand the list of options beneath it.
4. Select Cookies.
5. Choose *Allow cookies for originating web site only.*
6. Choose *Accept cookies for* and then limit cookie lifetime to two days. This limit means that any cookie on your machine will be deleted after two days.

   (Note that Internet Explorer does not provide a mechanism for setting the lifetime of a cookie.)
7. Click OK to close the Preferences dialog box. Close the browser.

Exercise 8.3: Using an Alternative Web Browser

1. Download the Mozilla browser from **www.mozilla.org**.

Caution

Appropriate Chat Room Behavior

The purpose of this exercise is merely to show you how easy it is for someone to learn about another person from his online activities. In no case would you consider using this information to invade another person's privacy or to harass or embarrass another person.

FYI: Settings in Mozilla

You should note that the newer versions of Mozilla (specifically Firefox) do not have menus like Netscape. To alter your settings in this browser or others, you may have to use the Help system to learn more or explore the options available.

2. Locate the settings for cookies and privacy in this browser. Use Help if necessary.
3. Set your Mozilla browser's cookie settings identical to how you set your Navigator settings.
4. Exit the settings dialog boxes.
5. Open the browser and then enter an URL for a Web site.
6. Answer these questions: Do you see any messages about cookies being set? Do you notice any other differences?
7. Close the browser.

Exercise 8.4: Tracking in a Chat Room

The purpose of this exercise is to grasp how easy it is to obtain personal information about someone from his online activities.

1. Enter any chat room. If you are not familiar with chat rooms or have not used them before, any of the following Web sites would make a good starting point for you:

   chat.yahoo.com/?myHome

   www.aol.com/community/chat/allchats.html

   www.javachatrooms.net/

   www.chathouse.com/

2. Note those people who use their real names.
3. Note those people who reveal personal details.
4. Compile as much information as you can about those posting in the chat room.

Exercise 8.5: Using Anti-Spyware

You should be aware that there are many products on the Web that help you to prevent spyware and cookies from being installed on your computer. One of the easiest to use is Spy Sweeper, which is available at **www.Webroot.com**.

1. Download and install the evaluation version of Spy Sweeper. (Complete instructions are available on the Web.)
2. Scan your computer for spyware and cookies. This review may take several minutes
3. Note what is found on your machine.
4. Delete the spyware and cookies.

PROJECTS

Project 8.1: Finding out About Cyber Stalking and the Law

1. Using the Web or other resources, find out what your state, country, or province's laws are regarding cyber stalking.
2. Write a brief essay describing those laws and what they mean. You may select to do a quick summary of several laws or a more in-depth examination of one law. If you choose the former, list the laws and write a brief paragraph explaining what they cover. If you choose the latter option, discuss the law's authors, why it was written, and possible ramifications of the law.

Project 8.2: Looking for Auction Fraud

Go to any auction site and try to identify whether there are any sellers you feel might be fraudulent. Write a brief essay explaining what indicated to you that the seller may not be dealing honestly.

Project 8.3: Examining Cyber Stalking Case Studies

1. Using the Web, find a case of cyber stalking not mentioned in this chapter. You may find some of the following Web sites helpful:

   www.safetyed.org/help/stalking/

   www.cyber-stalking.net/

   www.technomom.com/harassed/index.shtml

2. Write a brief essay discussing the case you chose. Mention the steps that you think might have helped avoid or ameliorate the situation.

Case Study

Consider the case of an intrepid identity thief named Jane. Her victim is John. Jane encounters John online in a chat room. John is using his real first name, but only his last initial. However, over a series of online conversations, he does reveal personal details about his life (marital status, children, occupation, region he lives in, and so forth). Eventually, Jane offers John some piece of information (i.e., an investment tip) as a trick to get John's e-mail address. Once she gets his e-mail address, an e-mail exchange begins outside of the chat room, wherein Jane purports to give John her real name, thus encouraging John to do the same. Of course, she uses "Mary" as a fictitious name. Jane now has John's real name, city, marital status, occupation, and so on, and John really knows nothing about Jane.

Jane has a number of options she can try, but she begins by using the phone book or the Web to get John's home address and phone number. She can then use this information to obtain John's social security number in a variety of ways. The most straightforward would be to go through John's trash while he was at work. However, if John works in a large company, Jane can just call (or enlist someone to call), claiming to be John's wife or another close relative and wanting to verify personnel data. If Jane is clever enough, she may come away with John's social security number. It is then a trivial matter (as we will see in Chapter 11) to get John's credit report and receive credit cards in his name.

From this scenario, consider the following questions:

1. What reasonable steps could John have taken to protect his identity in the chat room?
2. What steps should any employer take to prevent being unwittingly complicit in identity theft?

Chapter 9

Industrial Espionage in Cyberspace

Chapter Objectives

After reading this chapter and completing the exercises, you will be able to do the following:

- Know what is meant by industrial espionage.
- Understand the low-technology methods used to attempt industrial espionage.
- Be aware of how spyware is used in espionage.
- Know how to protect a system from espionage.

Introduction

When you hear the word ***espionage,*** perhaps you conjure up a number of exciting and glamorous images. Perhaps you have visions of a well-dressed man who drinks martinis, shaken but not stirred, traveling to glamorous locations with equally glamorous travel companions. Or perhaps you envision some exciting covert operation with high-speed car chases and guns blazing in far-away exotic lands. Contrary to popular media portrayals, espionage is often much less exciting than those visions. The ultimate goal of espionage is to obtain information that would not otherwise be made available. Generally, espionage is best done with as little fanfare as possible. Blazing gun battles and glamorous locations tend to be the antithesis of intelligence gathering. Rather, information is the goal. If possible, it is best to obtain that information without the target organization even realizing that its information has been compromised.

Many people assume that such spying is only engaged in by governments, intelligence agencies, and nefarious international organizations, such as Al Queda. While those entities do indeed engage in espionage, they are certainly not the only organizations that do so. The aforementioned organizations desire to acquire information for political and military goals. However, economic goals are also dependent on accurate and often sensitive data. With billions of dollars at stake, private companies can become engaged in industrial espionage as either a target or a perpetrator. What company would not like to know exactly what its competitor is doing? In fact, corporate or economic espionage is on the rise.

Corporate or economic espionage is a growing problem, but it can be difficult to accurately assess just how great a problem it is. Companies that perpetrate corporate espionage do not share the fact that they do it, for obvious reasons. Companies that are victims of such espionage often do not wish to reveal that fact, either. Revealing that their security was compromised could have a negative impact on their stock value. It is also possible, in certain cases, that such a breach of security might open the company to liability claims from customers whose data may have been compromised. For these reasons, companies often are hesitant to disclose any industrial espionage activities. Because you will want to protect yourself and your company, it is important that you learn about espionage methods and protections. In the exercises at the end of this chapter, you will run anti-spyware, key loggers, and screen capture software so you are aware of how they work and, hence, will be cognizant of the risks they pose.

What Is Industrial Espionage?

Industrial espionage is simply the use of spying techniques to find out key information that is of economic value. Such data might include details on a competitor's new project, a list of a competitor's clients, research data, or any information that might give the spying organization an economic advantage. While the rationale for corporate espionage is different from military espionage, corporate techniques are often the same as those methods employed by intelligence agencies and can include electronic monitoring, photocopying files, or compromising a member of the target organization. Not only does economic espionage use the same techniques as intelligence agencies, but it often also uses the same people. There have been a number of incidents in which former intelligence agents are found working in corporate espionage. When such individuals bring their skills and training to the world of corporate espionage, the situation becomes much more difficult for computer security experts.

IN PRACTICE: Leaving with Sensitive Data

While various computer experts and government agencies attempt to estimate the impact and spread of corporate espionage, its very nature makes accurate estimates impossible. Not only do the perpetrators not wish to disclose their crimes, but often the victims will not disclose the event, either. However, anecdotal evidence would suggest that the most common form of espionage is simply an employee who quits, takes a job with another firm, and leaves with sensitive data. In many cases, these employees choose data that is readily available within the company and, as such, the data is considered a "gray area" as to its confidentiality. For example, a salesperson may leave with a printout of contacts and customers so that he can solicit them on behalf of the next employer. It is critical that you have a very well-worded non-disclosure and non-compete agreement with all employees. It is best to solicit the services of an employment attorney to draw up this agreement. Additionally, you might consider limiting an employee's access to data prior to terminating their employment. You should also conduct exit interviews and consider confiscating items such as company phone books which may at first seem insignificant but which could contain data useful to another company.

Information as an Asset

Many people are used to viewing tangible objects as assets, but have difficulty appreciating how mere information can be a real asset. Companies spend billions of dollars every year on research and development. The discovered information is worth at least the amount of resources taken to derive the information, plus the economic gain produced by the information. For example, if a company spends $200,000 researching a process that will in turn generate $1 million in revenue, then that data is worth at least $1.2 million. You can think of this economic gain as a simple equation:

```
VI (value of information) = C (cost to produce)
            + VG (value gained)
```

While some people are not yet fully cognizant of the concept, data does indeed represent a valuable asset. When we speak of the "information age" or our "information-based economy," it is important to realize that these terms are not just buzzwords. Information is a real commodity. It is as much an economic asset as any other item in the company's possession. In fact, it is most often the case that the data residing on a company's computer is worth far more than the hardware and software of the computer system itself. It is certainly the case that the data is much more difficult to replace than the computer hardware and software.

To help you truly appreciate the concept of information as a commodity, consider the process of earning a college degree. You spend four years sitting in various classrooms. You pay a significant amount of money for the privilege of sitting in a room and listening to someone speak at length on some topic. At the end of the four years, the only tangible product you receive is a single piece of paper. Surely you can get a piece of paper for far less cost and with much less effort. What you actually paid for was the information you received. The same is true of the value of many professions. Doctors, attorneys, engineers, consultants, managers, and so forth all are consulted for their expert information. Information itself is the valuable commodity.

The data stored in computer systems has a high value for two reasons. First, there is a great deal of time and effort that goes into creating and analyzing the data. If you spend six months with a team of five people gathering and analyzing information, then that information is worth at least an amount equal to the salaries and benefits of those people for that length of time. Second, data often has intrinsic value, apart from the time and effort spent acquiring those facts. If the facts are about a proprietary process, invention, or algorithm, its value is obvious. However, any data that might provide a competitive edge is inherently valuable. For example, insurance companies frequently employ teams of statisticians and actuaries who use the latest technology to try to predict the risks associated with any given group of potential insureds. The resulting statistical information might be quite valuable to a competing insurance company. Even a customer contact list has a certain inherent value.

Thus, as you work in the computer security field, always keep in mind that any data that might have economic value is an asset to your organization and that such data provides an attractive target for any competitors who may not have ethical inhibitions against using espionage. If your company management thinks that this threat is not real, then they are very much mistaken. Any company is a potential victim of corporate espionage. You should take steps to protect your valuable information—and the first critical step in this process is asset identification.

Asset identification is the process of listing the assets that you believe support your organization. This list should include things that impact direct day-to-day operations as well as those that are tied to your company's services or products. The CERT Web site (**www.cert.org/archive/pdf/tutorial-workbook.pdf**) offers a very useful worksheet that you can use to itemize the assets in your organization. This workbook also offers a number of other useful worksheets for assuring information security

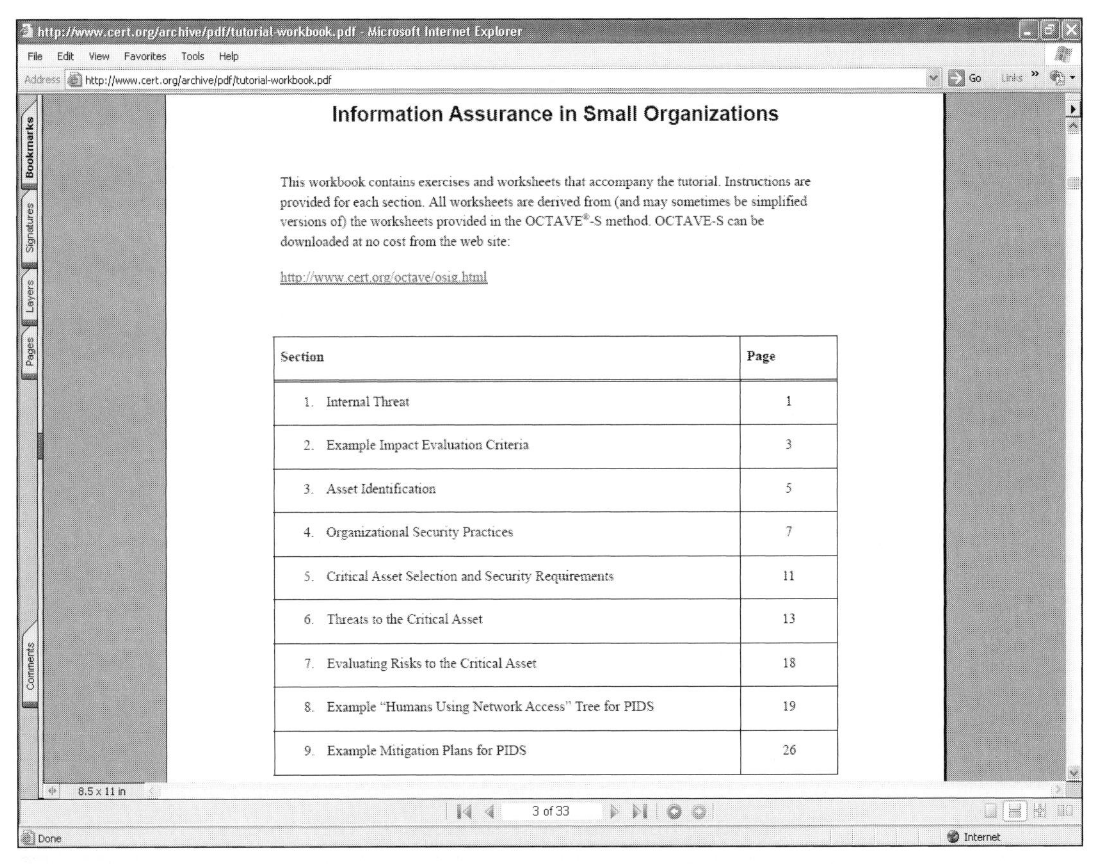
http://www.cert.org/archive/pdf/tutorial-workbook.pdf - Microsoft Internet Explorer

File Edit View Favorites Tools Help

Address http://www.cert.org/archive/pdf/tutorial-workbook.pdf

Information Assurance in Small Organizations

This workbook contains exercises and worksheets that accompany the tutorial. Instructions are provided for each section. All worksheets are derived from (and may sometimes be simplified versions of) the worksheets provided in the OCTAVE®-S method. OCTAVE-S can be downloaded at no cost from the web site:

http://www.cert.org/octave/osig.html

Section	Page
1. Internal Threat	1
2. Example Impact Evaluation Criteria	3
3. Asset Identification	5
4. Organizational Security Practices	7
5. Critical Asset Selection and Security Requirements	11
6. Threats to the Critical Asset	13
7. Evaluating Risks to the Critical Asset	18
8. Example "Humans Using Network Access" Tree for PIDS	19
9. Example Mitigation Plans for PIDS	26

FIGURE 9.1 Table of contents from the CERT Information Assurance on Small Organizations Workbook.

within your organization. As the table of contents in Figure 9.1 shows, this workbook is also a tutorial that steps you through all the information security considerations.

Table 9–1 is a variation on the worksheet provided by CERT. Armed with this table and based on your knowledge and experience with the company, you can complete your asset identification following the steps outlined below.

1. In the first column of the table, list the information assets. You should list the types of information used by people in your company—the information people need to do their jobs. Examples are product designs, software programs, system designs, documentation, customer orders, and personnel data.
2. For each entry in the *Information* column, fill in the names of the systems on which the information resides. In each case, ask yourself which systems people need to perform their jobs.

TABLE 9.1 Asset Identification Worksheet

Information	Systems	Services and Applications	Other Assets

3. For each entry in the *Information* column, fill in the names of the related applications and services. In each case, ask yourself what applications or services are needed for individuals to perform their jobs.
4. In the last column, list any other assets that may or may not be directly related to the other three columns. Examples are databases with customer information, systems used in production, word processors used to produce documentation, compilers used by programmers, and human resources systems.

Once you complete the proceeding steps and fill out the Asset Identification worksheet, you will have a good understanding of the critical assets for your organization. With this information, you will know how best to devote your defensive efforts. Some specific protective steps will be examined later in this chapter.

How Does Espionage Occur?

There are two ways that espionage can occur. An easy, low-technology avenue would be for current or former employees to simply take the data or for someone to use social engineering methods (discussed in Chapter 3) to extract data from unsuspecting company employees. The second, more technology-oriented method is for the individuals to use spyware, which includes the use of cookies and key loggers.

Low-Tech Industrial Espionage

Corporate espionage can occur without the benefit of computers or the Internet. Disgruntled former (or current) employees can copy sensitive documents, divulge corporate strategies and plans, or perhaps reveal sensitive information. In fact, whether the method used is technological or not, disgruntled employees are the single greatest security risk to any organization. A corporate spy need not hack into a system in order to obtain sensitive and confidential information if an employee is willing to simply hand over the information. Just as with military and political espionage, the motives for the employee to divulge the information vary. Some engage in such acts for obvious financial gains. Others may elect to reveal company secrets merely because they are angry over some injustice (real or imagined). Whatever the motive, any organization has to be cognizant of the fact that it has any number of employees who may be unhappy with some situation and have the potential to divulge confidential information.

Certainly one can obtain information without the benefit of modern technology; however, computer technology (and various computer-related tactics) can certainly assist in corporate espionage, even if only in a peripheral manner. Some incidents of industrial espionage are conducted with technology that requires little skill on the part of the perpetrator as illustrated in Figures 9.2 and 9.3. This technology can include using Universal

FIGURE 9.2 Low-tech espionage is easy.

FIGURE 9.3 Low-tech espionage is portable.

Serial Bus (USB) flash drives, CD ROMs, or other portable media to take information out of the organization. Even disgruntled employees who wish to undermine the company or make a profit for themselves will find it easier to burn a wealth of data onto a compact disk (CD) and carry that out in their coat pocket rather than attempting to photocopy thousands of documents and smuggle them out. And the new USB flash drives, smaller than your average key chain, are a dream come true for corporate spies. These drives can plug into any USB port and store 256 megabytes or more of data.

While information can be taken from your company without overt hacking of the system, you should keep in mind that if your system is insecure, it is entirely possible that an outside party would compromise your system and obtain that information without an employee as an accomplice. In addition to these methods, there are other low-tech, or virtually "no-tech," methods used to extract information. Social engineering, which was discussed at great length in Chapter 3, is the process of talking a person into giving up information she otherwise would not divulge. This technique can be applied to industrial espionage in a number of ways.

The first and most obvious use of social engineering in industrial espionage is in direct conversation in which the perpetrator attempts to get the targeted employee to reveal sensitive data. As illustrated in Figure 9.4,

FIGURE 9.4 Social engineering used as low-tech espionage.

employees will often inadvertently divulge information to a supplier, vendor or salesperson without thinking the information is important or that it could be given to anyone. A more interesting way of using social engineering would be via e-mail. In very large organizations, one cannot know every member. This loophole allows the clever industrial spy to send an e-mail message claiming to come from some other department and perhaps simply asking for sensitive data. A corporate spy might, for example, forge an e-mail to appear to be coming from the legal office of the target company, requesting an executive summary of some research project.

Computer security expert Andrew Briney (Briney, 2003) places people as the number one issue in computer security.

Spyware Used in Industrial Espionage

Clearly, any software that can monitor activities on a computer can be used in industrial espionage. *Security IT World,* an online e-zine, featured an article in their October 2003 issue that dealt with the fact that monitoring a computer is an easy thing to do in the 21st century. One method to accomplish monitoring is via spyware, which we discussed in detail in Chapter 5. Clearly, software or hardware that logs key strokes or takes screen shots would be most advantageous to the industrial spy.

The application of this type of software to espionage is obvious. A spy could get screen shots of sensitive documents, capture logon information for databases, or in fact capture a sensitive document as it is being typed. Any of these methods would give a spy unfettered access to all data that is processed on a machine that contains spyware.

Protecting Against Industrial Espionage

By now, you are aware that there are many ways that your organization's valuable information assets can be compromised. The question thus becomes: What steps can you take to alleviate the danger? Note that I said "alleviate" the danger. There is nothing you can do to make any system, any information, or any person totally secure. Totally unbreakable security is simply a myth. The best you can do is work to achieve a level of security that makes the effort required to get information more costly than the value of the information.

One obvious protection is to employ anti-spyware software. This software, coupled with other security measures such as firewalls and intrusion-detection software (both examined in Chapter 6), should drastically reduce the chance that an outside party will compromise your organization's data. Furthermore, implementing organizational policies (also discussed in Chapter 6) that help guide employees on safely using computer and Internet resources will make your system relatively secure. If you add to your protection arsenal the strategy of encrypting all transmissions, your system will be as secure as you can reasonably make it. (Chapter 7 is devoted to encryption.) However, all of these techniques (firewalls, company policies, anti-spyware, encryption, and so forth) will only help in cases in which the employee is not the spy. What do you do to ameliorate the danger of employees intentionally stealing or compromising information? Actually, there are several courses of action any organization can take to lesson risks due to internal espionage. Here are 11 steps you can use:

1. Always use all reasonable network security: firewalls, intrusion-detection software, anti-spyware, patching and updating the operating system, and proper usage policies.
2. Give the personnel of the company access to only the data that they absolutely need to perform their jobs. Use a "need-to-know" approach. One does not want to stifle discussion or exchange of ideas, but sensitive data must be treated with great care.
3. If possible, set up a system for those employees with access to the most sensitive data in which there is a rotation and/or a separation of duties. In this way, no one employee has access and control over all critical data at one time.
4. Limit the number of portable storage media in the organization (such as CD burners, zip disks, and flash drives) and control access to these media. Log every use of such media and what was stored. Some organizations have even prohibited cell phones because many phones allow the user to photograph items and send the pictures electronically.
5. Do not allow employees to take documents/media home. Bringing materials home may indicate a very dedicated employee working on her own time or a corporate spy copying important documents and information.
6. Shred documents and melt old disks/tape backups/CDs. A resourceful spy can often find a great deal of information in the garbage.
7. Do employee background checks. You must be able to trust your employees, and you can only do this with a thorough background check. Do not rely on "gut feelings." Give particular attention to information technology (IT) personnel who will, by the nature of their jobs, have a greater access to a wider variety of data. This scrutiny is most important with positions such as database administrators, network administrators, and network security specialists.
8. When any employee leaves the company, scan their PC carefully. Look for signs that inappropriate data was kept on that machine. If you have any reason to suspect any inappropriate usage, then store the machine for evidence in any subsequent legal proceedings.

9. Keep all tape backups, sensitive documents, and other media under lock and key, with limited access to them.
10. If portable computers are used, then encrypt the hard drives. Encryption prevents a thief from extracting useable data from a stolen laptop. There are a number of products on the market that accomplish this encryption, including the following:
    - CryptoEx from Navastream (**www.navastream.com**). As Figure 9.5 shows, the CryptoEx family of products has different components to suit different needs. CryptoEx Pocket enables you to protect a personal digital assistant (PDA) and CryptoEx Volume enables you to encrypt hard drives.

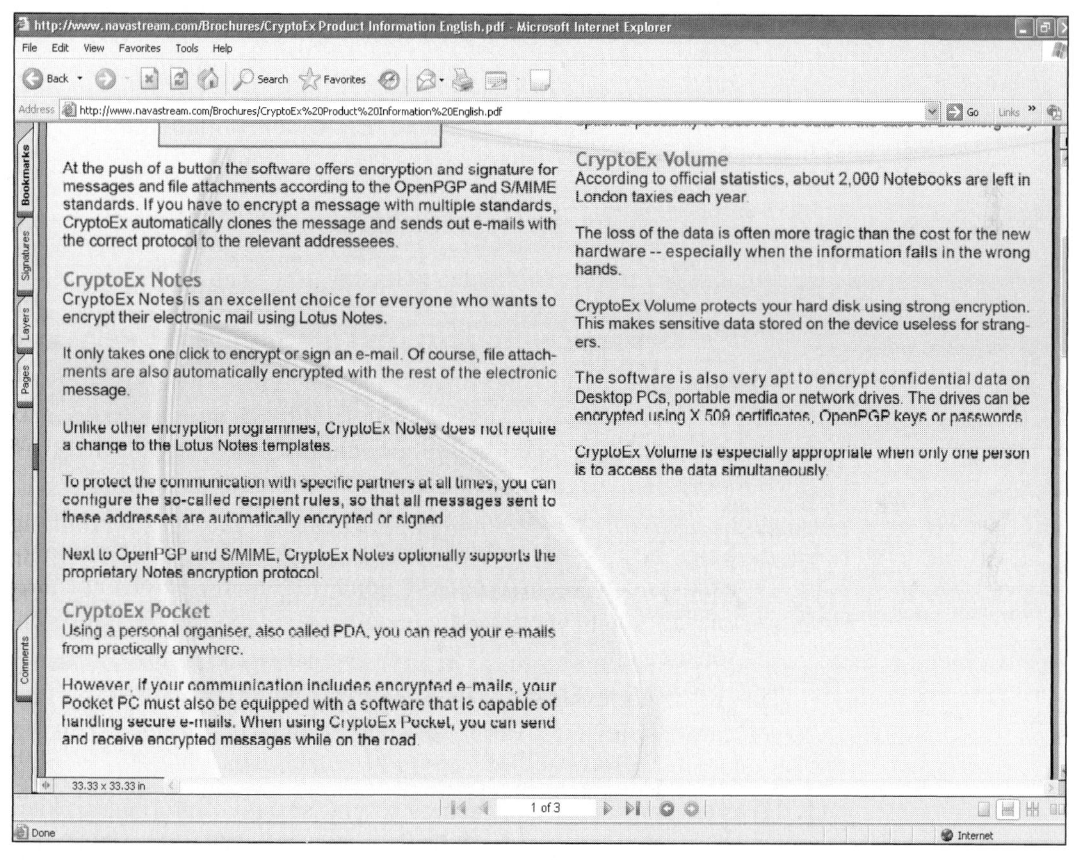

FIGURE 9.5 Navastream's CryptoEx

    - CryptoGram Folder from Imecom Group (**www.secure-messaging.com/products/cgfolder/index.htm**). As Figure 9.6 shows, CryptoGram Folder provides features that enable you to protect your files, hard drive, and e-mail.

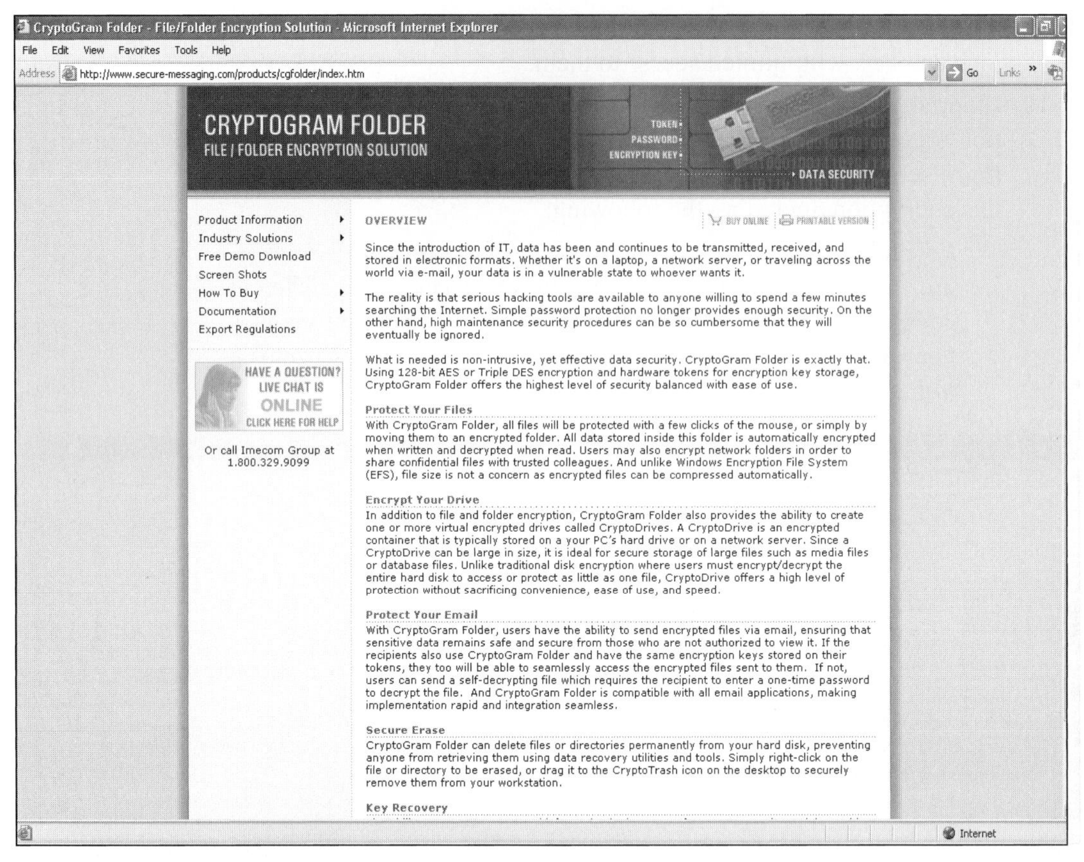

FIGURE 9.6 Overview of CryptoGram Folder.

- Safe House from Envoy Data Corporation (**www.smartcardsys.com/security/**). As Figure 9.7 shows, SafeHouse also enables you to encrypt data on either a notebook or desktop personal computer.

This list is not exhaustive; therefore, it is highly recommended that you carefully review a variety of encryption products before making a selection.

11. Have all employees with access to any sensitive information sign non-disclosure agreements. Such agreements give you, the employer, a recourse should an ex-employee divulge sensitive data. It is amazing how many employers do not bother with this rather simple protection.

Unfortunately, following these simple rules will not make you totally immune to corporate espionage. However, using these strategies will make any such attempts much more difficult for any perpetrator and, thus, you will improve your organization's data security.

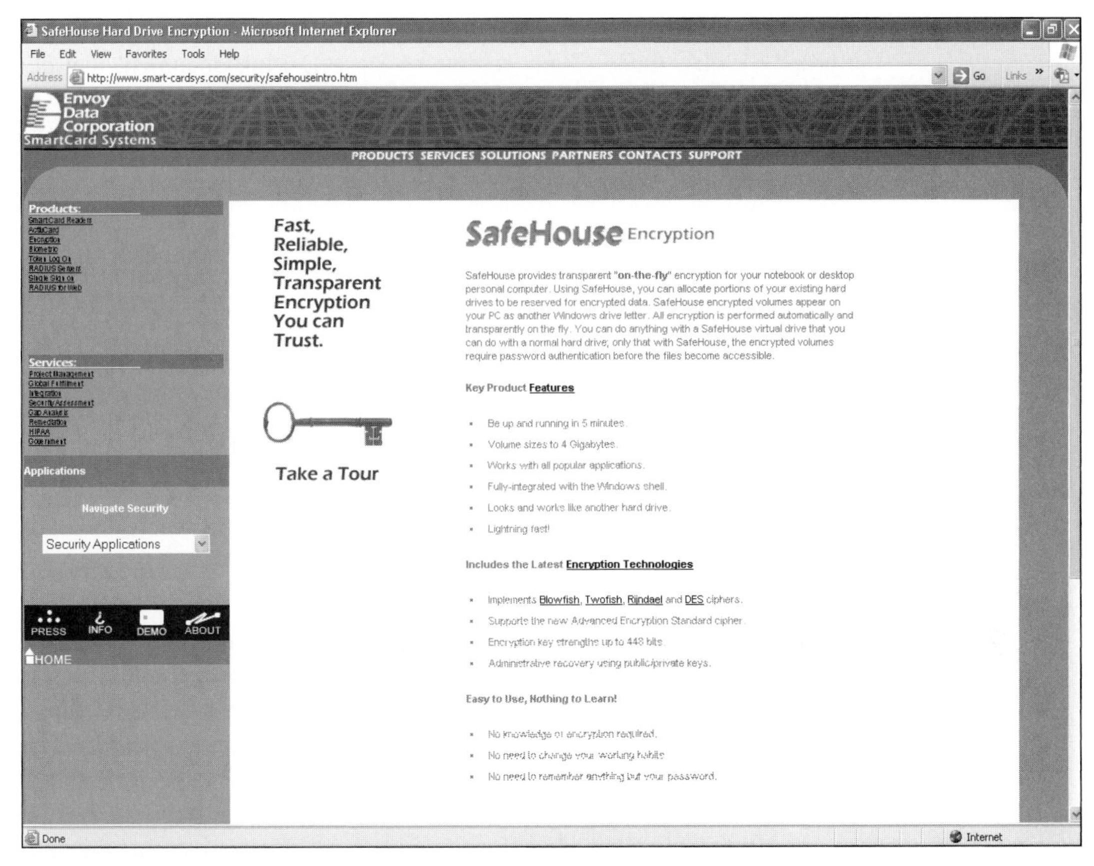

FIGURE 9.7 Overview of Safe House encryption.

Real-World Examples of Industrial Espionage

Now that you have been introduced to the concept of corporate espionage, let's look at five actual cases. These case studies are of real-world espionage found in various news sources. This section should give you an idea for what types of espionage activities actually occur.

Example 1: VIA Technology

VIA Technology actually provides two examples of industrial espionage. In the first instance, the chief executive officer (CEO) of the firm, which was based in Taipei, was indicted for copyright infringement for allegedly stealing technology from one of his own customers, a networking company called D-Link (Lemon, 2003).

According to the allegations, VIA engineer Jeremy Chang left VIA to work for D-Link. For several months while at D-Link, Chang continued to receive a paycheck from VIA. Then he promptly resigned from D-Link and returned to VIA. Once Chang rejoined VIA, a D-Link document that detailed one of their simulation programs for testing integrated circuits was posted to an FTP server owned by VIA.

The prosecutors allege that Chang continued to receive a check from VIA because he had never really resigned. They allege that Chang was in fact a "plant" sent to D-Link to acquire D-Link's technology for VIA. VIA maintains that his continuation to receive a check was simply an oversight, and Chang denies that he posted the document in question. Whatever the truth of the case, it should make any employer think twice about hiring decisions and non-disclosure agreements.

To make matters worse for VIA, another company accused VIA of stealing code for its optical readers. In both cases, the story of the possible theft of technology alone has had a negative impact on the stock value of both companies.

Example 2: General Motors

In 1993, General Motors (GM) and one if its partners began to investigate a former executive, Inaki Lopez. GM alleged that Lopez and seven other former GM employees had transferred GM proprietary information to Volkswagen (VW) in Germany via GM's own network (Szczesny, 2000). The information allegedly stolen included component price data, proprietary construction plans, internal cost calculations, and a purchasing list.

In 1996, GM followed up the ongoing criminal investigation with civil litigation against Lopez, VW, and the other employees. In November of 1996, GM expanded its legal battle by invoking the various Racketeer Influenced and Corrupt Organizations Act (RICO) statutes, originally intended to be used against organized crime conspiracies (Dever, 1996). By May of 2000, a federal grand jury indicted Lopez on six counts related to fraud and racketeering. As of this writing, the case is not resolved (*USA Today,* 2000). At the time Lopez was indicted, he was residing in Spain and the U.S. Justice Department was negotiating for his extradition. Thus, you can see that corporate espionage is neither new nor restricted to technology companies.

Example 3: Interactive Television Technologies, Inc.

On August 13, 1998, someone broke into the computer systems of Interactive Television Technologies, Inc. and stole the data for a project the company was working on (Secur Telecom, 1998). That project involved four years of intense research and a substantial financial investment. The product was to be a way whereby anyone with a television could have Internet access via the Web. This product, code-named "Butler," would have been worth a substantial amount to its inventors. However, with all the research material stolen, it was only a matter of time before several other companies came out with competing products, thus preventing Interactive Television Technologies from pursuing a patent.

To date, no arrests have been made and no leads are available in this case. This situation was a case of very skillful hackers breaking into a computer system and taking exactly what they needed. One can only speculate about their motives. They may well have sold the research data to competitors of Interactive Television Technologies, or they may have simply put the data out in the open via the Internet. Whatever the motives or profits for the perpetrators, the outcome for the victim company was catastrophic.

Example 4: Bloomberg, Inc.

According to the *American Bar Association Journal* (U.S. Department of Justice, 2003), in August 2003, Oleg Zezev, a 29-year-old PC technician from Kazakhstan, broke into the Bloomberg Inc. computer system and used the alias "Alex" to obtain information and then blackmail the firm.

Zezev entered Bloomberg's computer system and accessed various accounts, including Michael Bloomberg's (CEO and founder of Bloomberg L.P.) personal account as well as accounts for other Bloomberg employees and customers. Zezev copied information from these accounts including e-mail inbox screens, Michael Bloomberg's credit card numbers, and screens relating to the internal functions of Bloomberg. He also copied internal information that was only accessible by Bloomberg employees.

Zezev then threatened to expose the data he had stolen to the public and, in essence, tell everyone exactly how he had broken into Bloomberg's network unless he received $200,000.

After deliberating for less than six hours, the jury in the U.S. District Court in Manhattan found the perpetrator guilty of all four charges: conspiracy, attempted extortion, sending threatening electronic messages, and computer intrusion. Although this is not industrial espionage in the classic sense, it does illustrate the compromising situations in which a company and its employees can be placed when security is breached.

Example 5: Avant Software

In 1997, executives at Avant Software in Santa Clara County, California, were charged with attempting to steal secrets from their rival, Cadence Design. The case focused on a former consultant for Avant, Mitsuru "Mitch" Igusa. After Igusa had taken a job at Cadence, he began e-mailing files to his home; it is alleged that he later turned those files over to Avant.

Industrial Espionage and You

These five cases notwithstanding, most companies will deny any involvement in anything that even hints at espionage. However, not all companies are quite so shy about the issue. Larry Ellison, CEO of Oracle Corporation, has openly defended his decision to hire private investigators to sift through Microsoft garbage in an attempt to garner information (Konrad, 2000). Clearly, espionage is no longer a problem just for governments and defense contractors. It is a very real concern in the modern business world. The savvy computer security professional will be aware of this concern and will take the appropriate proactive steps.

Summary

A number of conclusions can be drawn from the examination of industrial espionage. The first conclusion: It does indeed occur. The case studies clearly demonstrate that industrial espionage is not some exotic fantasy dreamed up by paranoid security experts. It is an unfortunate, but quite real, aspect of modern business. If your firm's management chooses to ignore these dangers, then they do so at their own peril.

The second thing that can be concluded from this brief study of industrial espionage is that there are a variety of methods by which espionage can take place. An employee revealing confidential information is perhaps the most common. However, compromising information systems is another increasingly popular means of obtaining confidential and potentially valuable data. You will want to know the best way to protect your company and yourself. In the upcoming exercises at the end of this chapter, you will run screen capture software, key loggers, and anti-spyware.

Test Your Skills

MULTIPLE CHOICE QUESTIONS

1. What is the ultimate goal of espionage?
   A. To subvert a rival government
   B. To obtain information that has value
   C. To subvert a rival business
   D. To obtain information not otherwise available

2. What is the best outcome for a spy attempting an espionage activity?
   A. To obtain information without the target even realizing he did so
   B. To obtain information with or without the target realizing he did so
   C. To obtain information and discredit the target
   D. To obtain information and cause harm to the target

3. What is the usual motivating factor for corporate/industrial espionage?
   A. ideological
   B. political
   C. economic
   D. revenge

4. Which of the following types of information would be a likely target for industrial espionage?
   A. A new algorithm that the company's IT department has generated
   B. A new marketing plan that the company has formulated
   C. A list of all the company's customers
   D. All of the above are correct.

5. Which of the following is a likely reason that an organization might be reluctant to admit it has been a victim of corporate espionage?
   A. It would embarrass the IT department.
   B. It would embarrass the CEO.
   C. It might cause stock value to decline.
   D. It might lead to involvement in a criminal prosecution.

6. What is the difference between *corporate* and *industrial* espionage?
   A. None; they are interchangeable terms.
   B. Industrial espionage only refers to heavy industry, such as factories.
   C. Corporate espionage only refers to executive activities.
   D. Corporate espionage only refers to publicly traded companies.

7. You can calculate the value of information by what formula?
   A. Resources needed to produce the information, plus resources gained from the information
   B. Resources needed to produce the information, multiplied by resources gained from the information
   C. Time taken to derive the information, plus money needed to derive the information
   D. Time taken to derive the information, multiplied by money needed to derive the information

8. If a company purchases a high-end Unix server to use for its research and development department, what is probably the most valuable part of the system?
   A. The high-end Unix server
   B. The information on the server
   C. The devices used to protect the server
   D. The room to store the server

9. Information is an asset to your company if it:
   A. Cost any sum of money to produce.
   B. Cost a significant sum of money to produce.
   C. Might have economic value.
   D. Might cost significant money to reproduce.

10. What is the greatest security risk to any company?
    A. disgruntled employees
    B. hackers
    C. industrial spies
    D. faulty network security

11. Which of the following is the best definition for *spyware*?
    A. Software that assists in corporate espionage
    B. Software that monitors activity on a computer
    C. Software that logs computer keystrokes
    D. Software that steals data

12. What is the highest level of security you can expect to obtain?
    A. A level of security that makes the effort required to get information more than the value of the information
    B. A level of security comparable with government security agencies, such as the Central Intelligence Agency
    C. A level of security that has a 92.5% success rate in stopping intrusion
    D. A level of security that has a 98.5% success rate in stopping intrusion

13. In the context of preventing industrial espionage, why might you wish to limit the number of company CD burners and control access to them in your organization?
    A. An employee could use such media to take sensitive data out.
    B. An employee could use such media to copy software from the company.
    C. CDs could be a vehicle for spyware to get on your system.
    D. CDs could be a vehicle for a virus to get on your system.

14. Why would you want to scan an employee's computer when he leaves the organization?
    A. To check the work flow prior to leaving
    B. To check for signs of corporate espionage
    C. To check for illegal software
    D. To check for pornography

15. What is the reason for encrypting hard drives on laptop computers?
    A. To prevent a hacker from reading that data while you are online
    B. To ensure that data transmissions are secure
    C. To ensure that another user on that machine will not see sensitive data
    D. To prevent a thief from getting data off of a stolen laptop

EXERCISES

Exercise 9.1: Learning about Industrial Espionage

1. Using the Web, library, journals, or other resources, look up a case of industrial or corporate espionage not already mentioned in this chapter. The following Web sites might be of some help to you in finding a case:
    - citeseer.ist.psu.edu/320204.html
    - www.newhaven.edu/california/CJ625/p6.html
    - www.fidex.com/hackinglaws.htm
2. Write a brief essay describing the facts in the case. The parties in the case and the criminal proceeding are of interest, but most of your discussion should focus on the technical aspects of the case. Be sure to explain how the espionage was conducted.

Exercise 9.2: Using Anti-Spyware

Note that this exercise may be repeated with different anti-spyware products. It is a good idea for any person interested in computer security to be familiar with multiple anti-spyware products.

1. Go to the Web site of one of the anti-spyware utilities. (See Chapter 5 if you need more direction.)
2. Find instructions on the vendor's Web site.
3. Download the trial version of that software.
4. Install it on your machine.
5. After installation, run the utility. What did it find? Record your results.
6. Let the utility remove or quarantine anything it found.

Exercise 9.3: Learning about Key Loggers

Note that this exercise may only be completed on machines where you have explicit permission to do so (no public computers).

1. Using any Web site, find and download a key logger. The following Web sites might help you locate a key logger:
   - home.rochester.rr.com/artcfox/TinyKL/
   - www.kmint21.com/familykeylogger/
   - www.blazingtools.com/bpk.html
2. Install the key logger on your PC.
3. Examine how it behaves on your machine and if you notice anything that might indicate the presence of illicit software.
4. Run the anti-spyware software you downloaded in Exercise 2. Does the anti-spyware software detect the key logger?

Exercise 9.4: Screen Capture Spyware

1. Using the Web, find and download a screen-capturing spyware application. The following Web sites might be helpful to you in selecting an appropriate product:
   - www.win-spy.com/doorway/index80.htm
   - marketwatch-cnet.com.com/3000-2384-10188787.html?tag=lst-0-2

- www.softforall.com/Multimedia/Screencapture/River_Past_Screen_Recorder07090011.htm

2. Install and configure the application on your computer.
3. Run the application and note what it finds.
4. Run the anti-spyware from Exercise 2 and see whether it detects your spyware program.

Exercise 9.5: Learning about Hardware-Based Key Loggers

In this chapter, as well as Chapter 5, we discussed software-based key loggers. However, there are also hardware-based key loggers.

1. Use the Internet to learn more about hardware-based key loggers. (You may wish to search for "Keykatcher" as a starting point.)
2. Write an essay outlining the way in which these key loggers work and how they could be implemented for either security or industrial espionage.

PROJECTS

Project 9.1: Preventing Corporate Espionage

Using one of the Web sites listed in this book (you can also choose from the preferred resources in Chapter 1) or other resources, find a set of guidelines on general computer security. Write a brief essay comparing and contrasting those guidelines against the ones given in this chapter. Keep in mind that the guidelines in this chapter relate specifically to corporate espionage and not to general computer security.

Project 9.2: Handling Employees

Write a brief essay describing steps regarding the handling of employees. These steps should include all steps that you believe any organization should take to prevent corporate espionage. It is important that you support your opinions with sources and reasons.

If possible, visit a company and talk with someone in either the IT or personnel departments to determine how that company handles issues such as employee termination, rotation of duties, control of access to data, and so forth. Compare and contrast your steps to those used by the company you visited.

Project 9.3: Asset Identification in Your Organization

Using the Asset Identification table found in this chapter or a similar table of your own design, identify the most valuable data in your organization (school or business) and what parties would most likely wish to access that data. Then write a brief guideline on how you might go about securing that data. In this project, you should tailor your security recommendations to the specific type of data you are trying to protect and against the most likely perpetrators of industrial espionage.

Case Study

David Doe is a network administrator for the ABC Company. David is passed over for promotion three times. He is quite vocal in his dissatisfaction with this situation. In fact, he begins to express negative opinions about the organization in general. Eventually, David quits and begins his own consulting business. Six months after David's departure, it is discovered that a good deal of the ABC Company's research has suddenly been duplicated by a competitor. Executives at ABC suspect that David Doe has done some consulting work for this competitor and may have passed on sensitive data. However, in the interim since David left, his computer has been formatted and reassigned to another person. ABC has no evidence that David Doe did anything wrong.

What steps might have been taken to detect David's alleged industrial espionage? What steps might have been taken to prevent his perpetrating such an offense?

Chapter 10

Cyber Terrorism and Information Warfare

Chapter Objectives

After reading this chapter and completing the exercises, you will be able to do the following:

- Explain what cyber terrorism is and how it has been used in some actual cases.
- Understand the basics of information warfare.
- Have a working knowledge of some plausible cyber terrorism scenarios.
- Have an appreciation for the dangers posed by cyber terrorism.

Introduction

Throughout this book, various ways have been examined in which a person might use a computer to commit a crime. This book has also looked into specific methods to make a system more secure. One issue that has not been addressed is that of cyber terrorism. People in countries around the world have grown accustomed to the ever-present threat of a terrorist attack, which could come in the form of a bomb, a hijacking, releasing a biological agent, or other means. Most people have not given much thought to the possibility of cyber terrorism.

The first question might be: What is cyber terrorism? According to the FBI, ***cyber terrorism*** is the premeditated, politically motivated attack against information, computer systems, computer programs, and data that results in violence against noncombatant targets by sub-national groups or

FYI: The U.S. Government Takes Information Security Seriously

Throughout 2003 and 2004, there have been a number of reports in reliable news sources, such as Cable News Network (CNN), of the U.S. government hiring hackers to test the security of various systems. The job of these hackers is to attempt to breach security of a sensitive system in order to find security flaws so they can be corrected before a more maliciously motivated hacker exploits them. Clearly, the U.S. government considers the concept of cyber terrorism to be a real threat and is taking steps to secure information.

clandestine agents (Dick, 2002). Cyber terrorism is simply the use of computers and the Internet connectivity between them in order to launch a terrorist attack. In short, cyber terrorism is just like other forms of terrorism—it is only the milieu of the attack that has changed. Clearly the loss of life due to a cyber attack would be much less than that of a bombing. In fact, it is highly likely that there would be no loss of life at all. However, significant economic damage, disruptions in communications, disruptions in supply lines, and general degradation of the national infrastructure are all quite possible via the Internet.

It is a strong possibility that, in time, someone or some group will try to use computer methods to launch a military or terrorist attack against our nation. Some experts make the case that the MyDoom virus (discussed in Chapter 4) was an example of domestic economic terrorism. However, an attack such as that may be only the tip of the iceberg. Sometime in the near future, our nation may be the target of a serious cyber terrorism attack. This chapter will examine some possible cyber terrorism scenarios, with the purpose of giving you a realistic assessment of just how serious a threat this is. In the exercises at the end of the chapter, you will have the opportunity to examine current acts of cyber terrorism, as well as potential threats, and the actions you can take to help prevent them.

Economic Attacks

There are a variety of ways that a cyber attack can cause economic damage. Lost files and lost records are one way. Chapter 9 discussed cyber espionage and mentioned the inherent value of data. In addition to stealing that data, it could simply be destroyed, in which case the data is gone and the resources used to accumulate and analyze the data are wasted. To use an analogy, consider that a malicious person could choose to simply destroy your car rather than steal it. In either case, you are without the car and will have to spend additional resources acquiring transportation.

In addition to simply destroying economically valuable data (remember that there is very little data that does not have some intrinsic value), there are other ways to cause economic disruption. Some of those ways include stealing credit cards, transferring money from accounts, and fraud. But it is a fact that anytime IT staff is involved with cleaning up a virus rather than developing applications or administering networks and databases, there is economic loss. The mere fact that companies now need to purchase antivirus software, intrusion-detection software, and hire computer security professionals means that computer crime has already caused economic damage to companies and governments around the world. However, the general damage caused by random virus outbreaks, lone hacking attacks, and online fraud is not the type of economic damage that is the focus of this chapter. This chapter is concerned with a concerted and deliberate attack against a particular target or targets for the exclusive purpose of causing direct damage.

A good way to get a firm grasp on the impact of this type of attack is to walk through a scenario. Group X (which could be an aggressive nation, terrorist group, activist group, or literally any group with the motivation to damage a particular nation) decides to make a concerted attack on our country. They find a small group of individuals (in this case, six) that are well versed in computer security, networking, and programming. These individuals, motivated either by ideology or monetary needs, are organized to create a coordinated attack. There are many possible scenarios under which they could execute such an attack and cause significant economic harm. The example outlined below is just one of those possible attack modalities. In this case, each individual has an assignment, and all assignments are designed to be activated on the same specific date.

- Team member one sets up several fake e-commerce sites. Each of these sites is only up for 72 hours and portends to be a major stock brokerage site. During the brief time they are up, the site's real purpose is only to collect credit card numbers/bank account numbers and so forth. On the predetermined date, all of those credit card and bank numbers will be automatically, anonymously, and simultaneously posted to various bulletin boards/Web sites and newsgroups, making them available for any unscrupulous individual that wishes to use them.

- Team member two creates a virus. This virus is contained in a Trojan horse. Its function is to delete key system files on the predetermined date. In the meantime, it shows a series of business tips or motivational slogans, making it a popular download with people in business.

- Team member three creates another virus. It is designed to create distributed Denial of Service attacks on key economic sites, such as those for stock exchanges or brokerage houses. The virus spreads harmlessly and is set to begin its distributed Denial of Service attack on the predetermined date.
- Team members four and five begin the process of footprinting major banking systems, preparing to crack them on the predetermined date.
- Team member six prepares a series of false stock tips to flood the Internet on the predetermined date.

If each of these individuals is successful in their mission, on the predetermined date, several major brokerages and perhaps government economic sites are taken down, viruses flood networks, and files are deleted from the machines of thousands of businessmen, economists, stock brokers. Thousands of credit cards and bank numbers are released on the Internet, guaranteeing that many will be misused. It is also highly likely that the cracking team members four and five will have some success—meaning that possibly one or more banking systems are compromised. It does not take an economist to realize that this would easily cost hundreds of millions of dollars, perhaps even billions of dollars. A concerted attack of this nature could easily cause more economic damage to our country than most traditional terrorists attacks (i.e., bombings) have ever done.

FIGURE 10.1 A team member of Group X?

You could extrapolate on this scenario and imagine not just one group of six cyber terrorists, but five groups of six—each group with a different mission and each mission designed to be committed approximately two weeks apart. In this scenario, the nation's economy would literally be under siege for two and one-half months.

This scenario is not particularly far-fetched when you consider that, in past decades, nuclear scientists were sought after by various nations and terrorist groups. More recently, experts in biological weapons have been sought by these same groups. It seems extremely likely that these groups will see the possibilities of this form of terrorism and seek out computer security/hacking experts. Given that there are literally thousands of people with the requisite skills, it seems likely that a motivated organization could find a few dozen people willing to commit these acts.

Military Operations Attacks

When computer security and national defense are mentioned together, the obvious thought that comes to mind is the possibility of some hacker breaking into ultra-secure systems at the Department of Defense, Central Intelligence Agency (CIA), or National Security Agency (NSA). However, such an intrusion into one of the most secure systems in the world is very unlikely—not impossible, but very unlikely. The most likely outcome of such an attack would be that the attacker is promptly captured. Such systems are hyper-secure and intruding upon them is not as easy as some movies might suggest. However, there are a number of scenarios in which breaking into less secure systems could jeopardize our national defense or put military plans at risk.

Consider less sensitive military systems for a moment, for example, systems that are responsible for basic logistical operations (e.g., food, mail, fuel). If someone cracks one or more of these systems, he could perhaps obtain information that several C-141s (an aircraft often used for troop transports and parachute operations) are being routed to a base that is within flight distance of some city — a city that has been the focal point of political tensions. This same cracker (or team of crackers) also finds that a large amount of ammunition and food supplies, enough for perhaps 5000 troops for two weeks, is simultaneously being routed to that base. Then, on yet another low-security system, the cracker (or team of crackers) notes that a given unit, such as two brigades of the 82nd airborne division, have had all military leaves cancelled. It does not take a military genius to conclude that these two brigades are preparing to drop in on the target city and secure that target. Therefore, the fact that a deployment is going to occur, the size of the deployment, and the approximate time of that deployment have all been deduced without ever attempting to break into a high-security system.

Taking the previous scenario to the next level, assume the hacker gets deep into the low-security logistical systems. Then assume that he does nothing to change the routing of the members of the brigades or the transport planes—actions that might draw attention. However, he does alter the records for the shipment of supplies so that the supplies are delivered two days late and to the wrong base. So there would be two brigades potentially in harms way, without a re-supply of ammunition or food en route. Of course, the situation could be rectified, but the units in question may go for some time without re-supply—enough time, perhaps, to prevent them from successfully completing their mission.

These are just two scenarios in which compromising low-security/low-priority systems can lead to very significant military problems. This further illustrates the serious need for high security on all systems. Given the interconnectivity of so many components of both business and military computer systems, there clearly are no truly "low-priority" security systems.

General Attacks

The previously outlined scenarios involve specific targets with specific strategies. However, once a specific target is attacked, defenses can be readied for it. There are many security professionals that work constantly to thwart these specific attacks. What may be more threatening is a general and unfocused attack with no specific target. Consider the various virus attacks of late 2003 and early 2004. With the exception of My Doom, which was clearly aimed at the Santa Cruz Organization, these attacks were not aimed at a specific target. However, the shear volume of virus attacks and network traffic did cause significant economic damage. IT personnel across the globe dropped their normal projects to clean infected systems and shore up the defenses of systems.

This leads to another possible scenario in which various cyber terrorists continuously release new and varied viruses, perform Denial of Systems attacks, and work to make the Internet in general, and e-commerce in particular, virtually unusable for a period of time. Such a scenario would actually be more difficult to combat, as there would not be a specific target to defend or a clear ideological motive to use as a clue to the identity of the perpetrators.

Information Warfare

Information warfare certainly predates the advent of the modern computer and, in fact, may be as old as conventional warfare. In essence, information warfare is any attempt to manipulate information in pursuit of a military or political goal. When you attempt to use any process to gather information on an opponent or when you use propaganda to influence opinions in a conflict, these are both examples of information warfare. Chapter 9 discussed the role of the computer in corporate espionage. The same techniques can be applied to a military conflict in which the computer can be used as a tool in espionage. Although information gathering will not be re-examined in this chapter, information gathering is only one part of information warfare. Propaganda is another aspect of information warfare. The flow of information impacts troop morale, citizens' outlooks on a conflict, the political support for a conflict, and the involvement of peripheral nations and international organizations.

Propaganda

Computers and the Internet are very effective tools that can be used in the dissemination of propaganda. Many people now use the Internet as a secondary news source, and some even use it as their primary news source. This means that a government, terrorist group, political party, or any activist group could use what appears to be an Internet news Web site as a front to put their own political spin on any conflict. Such a Web site does not need to be directly connected to the political organization whose views are being disseminated; in fact, it is better if it is not directly connected. The Irish Republican Army (IRA), for example, has always operated with two distinct and separate divisions: one that takes paramilitary/terrorist action and another that is purely political. This allows the political/information wing, called Sinn Fein, to operate independently of any military or terrorist activities. In fact, Sinn Fein now has their own Web site shown in Figure 10.2 where they disseminate news with their own perspective (**www.sinnfein.org**). In this situation, however, it is fairly clear to whoever is reading the information that it is biased toward the perspective of the party sponsoring the site. A better scenario (for the party concerned) occurs when there is an Internet news source that is favorably disposed to a political group's position without having any actual connection at all. This makes it easier for the group to spread information without being accused of any obvious bias. The political group (be it a nation, rebel group, or terrorist organization) can then "leak" stories to this news agency.

Information Control

Since World War II, control of information has been an important part of political and military conflicts. Below are just a few examples.

- Throughout the Cold War, Western democracies invested time and money for radio broadcasts into communist nations. This well-known campaign was referred to as Radio Free Europe. The goal was to create dissatisfaction among citizens of those nations, hopefully encouraging defection, dissent, and general discontent. Most historians and political analysts agree that this was a success.

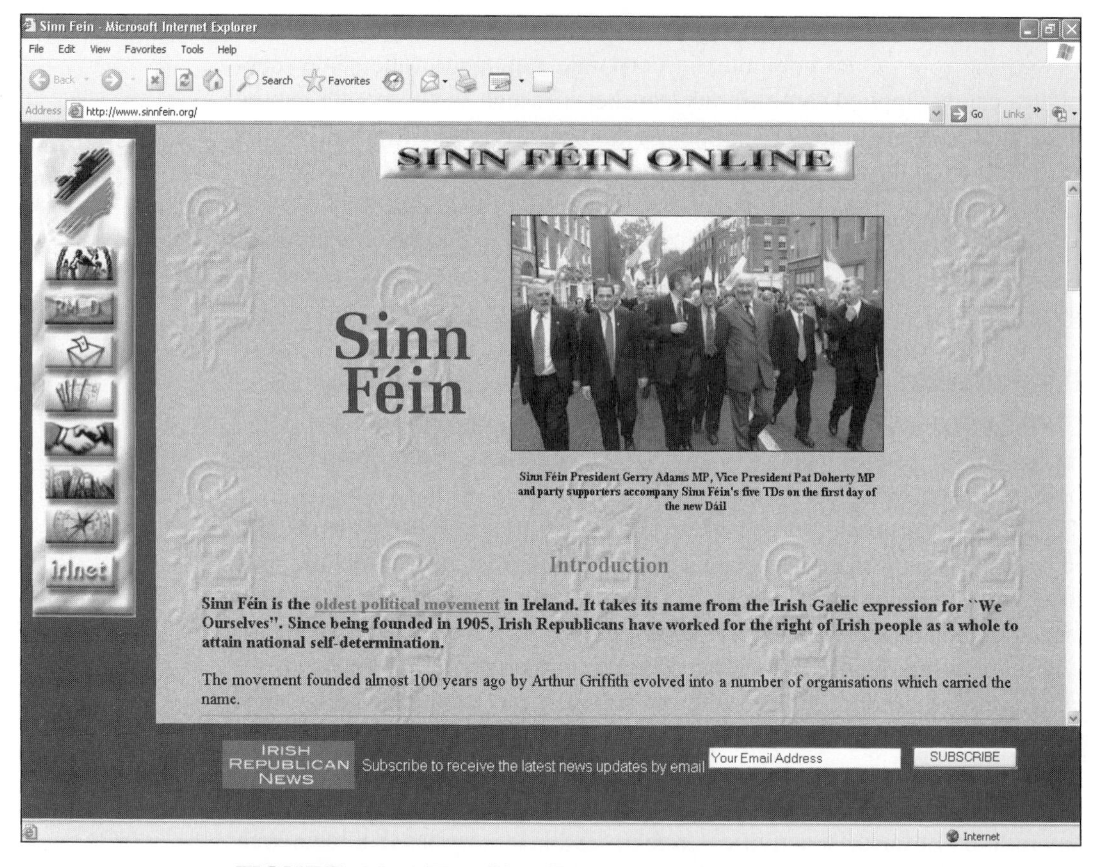

FIGURE 10.2 The Sinn Fein Web site.

- The Vietnam War was the first modern war in which there was strong and widespread domestic opposition. Many analysts believe that opposition was due to the graphic images being brought home via television.
- Today, the government and military of every nation are aware of how the phrases they use to describe activities can affect public perception. They do not say that innocent civilians were killed in a bombing raid. Rather, they state that there was "some collateral damage." Governments do not speak of being the aggressor or starting a conflict. They speak of "preemptive action." Dissenters in any nation are almost always painted as treasonous or cowards.

Public perception is a very important part of any conflict. Each nation wants their own citizens to be totally in support of what they do and to maintain a very high morale. High morale and strong support lead to volunteers for military service, public support for funding the conflict, and political success for the nation's leader. At the same time, you want the enemy to have low morale—to doubt not only their ability to be successful in the conflict, but also their moral position relative to the conflict. You want them to doubt their leadership and to be as opposed to the conflict as possible. The Internet provides a very inexpensive vehicle for swaying public opinion.

Web pages are just one facet of disseminating information. Having people post to various discussion groups can also be effective. One full-time propaganda agent could easily manage 25 or more distinct online personalities, each spending time in different bulletin boards and discussion groups, espousing the views that his political entity wants to espouse. These can reinforce what certain Internet news outlets are posting or they could undermine those postings. They can also start rumors. Rumors can be very effective even when probably false. People often recall hearing something with only a vague recollection of where they heard it and whether it was supported by any data.

Such an agent could have one personality that purports to be a military member (it would take very little research to make this credible) and could post information "not seen in newscasts" that would cast the conflict in either a positive or negative light. She could then have other online personas that entered the discussion who would agree with and support the original position. This would give the initial rumor more credibility. Some people suspect this is already occurring in Usenet newsgroups and Yahoo discussion boards.

FYI: Cyber Information Warfare Now

Anyone familiar with Yahoo news boards has probably noticed an odd phenomenon. At certain times, there will be a flood of posts from anonymous users, all saying essentially the exact same things—even using the exact same grammar, punctuation, and phrasing—and all in support of some ideological perspective. These flurries often happen in times when influence of public opinion is important, such as when an election is nearing. Whether or not these postings are coordinated by any well-known or official organization is debatable. However, they are an example of information warfare. One person or group of people attempt to sway opinion by flooding one particular media (Internet groups) with various items advocating one view. If they are lucky, some individuals will copy the text and e-mail it to friends who do not participate in the newsgroups, thus crossing over to another media and spreading opinions (in some cases entirely unfounded) far and wide.

FYI: Disinformation—A Historical Perspective

While disinformation campaigns are certainly easier to conduct since the advent of mass communication, particularly the Internet, such activities did exist prior to the Internet, or even television. For example in the weeks leading up the famous D-Day invasion of World War II, the Allied forces used a number of disinformation techniques:

- They created documents and communiqués listing fictitious military units that would invade from an entirely different location than the real invasion was planned.
- They used Allied double agents to spread similar disinformation to the Germans.
- A few small groups simulated a large scale invasion to distract the German army.

Disinformation

Another category of information warfare that is closely related to propaganda is disinformation. It is a given that a military opponent is attempting to gather information about troop movements, military strength, supplies, and so forth. A prudent move would be to set up systems that had incorrect information and were just secure enough to be credible, but not secure enough to be unbreakable. An example would be to send an encrypted coded message such that, when the message is decrypted, it seems to say one thing, but to those who can complete the code, it has a different message. The actual message is "padded" with "noise." That noise is a weakly encrypted false message, whereas the real message is more strongly encrypted. In this way, if the message is decrypted, there exists a high likelihood that the fake message will be decrypted and not the real one. General Gray USMC put it best when he said, "Communications without intelligence is noise; intelligence without communications is irrelevant." (Institute for the Advanced Study of Information Warfare, 2004)

The goal of any military or intelligence agency is to make certain our communications are clear and that the enemy can only receive noise.

Actual Cases

It should be noted that there are voices in the computer security industry that think cyber terrorism or cyber war are simply not realistic scenarios. Marcus Ranum of Information Security magazine states as much in the

April 2004 issue. He and others claim that there is no danger from cyber terrorism and that, in fact, "The whole notion of cyberwarfare is a scam." (Ranum, 2004) However, computer warfare and cyber terrorism have already been used on a small scale. It seems quite plausible that, in a matter of time, it will be seen on a much larger scale.

Even if you believe that the scenarios outlined in the earlier sections of this chapter are merely the product of an overactive imagination, you should consider that there have already been a few actual incidents of cyber terrorism—although much less severe than the theoretical scenarios. This section examines some of these cases so as to show you how such attacks have been carried out in the past.

The incidents listed below were reported in testimony before the Special Oversight Panel on Terrorism Committee on Armed Services U.S. House of Representatives (Denning, 2000).

- In 1996, a computer hacker allegedly associated with the White Supremacist movement temporarily disabled a Massachusetts ISP and damaged part of the ISP's record-keeping system. The ISP had attempted to stop the hacker from sending out worldwide racist messages under the ISP's name. The hacker signed off with the threat, "You have yet to see true electronic terrorism. This is a promise."
- In 1998, ethnic Tamil guerrillas swamped Sri Lankan embassies with 800 e-mails a day over a two-week period. The messages read, "We are the Internet Black Tigers and we're doing this to disrupt your communications." Intelligence authorities characterized it as the first known attack by terrorists against a country's computer systems.
- During the Kosovo conflict in 1999, NATO computers were blasted with e-mail bombs and hit with Denial of Service attacks by ***hacktivists*** (the name applied to individuals who work for their causes using cyber terrorism) protesting the NATO bombings. In addition, businesses, public organizations, and academic institutes received highly politicized virus-laden e-mails from a range of Eastern European countries, according to reports. Web defacements were also common. After the Chinese Embassy was accidentally bombed in Belgrade, Chinese hacktivists posted messages such as, "We won't stop attacking until the war stops!" on U.S. government Web sites.

The good news is that these particular attacks caused little damage and were clearly the product of amateurs. However, it may only be a matter of time before more damaging attacks are perpetrated by far more skilled cyber terrorists. Yet it is clear that cyber terrorism, at least on a low-intensity scale, is already beginning. These warnings can be heeded and the issues taken seriously, or they can simply be ignored until disaster strikes.

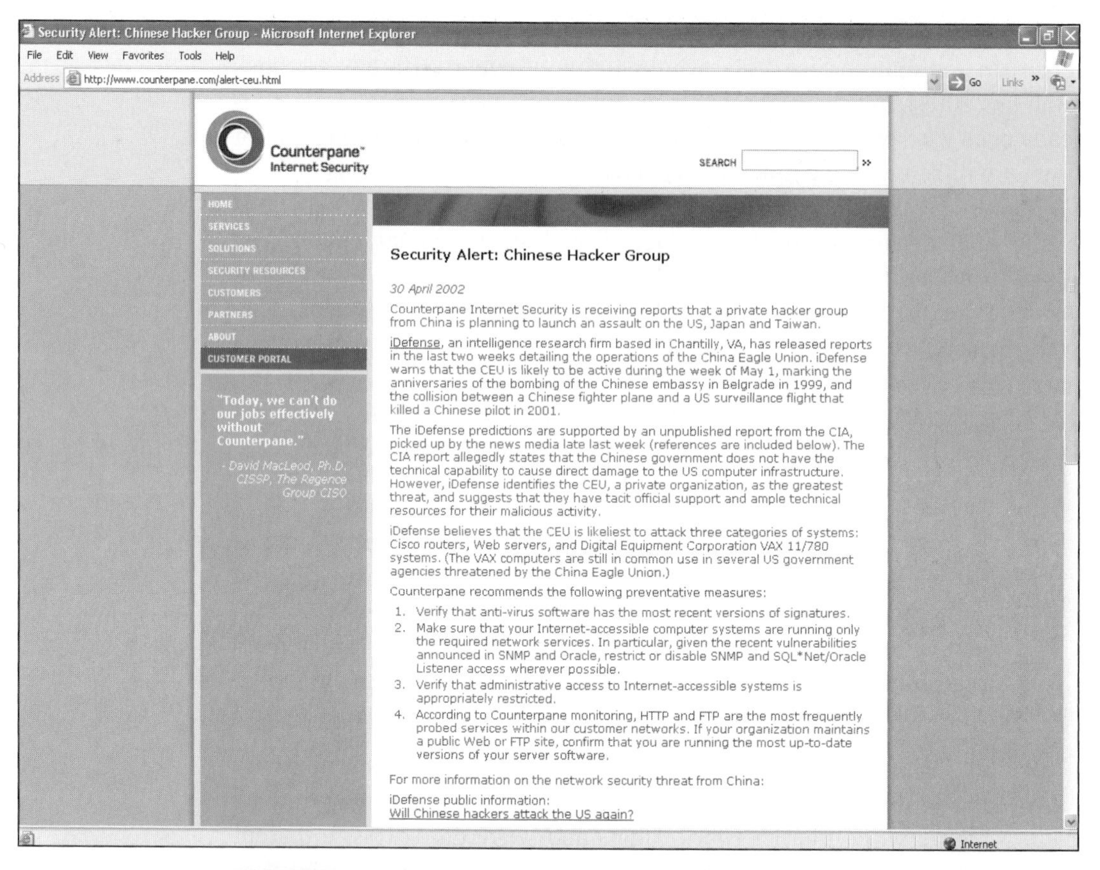
Security Alert: Chinese Hacker Group - Microsoft Internet Explorer

http://www.counterpane.com/alert-ceu.html

Counterpane Internet Security

HOME
SERVICES
SOLUTIONS
SECURITY RESOURCES
CUSTOMERS
PARTNERS
ABOUT
CUSTOMER PORTAL

"Today, we can't do our jobs effectively without Counterpane."

- David MacLeod, Ph.D. CISSP, The Regence Group CISO

Security Alert: Chinese Hacker Group

30 April 2002

Counterpane Internet Security is receiving reports that a private hacker group from China is planning to launch an assault on the US, Japan and Taiwan.

iDefense, an intelligence research firm based in Chantilly, VA, has released reports in the last two weeks detailing the operations of the China Eagle Union. iDefense warns that the CEU is likely to be active during the week of May 1, marking the anniversaries of the bombing of the Chinese embassy in Belgrade in 1999, and the collision between a Chinese fighter plane and a US surveillance flight that killed a Chinese pilot in 2001.

The iDefense predictions are supported by an unpublished report from the CIA, picked up by the news media late last week (references are included below). The CIA report allegedly states that the Chinese government does not have the technical capability to cause direct damage to the US computer infrastructure. However, iDefense identifies the CEU, a private organization, as the greatest threat, and suggests that they have tacit official support and ample technical resources for their malicious activity.

iDefense believes that the CEU is likeliest to attack three categories of systems: Cisco routers, Web servers, and Digital Equipment Corporation VAX 11/780 systems. (The VAX computers are still in common use in several US government agencies threatened by the China Eagle Union.)

Counterpane recommends the following preventative measures:

1. Verify that anti-virus software has the most recent versions of signatures.
2. Make sure that your Internet-accessible computer systems are running only the required network services. In particular, given the recent vulnerabilities announced in SNMP and Oracle, restrict or disable SNMP and SQL*Net/Oracle Listener access wherever possible.
3. Verify that administrative access to Internet-accessible systems is appropriately restricted.
4. According to Counterpane monitoring, HTTP and FTP are the most frequently probed services within our customer networks. If your organization maintains a public Web or FTP site, confirm that you are running the most up-to-date versions of your server software.

For more information on the network security threat from China:

iDefense public information:
Will Chinese hackers attack the US again?

FIGURE 10.3 Counterpane Internet Security report on a planned cyberattack.

In addition to those cases listed above, there have been other credible threats or actual incidents of cyber attacks in the past several years.

- In 2002, Counterpane Internet Security reported (as shown in Figure 10.3) a credible threat of a Chinese-backed, all-out cyber attack planned on the United States and Taiwan (2002). A private group of Chinese hackers, called the Chinese Eagle Union, planned to attack routers and Web servers across the United States and Taiwan. The attack never materialized, but unconfirmed reports suggested that the CIA took the threat seriously.
- In June of 2000, Russian authorities arrested a man they accused of being a CIA-backed hacker. As shown in Figure 10.4, this man allegedly hacked into systems of the Russian Domestic Security Service (FSB) and gathered secrets that he then passed on to the CIA (BBC News, 2000). This example illustrates the potential for a

BBC News | EUROPE | Russians arrest 'CIA hacker' - Microsoft Internet Explorer

File Edit View Favorites Tools Help

Address http://news.bbc.co.uk/1/hi/world/europe/806984.stm

BBC HOMEPAGE | WORLD SERVICE | EDUCATION low graphics version | feedback | help

BBC NEWS

You are in: World: Europe

Front Page
World
Africa
Americas
Asia-Pacific
Europe
Middle East
South Asia
From Our Own Correspondent
Letter From America
UK
UK Politics
Business
Sci/Tech
Health
Education
Entertainment
Talking Point
In Depth
AudioVideo

Monday, 26 June, 2000, 17:31 GMT 18:31 UK

Russians arrest 'CIA hacker'

The hacker was allegedly passing secrets to the CIA

The Russian authorities say they have arrested a man who allegedly spied for the United States by hacking into Russian security service computers.

The man's name has not been revealed, but he is said to be a Lithuanian who passed secrets to his own government as well as to the US.

News of the arrest was given by the Russian domestic security service, the FSB - the successor to the KGB.

It said the man had hacked into FSB computers and passed on secrets to the US Central Intelligence Agency.

"The most important thing for the Americans was to use the agent to penetrate information systems used by the Russian FSB"

FSB statement

The man is said to have given "detailed testimony" about his spying activities for both the Lithuanian state security department and the CIA.

The statement said the man had been "active

Search BBC News Online

GO

Advanced search options

Launch console for latest audio/video

BBC RADIO NEWS
BBC ONE TV NEWS
WORLD NEWS SUMMARY
BBC NEWS 24 BULLETIN
PROGRAMMES GUIDE

See also:

- 05 Apr 00 | Europe
  US 'spy' held in Moscow
- 15 Mar 00 | Europe
  Moscow arrests 'British spy'
- 14 Oct 98 | Americas
  US army analyst accused of spying
- 02 Dec 99 | Europe
  US 'spy' recalled
- 04 Jun 00 | Europe
  Analysis: Cautious start for Clinton and Putin
- 13 Sep 99 | Britain betrayed
  Who's being spied on?
- 05 Apr 00 | Europe
  Analysis: Spymasters change focus

Internet links:

- CIA
- US intelligence website on Russia
- US Embassy in Russia
- Russian Information Centre
- FSB (in Russian)
- Lithuanian Government

The BBC is not responsible for the content of external internet sites

Top Europe stories now:

- Mass resignations rock

Internet

FIGURE 10.4 BBC report on an arrested hacker.

skilled hacker using his knowledge to conduct espionage operations. This espionage is likely occurring much more often than is reported in the media, and many such incidents may never come to light.

Alternative media sources have been reporting that both the CIA and NSA have employed hackers for some time. This might be easily dismissed as false were it not for the fact that such hackers have actually been caught, as in the Russian story. One might even go so far as to say that, in our

FYI: The Threat of Cyber Terrorism

Fortunately, to date, the examples given in this text, are about the most dramatic that have been made public. Cyber terrorism is not a big problem today; it is the problem that is looming on our horizon.

modern age, for intelligence gathering agencies not to employee cyber intelligence-gathering techniques would be a dereliction of their duty.

What is also frightening to consider are reports that our satellites, used for communication, weather, and military operations, could be vulnerable to hacking (Roberts, 2002). Such vulnerabilities seem less likely simply because of the skill level required to execute such an attack. As previously mentioned, hacking/cracking is like any other human endeavor—by the law of averages, most people are mediocre. The level of skill required to compromise security on a satellite system is far greater than that required to compromise the security of a Web site. Of course, that does not mean that such an attack is impossible, but simply that it is less likely.

Future Trends

By carefully analyzing what is occurring presently in cyber crime and terrorism along with the recent history of that field, you can extrapolate and make reasonably accurate estimates for what trends will dominate in the

FIGURE 10.5 The Cyberterrorism Preparedness Act of 2002.

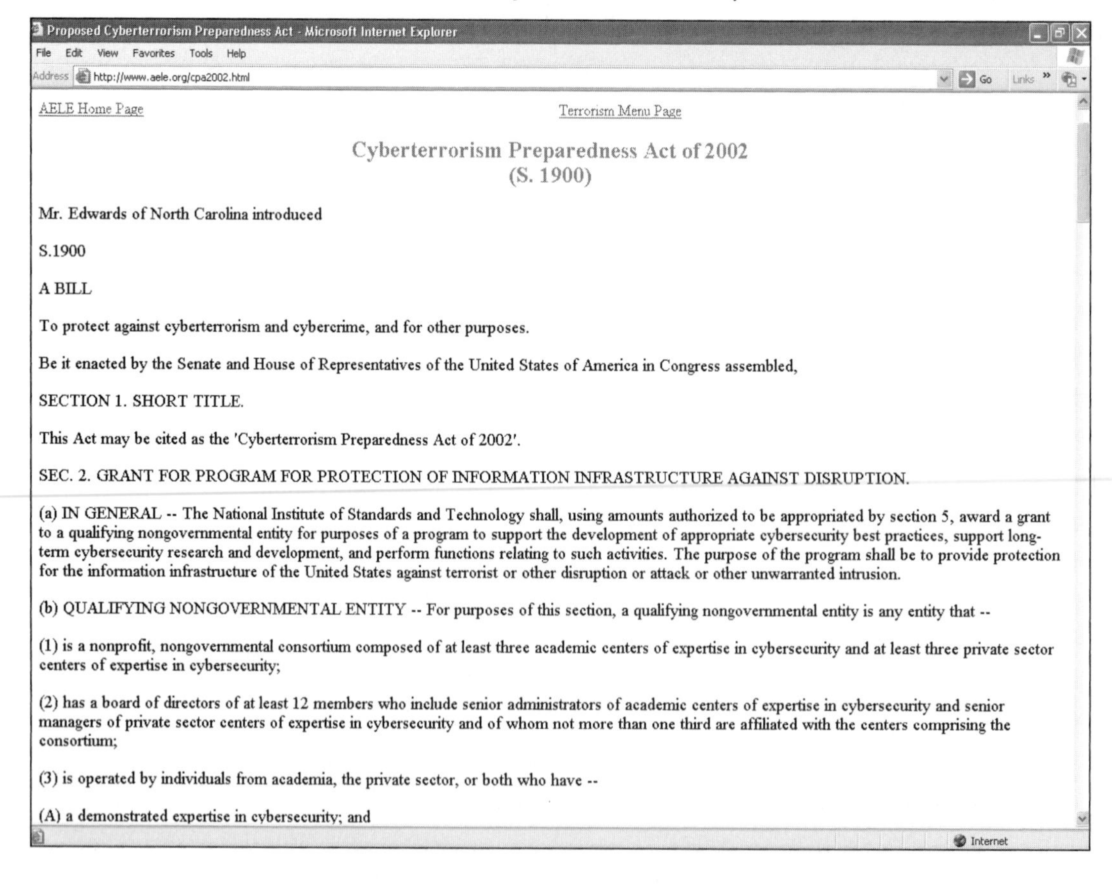

Proposed Cyberterrorism Preparedness Act - Microsoft Internet Explorer

File Edit View Favorites Tools Help

Address http://www.aele.org/cpa2002.html

AELE Home Page

Terrorism Menu Page

Cyberterrorism Preparedness Act of 2002
(S. 1900)

Mr. Edwards of North Carolina introduced

S.1900

A BILL

To protect against cyberterrorism and cybercrime, and for other purposes.

Be it enacted by the Senate and House of Representatives of the United States of America in Congress assembled,

SECTION 1. SHORT TITLE.

This Act may be cited as the 'Cyberterrorism Preparedness Act of 2002'.

SEC. 2. GRANT FOR PROGRAM FOR PROTECTION OF INFORMATION INFRASTRUCTURE AGAINST DISRUPTION.

(a) IN GENERAL -- The National Institute of Standards and Technology shall, using amounts authorized to be appropriated by section 5, award a grant to a qualifying nongovernmental entity for purposes of a program to support the development of appropriate cybersecurity best practices, support long-term cybersecurity research and development, and perform functions relating to such activities. The purpose of the program shall be to provide protection for the information infrastructure of the United States against terrorist or other disruption or attack or other unwarranted intrusion.

(b) QUALIFYING NONGOVERNMENTAL ENTITY -- For purposes of this section, a qualifying nongovernmental entity is any entity that --

(1) is a nonprofit, nongovernmental consortium composed of at least three academic centers of expertise in cybersecurity and at least three private sector centers of expertise in cybersecurity;

(2) has a board of directors of at least 12 members who include senior administrators of academic centers of expertise in cybersecurity and senior managers of private sector centers of expertise in cybersecurity and of whom not more than one third are affiliated with the centers comprising the consortium;

(3) is operated by individuals from academia, the private sector, or both who have --

(A) a demonstrated expertise in cybersecurity; and

Internet

near future. This section will endeavor to do that. There are certainly positive and negative trends that should be considered.

Positive Trends

It does seem that various governments are beginning to take notice of this problem and are taking some steps to ameliorate the dangers. For example, U.S. senator John Edwards (D-NC) proposed two bills in 2002 aimed at allocating $400 million for cybersecurity efforts. The first measure, called the Cyberterrorism Preparedness Act of 2002 (Tech Law Journal, 2002), a portion of which is shown in Figure 10.5, would set aside $350 million over five years for improving network security, first for Federal systems and then for the private sector. It would also create a group assigned to gather and distribute information about the best security practices. The Cybersecurity Research and Education Act of 2002 (The Orator, 2002), a portion of which is shown in Figure 10.6, would provide $50 million over four years for fellowships that would be used to train IT specialists in cyber security. It also

FIGURE 10.6 Cybersecurity Research and Education Act of 2002.

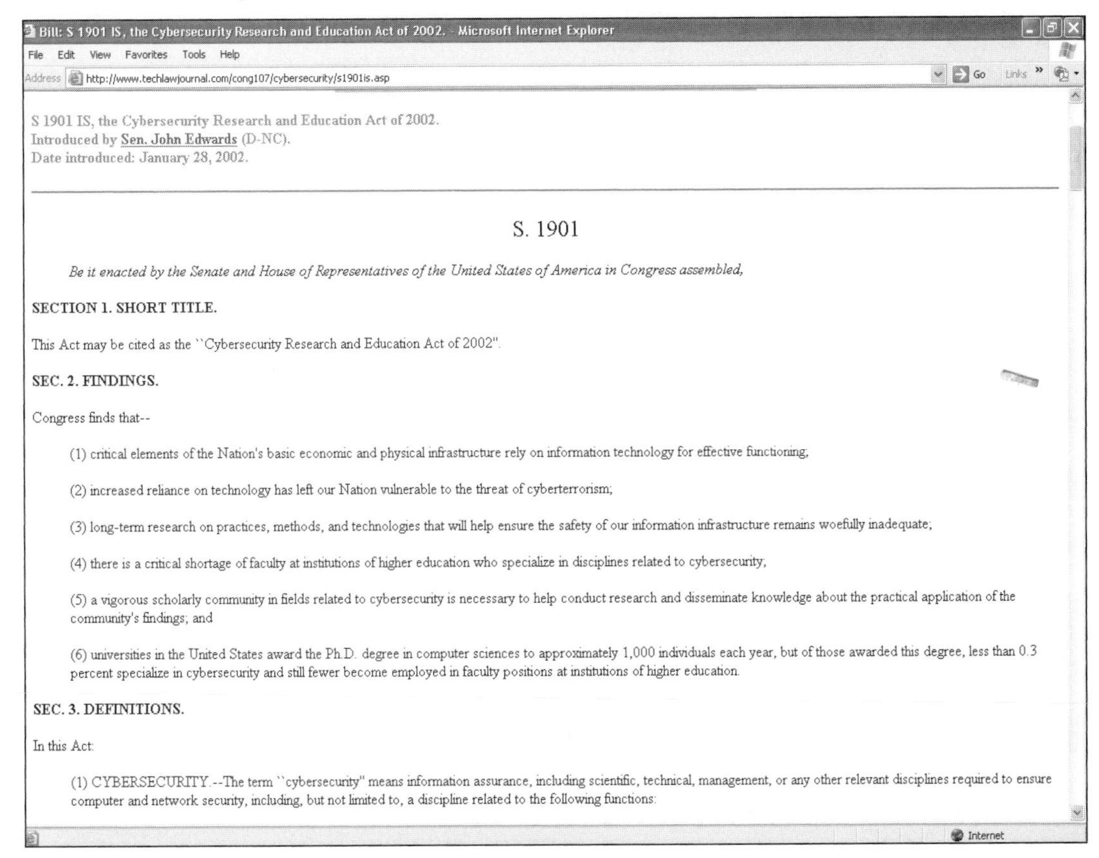

Bill: S 1901 IS, the Cybersecurity Research and Education Act of 2002. - Microsoft Internet Explorer

File Edit View Favorites Tools Help

Address http://www.techlawjournal.com/cong107/cybersecurity/s1901is.asp

S 1901 IS, the Cybersecurity Research and Education Act of 2002.
Introduced by Sen. John Edwards (D-NC).
Date introduced: January 28, 2002.

S. 1901

Be it enacted by the Senate and House of Representatives of the United States of America in Congress assembled,

SECTION 1. SHORT TITLE.

This Act may be cited as the "Cybersecurity Research and Education Act of 2002".

SEC. 2. FINDINGS.

Congress finds that--

(1) critical elements of the Nation's basic economic and physical infrastructure rely on information technology for effective functioning;

(2) increased reliance on technology has left our Nation vulnerable to the threat of cyberterrorism;

(3) long-term research on practices, methods, and technologies that will help ensure the safety of our information infrastructure remains woefully inadequate;

(4) there is a critical shortage of faculty at institutions of higher education who specialize in disciplines related to cybersecurity;

(5) a vigorous scholarly community in fields related to cybersecurity is necessary to help conduct research and disseminate knowledge about the practical application of the community's findings; and

(6) universities in the United States award the Ph.D. degree in computer sciences to approximately 1,000 individuals each year, but of those awarded this degree, less than 0.3 percent specialize in cybersecurity and still fewer become employed in faculty positions at institutions of higher education.

SEC. 3. DEFINITIONS.

In this Act:

(1) CYBERSECURITY.--The term "cybersecurity" means information assurance, including scientific, technical, management, or any other relevant disciplines required to ensure computer and network security, including, but not limited to, a discipline related to the following functions:

Internet

calls for the creation of a Web-based university where administrators can get updated training. As of this writing, both bills are in committee and have not come before the entire Senate for a vote. However, the fact that bills such as this, and others, are being considered by various governments, including the U.S. government, is a step in the right direction.

Negative Trends

Unfortunately, as legislative bodies become aware of this problem and focus some resources on the issue, the threats continue to grow. In a paper commissioned by the Rand Corporation (Hoffman, 2003), it is noted that even groups such as Al Queda—who have not used cyber terrorism as one of their attack modalities as of this writing—have used Internet and computer technology resources to plan their various activities and coordinate training.

As early as 2000, the U. S. General Accounting Office warned of several possible cyber terrorism scenarios (Tech Law Journal, 2000). As shown in Figure 10.7, their concerns involved far more lethal attackers than any of

FIGURE 10.7 Rand report on cyber terrorism.

Story: Advisory Panel Reports on Cyber Terrorism - Microsoft Internet Explorer

File Edit View Favorites Tools Help

Address http://www.techlawjournal.com/security/20001214.asp

Home | Calendar | Subscribe | Back Issues | Reference

Advisory Panel Reports on Cyber Terrorism

(December 14, 2000) A national domestic terrorism advisory panel released its second annual report on terrorism, weapons of mass destruction, and cyber terrorism. The panel's Chairman, Gov. James Gilmore, stated that cyber terrorism "can be a very deliberate attack on the capabilities of the United States to respond to any other type of attack." The panel recommended the creation of an executive branch office, and Congressional committees, with responsibility for combating terrorism.

The report references two possible cyber terrorist scenarios. First, "It is easy to envision a coordinated attack by terrorists, using a conventional or small-scale chemical device, with cyber attacks against law enforcement communications, emergency medical facilities, and other systems critical to a response."

Second, "it is conceivable that terrorists could mount a cyber attack against power or water facilities or industrial plants -- for example, a commercial chemical plant that produces a highly toxic substance -- to produce casualties in the hundreds of thousands."

The report adds that "the most likely perpetrators of cyber-attacks on critical infrastructures are terrorists and criminal groups rather than nation-states."

Related Documents
See, Second Annual Report of the Advisory Panel to Assess Domestic Response Capabilities for Terrorism Involving Weapons of Mass Destruction, dated Dec. 15, 2000.
The full report with appendices is a 191 page PDF file in a Rand Corporation web site.
See also, Rand page with links to other related documents.

Virginia Governor James Gilmore released the panel's second annual report at a press conference at the National Press Club in Washington DC on Thursday morning, December 14. He was joined by the panel's Vice Chairman, Lt. Gen. Clapper (ret.), former Army Secretary John Marsh, and Executive Director of the panel, Mike Wormouth. In addition, Sen. John Warner (R-VA), Chairman of the Senate Armed Services Committee, attended the event, but did not participate.

The panel is named the Advisory Panel to Assess Domestic Response Capabilities for Terrorism Involving Weapons of Mass Destruction. It was created by an Act of Congress in April 1999, and charged with writing three annual reports on terrorist threats. The report just released is the second of three.

Gov. James Gilmore

"These recommendations concern the terrorist threat, the need for a national strategy and its components, the role of the executive branch and the Congress, the emphasis on protecting our civil liberties, the intelligence community, and the Department of Defense, and state and local first responders," said Gov. Gilmore.

"Terrorism is not solely a federal issue. It is also a state issue, and community issue. As such, it makes it a truly national issue for all the people of the United States."

"Some have suggested that we are totally unprepared to meet the threat of terrorism in our own front yard. That is inaccurate, and it is untrue. But, we can be better prepared. Indeed, we must become better prepared," said Gov. Gilmore.

"No one, as they listen to this report, and the discussions of our panel, anywhere in the world should make any mistake about our commitment to preparation, our capacities that we

Gov. Gilmore's Comments on Cyber Terrorism

Internet

the scenarios that have been outlined in this chapter. They proposed possible attack scenarios in which the computer-controlled machinery in a chemical plant was altered in order to cause a release of toxic chemicals into the environment. This could be done in a variety of ways including simply causing the machinery to drastically over-produce, overheat, or perhaps prematurely shut down equipment. The panel also contemplated scenarios in which water and power supplies were interrupted or compromised via computer systems. In essence, their focus was on the potential for massive casualties as a direct result of a cyber-based attack rather than the economic damage on which this chapter's scenarios focused.

Defense Against Cyber Terrorism

As the world becomes more dependent upon computer systems, the danger of cyber terrorism will grow. Clearly, there must be a much stronger emphasis on computer security. In addition to the basic security measures already recommended in this book, there are also some recommendations for preparing for and protecting systems against cyber terrorism.

- Many recommend a Manhattan Project-level government program designed to prepare for and defend against cyber warfare.
- Major academic institutions must begin dedicated research and academic programs that are devoted solely to computer security.
- Computer crime must be treated far more seriously, with stronger punishments and more active investigation of suspected crimes.
- It is unreasonable to ask every police department to have a computer-crime specialist on staff. However, state-level investigative agencies should be able to hire such personnel. Rather than take law enforcement officers and train them in basic computer crime, the recommendation exists to take highly skilled computer professionals and train them in law enforcement. To adequately combat cyber terrorism, one absolutely must first and foremost be a highly qualified computer expert.
- An emergency reporting system may need to be implemented so that security professionals from various industries have a single source where they can report attacks on their systems and can view the issues with which other security professionals are dealing. This could enable security professionals as a group to more quickly recognize when a coordinated attack is occurring.

In addition, you can make some additions to and variations on your existing security measures. For example, you should have a recovery process in place so that data can be quickly recovered should someone delete important files. You should also, as recommended in Chapter 9, assess what data is of most value and focus your attention on that data. But, as this chapter points out, you must also consider how data that would at first appear to be of less value may actually reveal more information about you personally or your company then is prudent.

Summary

It is clear that there are a variety of ways in which cyber terrorist attacks could be used against any industrialized nation. Many experts, including various government panels, senators, and terrorism experts, believe that this is a very real threat. This means that it is more important than ever to be extremely vigilant in securing your computer systems. You must also look beyond the obvious uses of data and see how someone with an intent to harm or cause economic hardship could use seemingly unimportant information. In the exercises at the end of this chapter, you will have a chance to explore various cyber terrorism and information warfare threats.

Test Your Skills

MULTIPLE CHOICE QUESTIONS

1. What is the most likely damage from an act of cyber terrorism?
   A. loss of life
   B. military strategy compromised
   C. economic loss
   D. disrupted communications

2. Which of the following is not an example of financial loss due to cyber terrorism?
   A. lost data
   B. transferring money from accounts
   C. damage to facilities including computers
   D. computer fraud

3. Which of the following military/government systems would most likely be the target of a successful computer hack?
   A. The most sensitive systems of the CIA
   B. Nuclear systems at NORAD
   C. Low-security logistical system
   D. Military satellite control systems
4. Which of the following might be an example of domestic cyber terrorism?
   A. Sasser virus
   B. Mimail virus
   C. Sobig virus
   D. MyDoom virus
5. What differentiates cyber terrorism from other computer crimes?
   A. It is organized.
   B. It is politically or ideologically motivated.
   C. It is conducted by experts.
   D. It is often more successful.
6. Which of the following is a political group that has already used the Internet for political intimidation?
   A. Internet Black Tigers
   B. Al Queda
   C. Mafia
   D. IRA
7. What is information warfare?
   A. Only spreading disinformation
   B. Spreading disinformation or gathering information
   C. Only gathering information
   D. Spreading disinformation or secure communications
8. Which of the following would most likely be considered examples of information warfare?
   A. Radio Free Europe during the Cold War
   B. radio political talk show
   C. normal news reports
   D. military press releases

9. Which of the following is a likely use of Internet newsgroups in information warfare?
   A. To spread propaganda
   B. To monitor dissident groups
   C. To send encoded messages
   D. To recruit supporters

10. Sending a false message with weak encryption, intending it to be intercepted and deciphered, is an example of what?
    A. poor communications
    B. need for better encryption
    C. disinformation
    D. propaganda

11. Which of the following best describes the communication goal of any intelligence agency?
    A. To send clear communications to allies and noise to all other parties
    B. To send clear communications to allies and noise only to the enemy
    C. To send disinformation to the enemy
    D. To send clear communications to allied forces

12. Which of the following conflicts had a cyber warfare component?
    A. 1989 invasion of Panama
    B. 1990 Kosovo crisis
    C. 1990 Somalia crisis
    D. Vietnam War

13. Which of the following agencies has allegedly had one of its cyber spies actually caught?
    A. NSA
    B. KGB
    C. FBI
    D. CIA

14. According to the October 2002 *InfoWorld* magazine article, which of the following systems may be vulnerable to attack?

    A. NORAD nuclear weapons control

    B. low-level logistical systems

    C. satellites

    D. CIA computers

15. Which of the following is a cyber attack that would likely cause imminent loss of life?

    A. disruption of banking system

    B. disruption of water

    C. disruption of security systems

    D. disruption of chemical plant control systems

EXERCISES

Exercise 10.1: Finding Information Warfare

1. Pick a current political topic.
2. Track that topic on multiple bulletin boards, Yahoo newsgroups, or blogs.
3. Look for signs that might indicate an organized effort to sway opinion or information warfare. This might include posts allegedly made by separate individuals that have highly similar points, grammar, and syntax.
4. Write a brief essay discussing what you found and why you think it constitutes information warfare.

Exercise 10.2: Cyber Terrorism Threat Assessment

1. Pick some activist group (e.g., political, ideological) that you find intriguing.
2. Using only the Web, gather as much information about that organization as you can.
3. Write a brief dossier on that group, including what you think is the likelihood that such a group would engage in information warfare or cyber terrorism and why.

Exercise 10.3: Finding Information Policies

1. Using the Web or other resources, locate several examples of organizational policies regarding information dissemination.
2. Find points common to all such policies.
3. Write a brief essay explaining why these policies might be related to either propagating or preventing information warfare.

Exercise 10.4: How Companies Defend Against Cyber Terrorism

1. Interview the IT staff of a company to find out whether they take information warfare or cyber terrorism into direct account when they are securing their systems.
2. Find out what steps they take to protect their company's systems from these threats.
3. Write a brief essay explaining what you have found out.

Exercise 10.5: Pulling it All Together

Pulling together what you have learned from previous chapters, what information can you apply to the protection of a system against cyber terrorism or information warfare? Write a brief outline of the steps you would take to secure a system against these threats.

PROJECTS

Project 10.1: Computer Security and Cyber Terrorism

Consider the various security measures you have examined thus far in this book. Given the threat of cyber terrorism, write an essay discussing how those methods might relate to cyber terrorism. Also discuss whether or not the threat of computer-based terrorism warrants a higher security standard than you might have otherwise used, and explain why or why not.

Project 10.2: The Law and Cyber Terrorism

Note: This is meant as a group project.

Using the Web or other resources, find and examine laws that you feel relate to cyber terrorism. Then write an essay describing legislation you believe needs to be written regarding cyber terrorism. Essentially, your group should act as if it were technical advisors to a congressional committee drafting new legislation.

Project 10.3: Cyber Terrorism Scenario

Considering any of the theoretical cyber terrorism scenarios presented in this chapter, write a security and response plan that you feel addresses that scenario and protects against that specific threat.

Case Study

Jane Doe is the network administrator responsible for security for a small defense contractor. Her company does handle some low-level classified material. She has implemented a strong security approach that includes:

- A firewall has all unneeded ports closed.
- Virus scanners are placed on all machines.
- Routers between network segments are secured.
- All machines have the operating systems patched monthly.
- Passwords are long, complex, and change every 90 days.

What other recommendations would you make to Jane Doe? Explain the reasons for each of your recommendations.

Chapter 11

Cyber Detective

Chapter Objectives

After reading this chapter and completing the exercises, you will be able to do the following:

- Find contact information on the Web.
- Locate court records on the Web.
- Locate criminal records on the Web.
- Use Usenet newsgroups to gather information.

Introduction

In the preceding chapters we have examined many facets of computer security. Three of those issues lead us to the content of this chapter. The first is identity theft, the second is hacking, and the third is investigating potential employees for sensitive positions.

In order for a criminal to perpetrate identity theft they have to take a small amount of information they find on their target and use that to garner even more information. Perhaps a discarded credit card receipt, or utility bill becomes the starting point from which the perpetrator finds enough information to assume the victim's identity. This chapter will show you some techniques that use the Internet to find additional information about a person. You need to be aware of how this is done, in order to be better prepared to defend against it and so that you are aware of what information about you personally is available.

Hackers, at least skilled hackers, will want information about a target person, organization, and system in order to assist in compromising security. Whether the perpetrator is attempting to use social engineering, or simply trying to guess a password, having information about the target will facilitate the task. Once you realize how easy it is to gain personal information about someone, you will realize why security experts are so adamant that you must not use passwords that are in any way associated with you, your profession, your hobbies, or anything that might be traced back to you.

Finally, when you are hiring employees that might have access to sensitive data, simply calling the references they provide is not an adequate method of checking into their background. And hiring a private investigator may be impractical. The information in this chapter might be of use to you in conducting some level of investigation on your own.

This may surprise some readers, but network administrators are of particular significance to be investigated before hiring. Most companies perform the same cursory check of network administrators as they do of any other person. That usually consists of verifying degrees/certifications and calling references. With some companies it might include a credit check and a local criminal check. However, a network administrator should be more thoroughly investigated. The reason is quite simple, regardless of how tight your security is, it cannot keep out the person who sets it up and maintains it. If you are considering hiring a network administrator for your company, knowing that he or she has been affiliated with hacking groups might be of interest to you. Or simply knowing that they have had lapses in judgment might indicate a stronger possibility that they will have similar lapses in the future. This may seem a bit paranoid, but by this point in this book you should have developed a little healthy paranoia.

The Internet can be a valuable investigation tool. It can be used to find out about potential employees, baby sitters, etc. Much of the information on the Internet is also free. Many states have court records online, and there are many other resources you can use to find information. In this chapter we will examine some of the various resources you can use on the Internet to locate critical information.

Before beginning this discussion, a few points need to be made clear. The first being that this information is a two edged sword. Yes, you can use it to find out if a potential business partner has previously been sued or declared bankruptcy, or if your child's little league coach has a criminal record. However as we briefly mentioned, a less scrupulous person can also use these techniques to gather detailed information about you, either for the purpose of identity theft or perhaps stalking. Some people have suggested to me that perhaps I should not put this information (and some other items that appear in various chapters) in this book. However my opinion is that the hackers, crackers, and perpetrators of identity theft already know about these resources, my hope is to level the playing field. I would also warn all readers that invading other people's privacy is fraught with ethical, moral, and in many cases legal, ramifications. It would be advisable to obtain written permission before running a background check on any person—or, better yet, play it safe and only perform searches on your own name. It must also be stressed that I am neither an attorney nor a law enforcement officer. I am simply providing you with techniques and resources. If you have questions about legality, you should refer those questions to an attorney.

General Searches

Sometimes you simply want to find an address, phone number, or e-mail address for a person. Or perhaps that is the starting point for a more thorough investigation. There are a number of absolutely free services on the Web that will allow you to perform this sort of search. Some are better than others, and obviously the more common the name you are searching for the harder it will be to find the right one. If you do a search for John Smith in California, you might have a tough time dealing with all the results you get.

A fairly easy to use service is the Yahoo People Search. When you go to **www.yahoo.com** you see a number of options on the page. One option is the 'People Search' shown in Figure 11.1.

When you select this option you will see a screen similar to the one shown in Figure 11.2. In this screen you enter a first and last name, as well as a city or state. You can then search for either a phone number/address or an email.

FIGURE 11.1 Yahoo People Search

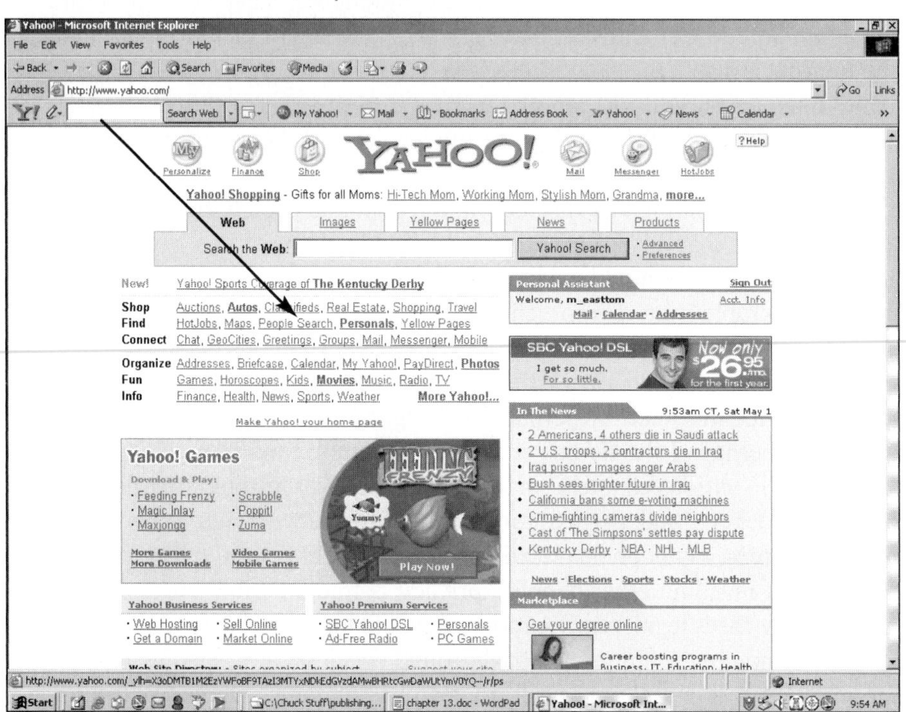

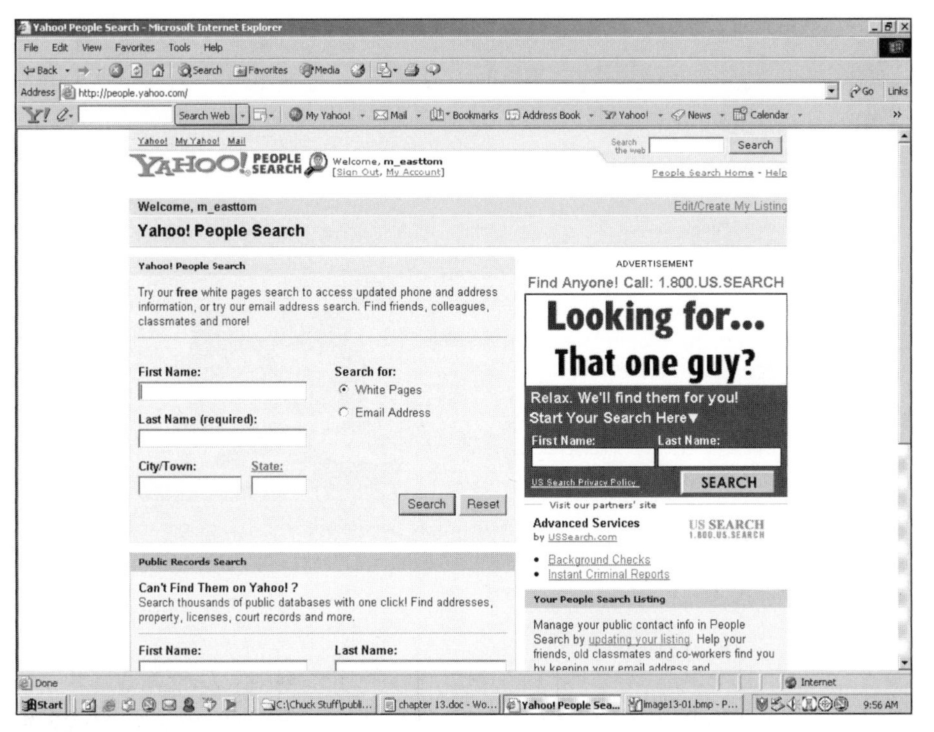

FIGURE 11.2 Search options

To illustrate how this works, I did a search on my own name, in Texas (where I live). As Figure 11.3 shows, that search results in my home address and phone number, as well two listings for my wife, Misty—one that shows our current address and phone number and one that shows our previous address and phone number.

Another useful site for addresses and phone numbers around the world is **www.infobel.com**. This site has the advantage of being international, allowing you to seek out phone numbers and addresses in a variety of countries. As you can see from Figure 11.4, the first step is to select a country to search in.

Once you have selected your country, you can then narrow your search further by providing as much information as you can on the person you are trying to locate. A first and last name, however, is a minimum.

These are just two of the many sites that allow you to investigate and discover a person's home address or telephone number. Several other good sites you should consider are listed below.

- www.smartpages.com
- www.theultimates.com/white/
- www.bigfoot.com/

Caution

Multiple Results

When searching for phone numbers and addresses, you can frequently find multiple wrong results, especially when searching for a common name. For example if you search for John Smith in the state of New York, the chances are you will get a huge number of results. The more information you have to narrow your search, the better. Even the search on "Easttom" in "Texas", a fairly uncommon name and, hence, a narrow search, resulted in one right listing and one wrong listing for Misty Easttom.

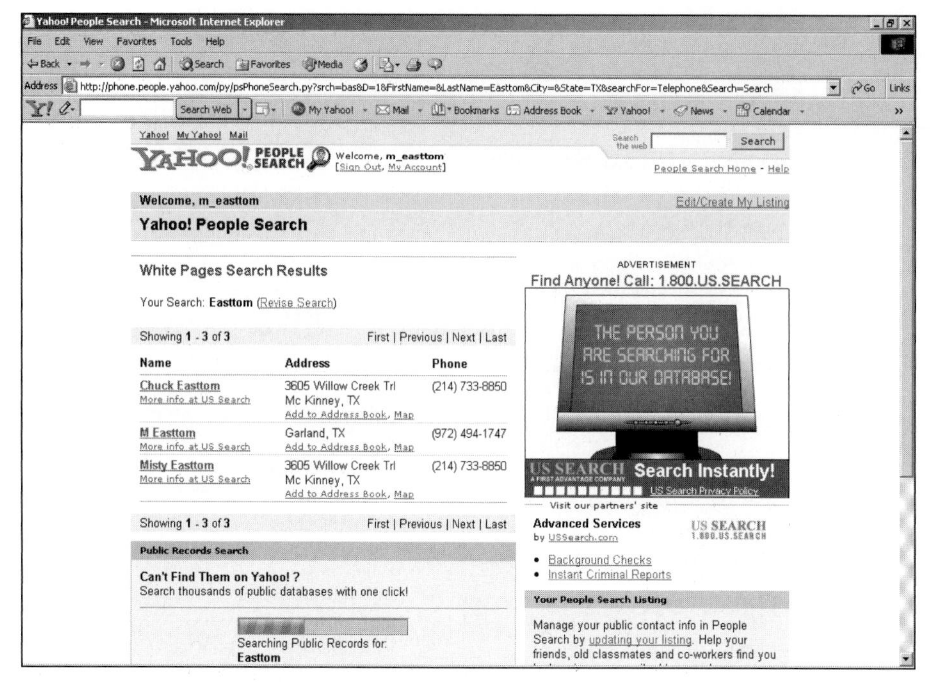

FIGURE 11.3 People Search results

FIGURE 11.4 Infobel home page

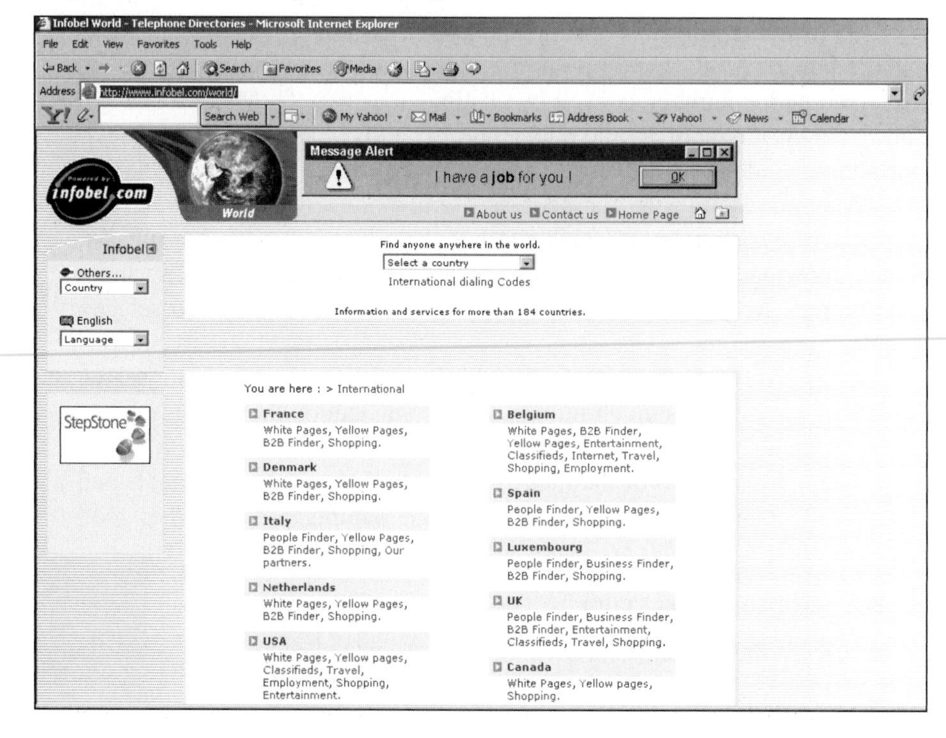

FYI: Respecting Privacy

You might wonder why I would be willing to put my home address and phone number in a published book. To begin with, anyone reading this chapter could easily have done their own search and found my information. And, in order to illustrate the process, I needed a name to use. For the liability reasons mentioned earlier I could not have used someone else's name. However, should readers wish to contact me, they are strongly encouraged to do so via my Web site (**www.chuckeasttom.com**) and email address (**chuckeasttom@yahoo.com**) rather than via phone. I try to answer all my email, but frequently avoid my phone. And I am certainly not encouraging anyone to make a surprise visit to my home!

Caution

Mistaken Identity

There have been cases of mistaken identity with sex offender lists. Any time you find negative information on a person you are investigating—whatever the source—you have an ethical responsibility to verify that information before you take any action on it.

- www.whowhere.com
- www.switchboard.com
- www.people.icq.com/whitepages

It is important to remember that the more information you can provide, and the more you narrow down your search, the greater the likelihood of finding what you are looking for. All of these Web sites can assist you in finding phone numbers and addresses, both current and past. For a background check on an employee this can be useful in verifying previous addresses.

Court Records and Criminal Checks

A number of states are now putting a variety of court records online. Everything from general court documents to specific records of criminal history and even lists of pedophiles. This sort of information can be critical before you hire an employee, use a babysitter, or send your child to little league. In the following sections, we discuss a variety of resources for this sort of information.

Sex Offender Registries

First, you should become familiar with the online sex offender registries. The FBI maintains a rather exhaustive list of individual state registries. You can access this information at **www.fbi.gov/hq/cid/cac/registry.htm**. Every state that has an online registry is listed on this Web site, as shown in Figure 11.5. Obviously some states have done a better job of making accurate information public, than have others. For example, Texas has a rather

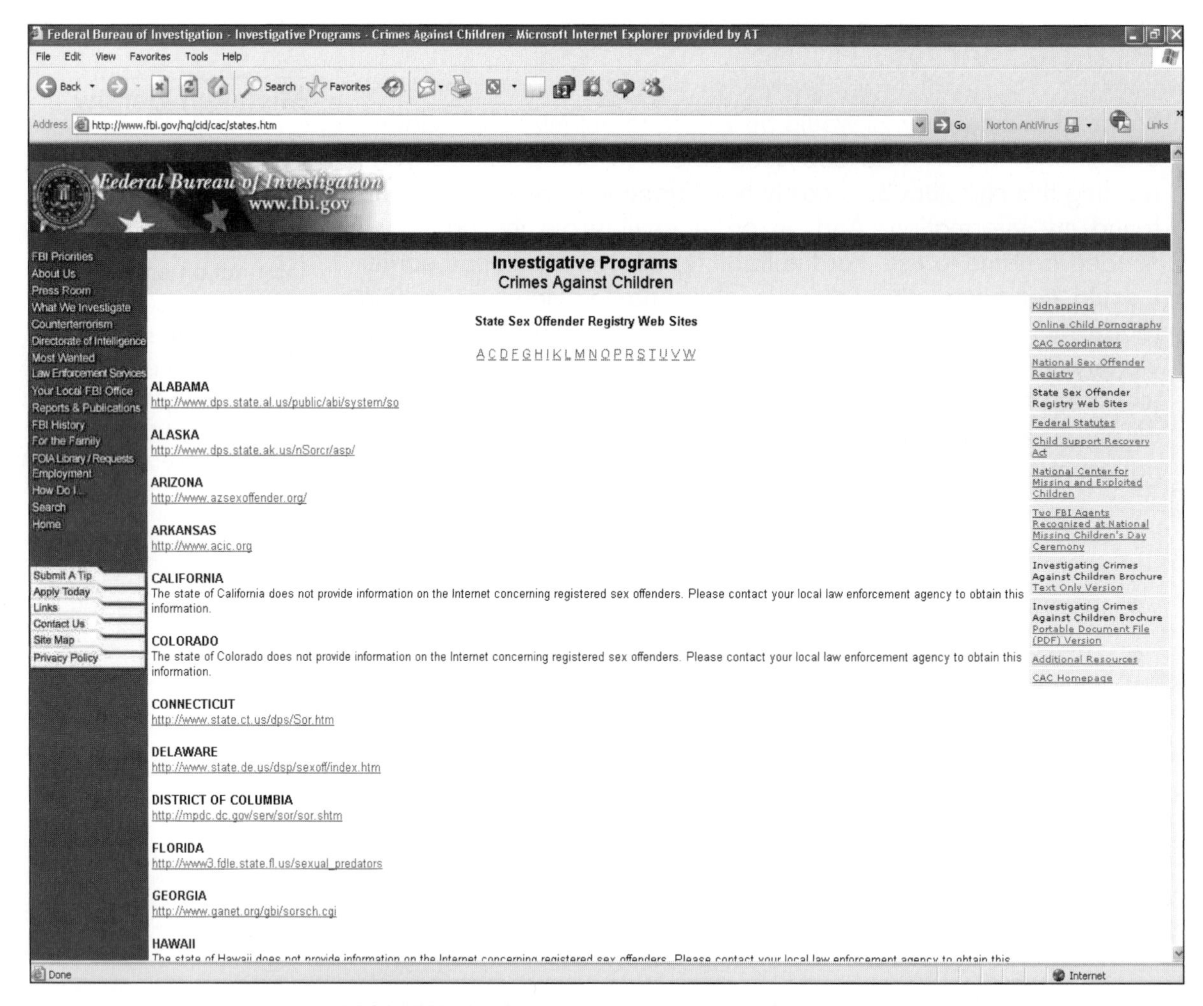

FIGURE 11.5 FBI state registry of sex offenders.

comprehensive site. You can find it at **records.txdps.state.tx.us/**. This site allows you to either look up an individual person, or to put in a zip code (or city name) and find out any registered sex offenders in that area. Figure 11.6 shows the search screen for the Texas site mentioned.

One of the most compelling things about the Texas sex offender registry is that it lists the offense the person was convicted of as well as a photo of the offender. This is important since the term 'sex offender' covers a wide variety of crimes. Some of which may not, for example, impact whether you should hire this person. It is important to know what a person was convicted of before you decide they are unsuitable to be interacting with your children or working in your organization.

Some sex offenders have committed heinous crimes and many parents will want to use this information to find out about potential baby sitters and

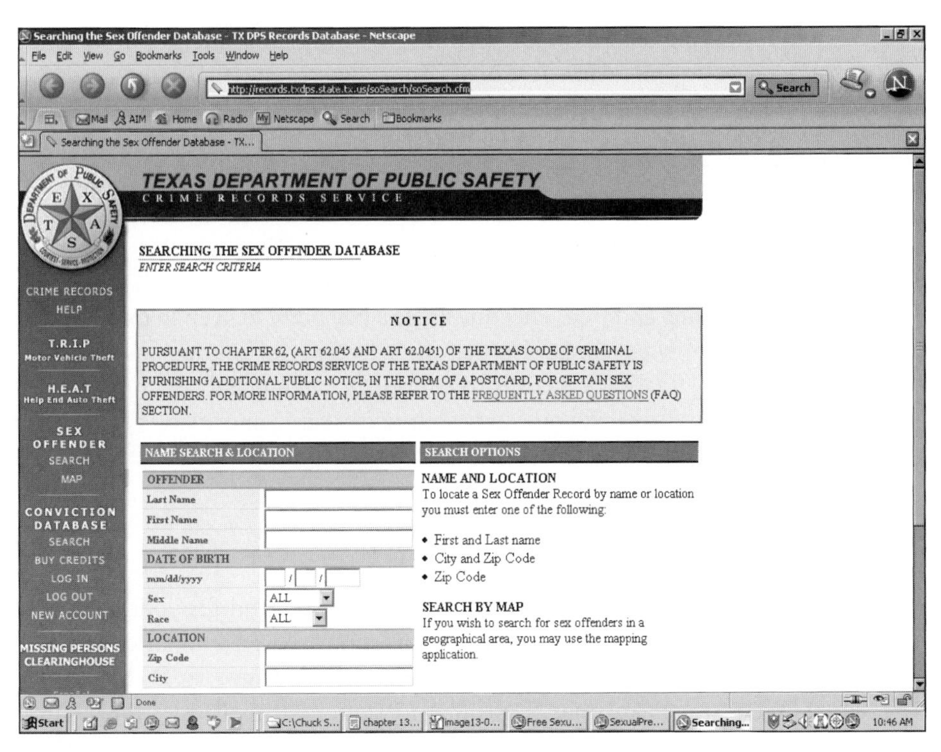

FIGURE 11.6 Texas sex offender search page

coaches. This information may also be applicable to employment screenings. However, anytime any information is used for employment screening it is advisable to check the laws in your area. You may not legally be able to base employment decisions on certain information. As with all legal questions, your best course of action is to consult a reputable attorney.

Civil Court Records

There are a variety of crimes, as well as civil issues, a person might be involved in that would make them unsuitable for a particular job. If you are hiring a person to work in your human resources department and oversee equal opportunity issues, knowing if they had been involved in domestic violence, racially motivated graffiti, or other similar issues, might effect your employment decision. Or, if you are considering a business partnership, it would be prudent to discover if you prospective partner has ever been sued by other business partners, or has ever filed for bankruptcy. Unfortunately, in any of these cases, you cannot simply rely on the other parties honesty. You need to check these things out for yourself.

Unfortunately this area of legal issues has not been transferred to a Web format as well as sex crimes. However many states and federal courts do offer online records. One of the best organized and most complete on this issue, is the state of Oklahoma. You can find their Web site at **www.oscn.net/applications/oscn/casesearch.asp**, and their home search page is shown in Figure 11.7.

This site allows you to search by last name, last and first name, case number, and more. You will get a complete record of any case you find, including current disposition and any filings. This includes both civil and criminal proceedings. Oddly enough, there are at least five different Web sites offering information on Oklahoma court cases for a fee—when all of that information is online and free. This illustrates a key point to keep in mind. There are a number of sites/companies that offer to do searches for you, for fees ranging from $9.95 to $79.95. It is true that they can probably do it faster than you. But it is also true that you can find the exact same information these people do, for free. And hopefully this chapter will equip you with the information you need to do that successfully.

Other Resources

There are many other Web sites that can be quite helpful for your searches. There are a few that deserve particular attention. The National Center for State Courts has a Web site at **www.ncsconline.org/D_KIS/info_court_Web_sites.html** that lists links to state courts all over the United

FIGURE 11.7 Oklahoma Online Court Records

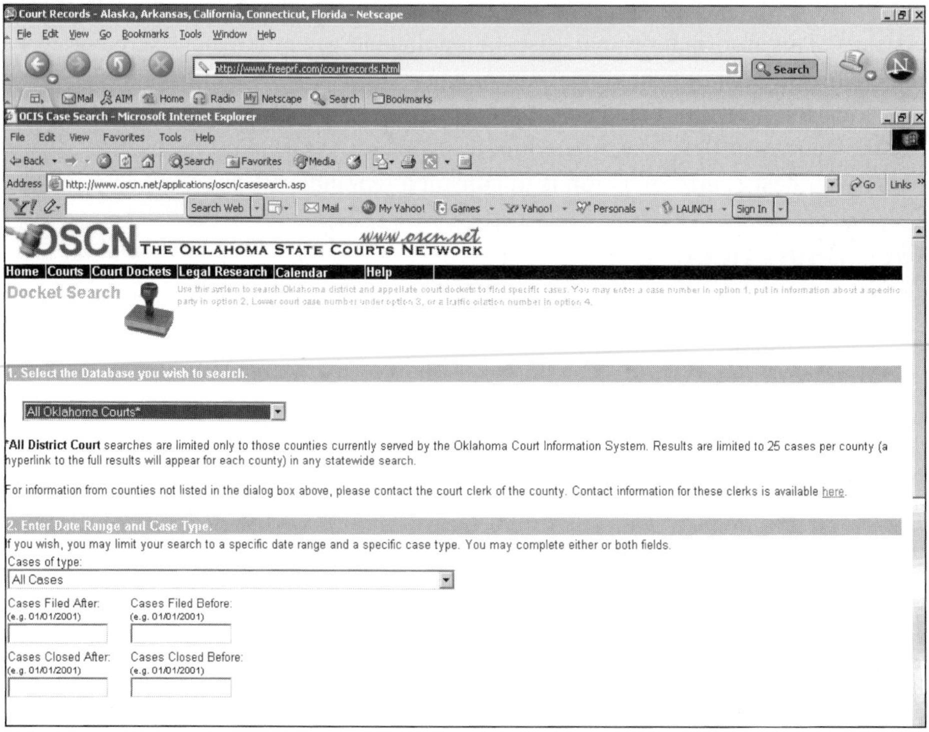

States. It also lists several international courts in countries like Australia, Brazil, Canada, and the United Kingdom. This Web site, as shown in Figure 11.8, is an excellent starting point if you are seeking court records. The Law School at Emory University has an interactive map that will help you find any federal court Web site in the United States. Their Web site is at **http://www.law.emory.edu/FEDCTS/**.

The following list is designed to give you a starting point for online Web searches across the United States. These Web sites should help you start your search for court records:

- Public Record Finder: **www.freeprf.com/courtrecords.html**
- Pacer: **www.pacer.psc.uscourts.gov/**

FIGURE 11.8 National Center for State Courts Web site.

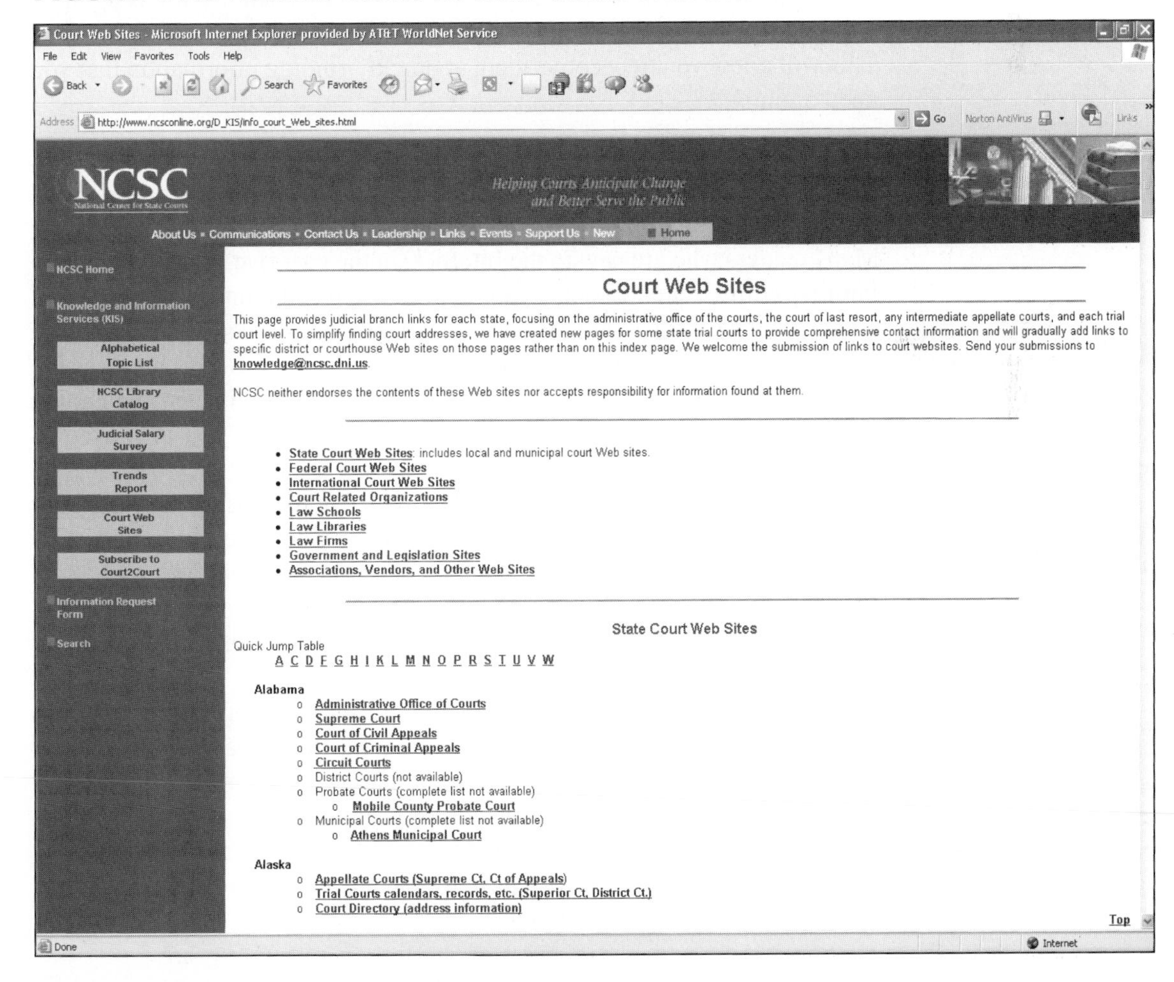

- The Boost: **www.theboost.net/court_records/**
- State Public Access: **www.ncsc.dni.us/NCSC/TIS/TIS99/PUBACS99/PublicAccesslinks.htm**
- Prison searches: **www.ancestorhunt.com/prison_search.htm**
- Federal Prison Records: **www.bop.gov/**
- Public Records: **www.searchsystems.net/**
- Public Records by State: **www.proagency.tripod.com/statesearchindex. html**
- United Kingdom Public Records: **www.pro.gov.uk/**

As you begin searching the Internet, you will find other sites that appeal to you. This may be due to their ease of use, content, or other factors. When you do find such sites, bookmark them. In a short time you will have an arsenal of online search engines. Also, your proficiency with using them will increase and you will learn which to use for which kind of information. This will allow you to become adept at quickly finding information that you need online.

Usenet

Many readers who are new to the Internet (in the past five years) may not be familiar with Usenet. Usenet is a global group of bulletin boards that exist on any subject you can imagine. There are specific software packages used to view these newsgroups, but for sometime now they have been accessible via Web portals. The search engine Google has an option on their main page, called 'Groups'. When you click on that option you are taken to Google's portal to Usenet newsgroups as shown in Figure 11.9.

As you can see, newsgroups are divided into broad categories. For example newsgroups devoted to science topics would be found under the heading *sci*. This includes groups like *sci.anthropology, sci.logic, sci.math.stat,* and more. The heading *alt* is a catch-all for anything and everything. This category includes things ranging from *alt.hacking* to *alt.adoption*.

You may be thinking that, while all this is fascinating, it does not have anything to do with tracking down information. But actually it does. If, for example, you were hiring a network administrator, you could see if she had posted in various network administration groups, and if those postings revealed key information about her network. This tool may be the single most important investigative tool you have, if you are willing to take the time and ferret out the information you need.

Caution

Usenet Information

Anyone can post anything on Usenet. There are no restrictions at all. So simply because you find a negative comment about a person on Usenet it is not wise to automatically assume that comment is true. These postings can only be viewed as part of an investigation and only credible if other facets of the investigation also support the postings you find.

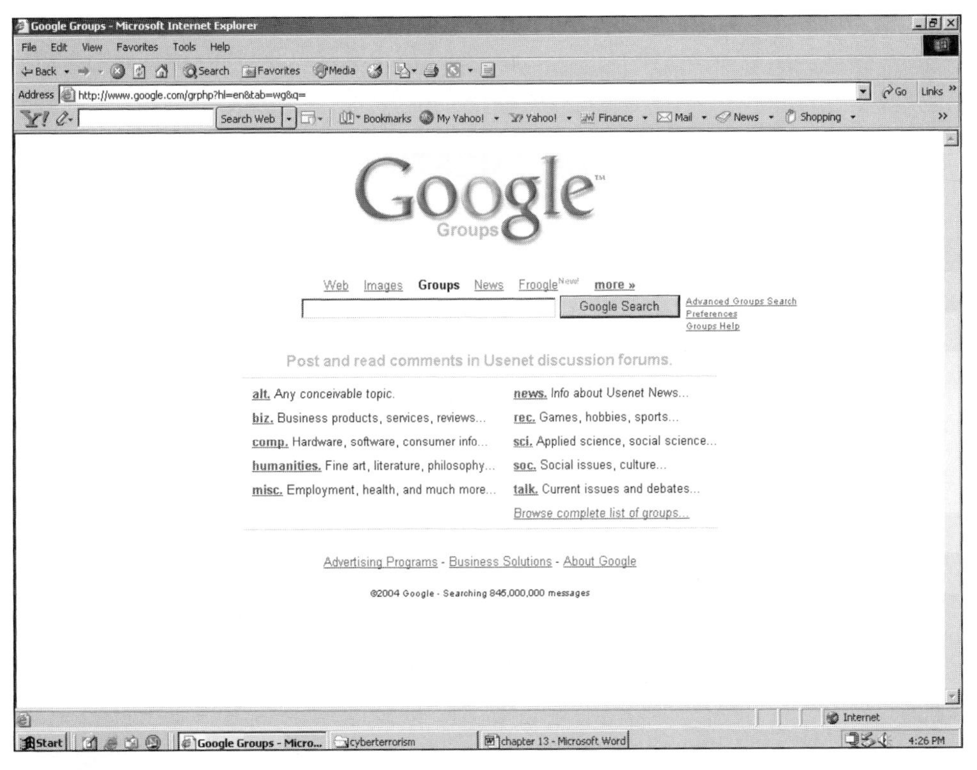

FIGURE 11.9 Google access to Usenet groups

Summary

We have seen in this chapter that the Internet can be a valuable resource for any sort of investigation. It is often one of the tools that hackers and identity thieves use to gain information about their target. However, it can also be a valuable tool for you in researching a prospective employee or business partner. It can also be invaluable for you to routinely find out what information is on the Internet about you. Seeing strange data that is not accurate can be an indication that you have already been the victim of identity theft.

Test Your Skills

MULTIPLE CHOICE QUESTIONS

1. How might an identity thief use the Internet to exploit his or her victim?

   A. He or she might find even more information about the target, and use this information to conduct their crime.

   B. He or she could find out how much the target has in their savings account.

   C. The identity thief usually does not use the Internet to accomplish his or her task.

   D. Identity thieves use the Internet to intercept your email and thus get access to your personal life.

2. Which of the following is not an ideal place to seek out phone numbers and addresses?

   A. Yahoo People Find

   B. People Search

   C. The international phone registry

   D. Infobell

3. Why do you not want too much personal data about you on the Internet?

   A. It might reveal embarrassing facts about you.

   B. It might be used by an identity thief to impersonate you.

   C. It might be used by a potential employer to find out more about you

   D. There is no reason to worry about personal information on the Internet.

4. How could a hacker use information about you found through Internet searches?
    A. To guess passwords if your passwords are linked to personal information such as your birth date, address, or phone number
    B. To guess passwords if your passwords are linked to your interests or hobbies
    C. In social engineering, to ascertain more information about you or your computer system
    D. All of the above
5. If you are hiring a new employee, which of the following should you do?
    A. Verify degrees and certifications
    B. Call references
    C. Perform an Internet search to verify contact information and to check for a criminal record
    D. All of the above
6. Which of the following would be LEAST important to know about a potential business partner?
    A. Past bankruptcies
    B. A 15-year-old marijuana possession arrest
    C. A law suit from a former business partner
    D. A recent DUI
7. What information would provide the most accurate results for locating a person?
    A. First name and state
    B. First name, last name, and state
    C. Last name and state
    D. First name and last name

8. Of the Web sites listed in this chapter, which would be the most useful in obtaining the address and phone number of someone who does not live in the United States?
    A. The FBI Web site
    B. Yahoo
    C. Infobel
    D. Google

9. Where would you go to find various state sex offender registries?
   A. The FBI Web site
   B. The national sex offender online database
   C. The interstate online sex offender database
   D. The special victims unit Web site

10. What is most important to learn about a person listed in a sex offender registry?
    A. The extent of his punishment
    B. How old she was when she committed their crime
    C. How long he has been out of prison
    D. The nature of her specific crime

11. Which Web search approach is best when checking criminal backgrounds?
    A. Check primarily the person's state of residence
    B. Check primarily federal records
    C. Check the current and previous state of residence
    D. Check as many places as might have information

12. What advantages are there to commercial Web search services?
    A. They can get information you cannot.
    B. They can get the information faster than you can.
    C. They can do a more thorough job than you can.
    D. They are legally entitled to do searches, you are not.

13. Which would you use to begin a search for information on a United States court case?
    A. The National Center for State Courts Web site
    B. Infobel
    C. Yahoo People Search
    D. Google Groups

14. Which of the following is the most accurate description of Usenet?
    A. A nation wide bulletin board
    B. A repository of computer security information
    C. A large scale chat room
    D. A global collection of bulletin boards

15. Which of the following is the most helpful data you might get from Usenet on a person you are investigating?
    A. Postings by the individual you are investigating
    B. Security tips to help you investigate
    C. Criminal records posted
    D. Negative comments made by others about your target

EXERCISES

For all Exercises and Projects in this chapter, you will concentrate your investigation on some person. It is best if you investigate yourself (which makes it easier to evaluate the accuracy of what you find) or if someone in the class or the instructor volunteers to be the target of the investigation. There are ethical issues with simply investigating random people without their knowledge or permission. It is also important to avoid embarrassing someone in the classroom. So the volunteer targets of the investigation should be certain they will not be embarrassed by whatever is found. Substitute the name of the person you are investigating for John Doe or Jane Doe in the projects and exercises.

Exercise 11.1: Finding Phone Numbers

1. Beginning with Yahoo People search, seek out phone numbers and addresses for John Doe.
2. Use at least two other sources to look up John's phone number.

Did you get too little information or too much information? Were you able to determine the correct, current number?

Exercise 11.2: Criminal Records Checks

1. Using sources listed in this chapter or other Web sites, look for criminal background information about John Doe. Start with the state John currently resides in, then check other states, particularly those that might have shown up with John's name in Exercise 1.
2. Expand your search to check for Federal crimes as well.

Exercise 11.3: Checking Court Cases

1. Search court records for any court cases for Jane Doe's business.
2. Check state licensing agency Web sites, if applicable, for any history or complaints on John's business.

Exercise 11.4: Finding Business Information on Usenet

1. Access Usenet.
2. Search bulletin boards and other groups that Jane Doe may have posted to in connection with her business.

Were you able to find out more about Jane's business through her postings to a Usenet group?

Exercise 11.5: Blocking Information

This chapter illustrated the many ways you can access information about someone and pointed out the potential hazards of having too much personal information available on the Internet. So, what can you do to prevent unscrupulous individuals from finding out too much about you? Check the primary Web sites listed in this chapter (i.e., Yahoo and Google) to see if they provide any means to block your information from being distributed. Are there any other means of blocking access to your personal information?

PROJECTS

Project 11.1: Investigating a Person

Using all of the Web resources in this chapter, and any others you come across, do a complete investigation of Jane Doe. Try to determine her address, phone number, occupation, age, and any criminal history. You might even check Usenet postings and find out clues as to Jane's hobbies and personal interests as well. Create a brief report on Jane based on your findings.

Project 11.2: Investigating a Company

Using all of the Web resources in this chapter, and any others you come across, do a complete investigation of John Doe's business. How long has he been in business? Are there any complaints about the business with any regulatory agency? Any complaints on Usenet boards? Any business relationships? Any past court proceedings? Write a report discussing your analysis of this business based on your findings.

Project 11.3: The Ethics of Investigation

Write an essay discussing the ethics of online investigations. Do you feel these investigations are an invasion of privacy? Why or why not? If you do feel they are an invasion of privacy, what do you think can be done about it? Are there problems with getting inaccurate information?

Case Study

Henry Rice, the owner and CEO of a small company, has been conducting a search for a new human resource administrator. After many rounds of interviews, he has narrowed his search down to two individuals that he feels are the best candidates. Each has very similar qualifications so Henry's decision may very well be based on the information he finds when he checks their references and performs a background check.

Henry has received written permission from each to conduct a background check. Where should Henry begin his search? What sites or sorts of information would be most critical for him to check? What type of information could weigh heavily for a person working in human resources? Write a brief essay, outlining what steps Henry should take in conducting his research.

Chapter 12

Computer Security Hardware and Software

Chapter Objectives

After reading this chapter and completing the exercises, you will be able to do the following:

- Evaluate the effectiveness of a scanner based on how it works.
- Choose the best type of firewall for a given organization.
- Understand anti-spyware methods.
- Employ intrusion-detection systems to detect problems on your system.

Introduction

Throughout this book, various aspects of computer crime and computer security have been discussed. At this point in your studies, you should have a good idea of what the real dangers are and what adequate security policies include, as well as a basic understanding of the various forms of computer crime. However, if you are striving to secure your network, you will need more technical details on the various security devices and software you might choose to employ. This chapter reviews these items with enough detail to allow you to make intelligent decisions on which types of products you will see.

Most of these devices have been mentioned and briefly described in the preceding chapters. The intent of this chapter is to delve more deeply into details of how these devices work. This information is of particular value to those readers who intend to eventually enter the computer security profession. Simply having a theoretical knowledge of computer security is inadequate. You must have some practical skills. This chapter will be a good starting point for gaining those skills, and the exercises at the end of the chapter will give you a chance to practice setting up and evaluating various types of firewalls, IDSs, and antivirus applications.

Virus Scanners

A virus scanner is essentially software that tries to prevent a virus from infecting your system. This fact is probably abundantly obvious to most readers. Knowing how a virus scanner works, however, is another matter. This topic was discussed briefly in Chapter 5, but will be elaborated on in this chapter.

In general, virus scanners work in two ways. The first method is that they contain a list of all known virus files. Generally, one of the services that vendors of virus scanners provide is a periodic update of this file. This list is typically in a small file, often called a *.dat* file (short for data). When you update your virus definitions, what actually occurs is that your current file is replaced by the more recent one on the vendor's Web site.

The antivirus program can then scan your PC, network, and incoming e-mail for known virus files. Any file on your PC or attached to an e-mail is compared to the virus definition file to see whether there are any matches. With e-mails, this can be done by looking for specific subject lines and content. Known virus files often have specific phrases in the subject line and the body of the messages they are attached to. Yet viruses and worms can have a multitude of headers, some of which are very common, such as *re:hello* or *re:thanks.* Scanning against a list of known viruses alone would result in many false positives. Therefore, the virus scanner also looks at attachments to see whether they are of a certain size and creation date that matches a known virus or whether it contains known viral code. The file size, creation date, and location are the telltale signs of a virus.

How Does a Virus Scanner Work?

An article in the July 2004 issue of *Scientific American,* titled "How Does a Virus Scanner Work," stated that a virus scanner is essentially software that searches for the signature or pattern of known virus. Keep in mind that the scanner only works if you keep it updated. And, of course, it only works with known viruses.

The second way a virus scanner works is to watch for certain types of behaviors that are typical of a virus. This might include any program that attempts to write to your hard drive's boot sector, change system files, automate your e-mail software, or self-multiply. Another feature that virus scanners search for is a file that will stay in memory after it executes. This is called a ***Terminate and Stay Resident (TSR)*** program. Some legitimate programs do this, but it is often a sign of a virus. Additionally, some virus scanners use more sophisticated methods, such as scanning your system files and monitoring any program that attempts to modify those files.

It is also important to differentiate between on-demand virus scanning and ongoing scanners. An ***ongoing virus scanner*** runs in the background and is constantly checking your PC for any sign of a virus. ***On-demand virus scanners*** run only when you launch them. Many modern antivirus scanners offer both options.

Virus-Scanning Techniques

In general, there are five ways a virus scanner might scan for virus infections. Some of these were mentioned in the previous section, but they are outlined and defined below.

E-mail and Attachment Scanning Since the primary propagation method for a virus is e-mail, e-mail and attachment scanning is the most important function of any virus scanner. Some virus scanners actually examine your e-mail on the e-mail server before downloading it to your machine. Other virus scanners work by scanning your e-mails and attachments on your computer before passing it to your e-mail program. In either case, the e-mail and its attachments should be scanned prior to you having any chance to open it and release the virus on your system.

Download Scanning Anytime you download anything from the Internet, either via a Web link or through some FTP program, there is a chance you might download an infected file. Download scanning works much like e-mail and attachment scanning, but does so on files you select for downloading.

File Scanning This is the type of scanning in which files on your system are checked to see whether they match any known virus. This sort of scanning is generally done on an on-demand basis instead of an ongoing basis. It is a good idea to schedule your virus scanner to do a complete scan of the system periodically. I personally recommend a weekly scan, preferably at a time when no one is likely to be using the computer.

Heuristic Scanning This is perhaps the most advanced form of virus scanning. This sort of scanning uses rules to determine whether a file or program is behaving like a virus and is one of the best ways to find a virus that is not a known virus. A new virus will not be on any virus definition list, so you must examine its behavior to determine whether it is a virus. However, this process is not foolproof. Some actual virus infections will be missed, and some non-virus files might be suspected of being a virus.

FYI: How Commercial Scanners Work

Most commercial virus scanners use multiple methods, including most, if not all, of the methods listed here. Any virus scanner that uses only one scanning modality would be virtually worthless from a practical virus defense perspective.

Active Code Scanning Modern Web sites frequently embed active codes, such as Java applets and ActiveX. These technologies can provide some stunning visual effects to any Web site. However, they can also be a vehicle for malicious code. Scanning such objects before they are downloaded to your computer is an essential feature in any quality virus scanner.

Commercial Antivirus Software

There are two brands of antivirus software that virtually dominate the antivirus market today and a number of companies that offer a commercial scanner also offer a free version that does not provide as many features as the commercial product. For example, AVG Anti-Virus, available from **www.grisoft.com**, is a commercial product, but the company also offers the AVG Anti-Virus Free Edition: McAfee and Norton. Both products are very good choices, and both also come with additional options, such as spam filters and personal firewalls. Either product can be purchased for a home machine for about $30 to $60 dollars (depending on options you add). This purchase price includes a one-year subscription to update the virus files so that your antivirus software will recognize all known virus attacks. Organizational licenses are also available to cover an entire network.

Of course, there are other antivirus solutions available. Several free virus scanners can easily be found on the Internet. McAfee and Norton are mentioned here because they are so commonly used, and it is likely that you will encounter them frequently.

Firewalls

A firewall is, in essence, a barrier between your network and the outside world. At a minimum, it will filter incoming packets based on certain parameters such as packet size, source IP address, protocol, and destination port. As was mentioned in the discussion on firewalls in Chapter 2, Linux and Windows XP ship with a simple firewall. Additionally, Norton and McAfee both offer personal firewall solutions for individual PCs.

In an organizational setting, you will want a dedicated firewall between your network and the outside world. This might be a router that also has built-in firewall capabilities. (Cisco Systems is one company that is well-known for high quality routers and firewalls.) Or, it might be a server that is dedicated solely to running firewall software. There are a number of firewall solutions that you can examine, and Appendix B has some links to get you started. Selecting a firewall, however, is an important decision. If you lack the expertise to make that decision, then you should arrange for a consultant to assist you in this respect.

Firewall Types and Components

Up to this point, most discussion of firewalls has focused on packet-filtering firewalls. However, there are several other types of firewalls or components to firewalls that are listed below.

- Screening firewall
- Application gateway
- Circuit-level gateway

The following sections will discuss each of these and assess the advantages and disadvantages of each.

Screening Firewall ***Screening firewalls,*** the most basic type of firewall, are simply another name for packet-filtering firewalls. This type of firewall works in the "Network" layer of the OSI model (see Chapter 1). It simply examines incoming packets and either allows or denies them entrance based on a set of rules that were put into its configuration. They can filter packets based on packet size, protocol type used, destination IP address, source IP address, destination port, source port, and so forth. For example, a packet filter might deny all traffic on ports 1024 and up, or it might block all incoming traffic using the TFTP protocol. You can use incoming and outgoing filters to dictate what information passes into or out of your local network.

Many routers offer this type of firewall option. These firewalls are usually very easy to configure and quite inexpensive. As mentioned, some operating systems include built-in packet-filtering capabilities.

There are a few disadvantages to the screening/packet-filtering firewall solution. One disadvantage is that they do not actually examine the packet or compare it to previous packets; therefore, they are quite susceptible to either a ping flood or SYN flood. They also do not offer any user authentication. Additionally, in many cases, a packet-filtering firewall will be used as a bastion host. A ***bastion host*** is a single point of contact between the Internet and a private network. It usually will only run a limited number of services (those that are absolutely essential to the private network) and no others.

Application Gateway An ***application gateway*** (also known as ***application proxy*** or ***application-level proxy***) is a program that runs on a firewall. When a client program, such as a Web browser, establishes a connection to a destination service, such as a Web server, it connects to an application gateway, or proxy. The client then negotiates with the proxy server in order to gain access to the destination service. In effect, the proxy establishes the connection with the destination behind the firewall and acts on behalf of the client, hiding and protecting individual computers on the network behind the firewall. This process actually creates two connections. There is one connection between the client and the proxy server and another connection between the proxy server and the destination.

Once a connection is established, the application gateway makes all decisions about which packets to forward. Since all communication is conducted through the proxy server, computers behind the firewall are protected.

With an application gateway, each supported client program requires a unique program to accept client application data. This sort of firewall allows for individual user authentication, which makes them quite effective at blocking unwanted traffic. However, a disadvantage is that these firewalls use a lot of system resources and are susceptible to SYN floods and ping floods.

Circuit-Level Gateway A ***circuit-level gateway*** is similar to an application gateway, but is more secure and generally implemented on high-end equipment. A circuit-level gateway relays a TCP connection, but does no additional processing or filtering of the protocol (Wack, 1995). In this system, your username is checked and granted access before the connection to the router is established. This means that you as an individual, either by username or IP address, must be verified before any further communication can take place. Once this verification takes place and the connection between the source and destination is established, the firewall simply passes bytes between the systems. A virtual "circuit" exists between the internal client and the proxy server. Internet requests go through this circuit to the proxy server, and the proxy server delivers those requests to the Internet after changing the IP address. External users only see the IP address of the proxy server. Responses are then received by the proxy server and sent back through the circuit to the client. While traffic is allowed through, external systems never see the internal systems.

While highly secure, this approach may not be appropriate for some public situations, such as e-commerce sites. This type of firewall does not allow features, such as URL filtering. They also frequently offer only limited auditing capabilities.

How Firewalls Examine Packets

In addition to how the firewall operates, you can further differentiate firewalls based on how they examine incoming packets. There are two main approaches to this task, and each is briefly examined below.

Stateful Packet Inspection The ***Stateful Packet Inspection (SPI)*** firewall will examine each packet, denying or permitting access based not only on the examination of the current packet, but also on data derived from previous packets in the conversation. This means that the firewall is aware of the context in which a specific packet was sent. This makes these firewalls far less susceptible to ping floods and SYN floods, as well as being less susceptible to spoofing. For example, if the firewall detects that the current packet is an ICMP packet and a stream of several thousand packets have been continuously coming from the same source IP, it is clearly a Denial of Service attack and the packets will be blocked.

The SPI firewall can also look at the actual contents of the packet. This allows for some very advanced filtering capabilities. Most high-end firewalls use the Stateful Packet Inspection method; when possible, this is the recommended type of firewall.

Stateless Packet Inspection ***Stateless packet inspection*** does not involve actually examining the contents of each packet, which is a significant weakness in using such an inspection technology. Also, the stateless packet inspection does not examine a packet within the context of an ongoing TCP conversation. It does not know what the preceding or subsequent packets are doing, thus making it vulnerable to ping floods and other Denial of Service attacks.

Firewall Configurations

In addition to the various types of firewalls, there are also various configuration options. The type of firewall tells you how it will evaluate traffic and hence decide what to allow and not to allow. The configuration gives you an idea of how that firewall is set up in relation to the network it is protecting. Some of the major configurations/implementations for firewalls include:

- Network host-based
- Dual-homed host
- Router-based firewall
- Screened host

Each of these is discussed in the following sections.

Network Host-Based A ***network host-based firewall*** is a software solution installed on an existing machine with an existing operating system. The most significant concern in using this type of firewall is that, no matter how good the firewall solution is, it is contingent upon the underlying operating system. In such a situation, it is absolutely critical that the machine hosting the firewall have a hardened operating system.

Dual-Homed Host A ***dual-homed host*** is a firewall running on a server with at least two network interfaces. The server acts as a router between the network and the interfaces to which it is attached. To make this work, the automatic routing function is disabled, meaning that an IP packet from the Internet is not routed directly to the network. You can choose what packets to route and how to route them. Systems inside and outside the firewall can communicate with the dual-homed host, but cannot communicate directly with each other.

Router-Based Firewall As was previously mentioned, you can implement firewall protection on a router. In larger networks with multiple layers of protection, this is commonly the first layer of protection. Although one can implement various types of firewalls on a router, the most common type used is packet filtering. If you use a broadband connection in your home or small office, you can get a packet-filtering firewall router to replace the basic router provided to you by the broadband company.

Screened Host A ***screened host*** is really a combination of firewalls. In this configuration, you use a combination of a bastion host and a screening router. The screening router adds security by allowing you to deny or permit certain traffic from the bastion host. It is the first stop for traffic, which can continue only if the screening router lets it through.

Commercial and Free Firewall Products

There is a variety of commercial firewall products from which you can choose. If all you want is a basic packet-filtering solution, many software vendors offer this. Major antivirus software vendors (including those mentioned previously in this chapter) often offer the firewall software as a bundled option with their antivirus software. Other companies, such as Zone Labs, sell firewall and intrusion-detection software. Zone Labs, for example, offers the ZoneAlarm Security Suite, which provides all the tools for complete Internet security. Major manufacturers of routers and hubs, such as Cisco Systems, also offer firewall products. How much security you need is a difficult question to answer. A bare minimum recommendation is to have a packet-filtering firewall/proxy server between your network and the Internet—but that is a bare minimum. There are also many free firewall applications available. Zone Labs, mentioned above for their commercial product, also offers a free download of the ZoneAlarm firewall protection.

Outpost Firewall, available from **www.agnitum.com/products/outpost/** is a product designed for the home or small office user. Like the Zone Labs product, it has both a free version and an enhanced commercial version. Information on this product is shown in Figure 12.1. Note that the free versions is an older version of the software and does not include many of the enhancements of the commercial version. But it may be sufficient for your needs.

Listed and shown below are a number of other sources for information on free firewall protection. Each of these Web sites offers links to a number of sources for free firewall protection as well as to other useful security tools. You may want to explore these sites as well as add them to your list of resource sites.

- www.free-firewall.org/
- www.homenethelp.com/web/howto/free-firewall.asp
- www.firewallguide.com/freeware.htm

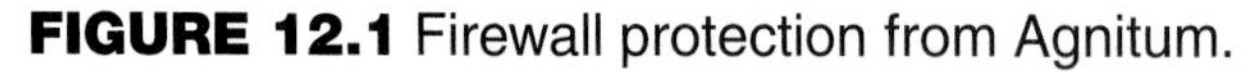

FIGURE 12.1 Firewall protection from Agnitum.

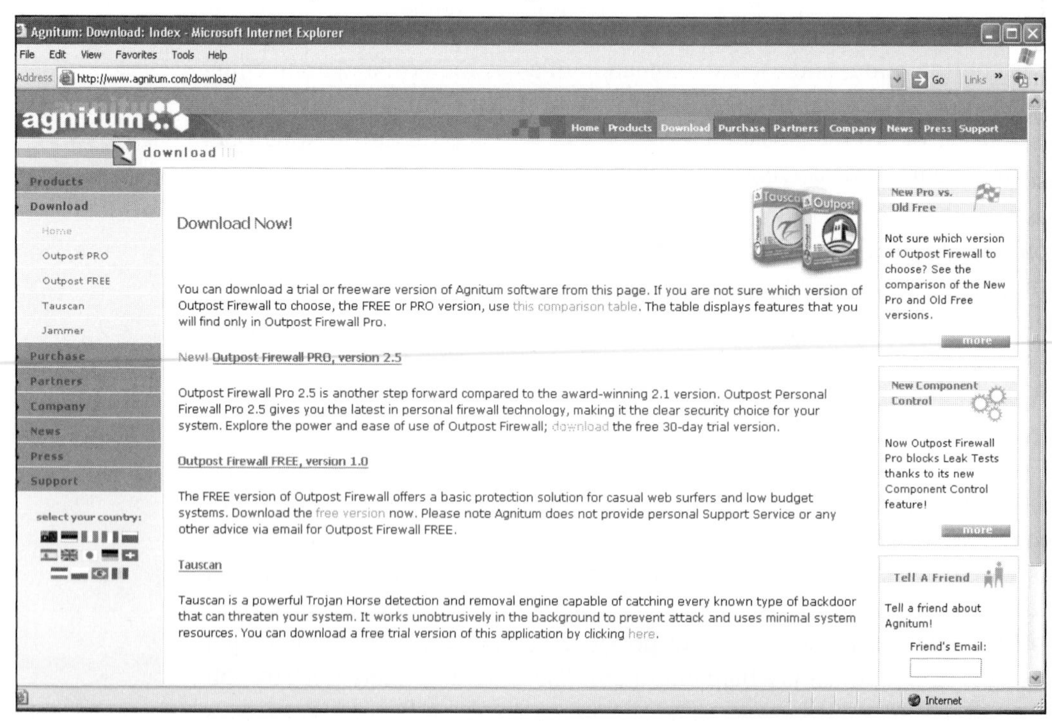

Firewall Logs

Firewalls are also excellent tools when attempting to ascertain what has happened after an incident occurs. Almost all firewalls, regardless of type or implementation, will log activity. These logs can provide valuable information that can assist in determining the source of an attack, methods used to attack, and other data that might help either locate the perpetrator of an attack or at least prevent a future attack using the same techniques. Any security-conscious network administrator should make it a routine habit to check the firewall logs.

Anti-Spyware

Anti-spyware, as discussed earlier in this book, scans your computer to see whether there is spyware running on your machine. This is an important element of computer security software that was at one time largely ignored. Even today, not enough people take spyware seriously or guard against it. Most anti-spyware works by checking your system for known spyware files. Each application must simply be checked against a list of known spyware. This means that you must maintain some sort of subscription service so that you can obtain routine updates to your spyware definition list.

In today's Internet climate, running anti-spyware is as essential as running antivirus software. Failing to do so can lead to serious consequences. Personal data, and perhaps sensitive business data, could easily be leaking out of your organization without your knowledge. And, as was pointed out in Chapter 9, it is entirely possible for spyware to be the vehicle for purposeful industrial espionage.

Barring the use of anti-spyware, or even in conjunction with such software, you can also protect yourself via your browser's security settings as was discussed in a previous chapter. Additionally, several times throughout this book, you have been warned to be cautious about attachments and Internet downloads. You would also be well advised to avoid downloading various Internet "enhancements," such as "skins" and "toolbars." If you are in an organization, prohibiting such downloads should be a matter of company policy.

Intrusion-Detection Software

Intrusion-detection software (IDS) has become much more widely used in the last few years. Essentially, an IDS will inspect all inbound and outbound port activity on your machine/firewall/system and look for patterns that might indicate an attempted break-in. For example, if the IDS finds that a series of ICMP packets were sent to each port in sequence, this probably indicates that your system is being scanned by network-scanning software, such as Cerberus. Since this is often a prelude to an attempt to breach your system security, it can be very important to know that someone is performing preparatory steps to infiltrate your system.

Entire volumes have been written on how IDS systems work. This chapter cannot hope to cover that much information. However, it is important that you have a basic idea of how these systems work.

The sections below will first examine the broad categories in which IDS systems tend to be viewed and then will also look at some specific approaches to IDS. While this information is not all-inclusive, it does address the more common terminology used.

IDS Categorization

There are a number of ways in which IDS systems can be categorized. The most common IDS categorizations are:

- misuse detection vs. anomaly detection
- passive systems vs. reactive systems
- network-based systems vs. host-based systems

Misuse Detection vs. Anomaly Detection An IDS that uses ***misuse detection*** analyzes the information it gathers and compares it to large databases of attack signatures (***IDS signatures***) (Webopedia, 2004) Much like a virus detection system, this form of IDS looks for specific attacks that have already been documented. However, similar to virus scanners, this form of IDS is only as good as the IDS signatures against which it compares the packets.

On the other hand, ***anomaly detection*** involves actual software that works to detect intrusion attempts and notify the administrator. This is what many people think of when they talk about intrusion-detection systems. The general process is simple: the system looks for any anomalous behavior. Any activity that does not match the pattern of normal user access is noted and logged. The software compares observed activity against expected normal usage profiles. Profiles are usually developed for specific users, groups of users, or applications. Any activity that does not match the definition of normal behavior is considered an anomaly and is logged.

Passive Systems vs. Reactive Systems In a ***passive system,*** the IDS detects a potential security breach, logs the information, and signals an alert. In a ***reactive system,*** the IDS responds to the suspicious activity by logging off a user or reprogramming the firewall to block network traffic from the suspected malicious source (Webopedia, 2004).

Network-Based System vs. Host-Based System In a network-based system (NIDS), the individual packets flowing through a network are analyzed. This system can detect malicious packets that are designed to be

> **FYI: Normal Activity Patterns**
>
> With anomaly-based IDS, it can take some time to create what is considered "normal" activity patterns. While these activity patterns are being established, you may experience a high rate of false alarms.
>
> You should also note that, if the network already contains malicious code, then the activity of this code would be considered "normal."

overlooked by a firewall's simplistic filtering rules (Webopedia, 2004). In a host-based system (HIDS), the activity of each individual computer or host is examined.

IDS Approaches

There are many approaches to detection and prevention. Some of these methods are implemented in various software packages, while others are simply strategies that an organization can employ to decrease the likelihood of a successful intrusion.

Preemptive Blocking This approach, sometimes called banishment vigilance, seeks to prevent intrusions before they occur. This is done by noting any danger signs of impending threats and then blocking the user or IP address from which these signs originate. Examples of this technique include attempting to detect the early foot printing stages of an impending intrusion, then blocking the IP or user that is the source of the foot printing activity. If you find that a particular IP address is the source of frequent port scans and other scans of your system, then you would block that IP address at the firewall.

This sort of intrusion detection and avoidance can be complicated. Usually, a software system will simply alert the administrator that suspicious activity has taken place. A human administrator will then make the decision whether or not to block the person. If the software automatically blocks any addresses it deems suspicious, you run the risk of blocking out legitimate users. It should also be noted that nothing prevents the offending user from moving to a different machine to continue their attack. This sort of approach should only be one part of an overall intrusion-detection strategy and not the entire strategy.

Infiltration This method refers to efforts on the part of the administrator or security specialist to acquire information from various illicit sources. Many administrators rely solely on various security bulletins from vendors.

With infiltration, the administrator proactively seeks out intelligence on potential threats and/or groups. In other words, it is not a software or hardware implementation, but rather a process of infiltrating hacker/cracker online groups in order to keep tabs on what sort of vulnerabilities are currently being exploited by these groups and what target systems are considered attractive targets. This form of intrusion detection is not widely used for two reasons. The first reason is that it is quite time-consuming. The second reason is that it requires spying skills, which many administrators may not possess.

Intrusion Deflection This method is becoming increasingly popular among the more security-conscious administrators. The essence of it is quite simple. An attempt is made to attract the intruder to a sub-system set up for the purpose of observing him. This is done by tricking the intruder into believing that he has succeeded in accessing system resources when, in fact, he has been directed to a specially designed environment. Being able to observe the intruder while he practices his art will yield valuable clues and can lead to his arrest.

This is often done by using what is commonly referred to as a *honey pot.* Essentially, you set up a fake system, possibly a server that appears to be an entire subnet. You make that system look very attractive by perhaps making it appear to have sensitive data, such as personnel files, or valuable data, such as account numbers or research. The actual data stored in this system is fake. The real purpose of the system is to carefully monitor the activities of any person who accesses the system. Since no legitimate user ever accesses this system, it is a given that anyone accessing it is an intruder.

Intrusion Deterrence This method involves simply trying to make the system seem like a less palatable target. In short, an attempt is made to make any potential reward from a successful intrusion attempt appear more difficult than it is worth. This approach includes tactics such as

FYI: Using Honey Pots

The use of honey pots and similar technologies is on the rise. In fact, some vendors are now selling pre-packaged, ready-to-use honey pots, including wireless honey pots. These devices are an admission that no system is 100% foolproof and are an attempt to at least capture the hacker after she has intruded the system.

attempting to reduce the apparent value of the current system's worth through camouflage. This essentially means working to hide the most valuable aspects of the system. The other tactic in this methodology involves raising the perceived risk of a potential intruder being caught. This can be done in a variety of ways, including conspicuously displaying warnings and warning of active monitoring. The perception of the security of a system can be drastically improved, even when the actual system security has not been improved.

Commercial IDS Providers

There are a number of vendors who supply IDS systems, each with its own strengths and weaknesses. Which system is best for your environment is contingent on many factors including the network environment, security level required, budget constraints, and the skill level of the person who will be working directly with the IDS. One popular open-source IDS is Snort, which can be downloaded for free from **www.snort.org/**.

Summary

It is absolutely critical that any network have a firewall and proxy server between the network and the outside world. It is critical that all machines in the network (servers and workstations alike) have updated virus protection. It is also a good idea to consider intrusion-detection software and anti-spyware as well. In the upcoming exercises, you will have an opportunity to practice setting up various types of firewalls and IDS systems.

Test Your Skills

MULTIPLE CHOICE QUESTIONS

1. Which of the following is the most common way for a virus scanner to recognize a virus?
   A. To compare a file to known virus attributes
   B. To use complex rules to look for virus-like behavior
   C. To only look for TSR programs
   D. To look for TSR programs or programs that alter the registry

2. What is one way of checking e-mails for virus infections?
   A. Block all e-mails with attachments
   B. Block all active attachments (e.g., ActiveX, scripting)
   C. Look for subject lines that are from known virus attacks
   D. Look for e-mails from known virus sources
3. What is a TSR program?
   A. Terminal Signal Registry programs that alter the system registry
   B. Terminate and System Remove that erase themselves when complete
   C. Terminate and Scan Remote that scan remote systems prior to terminating
   D. Terminate and Stay Resident that actually stay in memory after you shut them down
4. What is the name for scanning that depends on complex rules to define what is and is not a virus?
   A. Rules-based scanning (RBS)
   B. Heuristic scanning
   C. TSR scanning
   D. Logic-based scanning (LBS)
5. Which of the following is not one of the basic types of firewalls?
   A. Screening firewall
   B. Application gateway
   C. Heuristic firewall
   D. Circuit-level gateway
6. Which of the following is the most basic type of firewall?
   A. Screening firewall
   B. Application gateway
   C. Heuristic firewall
   D. Circuit-level gateway
7. Which of the following is a disadvantage to using an application gateway firewall?
   A. It is not very secure.
   B. It uses a great deal of resources.
   C. It can be difficult to configure.
   D. It can only work on router-based firewalls.

8. What is SPI?
   A. Stateful Packet Inspection
   B. System Packet Inspection
   C. Stateful Packet Interception
   D. System Packet Interception
9. What is the term for a firewall that is simply software installed on an existing server?
   A. Network host-based
   B. Dual-homed
   C. Router-based
   D. Screened host
10. What is a major weakness with a network host-based firewall?
    A. Its security is dependent on the underlying operating system.
    B. It is difficult to configure.
    C. It can be easily hacked.
    D. It is very expensive.
11. What is the term for blocking an IP address that has been the source of suspicious activity?
    A. Preemptive blocking
    B. Intrusion deflection
    C. Proactive deflection
    D. Intrusion blocking
12. What is the term for a fake system designed to lure intruders?
    A. Honey pot
    B. Faux system
    C. Deflection system
    D. Entrapment
13. Which of the following is the correct term for simply making your system less attractive to intruders?
    A. Intrusion deterrence
    B. Intrusion deflection
    C. Intrusion camouflage
    D. Intrusion avoidance

14. What method do most IDS software implementations use?
    A. Anomaly detection
    B. Preemptive blocking
    C. Intrusion deterrence
    D. Infiltration

15. How do most anti-spyware packages work?
    A. By using heuristic methods
    B. By looking for known spyware
    C. The same way antivirus scanners work
    D. By seeking out TSR cookies

EXERCISES

Exercise 12.1: Setting Up a Firewall

Microsoft Windows XP and Linux both offer built-in packet-filtering firewalls of some sort.

1. Using the documentation for whichever operating system you have, decide what packets you wish to block.

2. Set your firewall to filter those packets.

Note: Ideally, if you have access to both operating systems, the best exercise is to experiment setting up firewalls for both.

Exercise 12.2: Router-Based Firewalls

Note: This exercise is for those labs with access to a lab router-based firewall.

1. Consult your router documentation for instructions on how to configure the firewall.

2. Configure your router-based firewall to block the same items you chose to block in Exercise 2.

Exercise 12.3: Evaluating Firewalls

Write a brief essay explaining whether you think the router-based solution or the built-in operating system solution is best. Explain your reasons.

Exercise 12.4: Active Code

Using the Web or other resources, find out why blocking active code (e.g., ActiveX, Scripts) might or might not be a good idea for some situations. Write a brief essay explaining your position.

Exercise 12.5: Hardware Used by a Company

Visit the IT department of a company and ascertain what hardware they use in their computer system's defense. Do they use a hardware firewall in addition to a software firewall? What form of intrusion-detection software do they use? Do they use antivirus and anti-spyware on the workstations within the company? Write a brief report summarizing your findings.

PROJECTS

Project 12.1: How Does the Microsoft Firewall Work?

Using Microsoft documentation, the Web, and other resources, find out what methodologies the Microsoft Windows XP firewall uses. Write a brief essay explaining the strengths and weaknesses of that approach. Also discuss situations in which you feel that approach is adequate and those in which it might be inadequate.

Project 12.2: How Does Anti-Virus Software Work?

Using documentation from the vendor, the Web, or other resources, find out what methodology Norton AntiVirus uses, as well as the methods that McAfee uses. Armed with this information, write a brief essay comparing and contrasting any differences. Also discuss situations in which one might be recommended over the other.

Project 12.3: Using Snort

Note: This is a longer project and appropriate for groups.

Go to the Snort.org Web site (**www.snort.org/**) and download Snort. Using the vendor documentation or other resources, configure Snort. Then use port scanners on the machine that has Snort configured and note whether Snort detects the scan.

Case Study

Jane Smith is responsible for security at the ABC Company. She has a moderate budget with which to purchase security solutions. To date, she has installed a router-based firewall between the network and the out-side world. She also has a commercial virus scanner on every machine on the network. What other actions might you recommend to her? Would you recommend a different firewall? Why or why not?

Appendix A

Computer Security Professionals: Education and Certifications

This book has been an introduction to the world of computer security. It is not sufficient to make you a security professional. It is rather a gateway into the profession. The question naturally arises: What should you do if you wish to become a computer security professional? What education, training, and certifications will best prepare you to embark on a career in computer security? This appendix answers these questions.

Academic Training and Programs

Clearly a degree is going to be necessary to pursue a career in computer security. There are a variety of computer science, engineering, computer information systems, and even some computer security programs from which you could choose. It is likely that you are currently enrolled in some college program. The question is: What does a program need to provide you the appropriate training?

The first issue to address is the type of degree and length of program. While many institutions offer associates (two-year) degrees, you would be hard put to find many job advertisements that do not require a four-year bachelors degree. In general, with many computer-related jobs, employers view the two-year degree as simply not sufficient. This is often not true for technical support or sales jobs, but generally is true for programming, networking, and computer security positions. Therefore, first and foremost, you will need to obtain a bachelors degree.

The second issue to address is content. While there are some degree programs available in computer security, most institutions do not offer such a specific degree. For security professionals, the difference between computer information systems, computer science, and engineering is not as critical as the content of your degree. In any degree program, you generally have flexibility in choosing both electives and a minor. This flexibility should allow you to formulate an appropriate program. The list below details what training is required.

- **Network:** First, you should take as many network courses as possible. Expertise in computer networks is a cornerstone of computer security.
- **Programming and database:** You will need at least introductory courses in these fields. Security extends well beyond simple firewalls into software development, database management, and all other aspects of IT. It is therefore critical that you have at least a cursory understanding of these topics.
- **Telecommunications:** If at all possible, an introductory course in basic telecommunications should be taken.
- **Security:** Obviously, if your college offers any specific courses in computer security, take them.
- **Math:** If you intend to get a better understanding of encryption, you will need mathematics up to and including number theory. Number theory is generally a post-calculus course.
- **Law/Criminology:** Since computer security often involves data forensics, it can be useful to have a basic understanding of the law and basic criminology.

You can see that network security is a very broad field and touches on a number of other fields. This means a broad educational background is necessary to truly be effective in this endeavor. The real key to any training program, in any field, is an appropriate mix of solid grounding in theory, with hands-on practice. As in this book, you have had numerous hands-on exercises as well as reading/research projects. Any good program will combine theory and research with hands-on practice. Studying how firewalls work is not much use unless you have actual experience installing a firewall.

It is also important to know something about the instructors for security courses. Security is becoming the hottest buzzword in IT; unfortunately, some academic institutions are so eager to provide security courses that they might be tempted to use instructors that may not have adequate backgrounds. Has the instructor/professor had professional, hands-on security experience? What is their background in relation to security? Usually, faculty members are eager to announce their credentials on the college or university's Web site. If you don't see any security-related experience or credentials, this might be a matter of concern to you.

Industry Certifications

Industry certifications are a significant part of the computer industry. Microsoft Certified Software Engineers, Red Hat Certified Engineers, and Certified Java Programmers are all part of the IT profession. However, people's attitudes toward certifications vary a great deal. Some people will tell you that they would never hire a person who was not certified. Some job ads either require or prefer one certification or another. Other professionals will tell you certifications are worthless. Both extremes come from two factors: a misunderstanding of what certification means and the use of "cheat sheets."

- Misunderstanding what certification means: Some people think certification is meant to show complete mastery of a topic. Thus, if such a person hires a certified CompTIA A+ technician who has not completely mastered PC hardware, then the employer might decide certifications are not worthwhile. The problem is that one or both parties in this case misunderstood what certification means. Certifications indicate that the person holding them has achieved a certain *minimum* level of competency with that product or technology; they do not indicate that the person in question has completely mastered the topic at hand.
- Use of "cheat sheets": The Internet is replete with "study guides" that are, in fact, cheat sheets for certification exams. These study guides often have the real questions and answers from a particular certification exam. A person could quite easily memorize such a cheat sheet, pass a test, and not truly understand the material. Such study guides are very good resources for identifying areas in which you may need more study. If used in conjunction with hands-on experience and a thorough study of reference material, they are then useful study aids. However, they are often used simply as cheat sheets, thus demeaning the value of certifications.

Once you have a realistic idea of what certifications mean, the next question that arises is: What certifications are truly meaningful in security? Unfortunately, computer certifications are not regulated as are medical licenses, real estate licenses, and so on. Anyone can publish a certification and make bold claims about it. However, over time, certain certifications have gained acceptance in the IT security profession. The following sections will examine a few of these and discuss what they mean.

Security +

This certification is administered by the Computer Technology Industry Association (CompTIA), which is famous for A+, Network+, and Linux+ certifications (as well as others). The test itself covers security concepts. It is not a hands-on test, but rather a test of general security knowledge. This certification is a good gateway to other certifications. In and of itself, it would not be a sufficient indication of whether a person is qualified to be a security professional. However, combined with experience, formal education, and possibly other certifications (e.g., Microsoft Certified Systems Engineer, Certified Novel Engineer), it might be a good indicator. For the novice trying to enter the security profession, this test is an excellent place to start. Details can be found at the CompTIA Web site at **www.comptia.org/certification/security/**.

CIW Security Analyst

This exam is quite similar in content to the Security+ exam. It asks general security knowledge questions, and its content is a bit more broad and inclusive than that of Security+. It does not delve into hands-on security knowledge. However, it has one very significant advantage over Security+: before you can take this exam, you must first pass the CIW Security Professional exam and the CIW Foundations exam, as well as one of the following:

- Microsoft Certified Systems Administrator (MCSA)
- Microsoft Certified Systems Engineer (MCSE)
- Certified Novell Engineer (CNE)
- Cisco Certified Network Professional (CCNP)
- Cisco Certified Network Associate (CCNA)
- Cisco Certified Internetwork Expert (CCIE)
- Linux Professional Institute (LPI) Level 2

This means that, in addition to basic security knowledge, the holder of this certification has had at least two other CIW certifications, as well as at least one major network certification. This combination of certifications is a likely indicator of competence in network security. You can find out more about this exam at **www.ciwcertified.com/**.

MCSE Security Specialization

Microsoft is a widely used operating system, and Microsoft-based networks abound. Many companies prefer to hire Microsoft Certified Systems Engineers (MCSE) for administering such networks. Microsoft has added a specialized track within the MCSE specifically for those people interested in security. In addition to the basic fundamentals of the MCSE, the security specialization requires three security-specific certification tests:

- Designing Security for a Microsoft Windows 2000 Network
- Implementing and Administering Security in a Microsoft Windows 2000 Network
- Installing, Configuring, and Administering Microsoft Internet Security and Acceleration (ISA) Server 2000, Enterprise Edition

If your goal is to secure Microsoft networks, then this particular certification would be very important. You can find out more about it at **www.microsoft.com/learning/mcp/mcse/security/windows2000.asp**.

CISSP

The Certified Information Systems Security Professional (CISSP) designation is the gold standard in security certifications. This designation is simply the most sought-after security certification due to the rigorous standards required to achieve certification. The requirements are as follows:

- Pass a grueling exam that takes several hours.
- Have at least four years of security experience, or three years and a bachelors degree. This experience must be certified by either another CISSP or an officer in your corporation.
- Meet certain continuing education requirements every 36 months to retain your certification.
- A certain percentage of those who pass the exam are randomly selected for an audit and investigation of their background.

With the CISSP certification, the test itself is not what makes the certification meaningful. It is the requirement for verifiable work experience as well as ongoing continuing education. For someone looking to excel in the computer security profession, this certification is certainly desirable. You can find out more about this test at **www.isc2.org**.

SANS Institute Certifications

The Sans Institute (**www.sans.org**) is a well-respected source for security information. You have probably noticed that both their site and their documents have been referenced more than once in this book; you would probably find the same in other computer security books. However, their computer security certifications have not been widely used within the security industry, probably due to the fact that they are relatively new and not extensively marketed. However, it seems likely that, in the coming years, their certifications will gain wider acceptance. You can find more details at **www.giac.org/subject_certs.php**.

High Tech Crime Network Certifications

This certification is included for a very different reason than the others. The High Tech Crime Network (**www.htcn.org/**) sponsors a number of computer crime certifications; they also have a very professional-looking Web site. They offer seminars, certifications, and more. However, a thorough search did not reveal a single job advertisement on any of the major job boards (e.g., **www.computerjobs.com**, **www.hotjobs.com, www.monster.com**) that required or even mentioned their certifications. Also, a review of two dozen top-selling security books and several security journals revealed no reference to these certifications.

This does not mean that the certifications are not valid; they very well may be quite rigorous and demanding certifications. However, they simply have not gained any acceptance in the IT security industry and will not assist you in gaining employment. This certification is mentioned because it is important for you when seeking industry certifications to consider how widely those certifications are accepted in the industry. A plethora of certifications will not help you if no one has heard of the certification vendor.

Appendix B

Resources

General Computer Crime and Cyber Terrorism

Cyber crime: **www.cybercrime.gov/**

Computer security: **www.cert.org**

Department of Justice Computer Crime **www.usdoj.gov/criminal/cybercrime/compcrime.html**

Symantec's antivirus site: **www.symantec.com/avcenter/**

Computer Associates Virus Information Center **www3.ca.com/virusinfo/**

Department of Defense cyber crime: **www.dcfl.gov/dc3/home.htm**

General Hacking

IRC security: **www.irchelp.org/irchelp/security/**

Hacking link: **www.hideaway.net/home/public_html/index.php**

Hacking link: **www.xs4all.nl/~l0rd/**

Hacking link: **www.hackinthebox.org/**

IP spoofing: **www.iss.net/security_center/advice/Underground/Hacking/Methods/Technical/Spoofing/default.htm**

Hacker history: **www.tranquileye.com/hackerculture/home.html**

Hacker history: **www.sptimes.com/Hackers/history.hacking.html**

Cyber Stalking

www.crimelibrary.com/criminology/cyberstalking/

www.cyber-stalking.net/

Identity Theft

www.consumer.gov/idtheft/

www.idtheftcenter.org/index.shtml

www.usdoj.gov/criminal/fraud/idtheft.html

Port Scanners and Sniffers

Port scanners: **www.hackfix.org/software/port.html**

Port scanners and other tools: **www.all-internet-security.com/security_scanners.html**

More port scanners: **www.mycert.org.my/resource/scanner.htm**

More scanners and sniffers: **is-it-true.org/pt/ptips13.shtml**

www.prosolve.com/software/winscan.php

Password Crackers

Password crackers: **www.password-crackers.com/**

More password crackers: **www.pcmag.com/article2/0,4149,696,00.asp**

Counter Measures

Preventing port scanning: **www.nwfusion.com/links/Encyclopedia/P/792.html**

Various security and hacking tools: **www.insecure.org**

Snort, an open source IDS system: **www.snort.org/**

The Sans Institute IDS FAQ: **www.sans.org/resources/idfaq/**

The Association of Computing Machinery IDS page: **www.acm.org/crossroads/xrds24/intrus.html**

Spyware

www.youarethespy.com/spy-software.htm

www.keystrokekeyloggers.com/spy_anywhere.asp

www.keyloggers.com/

www.bestspyware.com/

www.spectorsoft.com/

www.spywareguide.com/

www.spywareinfo.com/

www.softactivity.com/

Counter Spyware

theplanet.tucows.com/preview/305123.html (free, removes spyware.)

www.webroot.com/wb/products/spysweeper/index.php

www.spywarenuker.com/overture.php

www.webroot.com

www.enigmasoftwaregroup.com/jump8.shtml

Cyber Investigation Tools

WhoIs tool: **www.whois.sc/**

Sam Spade for Windows: **www.samspade.org/ssw/**

Various search tools: **www.virtualgumshoe.com/**

General Tools

General tools: **www.maxwells-alley.com/tech/toolkit.html**

General tools: **www.all-internet-security.com/security_scanners.html**

Scanning tool: **www.rawlogic.com/netbrute/**

General tools: **www.totalshareware.com**

Virus Research

CNET Virus Center: **reviews.cnet.com/4520-6600_7-5020382-1.html?legacy=cnet**

Fsecure: **www.fsecure.com**

Symantec virus encyclopedia: **securityresponse.symantec.com/avcenter/vinfodb.html**

Computer Associates Virus Information Center: **www3.ca.com/securityadvisor/virusinfo/default.aspx**

Appendix C

Sample Security Policy Documents and Checklists

Throughout this text, you have been given many tips and, at times, lists of things to be done in order to secure a system. This appendix is a compilation of many of those tips and "to-do" lists, brought together in one convenient location. In addition, the material contained within this appendix is available on the companion Web site should you need these documents in electronic format. In particular, you may find the electronic sample Acceptable Use Policy and the sample Password Policy extremely helpful as a starting point for your own policies.

The sections contained within this appendix are:

- Basic Home PC Policies
- Basic PC Security Checklist
- Basic Network Security Checklist
- Online Fraud Checklist
- Sample Acceptable Use Policy
- Sample Password Policy
- Hiring a Security Professional

Basic Home PC Policies

This list of suggested policies is for all home users of PCs. You may wish to add other items to this list of personal recommendation from the author.

General Tips

Following are general tips that, if followed, will help to keep your home PC system secure.

- Virus scanning: You must have virus scanning software on your computer. It must be up to date and properly configured.
- Patches: You must have updated patches for your operating system and all software. I recommend a minimum of a quarterly audit during which you check the patches on all machines, including servers.
- Services: Any service you don't need, shut it off. That goes for all machines.
- Configure: Configure your browser for high security.
- Firewall: If your operating system has a firewall (Windows XP and Linux both do), then make sure it is on and properly configured.
- Anti-spyware: You should definitely consider anti-spyware.
- Information: Don't give out personal information on the Internet unless you must. Do not use your real name or address in any chat room, newsgroup, and so on.
- Attachments: When in doubt, don't open them. Have friends and colleagues use a codeword in the subject of an e-mail when they must send attachments. If you don't see that codeword, don't open the attachment. You can use something simple, yet unique, as a codeword. It can be anything that you agree on with friends and colleagues. For example, the subject line could be:

  Hey, this is the picture you asked for codeword:willow

  or

  Your letter is attached codeword:oaktree

Specific Tips for Windows Users

Much has been made of Microsoft Window's security flaws. It is not my intent to debate the merits of Windows, Linux, or any other operating system. It is simply my intent to help you secure whatever system you are using. If you are using Windows 2000, XP, or 2003, then there are several steps you can take to make your system more secure.

- Make it a scheduled item to routinely visit the Microsoft Windows Update page (**v5.windowsupdate.microsoft.com/v5consumer/**

default.aspx?ln=en-us) to obtain the latest patches/updates. Checking once a month would be sufficient for most people—perhaps even once per quarter.

- Do the same for Microsoft Office Updates (**office.microsoft.com/en-us/officeupdate/default.aspx**).
- If you have Windows XP or higher, turn on and configure the firewall as described on the Web site listed above.
- Run a well-known virus scanner, such as McAffee or Norton.
- Follow the basic rules (e.g., don't download unknown attachments).
- Go to Tools and Internet Options on your Internet Explorer and reconfigure it for much higher security. When you go to the security tab, make sure ALL zones are AT LEAST MEDIUM. If you feel more confident in your knowledge of security issues, then you may want to customize it further.
- If there is a service you don't need, shut it off. This is described in the section on how to find out information on a target system.
- Microsoft has a security analyzer tool. You should run this on your system a MINIMUM of once per quarter (MS Security Analyzer: **support.microsoft.com/default.aspx?scid+kb%3Ben-us%3Bq320454**).

Microsoft may not have developed the most secure operating system available; however, many "security flaws" are actually people using the operating system that have no idea what they are doing. Start with these basic tips, and your PC will be more secure than a great many people on the Internet.

Basic PC Security Checklist

This checklist is provided to assist you in ensuring that an individual computer—either a home PC or a workstation in a business—has appropriate security. This checklist can form the foundation for a basic audit.

Basic Security

Basic security is the absolute minimum standard that all computers should meet. Many computers will exceed this level.

____ Patches have been updated within the last 90 days.

____ Antivirus software is installed, updated, and running.

____ All unused/unneeded services have been shut down.

____ If the operating system has built in port filtering or a firewall, it is turned on.

____ The password is at least eight characters long and has been changed within the last six months.

____ The browser is configured to default medium-level security.

____ Only the administrator has full rights to the machine.

Enhanced Security

Enhanced security is for users who are willing to invest more resources in ensuring security. This assumes the basic security level has been met and adds or enhances those with the following steps:

____ Anti-spyware software is installed, updated, and running.

____ The browser is configured on a custom basis for levels exceeding medium security.

____ The password is at least eight characters long, contains a mixture of characters, and has been changed within the last 90 days.

____ All unneeded operating system components have been uninstalled.

____ The machine has been scanned for vulnerabilities with a security analyzer or port scanner within the last 120 days.

Basic Network Security Checklist

This checklist is provided to assist you in ensuring that an organizational network has appropriate security. This checklist can form the foundation for a basic audit.

Basic Security

Basic security simply provides minimum standards that any network should employ. If your network does not at least meet these standards, then you are in significant danger. Many networks will actually exceed these standards.

____ All workstations and servers are in compliance with the Basic PC Security Checklist (Basic Security level).

____ There is a packet-filtering firewall between the network and the outside world.

____ There is a proxy server between the network and the outside world.

____ All routers are configured to not repeat broadcast packets.

____ All passwords are at least eight characters long and have been changed within the last six months.

____ Servers are all physically secure, with only necessary personnel having access.

____ There are policies in place prohibiting downloads of any software from the Internet.

____ There are policies in place governing how e-mail attachments are handled.

____ There are policies in place on how to handle terminated employees.

____ All employees are made aware of security and organizational policies.

____ Server logs are kept and checked at least once per month.

____ All servers are backed up at least once per week, with once-per-month backups being moved offsite to a secure location.

____ Only the administrator has full rights to any machine.

Enhanced Security

Enhanced security is for users who are willing to invest more resources in ensuring security. This assumes that all workstations have enhanced security (see the Basic PC Security Checklist) and that the basic network level is achieved. Enhanced security adds the following:

____ There is a stateful packet inspection firewall on the perimeter.

____ All routers to subnets have packet-filtering firewalls built in.

____ All servers are backed up once per day, with once-per-week backups being moved offsite to a secure location.

____ A clearly written disaster recovery plan is in place and all IT personnel are familiar with it.

____ An intrusion detection software system is installed and running.

____ Server logs are kept and checked weekly.

____ Patches are checked and updated on all machines every 60 days or less.

____ All personnel with network administrative privileges have had an extensive background check (e.g., criminal, credit, references).

____ All browsers are configured on a custom basis for levels exceeding medium security.

____ All passwords are at least eight characters long, contain a mixture of characters, and have been changed within the last 90 days.

____ All servers are scanned with a security analyzer and a port scanner at least once every 90 days.

____ External logins to the network are only done on a very limited basis and are accomplished with a virtual private network.

____ All sensitive communications and all communications outside the network are encrypted.

____ All security activities (e.g., backups, scanning, downloading patches, changing passwords, adding/removing users, changing permissions) are logged with the name of the person performing the action, the date/time, and the name of the person authorizing the action.

____ Once each quarter, a basic audit is performed using a security analyzer on servers, including a check of patches and a spot check of logs and policies.

____ Once per year, the entire network is carefully audited including a review of administrative personnel backgrounds, a complete simulated breach attempt, packet sniffing to check encryption, review of logs, and so forth.

____ Users are given routine, brief security updates warning them of current scams, frauds, viruses, Trojan horse, and so forth.

____ Old media (e.g., hard drives, tapes) are thoroughly destroyed.

Online Fraud Checklist

This checklist is provided to assist you in ensuring that you are taking appropriate precautions to avoid online fraud. It is important to note that there is no way to guarantee you won't be a victim of fraud, but you can take steps to significantly reduce the chance of being a victim.

Investment Offers

____ Take investment advice only from well-known, reputable brokerage firms/sources.

____ Independently research and verify all claims.

____ View all claims/offers with skepticism.

____ Never invest when someone is using high-pressure tactics.

____ Only invest money you can afford to lose.

Online Auctions

____ Only work with well-known auction sites (eBay).

____ Only bid on items if the seller has a high positive rating (don't bid with unrated sellers).

____ Ask questions of the seller (usually via e-mail) before bidding.

____ If the product seems too good to be true, don't bid.

Sample Acceptable Use Policy

Overview

All technology-related systems—including, but not limited to, computer equipment, software, telephone systems, network equipment, operating systems, storage media, network accounts providing electronic mail, and Web browsers—are the property of <organization's name goes here>. These systems are to be used for business purposes in serving the interests of the organization and our clients and customers in the course of normal operations. The purpose of this document is to outline the acceptable use of computer equipment at <Company Name>. These rules are in place to protect the employee and <organizations name goes here>.

Policies

General Use

1. For security and network maintenance purposes, authorized individuals within <organizations name goes here> may monitor equipment, systems, and network traffic at any time, per <organization's name goes here> Audit Policy.
2. <organization's name goes here> reserves the right to audit networks and systems on a periodic basis to ensure compliance with this policy.

Security and Proprietary Information

1. All passwords must be kept secure. Employees are directed to never share accounts. Authorized users are responsible for the security of

their passwords and accounts. System-level passwords should be changed quarterly, and user-level passwords should be changed every six months.

2. All PCs, laptops, and workstations should be secured with a password-protected screensaver, with the automatic activation feature set at ten minutes or less, or by logging off (Ctrl+Alt+Delete for Windows 2000 users) when the host will be unattended.
3. Postings by employees from <organization's name goes here> e-mail address to newsgroups are prohibited unless part of normal business operations.
4. All hosts used by the employee that are connected to <organization's name goes here> Internet/Intranet/Extranet, whether owned by the employee or <organization's name goes here>, shall be continually executing approved virus-scanning software with a current virus database unless overridden by departmental or group policy.
5. Employees must use extreme caution when opening e-mail attachments received from unknown senders, which may contain viruses or Trojan horses.

Unacceptable Use

The following activities are, in general, prohibited. Unless your job duties specifically require you to violate these policies (such as a security administrator performing a vulnerability audit), you are directed to never engage in any of these activities. Under no circumstances is an employee of <organization's name goes here> authorized to engage in any activity that is illegal under local, state, federal, or international law while utilizing <Company Name>-owned resources.

The list below is by no means exhaustive, but attempts to provide a framework for activities which fall into the category of unacceptable use. You should not assume that any activity not listed is acceptable. The activities listed are strictly prohibited, with no exceptions.

1. Violations of the rights of any person or company protected by copyright, trade secret, patent, or other intellectual property, or similar laws or regulations, including, but not limited to, the installation or distribution of any software products that are not appropriately licensed for use by <organization's name goes here>.
2. Unauthorized copying of copyrighted material including, but not limited to, books, copyrighted music, or copyrighted software for which <organization's name goes here> does not have an active license is strictly prohibited.

3. Introduction of any programs into the network or server that are not approved by the appropriate IT personnel.
4. Revealing your account password or allowing use of your account by any other person.
5. Using <organization's name goes here> computing asset to actively engage in procuring or transmitting material that is in violation of sexual harassment laws in the user's local jurisdiction.
6. Making statements about warranty, expressly or implied, unless it is a part of normal job duties.
7. Attempting to perform security breaches or disruptions of network communication. This is a violation even if the attempt is unsuccessful. Security breaches include, but are not limited to, accessing data the employee is not authorized to access, attempting to guess or crack any password, and attempting to access any account or server the employee is not expressly authorized to access unless these duties are within the scope of regular duties.
8. Port scanning or security scanning is expressly prohibited unless it is a direct part of your duties, such as in the case of a network administrator performing an authorized vulnerability scan.
9. Executing any form of network monitoring that will intercept data not intended for the employee's host unless this activity is a part of the employee's normal job/duty.
10. Circumventing user authentication or security of any host, network, or account.
11. Sending unsolicited e-mail messages, including the sending of "junk mail" or other advertising material, to individuals who did not specifically request such material (e-mail spam).
12. Any form of harassment via e-mail, telephone, or paging, whether through language, frequency, or size of messages.
13. Creating or forwarding "chain letters" or "pyramid" schemes of any type.

Enforcement of Policies

Any employee found to have violated this policy may be subject to disciplinary action, up to and including termination of employment. In some cases, the employee who violates these policies may be subject to civil or criminal action.

Password Policy

1.0 Overview

Passwords are an important aspect of computer security. They are the front line of protection for user accounts. A poorly chosen password may result in the compromise of <Company Name>'s entire corporate network. As such, all <Company Name> employees (including contractors and vendors with access to <Company Name> systems) are responsible for taking the appropriate steps, as outlined below, to select and secure their passwords.

2.0 Purpose

The purpose of this policy is to establish a standard for creation of strong passwords, the protection of those passwords, and the frequency of change.

3.0 Scope

The scope of this policy includes all personnel who have or are responsible for an account (or any form of access that supports or requires a password) on any system that resides at any <Company Name> facility, have access to the <Company Name> network, or store any non-public <Company Name> information.

4.0 Policy

4.1 General

- All system-level passwords (e.g., root, enable, NT administration, application administration accounts) must be changed on at least a quarterly basis.
- All production system-level passwords must be part of the InfoSec-administered global password management database.
- All user-level passwords (e.g., e-mail, Web, desktop computer) must be changed at least every six months. The recommended change interval is every four months.
- User accounts that have system-level privileges granted through group memberships or programs such as "sudo" must have a unique password from all other accounts held by that user.
- Passwords must not be inserted into e-mail messages or other forms of electronic communication.

- Where SNMP is used, the community strings must be defined as something other than the standard defaults of "public," "private," and "system" and must be different from the passwords used to log in interactively. A keyed hash must be used where available (e.g., SNMPv2).
- All user-level and system-level passwords must conform to the guidelines described below.

4.2 Guidelines

A. General Password Construction Guidelines

Passwords are used for various purposes at <Company Name>. Some of the more common uses include user-level accounts, Web accounts, e-mail accounts, screensaver protection, voicemail password, and local router logins. Since very few systems have support for one-time tokens (i.e., dynamic passwords that are only used once), everyone should be aware of how to select strong passwords.

Poor, weak passwords have the following characteristics:

- The password contains less than eight characters.
- The password is a word found in a dictionary (English or foreign).
- The password is a common-usage word, such as
  - Names of family, pets, friends, co-workers, fantasy characters, and so forth
  - Computer terms and names, commands, sites, companies, hardware, or software
  - The words "<Company Name>," "sanjose," "sanfran," or any derivation
  - Birthdays and other personal information, such as addresses and phone numbers
  - Word or number patterns such as aaabbb, qwerty, zyxwvuts, 123321, and so forth
  - Any of the above spelled backwards
  - Any of the above preceded or followed by a digit (e.g., secret1, 1secret)

Strong passwords have the following characteristics:

- Contain both upper- and lowercase characters (e.g., a-z, A-Z)
- Have digits and punctuation characters as well as letters (e.g., 0-9,!@#$%^&*()_+|~-=\`{}[]:";'<>?,./)
- Are at least eight alphanumeric characters long.
- Are not words in any language, slang, dialect, or jargon
- Are not based on personal information, names of family, and so forth
- Passwords should never be written down or stored on line. Try to create passwords that can be easily remembered. One way to do this is create a password based on a song title, affirmation, or other phrase. For example, the phrase might be: ""This May Be One Way to Remember" and the password could be: "TmB1w2R!" or "Tmb1W>r~" or some other variation.

NOTE: Do not use either of these examples as passwords!

B. Password Protection Standards

Do not use the same password for <Company Name> accounts as for other non-<Company Name> access (e.g., personal ISP account, option trading, benefits). Where possible, don't use the same password for various <Company Name> access needs. For example, select one password for Engineering systems and a separate password for IT systems. Also, select a separate password to be used for an NT account and a UNIX account.

Do not share <Company Name> passwords with anyone, including administrative assistants or secretaries. All passwords are to be treated as sensitive, confidential <Company Name> information.

Following is a list of "don't's":

- Don't reveal a password over the phone to ANYONE.
- Don't reveal a password in an e-mail message.
- Don't reveal a password to the boss.
- Don't talk about a password in front of others.
- Don't hint at the format of a password (e.g., "my family name").
- Don't reveal a password on questionnaires or security forms.
- Don't share a password with family members.
- Don't reveal a password to co-workers while on vacation.

If someone demands a password, refer them to this document or have them call someone in the Information Security Department.

Do not use the "Remember Password" feature of applications (e.g., Eudora, OutLook, Netscape Messenger).

Again, do not write passwords down and store them anywhere in your office. Do not store passwords in a file on ANY computer system (including PDAs or similar devices) without encryption.

Change passwords at least once every six months (except system-level passwords, which must be changed quarterly). The recommended change interval is every four months.

If an account or password is suspected to have been compromised, report the incident to Information Security and change all passwords.

Password cracking or guessing may be performed on a periodic or random basis by Information Security or its delegates. If a password is guessed or cracked during one of these scans, the user will be required to change it.

C. Application Development Standards

Application developers must ensure that their programs contain the following security precautions:

- Should support authentication of individual users, not groups
- Should not store passwords in clear text or in any easily reversible form
- Should provide for some sort of role management so that one user can take over the functions of another without having to know the other's password
- Should support TACACS+, RADIUS, and/or X.509 with LDAP security retrieval wherever possible

D. Use of Passwords and Pass Phrases for Remote Access Users

Access to <Company Name> networks via remote access is to be controlled using either a one-time password authentication or a public/private key system with a strong pass phrase.

E. Pass Phrases

Pass phrases are generally used for public/private key authentication. A public/private key system defines a mathematical relationship between the public key that is known by all and the private key that is known only to the user. Without the pass phrase to "unlock" the private key, the user cannot gain access.

Pass phrases are not the same as passwords. A pass phrase is a longer version of a password and is, therefore, more secure. A pass phrase is typically composed of multiple words. Because of this, a pass phrase is more secure against "dictionary attacks."

A good pass phrase is relatively long and contains a combination of upper- and lowercase letters and numeric and punctuation characters. An example of a good pass phrase is "The*?#>*@TrafficOnThe101Was*&#!#ThisMorning."

All of the rules above that apply to passwords apply to pass phrases.

5.0 Enforcement

Any employee found to have violated this policy may be subject to disciplinary action, up to and including termination of employment.

6.0 Definitions

Terms	Definitions
Application Administration Account	Any account that is for the administration of an application (e.g., Oracle database administrator, ISSU administrator)

7.0 Revision History

Hiring a Security Professional

If you should decide to hire a security professional, whether as a permanent position or simply as a short-term consultant to assess your organization's security, the question becomes: How do you find a good one? Security is perceived as one of the more glamorous segments of the IT profession. It also does not take a great deal of knowledge to know more about security than the average person. By reading a few security books, you would probably know more than most people. This leads to a number of unqualified people posing as security experts. Therefore, how do you know if you are getting the real thing? This section contains a few guidelines that will help you.

Experience

The primary item to look for is experience—verifiable experience with references. There is no substitute for real-world experience. A security professional should have a minimum of five years of IT experience (e.g., networking, programming), with three years directly related to security.

Education/Training

It is certainly possible to be a security professional without any college or formal training. However, to be truly proficient at security, one needs to understand operating systems, networks, programming, and so forth. It is likely that a person with these qualifications would have a degree in computer science, engineering, MIS, or some related field. You will find that some colleges now offer security-specific degrees.

Certifications

Certifications are certainly not the end-all and be-all of any branch of IT, including security. You should never hire someone simply based on certifications. However, they can be one part of the entire picture. As with all professional designations, some security certifications mean more than others. Following are a few of the more common certifications. (For more information on certifications and links to more information, see Appendix C.)

- Security+: This is CompTIA's general security certification and is actually a test of general knowledge. Holding this certification alone is probably not sufficient to qualify someone as a security professional. However, it is a good starting place for someone wanting to pursue a computer security career.

- CIW Security Analyst: This test approximates the same level of knowledge as the Security+ test. However, what makes it valuable is that CIW will only award it to those who also have MCSA, MCSE, or CNE. In other words, you must have some solid knowledge of computer networks before you can take the CIW Security Analyst test, giving the holder of this certification a little more credibility.

- MSCE Security Specialist: This is the Microsoft Certified Systems Engineer (MSCE) test, with specific security tests taken as electives. If you are looking for someone to secure a 100% Microsoft network, this is probably a good certification.

- CISSP: This is the gold standard in security. This certification requires three years of real-world experience, a grueling exam, and continuing education credits to maintain. This certification is generally a strong indicator of a qualified security professional.

- Other: As stated earlier, to be good at security, you must understand networks. For this reason, you often see people that started out as Linux, Unix, Microsoft, or Novell administrators eventually specialize in security. This means that people will often have Linux +,

RHCE, MCSA, MCSE, CNE, CCNP, and other certifications related to networking and hardware.

Background

You must do a background check. Any security professional that objects to a criminal, credit, and drug screen should be avoided. You should always check the background of the person you hire, but this caution rings more true in the security field than for any other position.

Documentation

Especially when hiring a consultant, you should agree on documentation of what they do before you sign any contract. For example, if you want a consultant to assess your security system, you should receive both detail and summary documentation. The detail documents should tell you exactly what steps he or she took, what vulnerabilities and strengths were found, and a recommended course of action to follow. It is even better if these recommendations are supported by cited studies and industry standards rather than simply being opinion. The summary document should summarize all of this in easy-to-follow terms.

No set of guidelines is foolproof. However, these simple rules should help you avoid hiring an unqualified security professional who may falsely declare your system to be secure.

Links to Reputable Certifications and Societies

CIW Security Analyst: **www.ciwcertified.com/certifications/professionalcert.asp?comm=home&llm=2#5**

Security + Exam: **www.comptia.org/certification/security/default.aspx**

CISSP Exam: **www.cissp.com/**

Computer Security Institute: **www.gocsi.com/**

SANS Institute: **www.sans.org/**

Glossary

Some terms in this section are from the hacker community and others are from the security professional's community. To truly understand computer security, one must be familiar with both worlds. General networking terms are also included in this glossary.

A

admin Short for system administrator.

adware Software loaded onto your machine, often without your knowledge, that causes ads to pop up on your screen. This technology often works in a different manner than Web page pop-ups; thus, pop-up blockers will not stop them.

anomaly detection A process of looking for system behavior that is not normal. This process is used by many intrusion-detection systems.

application gateway A type of firewall that authenticates entire client applications.

application-level proxy Another name for an application gateway.

application proxy Another name for an application gateway.

asset identification Identifying all of the assets you must protect. This is a critical step in securing any system.

audit A check of systems security. This usually includes a review of documents, procedures, and system configurations.

authentication The process of verifying that a user is authorized to access a given resource. This is part of the logon system.

B

back door A hole in the security system deliberately left by the creator of the system.

backbones The central Internet connections to which Internet Service Providers must ultimately connect.

bagbiter Something, such as a program or a computer, that fails to work or works in a remarkably clumsy manner.

bastion host A gateway between an inside network and an outside network. Used as a security measure, it is designed to defend against attacks aimed at the inside network.

bid shielding The process of entering fake high bids in an online auction, then withdrawing them just before the auction concludes. This has the effect of protecting one bid (one entered before the fake bidding began) from competition.

bid siphoning Attempts to lure buyers from a legitimate auction site to an off-site auction that is a fraud.

binary numbers Numbers using the base 2. Ultimately, all data on a computer is stored in a base 2 format.

black hat hackers Hackers with malicious intent; synonymous with cracker.

block cipher Ciphers that encrypt blocks of text at a time, for example, 64 bytes at a time.

BlowFish A well known encryption algorithm.

brain dump The act of telling someone everything one knows.

breach To successfully break into a system; to *breach* the security.

brute force To try to crack a password by simply trying every possible combination.

buffer overflow An attack that involves loading a buffer with more data than it is designed to hold.

bug A flaw in a system.

C

Caesar cipher One of the oldest known encryption methods. It simply shifts each character by a given number of characters.

cipher Synonym for cryptographic algorithm.

cipher text Encrypted text.

circuit-level gateway A type of firewall that employs user authentication.

client errors Errors that occur on the client machine rather than the server.

code The source code for a program or the act of programming, as in "to *code* an algorithm."

code grinder An unflattering reference to one who works in an uncreative corporate programming environment.

cookie A small file containing information from a Web site.

cracker One who breaks into a system in order to do something malicious, illegal, or harmful. A hacker with malicious intent; synonymous with black hat hacker.

crash A sudden and unintended failure, as in "my computer *crashed*."

cryptography The study of encryption and decryption.

cyber fraud Using the Internet to defraud someone.

cyber stalking Using the Internet to harass someone.

cyber terrorism Using the Internet to terrorize someone or some group of individuals.

D

Data Encryption Standard (DES) A widely used block cipher encryption algorithm.

datagram A packet sent using the TCP protocol.

decryption To break encryption and discover the underlying message.

demigod A hacker with years of experience, or one with a national or international reputation.

Distributed Denial of Service (DDoS) A Denial of Service attack launched from multiple machines, often without the knowledge of the owners of those machines.

Domain Name Service (DNS) A protocol that translates names, such as **www.prenticehall.com**, into an IP addresses.

DNS servers/Domain Name Server A server that provides DNS Service.

Denial of Service (DoS) An attack that prevents legitimate users from accessing a resource.

dual-homed host A firewall that actually has two network interface cards, thus participating in two networks (although one might be the Internet itself).

dumpster diving The process of searching through trash looking for information that might be useful in hacking (particularly social engineering) or identity theft.

E

echo/chargen attack A type of Denial of Service attack that attempts to build up to much CPU activity with echos.

encryption The act of encrypting a message. This usually involves altering a message so that it cannot be read without the key and the decryption algorithm.

espionage Spying; the act of illicitly gaining confidential information.

ethical hacker One who hacks into systems in order to accomplish some goal that they feel is ethically valid.

F

firewall A device or software that provides a barrier between your machine or network and the rest of the world.

flood attack An attack that involves sending a large number of packets to a server in an attempt to overload the server.

footprinting A term hackers use for assessing a system looking for vulnerabilities.

G

gray hat hackers Hackers who normally behave legally but who may, for certain reasons and in limited situations, conduct illegal activities, usually for reasons they feel are ethically compelling.

H

hacker One who tries to learn about a system by examining it in detail and reverse-engineering it.

hacking The process of attempting to learn about a system by examining it and often exploiting flaws. This usually involves attempts to compromise the target system in some way.

hactivism Hacking conducted for ideological purposes.

hardening The process of securing all aspects of a server. This includes adding patches, shutting off unnecessary services, making sure all settings are secure, and so forth.

hub A device for connecting computers.

I

ICMP flood attacks An attack that attempts to overload the target system with too many ICMP packets for it to respond to.

identity theft The process of getting enough personal information on someone so that you might be able to pose as that person. Often done to secure credit or make purchases in the victim's name.

IDS signatures Characteristics of specific types of attacks that intrusion-detection systems look for.

industrial espionage The use of espionage for purely economic purposes.

information warfare The use of information in any conflict. This often involves propaganda and disinformation campaigns.

Internet Control Message Protocol (ICMP) A protocol used for a variety of purposes, including "pinging" other computers.

Internet Protocol (IP) A protocol that is part of the TCP/IP suite of protocols, which is the foundation for most networking and all Internet communications.

Internet Protocol Security (IPSec) A protocol that is critical for securing virtual private networks.

Internet Service Provider (ISP) A company that provides Internet access for clients.

intrusion-detection system (IDS) A system that is designed to detect signs of attacks in progress and to notify the administrator.

IP address A numerical designation for a computer consisting of four 1-byte binary numbers.

IPConfig A utility that provides extensive information about a computer's network connection.

K

key logger Software that logs key strokes on a computer.

L

land attack Sending a packet to a machine with the source host/port the same as the destination host/port, causing some systems to crash.

Layer 2 Tunneling Protocol (L2TP) A protocol that is used to create virtual private networks. It is a successor to the older point-to-point tunneling protocol (PPTP).

layered security approach An approach that attempts to fortify security within the network rather than just the perimeter.

loop back address An address used to test a machine's own network card, 127.0.0.1.

M

MAC addresses A unique hexadecimal number that is used to identify a network interface card.

malware Any software that has a malicious purpose, such as a virus or Trojan horse.

mono-alphabet substitution A primitive encryption algorithm in which there is one single substitute character for all plain text characters.

multi-alphabet substitution A primitive encryption algorithm in which there are multiple substitute characters for all plain text characters.

N

Network Access Points (NAP) Places where one can connect to a network. This often is used to refer to wireless network connectivity points.

network host-based firewall A firewall that is running software on an existing server.

network scanning The process of scanning a network looking for vulnerabilities.

NIC Network interface card, which is the card that allows network connectivity for a computer.

O

on-demand virus scanners Virus scanning that runs when requested by the user.

ongoing virus scanner Virus scanning that is continually running in the background.

OSI model A seven-layer model describing network connectivity, devices, and protocols.

P

packet A binary piece of data prepared for transmission over a network.

pass phrases A phrase that is used instead of a simple password.

password age How long a password is viable before it must be replaced.

password history How many old passwords a system remembers to prevent a user from reusing them.

penetration testing Assessing the security of a system by attempting to break into the system. This is the activity most sneakers engage in.

perimeter security approach An approach that simply tries to secure the barriers between a network and the Internet without concern for security within the network.

phishing The process of sending e-mails to people in which the e-mail purports to be from some legitimate financial institution, such as a bank or credit card company, and induces the recipient to provide personal information.

phreaking The process of hacking phone systems.

ping To send a single ICMP packet to a destination, usually in order to confirm that the destination can be reached.

Ping of Death (PoD) To send an extremely large packet to a target. For some older systems, this would cause the target to crash.

Point-to-Point Tunneling Protocol (PPTP) A protocol used in virtual private networks. It is based on the earlier point-to-point protocol (PPP).

port A numerical designation for a connection point on a computer. There are well defined ports for specific protocols such as FTP port 21, HTTP port 80, and so forth.

port scanning Scanning a target machine to see what ports are open in an attempt to assess vulnerabilities.

Pretty Good Privacy (PGP) A widely used encryption algorithm.

protocols Agreed-upon methods of communication in networking that refer to ways of performing certain types of communication, such as hypertext transfer protocol for Web pages.

proxy server A machine or software that hides all internal network IP addresses from the outside world. It provides a point of contact between a private network and the Internet.

public key encryption Encryption algorithms that use two keys. One is publicly distributed and is used to encrypt messages. The other is kept private and is used to decrypt the messages.

pump and dump Artificially inflating the price of a stock so you may sell your shares at a much higher value than they should have been sold.

R

reactive security Security that simply acts after something has gone wrong.

router A device that separates networks.

RSA A widely used encryption algorithm.

RST cookie A method for preventing Denial of Service attacks that actually uses a type of cookie to authenticate the client's connection.

S

screened host A firewall, usually on the perimeter of a network, that combines a packet-filtering router with an application gateway located on the protected subnet side of the router; also called a *screening firewall.*

script kiddy A hacker term for one who claims much greater hacking skill than they actually have.

server errors Errors that occur on the server rather than the client.

shill bidding A term for a seller putting in fake bids on his own item in order to drive up the price.

single-key encryption An encryption method in which the same key is used to both encrypt and decrypt a message. This is also referred to as *symmetric key encryption*.

smurf A specific type of distributed Denial of Service attack.

sneaker Someone who is attempting to compromise a system in order to assess its vulnerability.

social engineering Using interpersonal skills to extract information about a computer system and its security.

spoofing Pretending to be something else, as when a packet might spoof another return IP address (as in the smurf attack) or when a Web site is spoofing a well known e-commerce site.

spyware Software that monitors computer use.

stateful packet inspection (SPI) A type of firewall process in which each packet and its contents are examined.

stateless packet inspection A type of firewall in which the inspection does not involve actually examining the contents of each packet, nor does it examine a packet within the context of an ongoing TCP conversation.

stream cipher A type of cipher in which the original text is encrypted one byte at a time in a stream of bytes.

subnet A subsection of a network.

subnet mask A mask used to determine what subnet an IP address belongs to.

substitution alphabet The characters used to replace plain text in a substitution or multi-substitution encryption algorithm.

switch A device that works like a hub, but routes packets only out of the port that they need to go to rather than out of all ports.

SYN cookies Cookies used to authenticate connection requests and thus avoid certain types of Denial of Service attacks.

SYN flood A Denial of Service attack in which the target is flooded with connection requests that are never completed.

SYNACK The response a server sends back to a connection request from a client.

T

teardrop attack A type of attack against a TCP/IP stack based on using fragmented packets

Terminate and Stay Resident (TSR) Software that stays loaded in memory even if shuts down.

Tracert A utility similar to ping that also tells you what hops it made getting to the destination and how long it took to get there.

Transmission Control Protocol (TCP) A protocol used to send data over the Internet; part of the TCP/IP suite of protocols.

Transmission Control Protocol/Internet Protocol (TCP/IP) A suite of protocols used for various types of Internet and networking communication.

Trojan horse Software that appears to have a valid and benign purpose, but really has another nefarious purpose.

U

UDP flood attack A Denial of Service attack based on sending a huge number of UDP packets.

Uniform Resource Locator (URL) An Internet address, such as **www.prenticehall.com**.

User Datagram Protocol (UDP) A protocol very similar to TCP except that transmissions are merely sent without any attempt to confirm their arrival at the destination.

V

virtual private network (VPN) A network that is constructed by using public wires to connect nodes.

virus Software that is self-replicating and spreads like a biological virus.

W

war-dialing Dialing phones waiting for a computer to pick up. This is usually done via some automated system.

war-driving Driving and scanning for wireless networks that can be compromised.

white hat hackers Hackers who only hack for legal/ethical purposes.

Z

zone transfers DNS servers must update their list of what IP addresses go with what URL (Uniform Resource Locator). They periodically perform zone transfers to synchronize those lists.

References

Chapter 1

100th Congress. Computer Security Act of 1987. Public Law 100-235. **www.net.ohio-state.edu/security/links/csa-1987.html** (accessed 15 December 2004).

CNN/Technology. Hacker Accesses 5.6 Million Credit Cards. February 18, 2003. **www.cnn.com/2003/TECH/02/17/creditcard.hack/index.html** (accessed 15 December 2004).

Computer Security Institute. Cyber Crime Bleeds U.S. Corporations, Survey Shows; Financial Losses from Attacks Climb for Third Year in a Row. April 7, 2002. **www.gocsi.com/press/20020407.jhtml;jsessionid=J5CTJV4ZKSD3MQSNDBGCKHSCJUMEKJVN?_requestid=219439** (accessed 15 December 2004).

DefCon II. Wardriving Statistics. Las Vegas, NV. August 2003. **www.defcon.org/html/ defcon-11/defcon-11-postcon.html** (accessed 15 December 15, 2004).

F-Secure. F-Secure Virus Descriptions. 2003. **www.f-secure.com/v-descs/_new.shtml** (accessed 15 December 2004).

Glossary of Hacker Terminology. June 2003. **www.cs.usask.ca/undergrads/kwm519/490/project/details/glossary.htm** (accessed 15 December 2004).

Lemos, Robert. Mitnick Teaches Social Engineering. *ZDNet News*. July 16, 2000. **news.zdnet.com/2100-9595_22-522261.html ?legacy=zdnn** (accessed 15 December 2004).

Mitnick, Kevin D., William L. Simon, and Steve Wozniak. 2002. *The Art of Deception: Controlling the Human Element of Security*. Indianapolis, IN: Wiley Publishing Inc.

Online Banking Report. OBR Special Report Series. New Edition—2004 Factbook: Online Banking by the Numbers. November 2003. **www.onlinebankingreport.com/resources/sr7.html** (accessed 15 December 2004).

Poulsen, Kevin. War Driving by the Bay. *SecurityFocus*. April 12, 2001. **www.security focus.com/news/192** (accessed 15 December 2004).

Raymond, Eric S. 1993. *The New Hacker's Dictionary*. 3rd ed. Cambridge, MA: The MIT Press.

Symantec. What Is the Difference Between Viruses, Worms, and Trojans? Security Response FAQ Sheet. 2003. **service1.symantec.com/SUPPORT/nav.nsf/aab56492973adccd8825694500552355/024c927836400f528825675100593eb2?OpenDocument&src=sec_web_nam** (accessed 15 December 2004).

Webopedia. Proxy Server. 2004. **www.webopedia.com/TERM/p/proxy_server.html** (accessed 15 December 2004).

Chapter 2

Webopedia. IP. 2004. **www.webopedia.com/TERM/I/IP.html** (accessed 15 December 2004).

Webopedia. TCP. 2004. **www.webopedia.com/TERM/T/TCP.html** (accessed 15 December 2004).

Chapter 4

Gibson, Steve. Description and Analysis of a Potent, Increasingly Prevalent, and Worrisome Internet Attack. *Distributed Reflection Denial of Service*. February 22, 2002. **grc.com/dos/drdos.htm** (accessed 15 December 2004).

Moore, David, Vern Paxson, Stefan Savage, Colleen Shannon, Stuart Staniford, and Nicholas Weaver. Slammer Worm Dissection: Inside the Slammer Worm. *IEEE Security and Privacy*. 2004. **www.computer.org/security/v1n4/j4wea.htm** (accessed 15 December 2004).

Delio, Michelle. My Doom Targets Linux Antagonist. *Wired News*. January 27, 2004. **www.wired.com/news/linux/0,1411,62058,00.html** (accessed 15 December 2004).

SCO./Linux. 2003. **swpat.ffii.org/patente/wirkungen/sco/index.en.html** (accessed 15 December 2004).

Webopedia. DoS Attack. 2004. **www.webopedia.com/TERM/D/DoS_attack.html** (accessed 15 December 2004).

Chapter 5

finjan software. Mobile Code—A Necessary Evil. 2004. **www.finjan.com/SecurityLab/KnowledgeCenter/CurrentTopics/ActiveContentandMaliciousMobileCode.asp** (accessed 15 December 2004).

F-Secure. F-Secure Virus Descriptions: Sobig. April 23, 2003. **www.f-secure.com/v-descs/sobig.shtml** (accessed 15 December 2004).

Gudmundsson, Atli, and Scott Gettis. W32.Mimail.A@mm. *Symantec*. July 28, 2004. **securityresponse.symantec.com/avcenter/venc/data/w32.mimail.a@mm.html** (accessed 15 December 2004).

searchSecurity.com. Buffer Overflow. September 13, 2004. **searchsecurity.techtarget.com/sDefinition/0%2C%2Csid14_gci549024%2C00.html** (accessed 15 December 2004).

searchSecurity.com. Rootkit. December 7, 2004. **searchsecurity.techtarget.com/sDefinition/0,,sid14_gci547279,00.html** (accessed 16 December 2004).

SpywareGuide. 2004. **www.spywareguide.com/product_list_full.php** (accessed 16 December 2004).

Vmyths.com. jdbgmgr.exe Virus. July 7, 2002. **vmyths.com/hoax.cfm?id=275&page=3** (accessed 16 December 2004).

Yakabovicz, Ed. Expert Knowledgebase. *TechTarget Expert Answer Center*. March 29, 2003. **expertanswercenter.techtarget.com/eac/knowledgebaseAnswer/0,,sid63_gci980661,00.html** (accessed 16 December 2004).

Chapter 7

Burnett, Steve, and Stephen Paine. 2001. *RSA Security's Official Guide to Cryptography*. New York, NY: McGraw-Hill.

Curtin, Matt. Snake Oil Warning Signs: Encryption Software to Avoid. April 10, 1998. **www.interhack.net/people/cmcurtin/snake-oil-faq.html** (accessed 16 December 2004).

Federal Information Processing Standards. Data Encryption Standards (DES). Publication 46-2. December 30, 1993. **www.itl.nist.gov/fipspubs/fip46-2.htm** (accessed 16 December 2004).

International PGP. Home Page. **www. pgpi.org/** (accessed March 2004).

McCune, Tom. Tom McCune's Page for Pretty Good Privacy. **www.mccune.cc/PGP. htm** (accessed March 2004).

MyCrypto.net. Encryption Algorithms. **www.mycrypto.net/encryption/crypto_algorithms.html** (accessed April 2004).

Security in Computing. Letter Frequency Distributions in the English Alphabet. 1988. **arapaho.nsuok.edu/~rosener/mis4313/freq-distribution.html** (accessed 16 December 2004).

Singh, Simon. 2001. *The Code Book: How to Make It, Break It, Hack It, Crack It*. New York, NY: Delacorte Press, 10, 241-242.

Zimmermann, Philip. Philip Zimmermann: Creator of PGP. **www.philzimmermann.com/EN/background/index.html** (accessed March 2004).

Chapter 8

Garner, Bryan A. 2000. *Black's Law Dictionary*. 7th ed. West Group.

Fraud Bureau. Stock Scams 101. Pump and Dump Classic. 1999. **www.fraudbureau.com/investor/101/article15.html** (accessed November 2003).

California Youth Authority. OPVS Bulletin—Stalking Awareness. 2000. **www.cya.ca. gov/Staff/stalking.html** (accessed 16 December 2004).

National Conference of State Legislatures. 2004 Pending Identity Theft Legislation. October 14, 2004. **www.ncsl.org/programs/lis/privacy/IDTheft2004_Pending.htm** (accessed 16 December 2004).

Romanian Information Technology Initiative. Anti-corruption Law Title III on Preventing and Fighting Cyber-crime. *Romanian Cybercrime Law*. May 7, 2002. **www.riti-internews.ro/cybercrime.htm** (accessed 16 December 2004).

University of Dayton School of Law. Cybercrimes. 2001. **cybercrimes.net/** (accessed 16 December 2004).

U.S. Department of Justice. Cyberstalking: A New Challenge for Law Enforcement and Industry. February 7, 2003. **www.usdoj.gov/criminal/cybercrime/cyberstalking.htm** (accessed 16 December 2004).

U.S. Department of Justice. What Are Identity Theft and Identity Fraud? June 5, 2000. **www.usdoj.gov/criminal/fraud/idtheft.html** (accessed October 2003).

U.S. Federal Trade Commission. Identity Theft and Assumption Deterrence Act. October 30, 1998. **www.ftc.gov/os/statutes/itada/itadact.htm** (accessed December 2004).

U.S. Federal Trade Commission. Internet Auctions: A Guide for Buyers and Sellers. June 2004. **www.ftc.gov/bcp/conline/pubs/online/auctions.htm** (accessed 16 December 2004).

U.S. Secret Service. Public Awareness Advisory Regarding "4-1-9" or "Advance Fee Fraud" Schemes. 2002. **www.secretservice.gov/alert419.shtml** (accessed November 2003).

U.S. Securities and Exchange Commission. Internet Fraud: How to Avoid Internet Investment Scams. November 15, 2001. **www.sec.gov/investor/pubs/cyberfraud.htm** (accessed October 2003).

U.S. Securities and Exchange Commission. Pump&Dump.con: Tips for Avoiding Stock Scams on the Internet. September 28, 2000. **www.sec.gov/investor/online/pump.htm** (accessed November 2003).

Working to Halt Online Abuse. Home Page. September 28, 2004. **www.haltabuse.org/** (accessed 16 December 2004).

Chapter 9

Briney, Andrew. The Four P's: When It Comes to Security, People Matter Most. *Information Security*. September 2003, 8. **infosecuritymag.techtarget.com/ss/0,295796,sid6_iss81_art198,00.html** (accessed 17 December 2004).

Dever, Paul. Federal Judge Says VW Chairman Must Remain Defendant in GM Spy Suit. *The Auto Channel*. October 24, 1996. **www.theautochannel.com/news/date/19961024/news02344.html** (accessed 17 December 2004).

Konrad, R. Leaks and Geeks: International Espionage Goes High-Tech. *CNET News*. September 21, 2000. **news.com.com/2100-1001-242620.html?legacy=cnet** (accessed September 2001).

Lemon, Sumner. Top VIA Execs Indicted for Industrial Espionage. *NetworkWorldFusion, IDG News Service*. December 8, 2003. **www.nwfusion.com/news/2003/1208updattop.html** (accessed 17 December 2004).

Secur Telecom. Introduction to Espionage. Latest Trends in Industrial Espionage. 1998. **www.securtelecom.com/IndustrialEspionage/espionage.htm** (accessed 17 December 2004).

Szczesny, Joseph. Lopez Surfaces in Indictment. *CarConnection.com*. May 29, 2000. **www.thecarconnection.com/index.asp?n=156,175&sid=175&article=1908** (accessed 17 December 2004).

U.S. Department of Justice. Kazakhstan Hacker Sentenced to Four Years Prison for Breaking into Bloomberg Systems and Attempting Extortion. July 1, 2003. **www.usdoj.gov/criminal/cybercrime/zezevSent.htm** (accessed 17 December 2004).

USA Today. Former GM Exec Indicted in VW Scandal. May 23, 2000. **www.usatoday.com/money/consumer/autos/mauto646.htm** (accessed 17 December 2004).

Chapter 10

BBC News. Russians Arrest "CIA Hacker." June 26, 2000. **news.bbc.co.uk/1/hi/world/europe/806984.stm** (accessed 17 December 2004).

Counterpane Internet Security. Security Alert: Chinese Hacker Group. April 30, 2002. **www.counterpane.com/alert-ceu.html** (accessed 17 December 2004).

Denning, Dorothy E. Cyberterrorism. May 23, 2000. **www.cosc.georgetown.edu/~denning/infosec/cyberterror.html** (accessed 17 December 2004).

Dick, Ronald L. Cyber Terrorism and Critical Infrastructure Protection. U.S. Federal Bureau of Investigation. July 24, 2002. **www.fbi.gov/congress/congress02/nipc072402.htm** (accessed 17 December 2004).

Hoffman, Bruce. Al Qaeda, Trends in Terrorism and Future Potentialities: An Assessment. Santa Monica, CA: The Rand Corporation, 2003. **www.rand.org/publications/P/P8078/P8078.pdf** (accessed 17 December 2004).

Institute for the Advanced Study of Information Warfare. March 14, 2004. **www.psycom.net/iwar.1.html** (accessed April 2004).

Ranum, Marcus. Myths of Cyberwar. *Information Security*. April 2004. **infosecuritymag.techtarget.com/ss/0,295804,sid6_iss366,00.html** (accessed 17 December 2004).

Roberts, Paul. Government Report Finds Satellite Security Lax. *InfoWorld*. October 4, 2002. **archive.infoworld.com/articles/hn/xml/02/10/04/021004hnsatellites.xml?s=IDGNS** (accessed 17 December 2004).

Tech Law Journal. Advisory Panel Reports on Cyber Terrorism. December 14, 2000. **www.techlawjournal.com/security/20001214.asp** (accessed 17 December 2004).

Tech Law Journal. Cyberterrorism Preparedness Act of 2002. January 28, 2002. **www.techlawjournal.com/cong107/cybersecurity/s1900is.asp** (accessed 17 December 2004).

The Orator. Cybersecurity Research and Education Act of 2002. 107th Congress, 2nd Session. January 28, 2002. **www.theorator.com/bills107/s1901.html** (accessed 17 December 2004).

Chapter 12

How Does a Virus Scanner Work? *Scientific American* (7), 2004.

Wack, John. Circuit-Level Gateways. *Computer Security Resource Center*. February 9, 1995. **csrc.nist.gov/publications/nistpubs/800-10/node53.html** (accessed 8 December 2004).

Webopedia. Intrusion Detection System, 2004. **www.webopedia.com/TERM/I/Intrusion_detection_system.html** (accessed 17 December 2004).

Webopedia. NIDS. 2004. **www.webopedia.com/TERM/N/NIDS.html** (accessed 17 December 2004).

Index

D

E

F

G

H

N

O

P